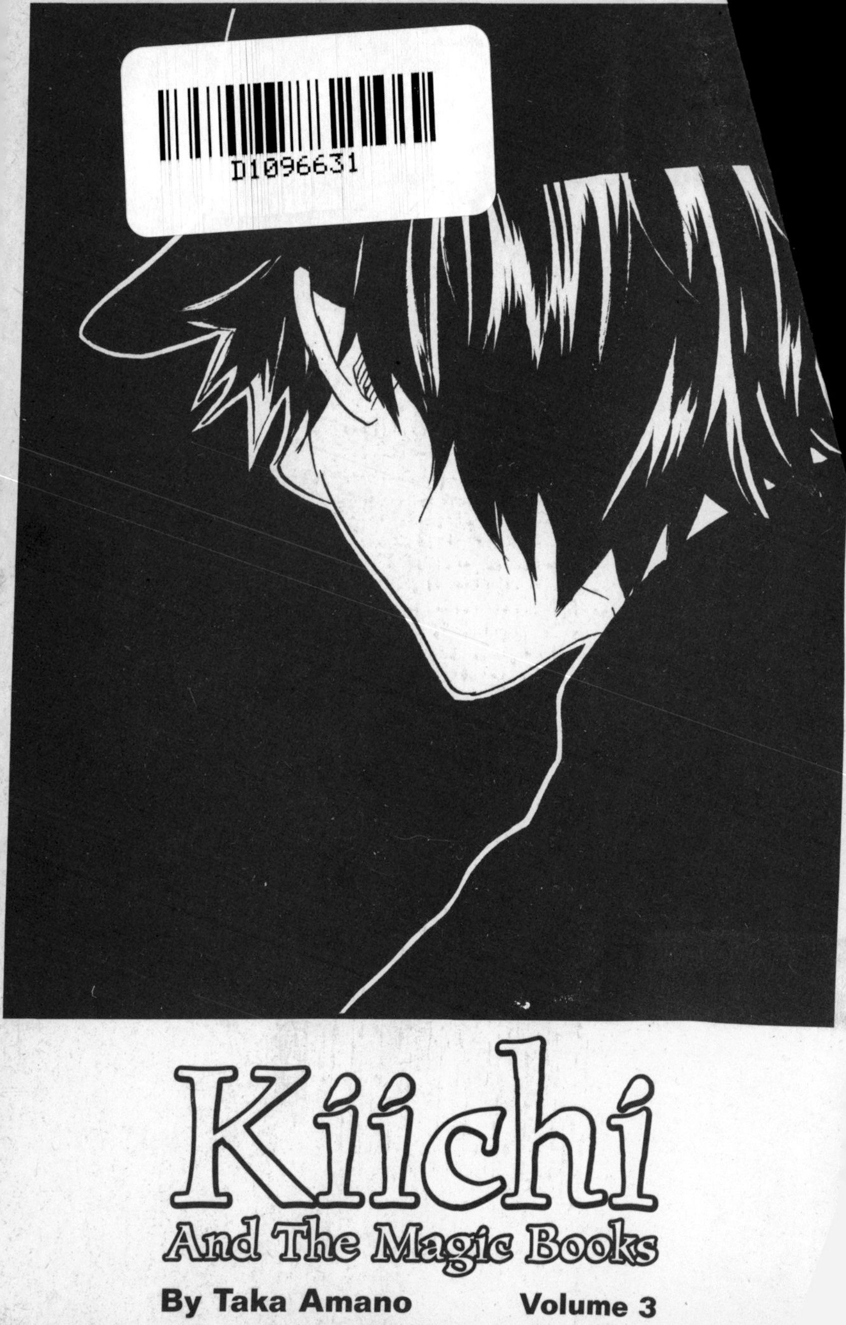

Kiichi And The Magic Books

By Taka Amano

Volume 3

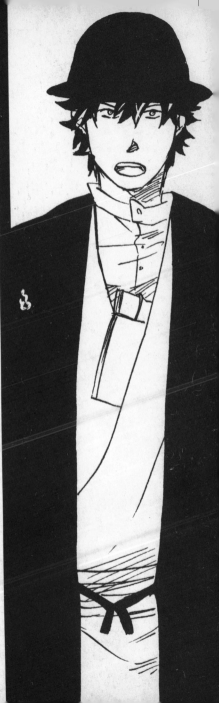

ok Ten

Book Eleven

Book Twelve

19   Book Thirteen

159   Afterword

FLEX
COMIX

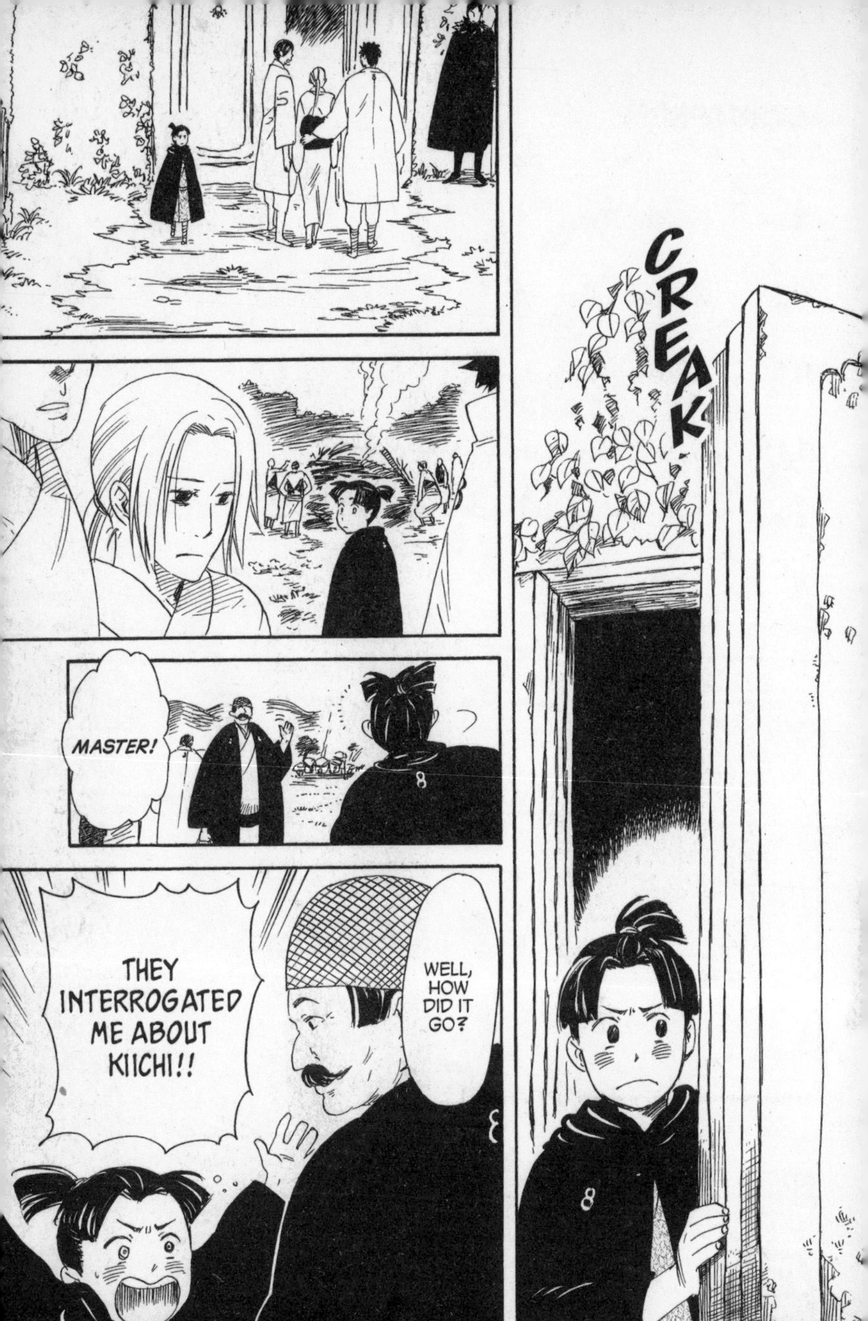
CREAK
MASTER!
WELL, HOW DID IT GO?
THEY INTERROGATED ME ABOUT KIICHI!!

BOOK TEN

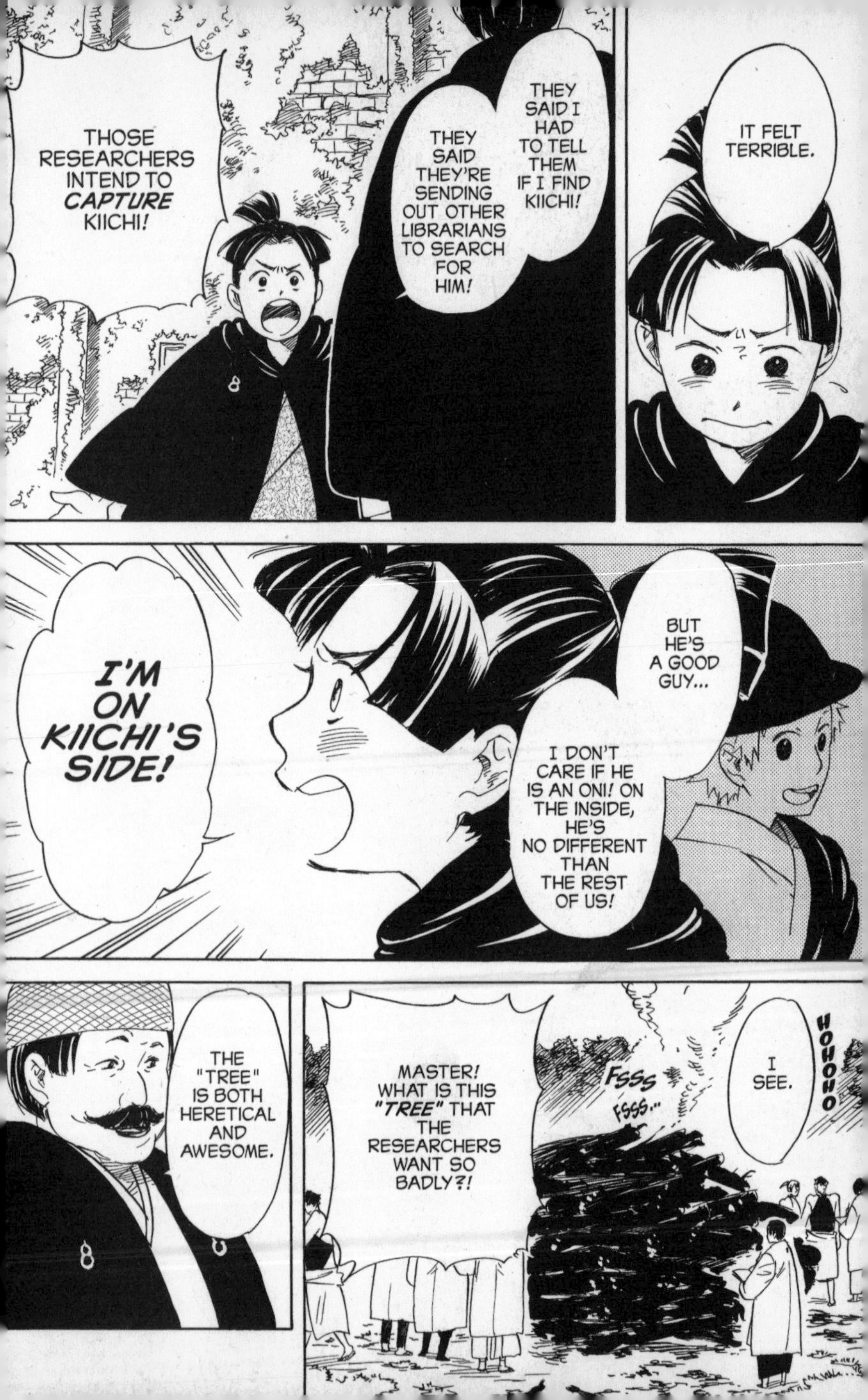
IT FELT TERRIBLE.
THEY SAID I HAD TO TELL THEM IF I FIND KIICHI!
THEY SAID THEY'RE SENDING OUT OTHER LIBRARIANS TO SEARCH FOR HIM!
THOSE RESEARCHERS INTEND TO *CAPTURE* KIICHI!
BUT HE'S A GOOD GUY...
I DON'T CARE IF HE IS AN ONI! ON THE INSIDE, HE'S NO DIFFERENT THAN THE REST OF US!
I'M ON KIICHI'S SIDE!
HOHOHO
I SEE.
FSSS
FSSS...
MASTER! WHAT IS THIS *"TREE"* THAT THE RESEARCHERS WANT SO BADLY?!
THE "TREE" IS BOTH HERETICAL AND AWESOME.

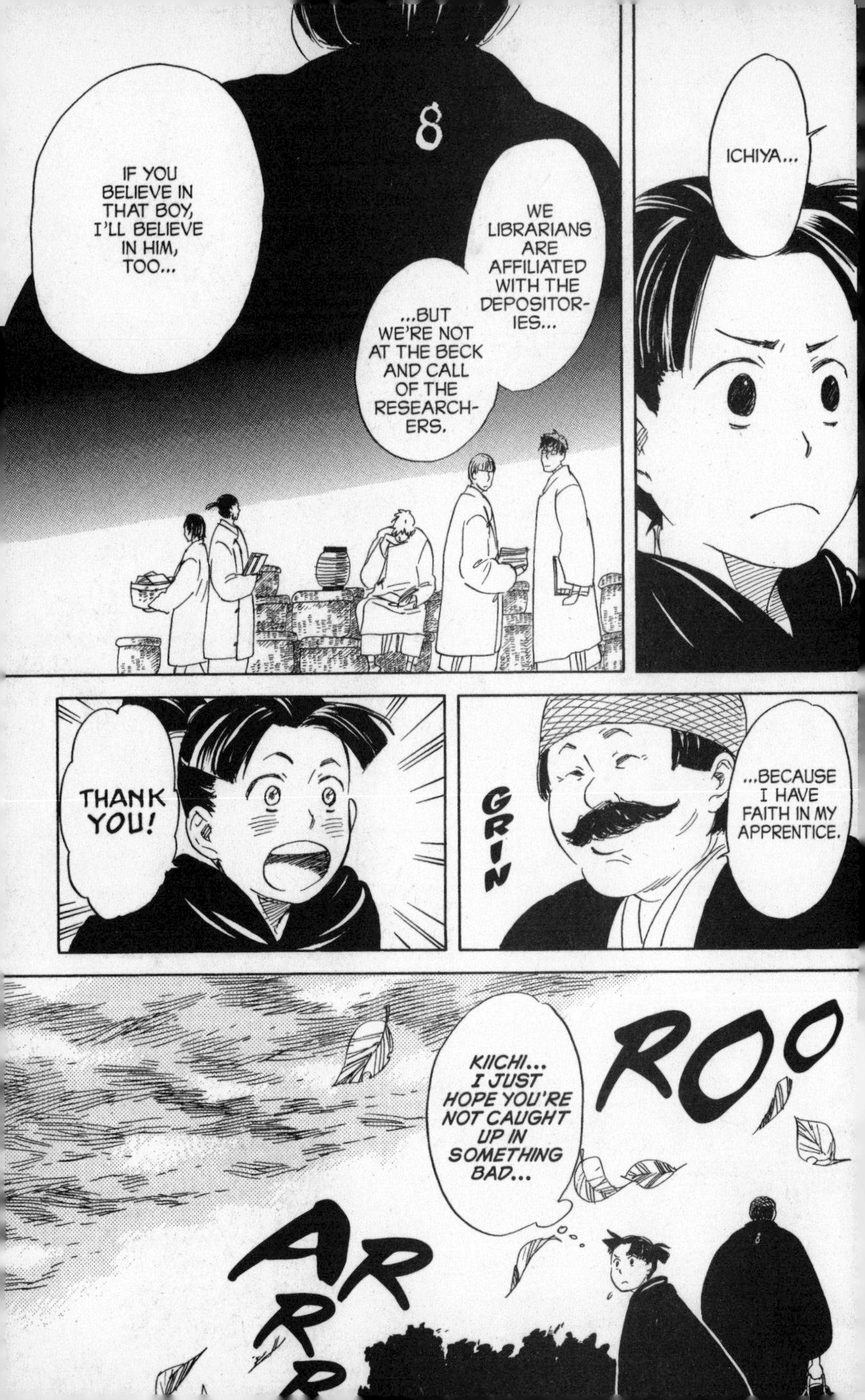
ICHIYA...
WE LIBRARIANS ARE AFFILIATED WITH THE DEPOSITORIES...
...BUT WE'RE NOT AT THE BECK AND CALL OF THE RESEARCHERS.
IF YOU BELIEVE IN THAT BOY, I'LL BELIEVE IN HIM, TOO...
...BECAUSE I HAVE FAITH IN MY APPRENTICE.
GRIN
THANK YOU!
ROO
KIICHI... I JUST HOPE YOU'RE NOT CAUGHT UP IN SOMETHING BAD...
ARR

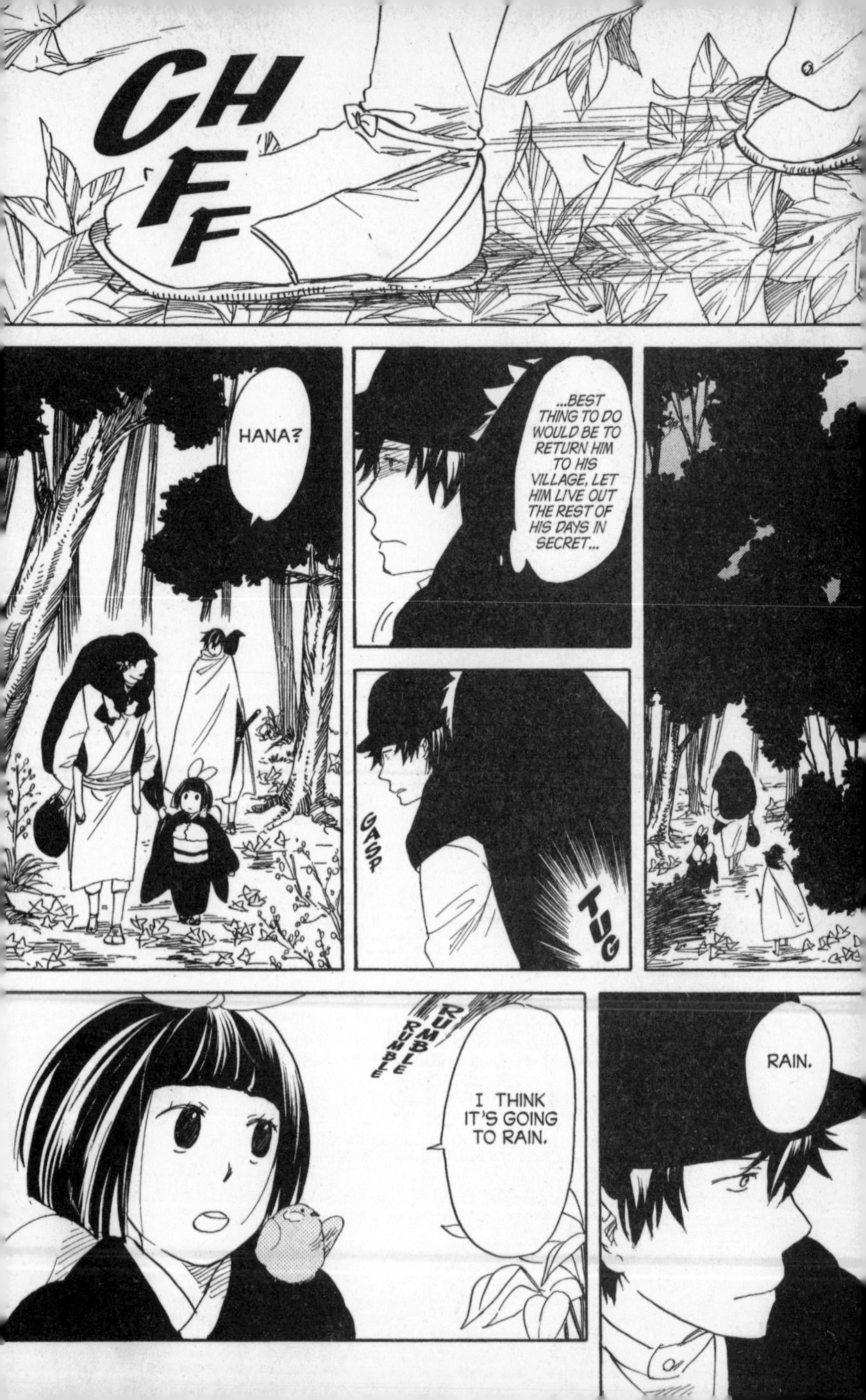
CHFF
...BEST THING TO DO WOULD BE TO RETURN HIM TO HIS VILLAGE, LET HIM LIVE OUT THE REST OF HIS DAYS IN SECRET...
GASP
TUG
HANA?
RAIN.
RUMBLE RUMBLE
I THINK IT'S GOING TO RAIN.

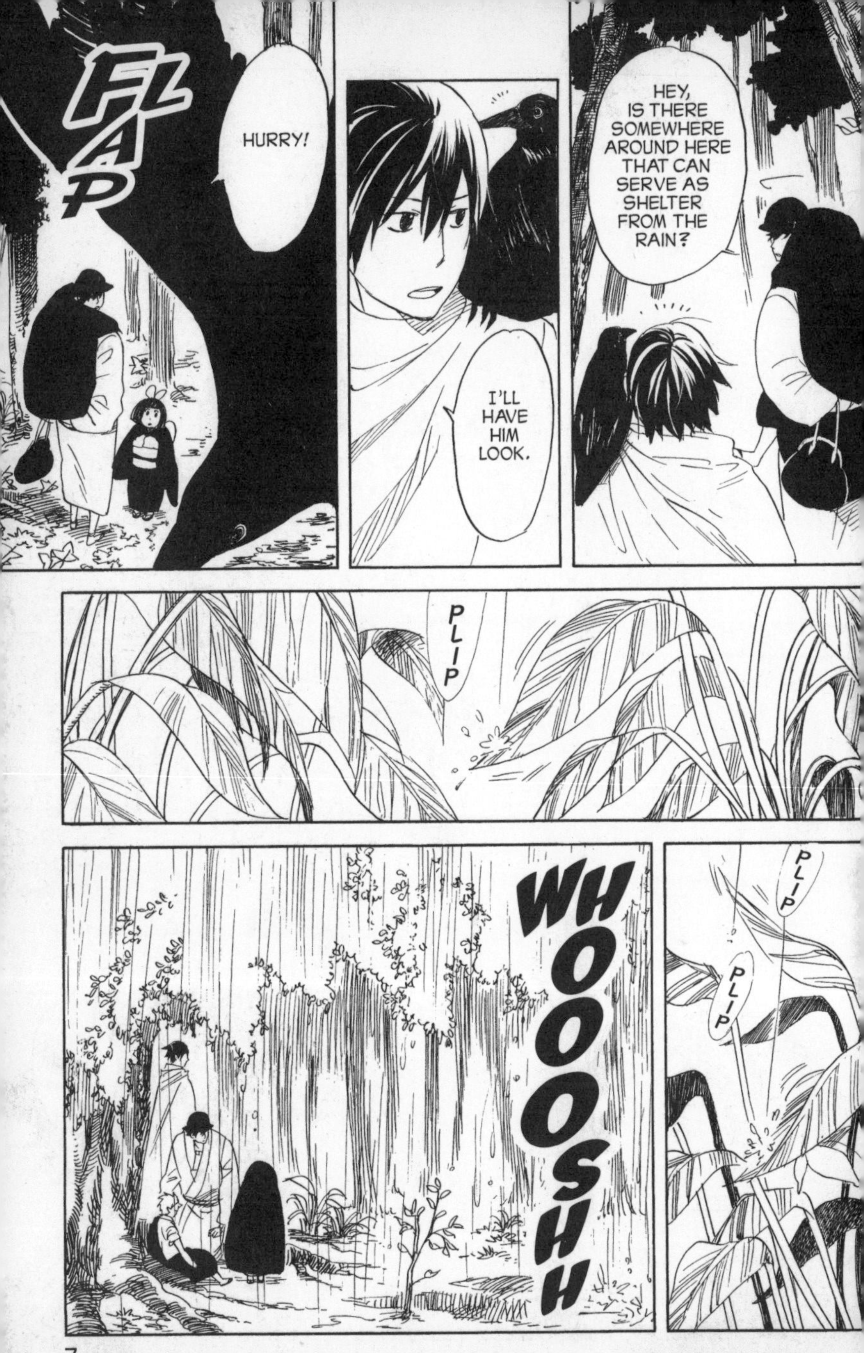
HEY, IS THERE SOMEWHERE AROUND HERE THAT CAN SERVE AS SHELTER FROM THE RAIN?
I'LL HAVE HIM LOOK.
FLAP
HURRY!
PLIP
PLIP
PLIP
WHOOOSHH

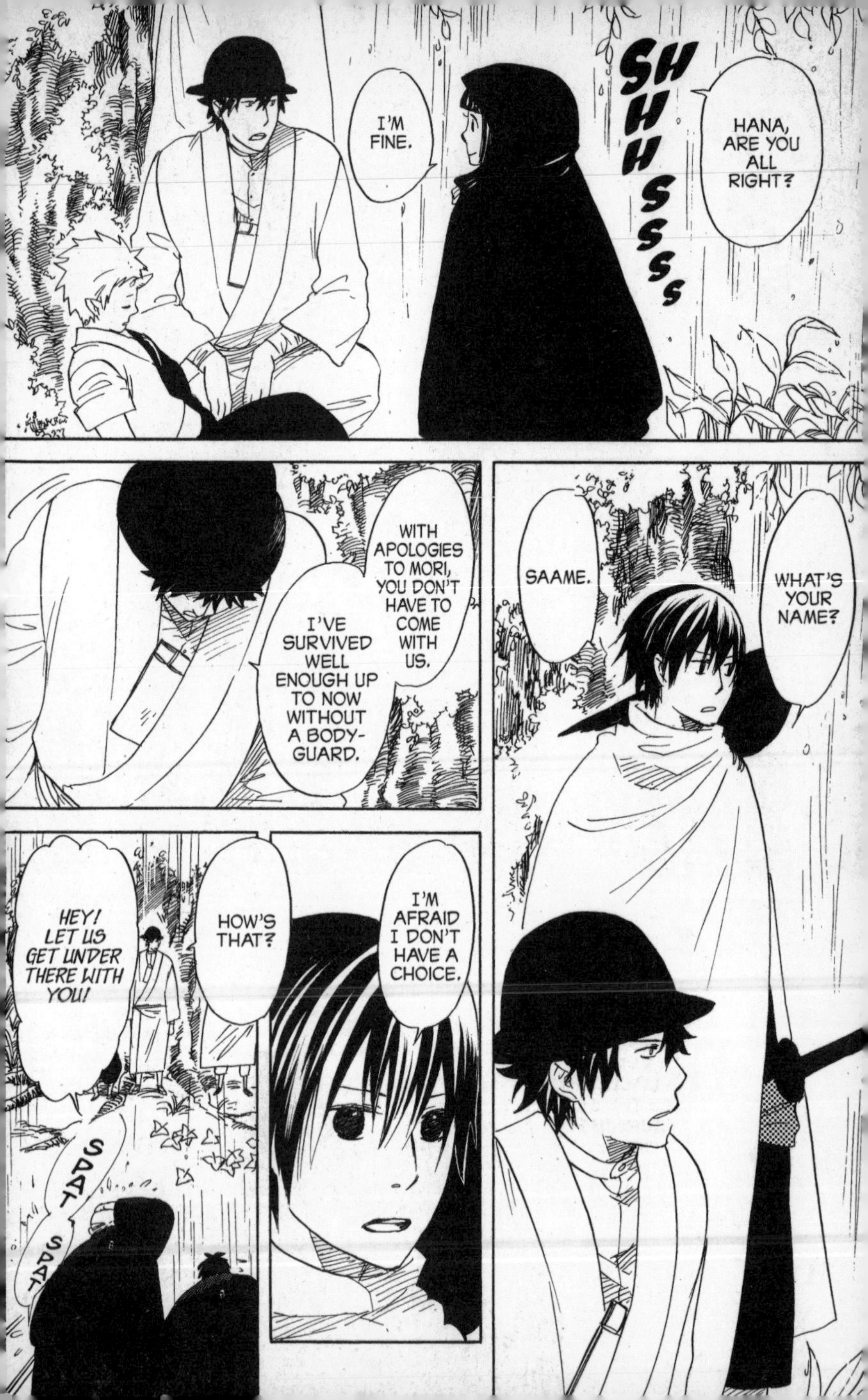
HANA, ARE YOU ALL RIGHT?
SHHHSSSS
I'M FINE.
WHAT'S YOUR NAME?
SAAME.
WITH APOLOGIES TO MORI, YOU DON'T HAVE TO COME WITH US.
I'VE SURVIVED WELL ENOUGH UP TO NOW WITHOUT A BODY-GUARD.
I'M AFRAID I DON'T HAVE A CHOICE.
HOW'S THAT?
HEY! LET US GET UNDER THERE WITH YOU!
SPAT SPAT

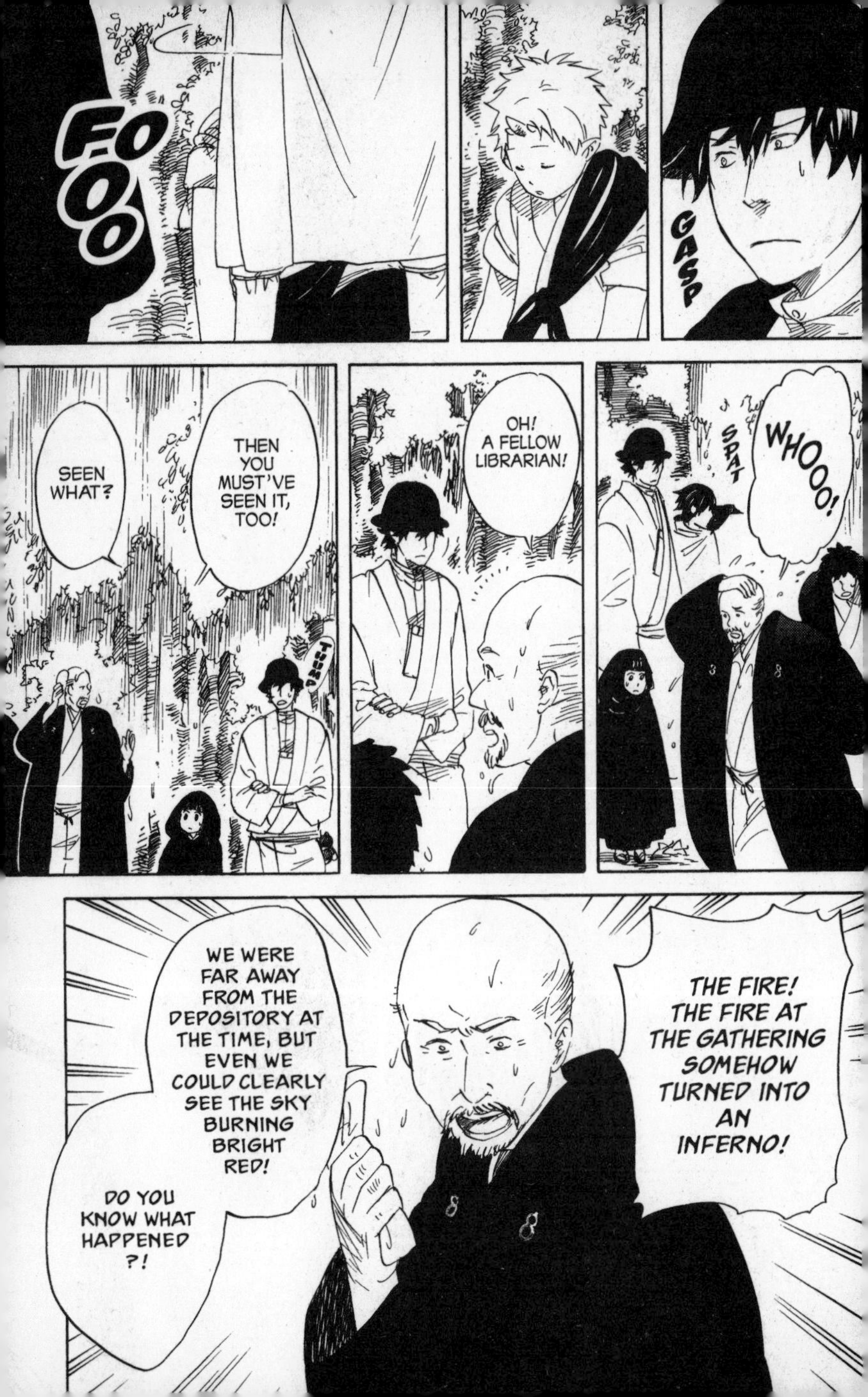
GASP
FOOO
WHOOO!
SPAT
OH! A FELLOW LIBRARIAN!
THEN YOU MUST'VE SEEN IT, TOO!
SEEN WHAT?
THUMP
THE FIRE! THE FIRE AT THE GATHERING SOMEHOW TURNED INTO AN INFERNO!
WE WERE FAR AWAY FROM THE DEPOSITORY AT THE TIME, BUT EVEN WE COULD CLEARLY SEE THE SKY BURNING BRIGHT RED!
DO YOU KNOW WHAT HAPPENED?!

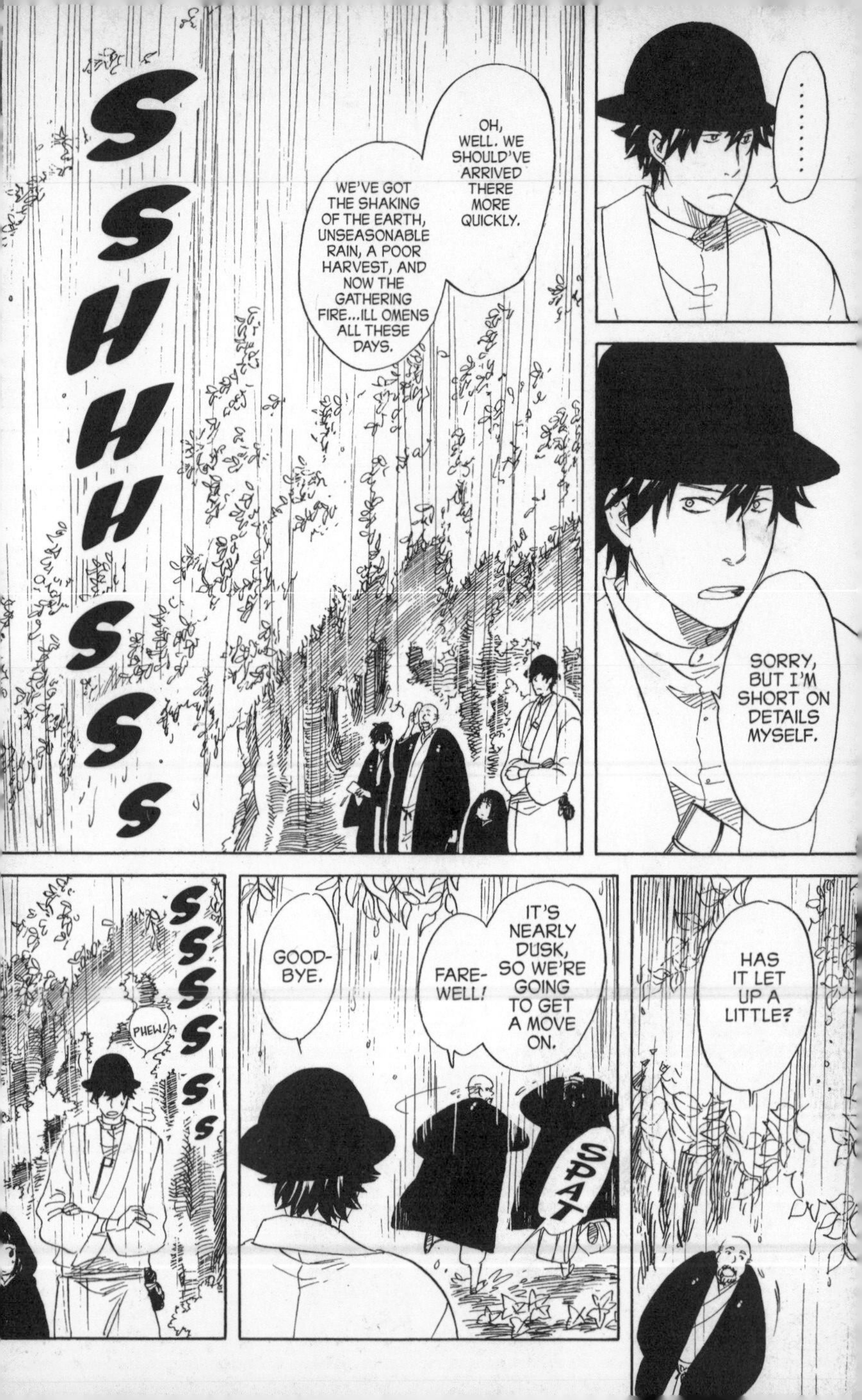
......
SORRY, BUT I'M SHORT ON DETAILS MYSELF.
OH, WELL. WE SHOULD'VE ARRIVED THERE MORE QUICKLY.
WE'VE GOT THE SHAKING OF THE EARTH, UNSEASONABLE RAIN, A POOR HARVEST, AND NOW THE GATHERING FIRE...ILL OMENS ALL THESE DAYS.
SSHHHSSS
HAS IT LET UP A LITTLE?
IT'S NEARLY DUSK, SO WE'RE GOING TO GET A MOVE ON.
FARE-WELL!
GOOD-BYE.
SPAT
SSSSSS
PHEW!

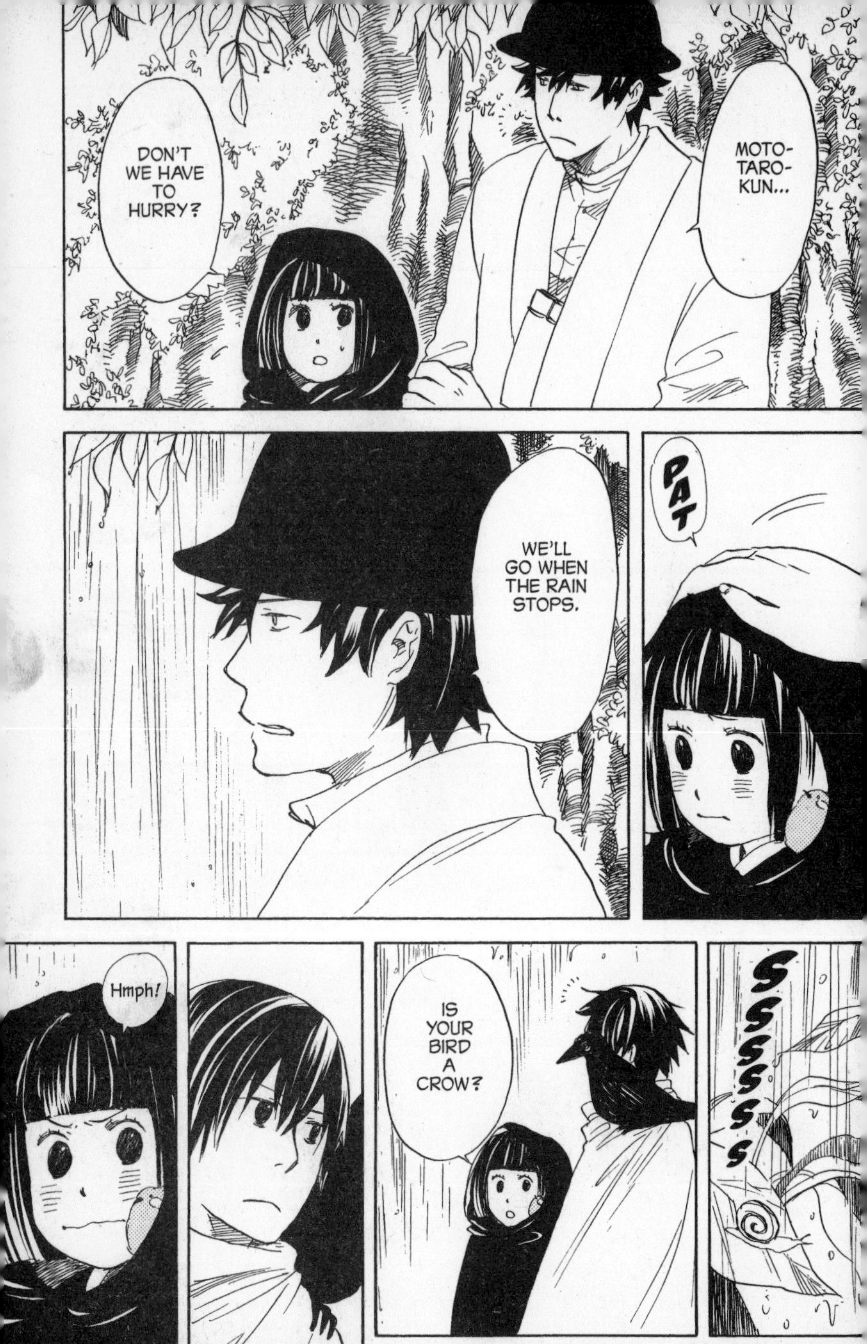
MOTO-TARO-KUN...
DON'T WE HAVE TO HURRY?
PAT
WE'LL GO WHEN THE RAIN STOPS.
SSSSSS
IS YOUR BIRD A CROW?
Hmph!

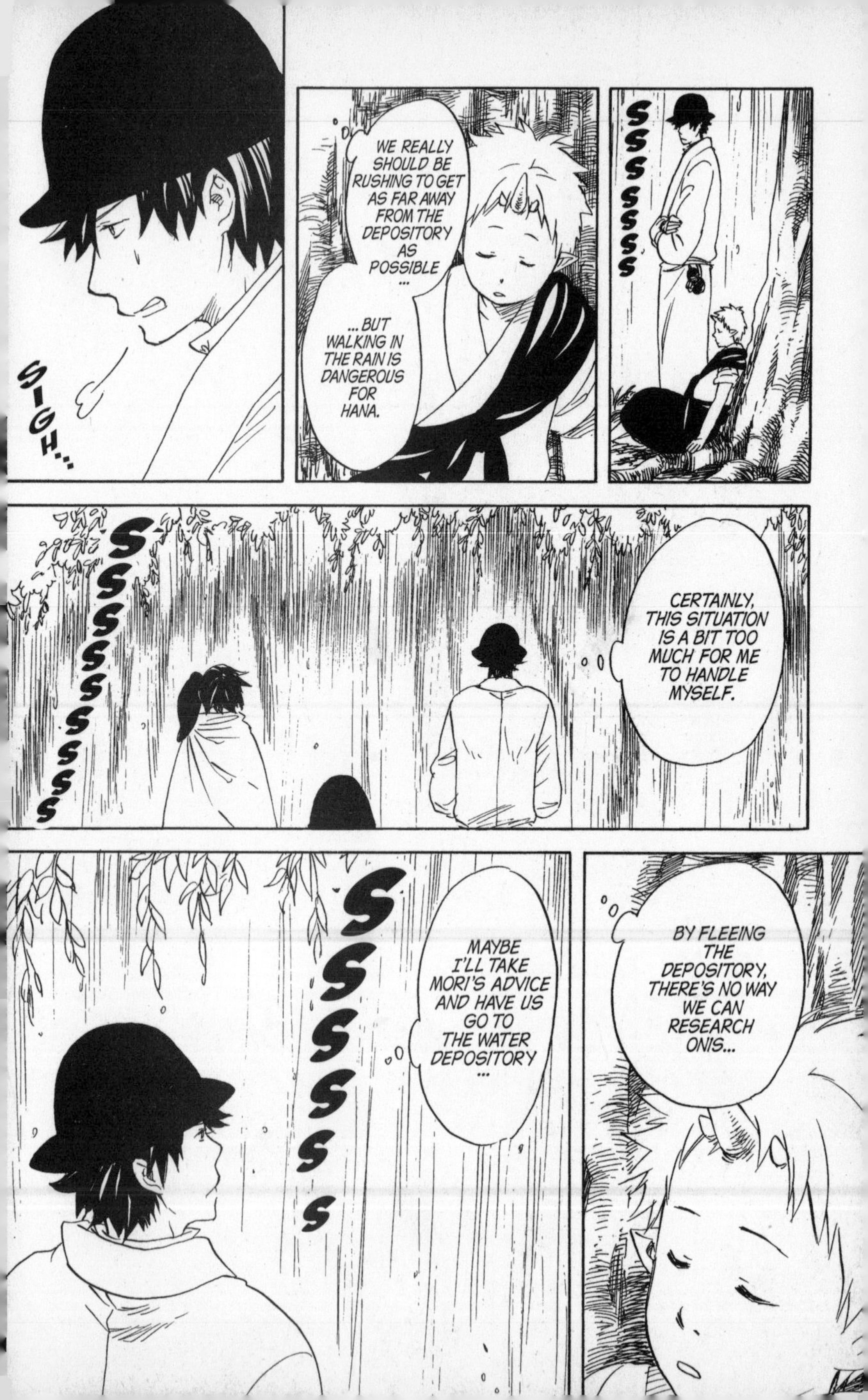
SSSSSSSS
WE REALLY SHOULD BE RUSHING TO GET AS FAR AWAY FROM THE DEPOSITORY AS POSSIBLE...
...BUT WALKING IN THE RAIN IS DANGEROUS FOR HANA.
SIGH...
CERTAINLY, THIS SITUATION IS A BIT TOO MUCH FOR ME TO HANDLE MYSELF.
SSSSSSSSSS
BY FLEEING THE DEPOSITORY, THERE'S NO WAY WE CAN RESEARCH ONIS...
MAYBE I'LL TAKE MORI'S ADVICE AND HAVE US GO TO THE WATER DEPOSITORY...
SSSSSSS

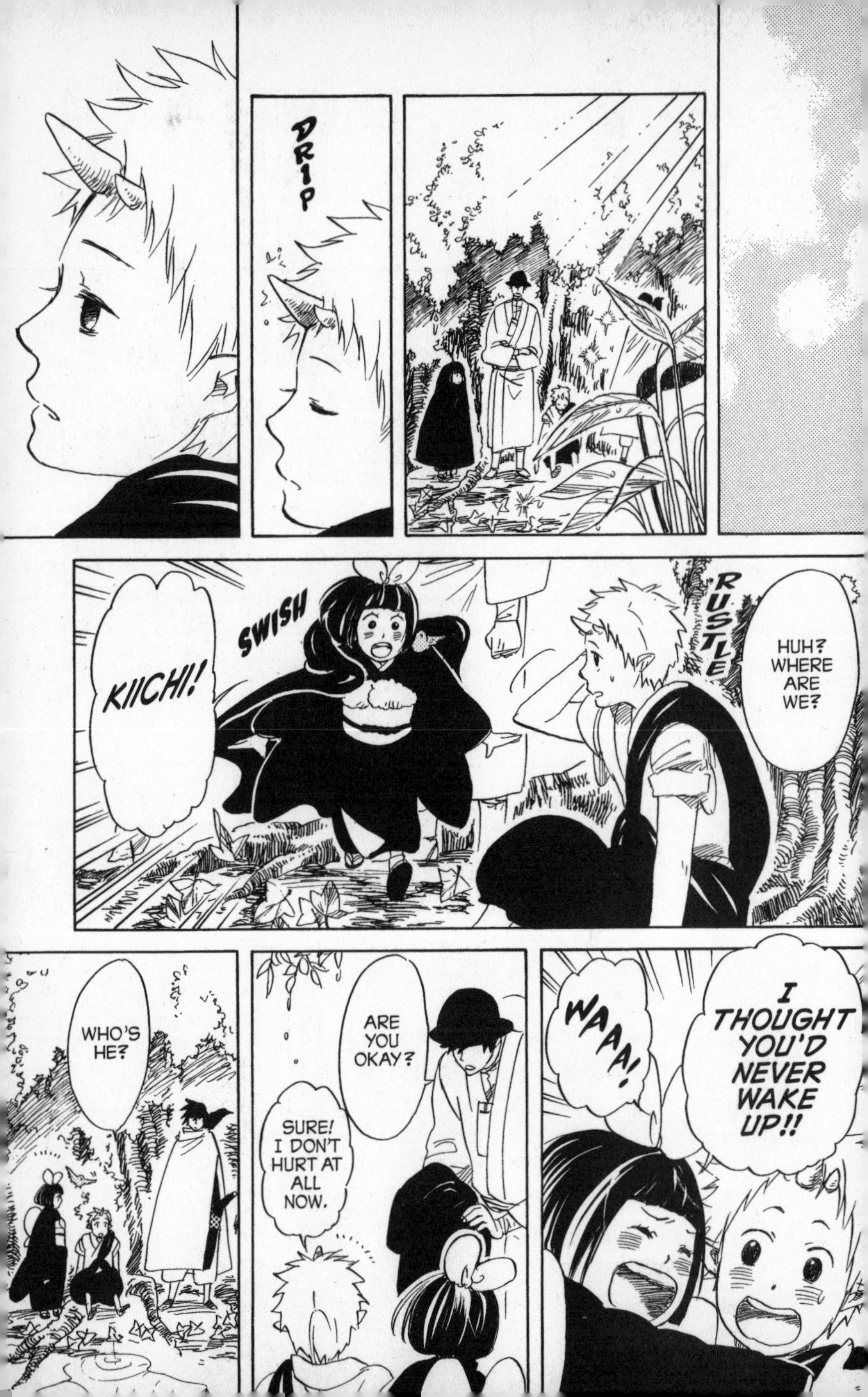
DRIP
RUSTLE
HUH? WHERE ARE WE?
SWISH
KIICHI!
I THOUGHT YOU'D NEVER WAKE UP!!
WAAA!
ARE YOU OKAY?
SURE! I DON'T HURT AT ALL NOW.
WHO'S HE?

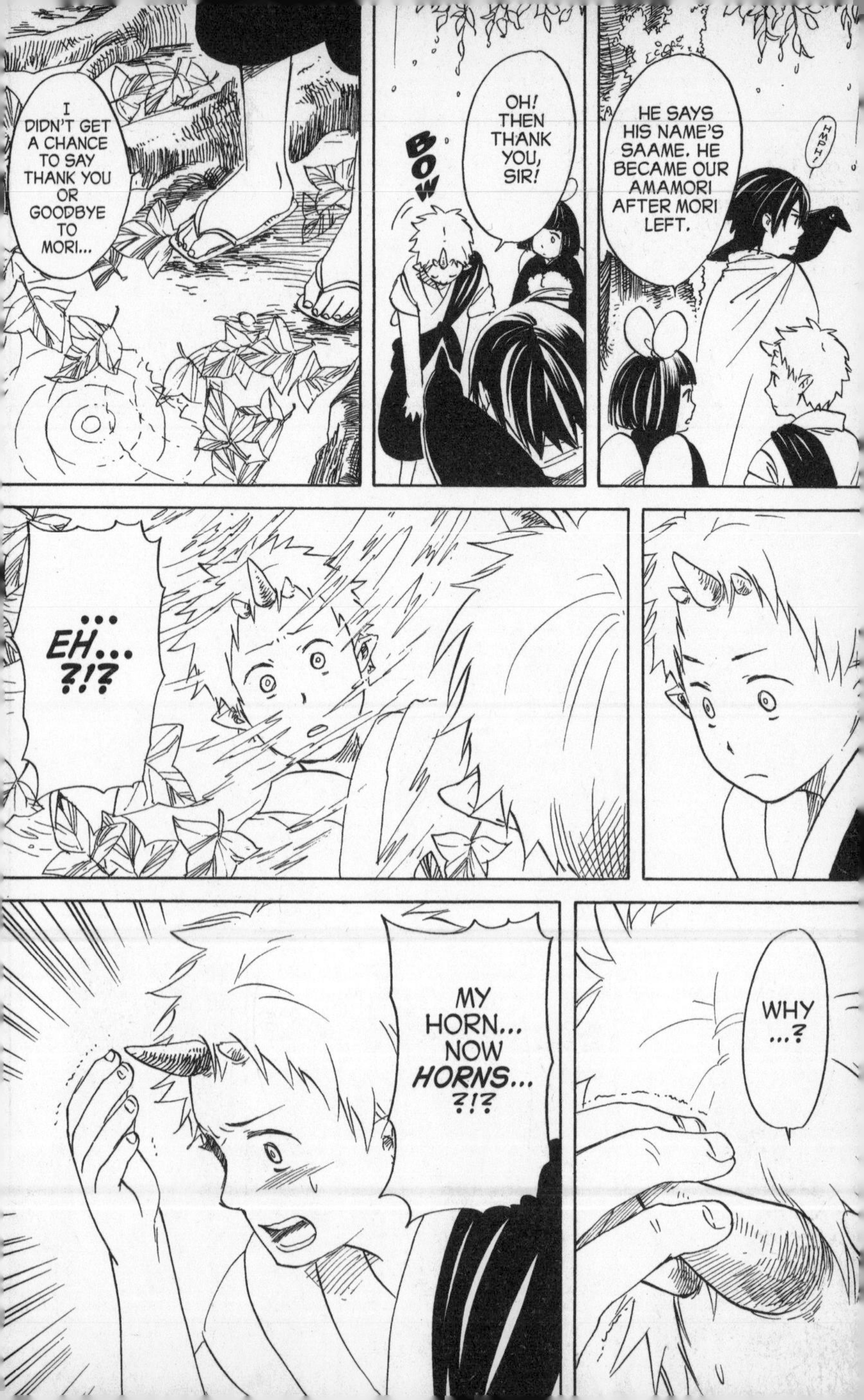
HMPH!
HE SAYS HIS NAME'S SAAME. HE BECAME OUR AMAMORI AFTER MORI LEFT.
OH! THEN THANK YOU, SIR!
BOW
I DIDN'T GET A CHANCE TO SAY THANK YOU OR GOODBYE TO MORI...
... *EH...* ?!?
WHY ...?
MY HORN... NOW *HORNS...* ?!?

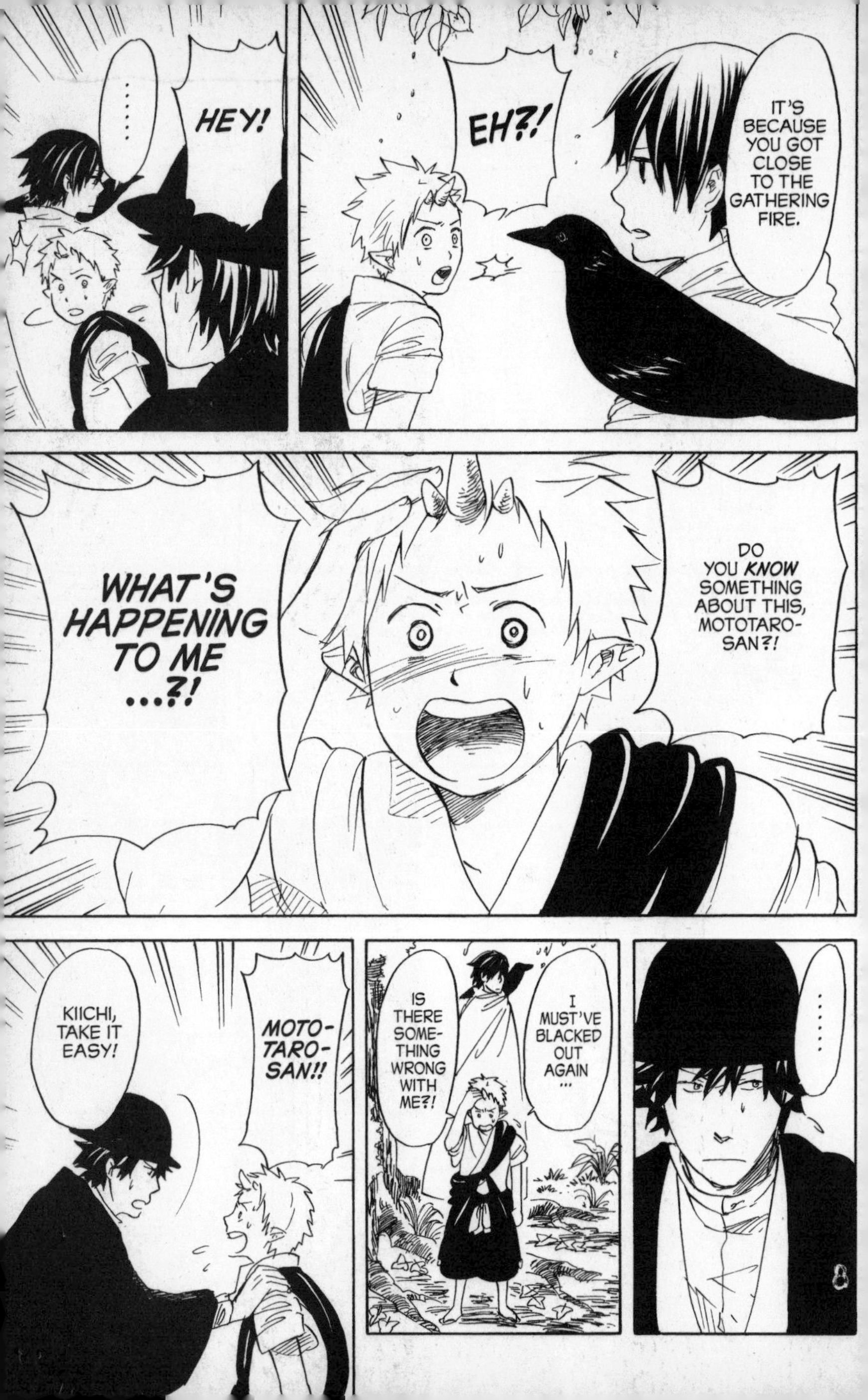
IT'S BECAUSE YOU GOT CLOSE TO THE GATHERING FIRE.
EH?!
HEY!
......
DO YOU KNOW SOMETHING ABOUT THIS, MOTOTARO-SAN?!
WHAT'S HAPPENING TO ME ...?!
......
I MUST'VE BLACKED OUT AGAIN ...
IS THERE SOMETHING WRONG WITH ME?!
MOTO-TARO-SAN!!
KIICHI, TAKE IT EASY!

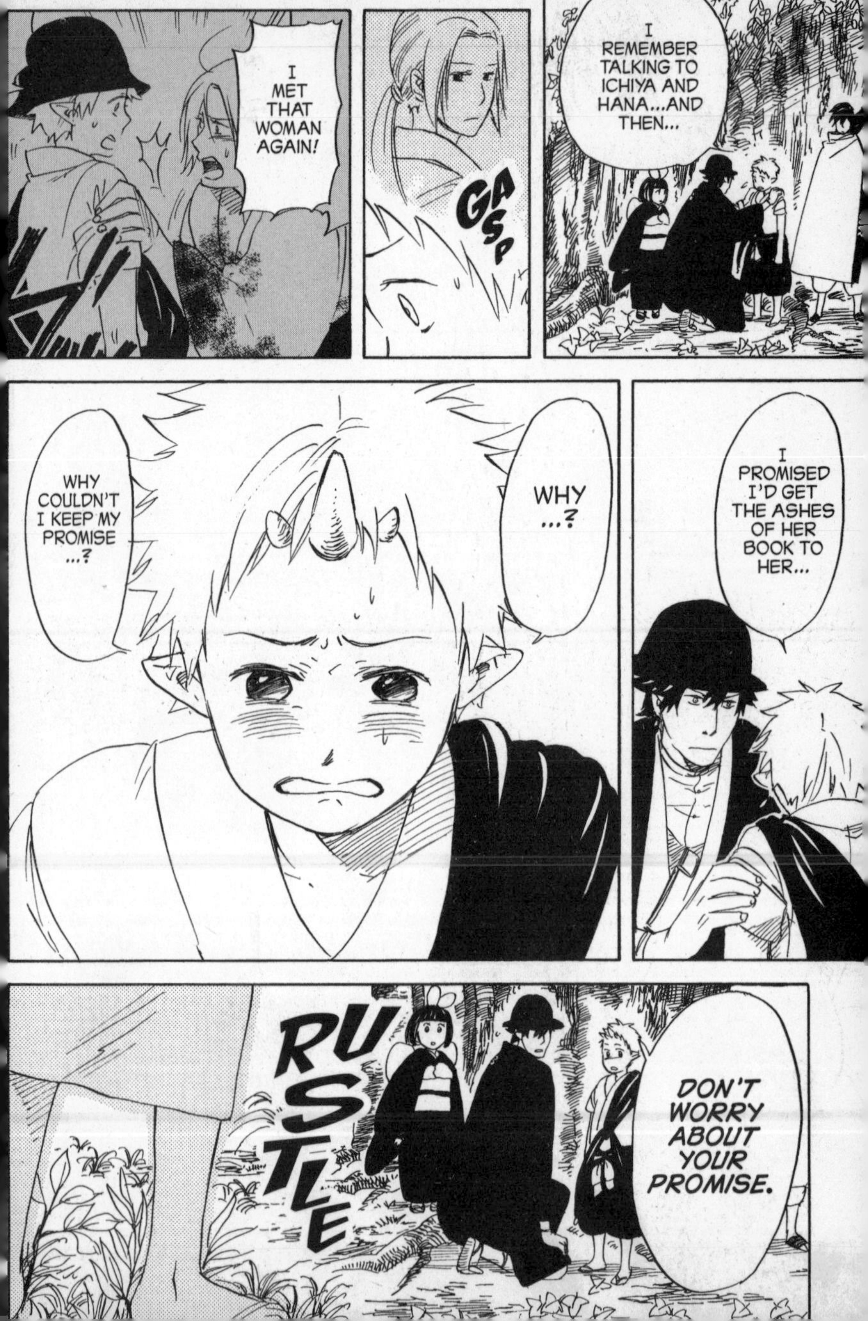
I REMEMBER TALKING TO ICHIYA AND HANA...AND THEN...
GASP
I MET THAT WOMAN AGAIN!
I PROMISED I'D GET THE ASHES OF HER BOOK TO HER...
WHY ...?
WHY COULDN'T I KEEP MY PROMISE ...?
DON'T WORRY ABOUT YOUR PROMISE.
RUSTLE

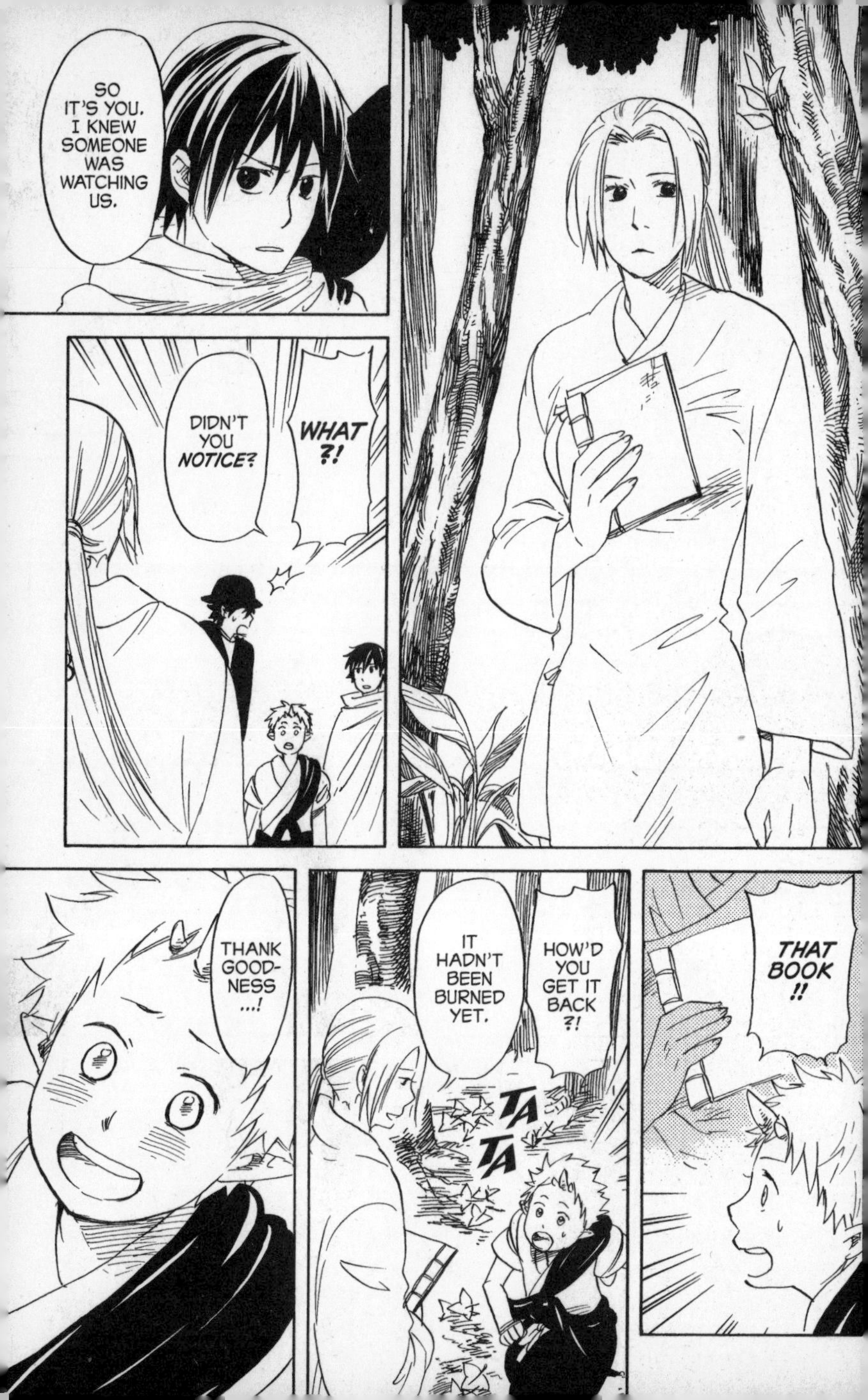
SO IT'S YOU. I KNEW SOMEONE WAS WATCHING US.
WHAT?!
DIDN'T YOU NOTICE?
THAT BOOK!!
HOW'D YOU GET IT BACK?!
IT HADN'T BEEN BURNED YET.
TA TA
THANK GOOD-NESS...!

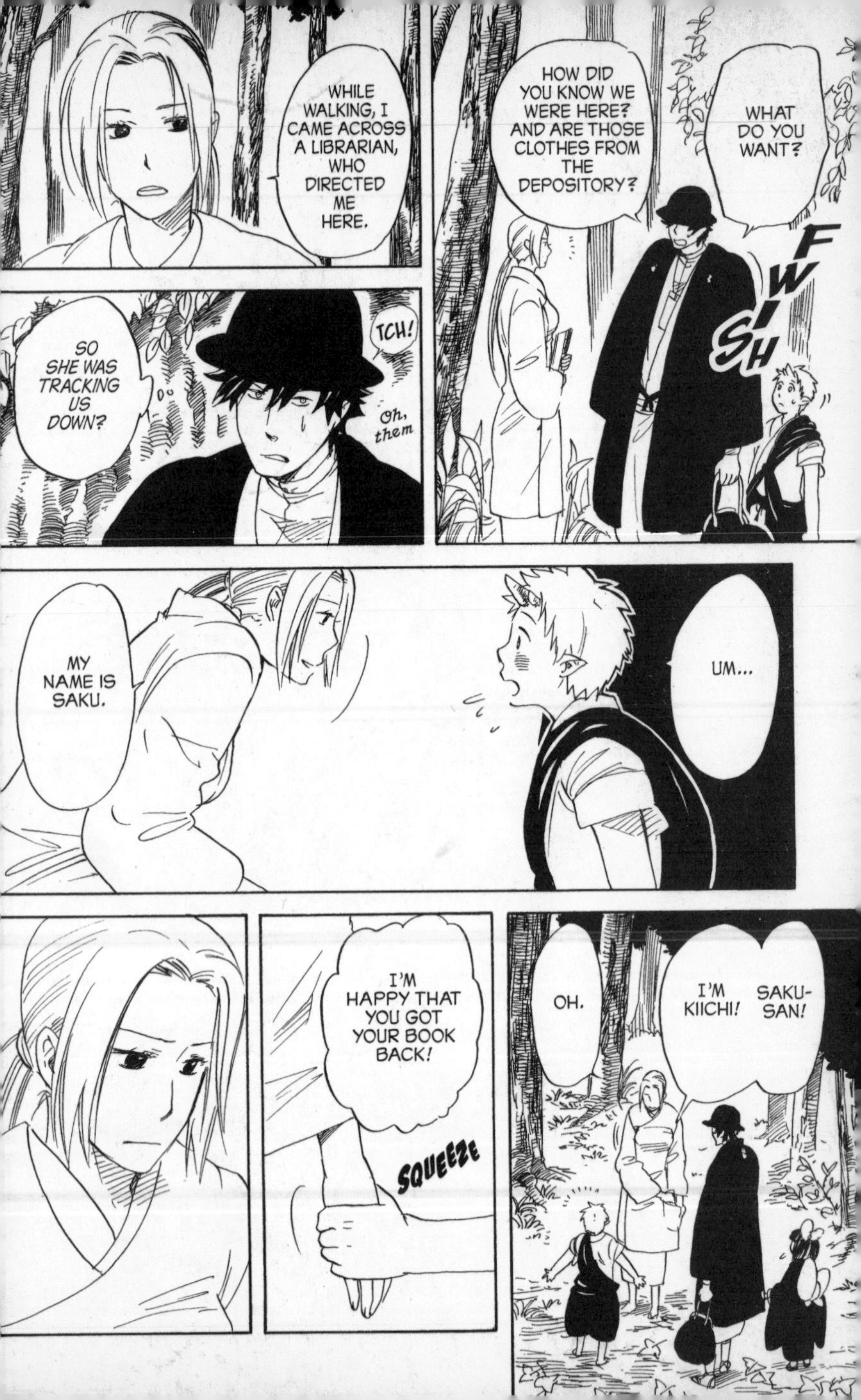
WHAT DO YOU WANT?
HOW DID YOU KNOW WE WERE HERE? AND ARE THOSE CLOTHES FROM THE DEPOSITORY?
FWISH
WHILE WALKING, I CAME ACROSS A LIBRARIAN, WHO DIRECTED ME HERE.
TCH!
Oh, them
SO SHE WAS TRACKING US DOWN?
UM...
MY NAME IS SAKU.
SAKU-SAN!
I'M KIICHI!
OH.
I'M HAPPY THAT YOU GOT YOUR BOOK BACK!
SQUEEZE

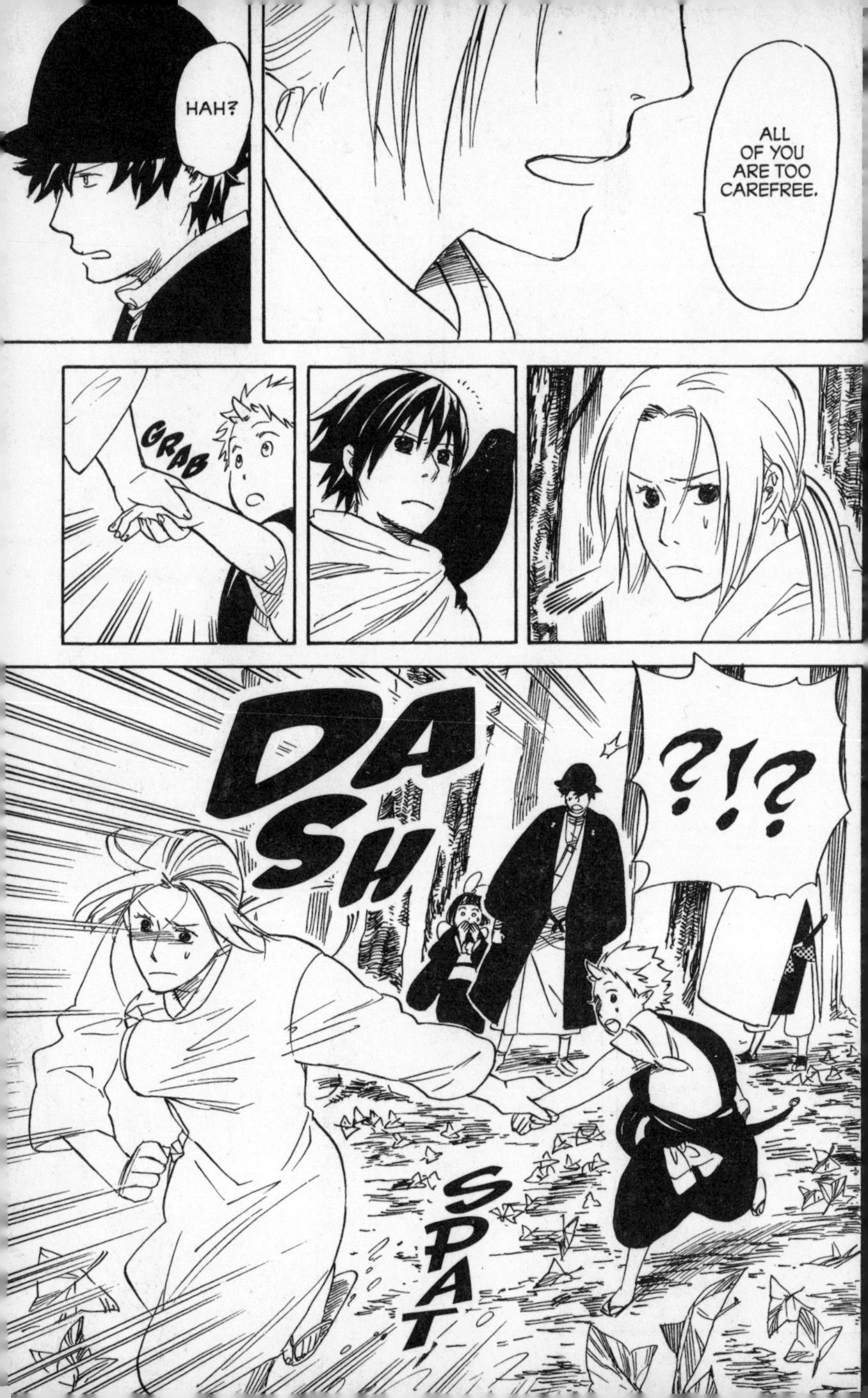
ALL OF YOU ARE TOO CAREFREE.
HAH?
GRAB
?!?
DASH
SPAT

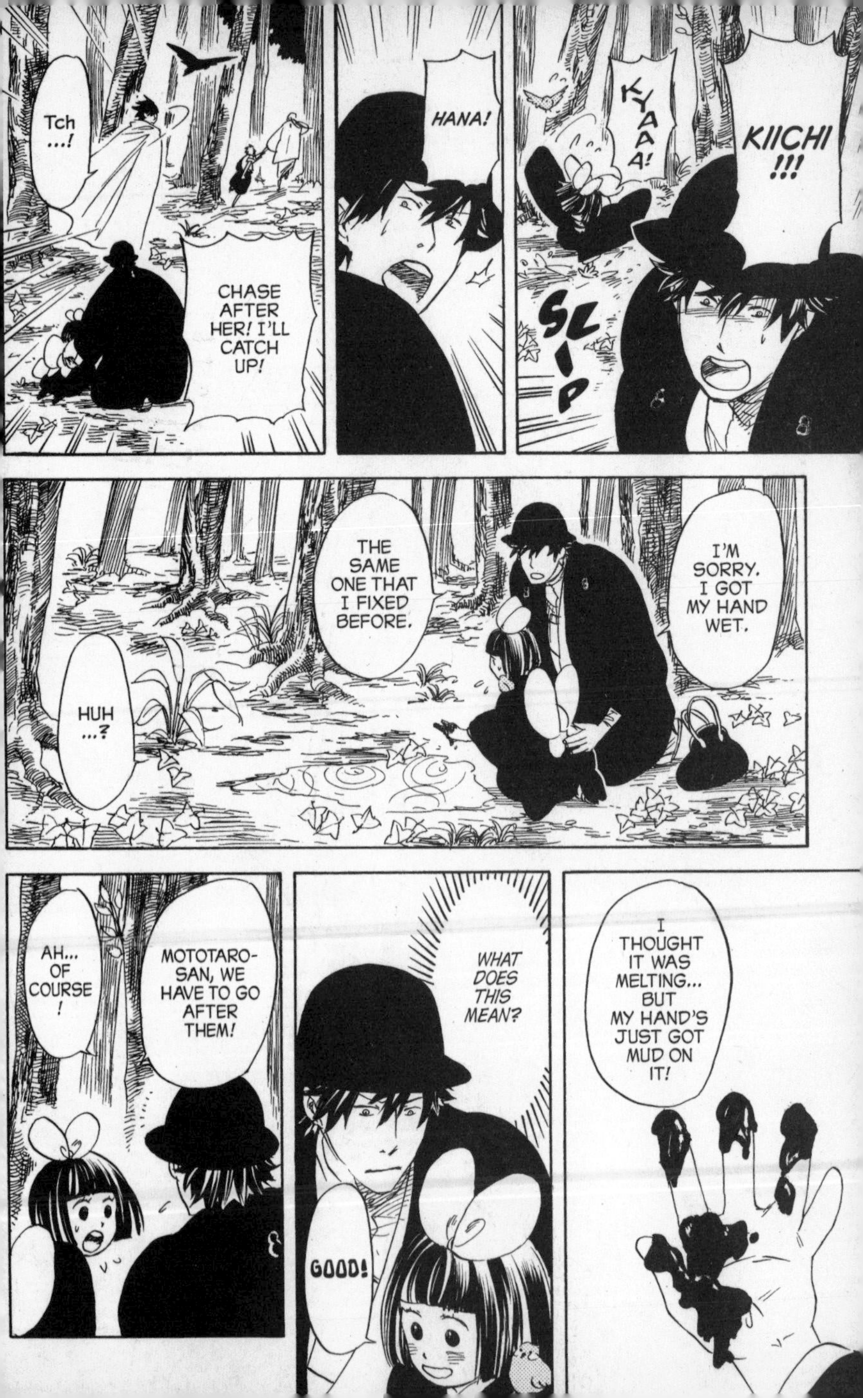
KIICHI !!!
KYAAA!
SLIP
HANA!
Tch ...!
CHASE AFTER HER! I'LL CATCH UP!
I'M SORRY. I GOT MY HAND WET.
THE SAME ONE THAT I FIXED BEFORE.
HUH ...?
I THOUGHT IT WAS MELTING... BUT MY HAND'S JUST GOT MUD ON IT!
WHAT DOES THIS MEAN?
GOOD!
MOTOTARO-SAN, WE HAVE TO GO AFTER THEM!
AH... OF COURSE!

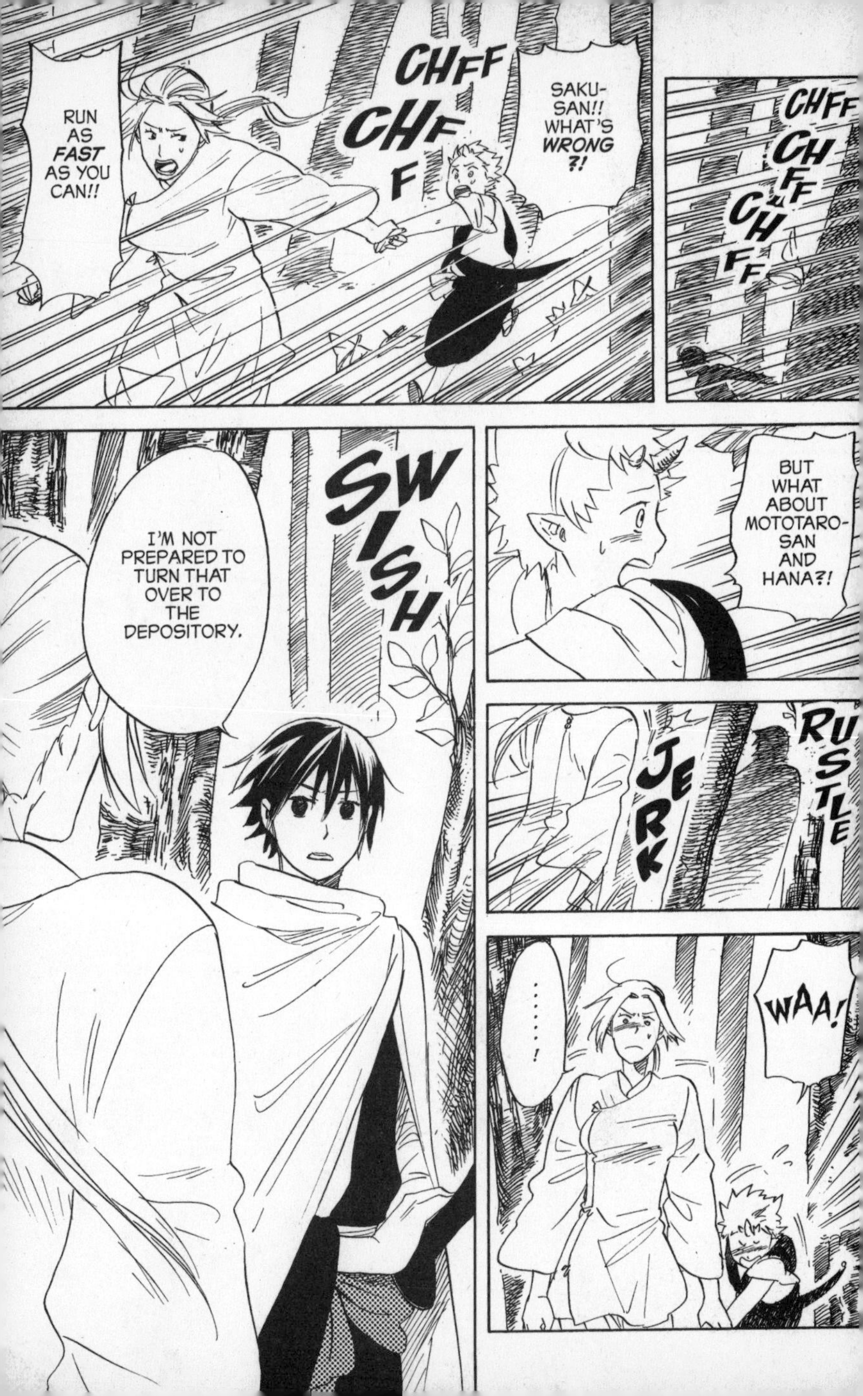
CHFF CHFF CHFF
SAKU-SAN!! WHAT'S *WRONG*?!
CHFF CHFF
RUN AS *FAST* AS YOU CAN!!
BUT WHAT ABOUT MOTOTARO-SAN AND HANA?!
RUSTLE
JERK
WAA!
......!
SWISH
I'M NOT PREPARED TO TURN THAT OVER TO THE DEPOSITORY.

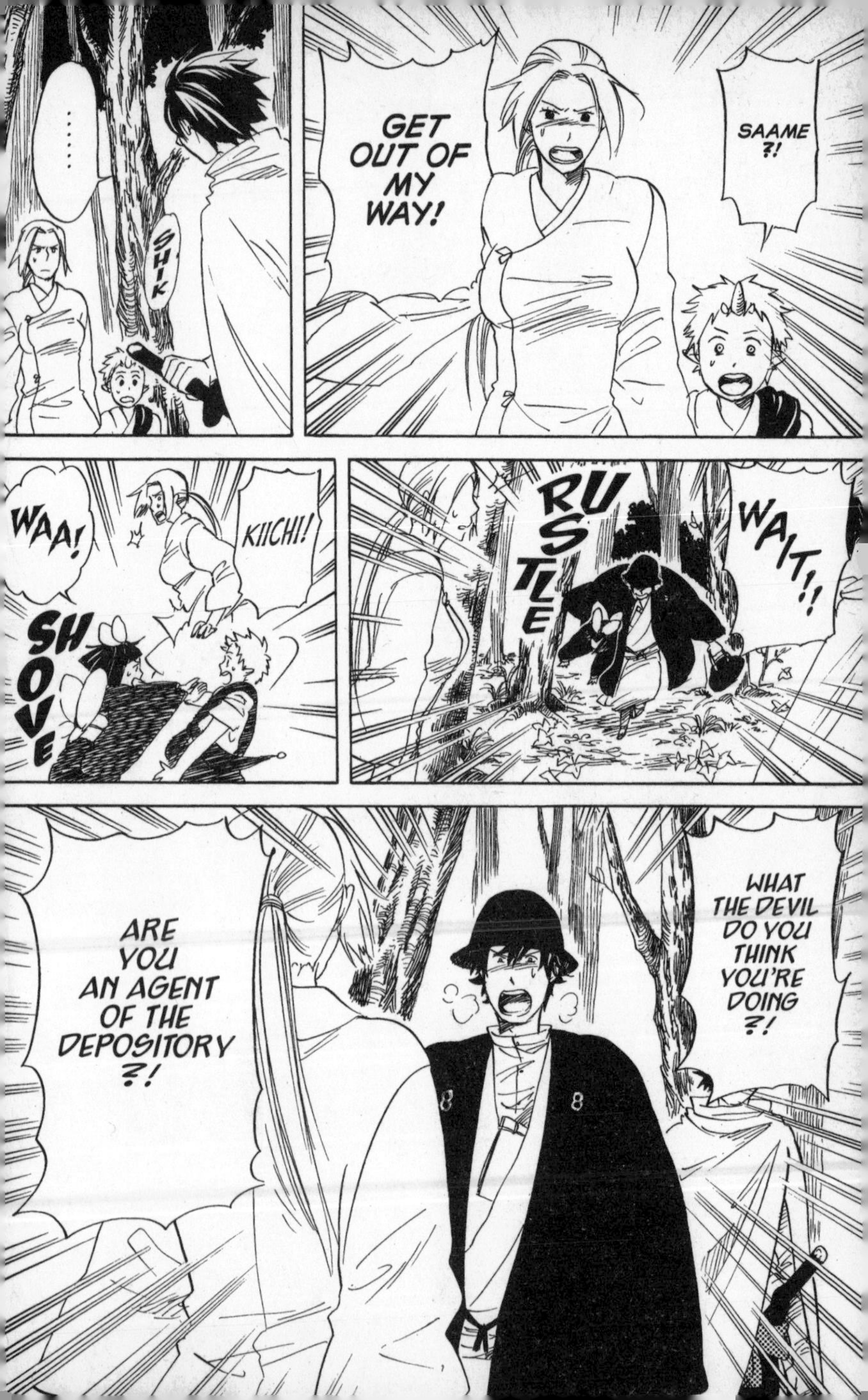
SAAME ?!
GET OUT OF MY WAY!
......
SHIK
WAIT!!
RUSTLE
KIICHI!
WAA!
SHOVE
WHAT THE DEVIL DO YOU THINK YOU'RE DOING ?!
ARE YOU AN AGENT OF THE DEPOSITORY ?!

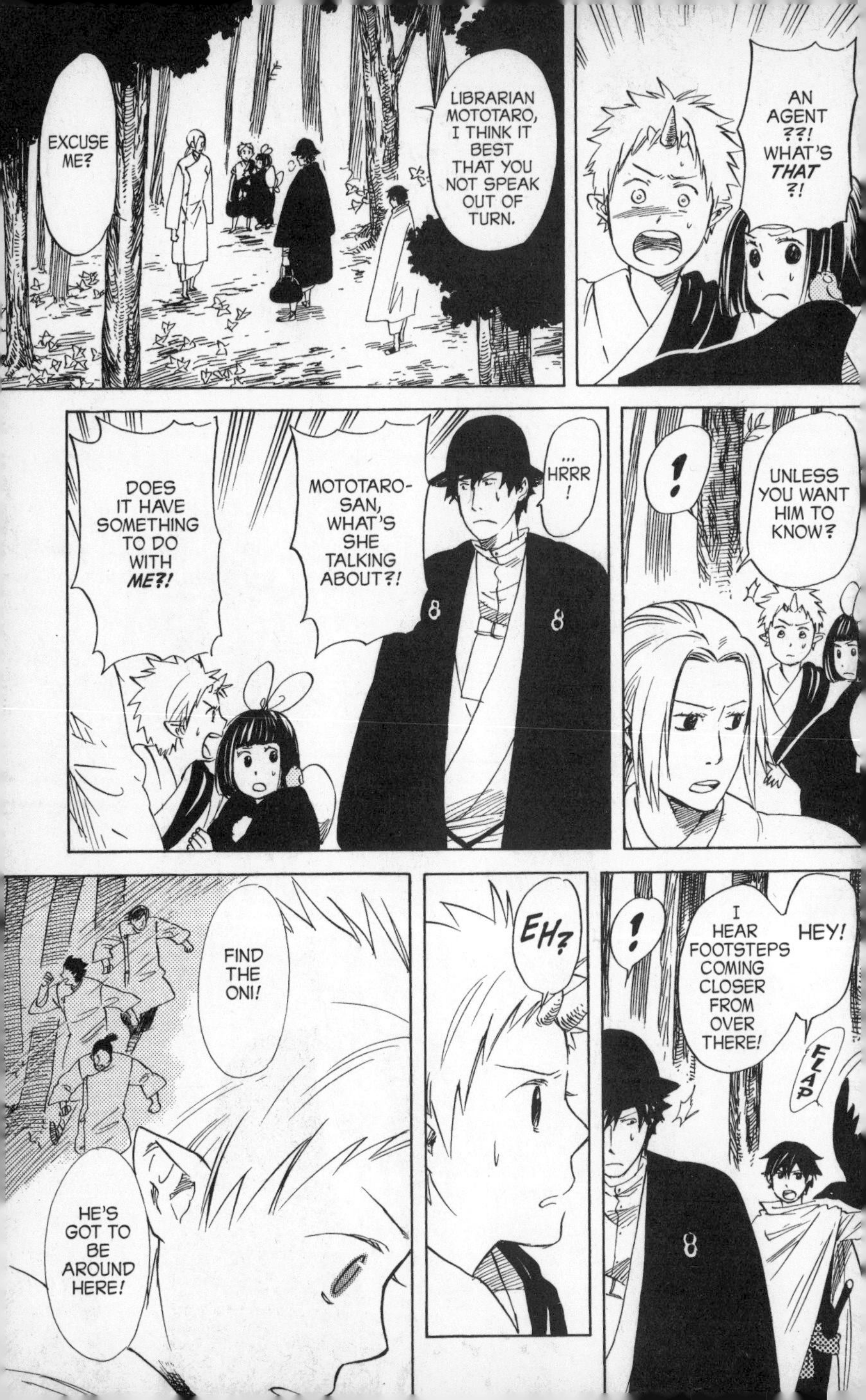
AN AGENT ??! WHAT'S *THAT* ?!
LIBRARIAN MOTOTARO, I THINK IT BEST THAT YOU NOT SPEAK OUT OF TURN.
EXCUSE ME?
UNLESS YOU WANT HIM TO KNOW?
!
... HRRR !
MOTOTARO-SAN, WHAT'S SHE TALKING ABOUT?!
DOES IT HAVE SOMETHING TO DO WITH *ME?!*
HEY!
I HEAR FOOTSTEPS COMING CLOSER FROM OVER THERE!
!
FLAP
EH?
FIND THE ONI!
HE'S GOT TO BE AROUND HERE!

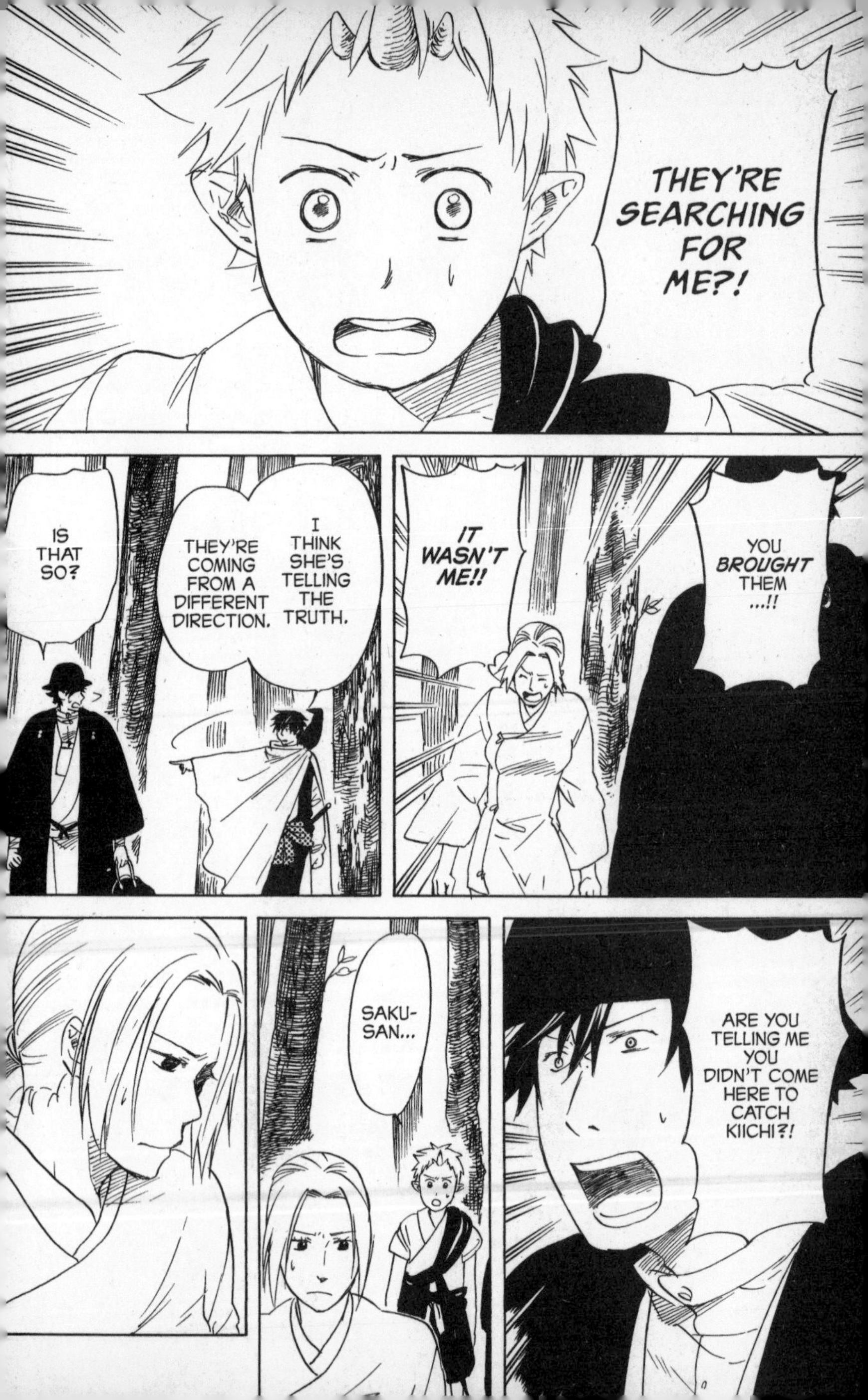
THEY'RE SEARCHING FOR ME?!
YOU BROUGHT THEM ...!!
IT WASN'T ME!!
I THINK SHE'S TELLING THE TRUTH.
THEY'RE COMING FROM A DIFFERENT DIRECTION.
IS THAT SO?
ARE YOU TELLING ME YOU DIDN'T COME HERE TO CATCH KIICHI?!
SAKU-SAN...

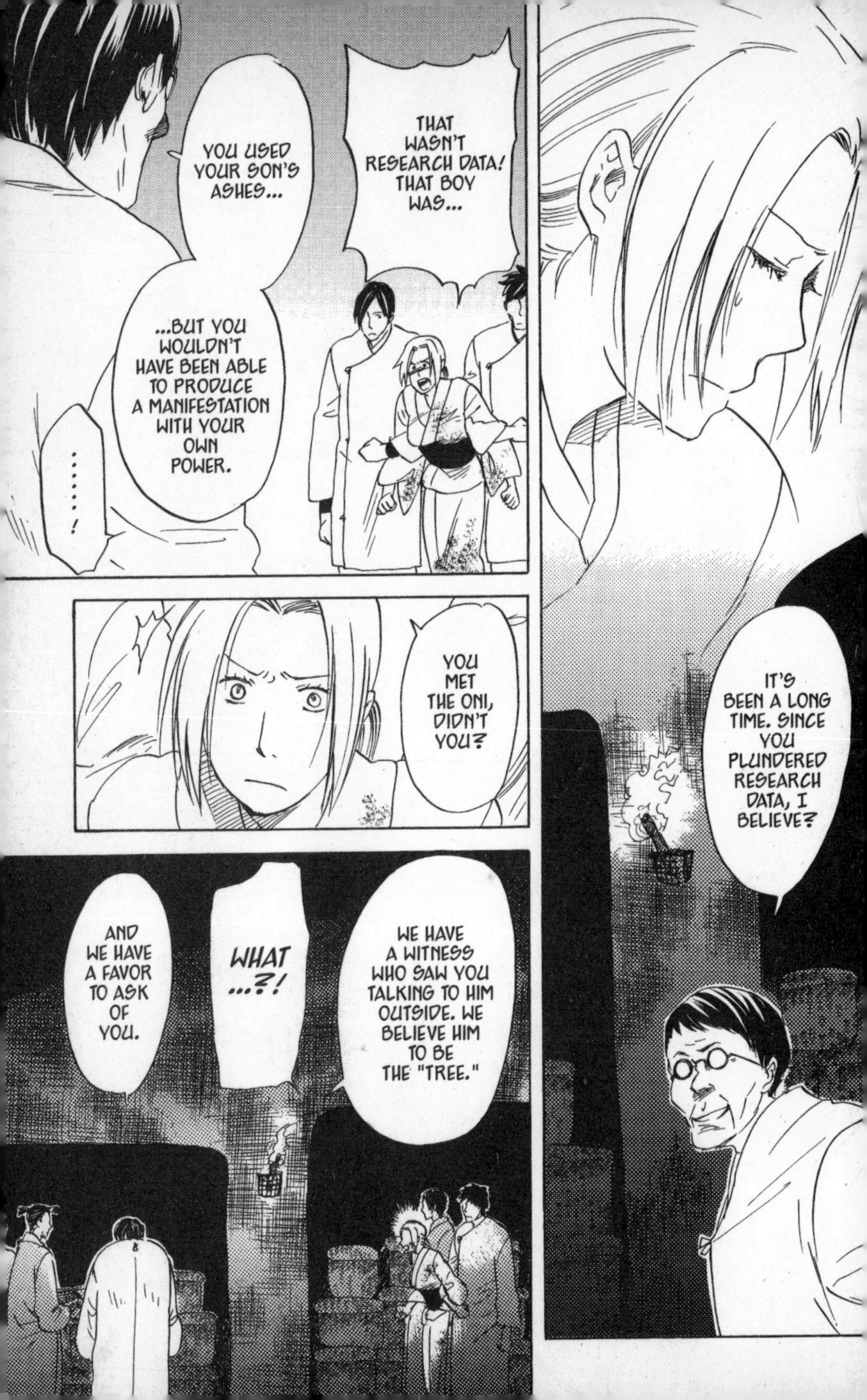
IT'S BEEN A LONG TIME. SINCE YOU PLUNDERED RESEARCH DATA, I BELIEVE?
THAT WASN'T RESEARCH DATA! THAT BOY WAS...
YOU USED YOUR SON'S ASHES...
...BUT YOU WOULDN'T HAVE BEEN ABLE TO PRODUCE A MANIFESTATION WITH YOUR OWN POWER.
......!
YOU MET THE ONI, DIDN'T YOU?
WE HAVE A WITNESS WHO SAW YOU TALKING TO HIM OUTSIDE. WE BELIEVE HIM TO BE THE "TREE."
WHAT ...?!
AND WE HAVE A FAVOR TO ASK OF YOU.

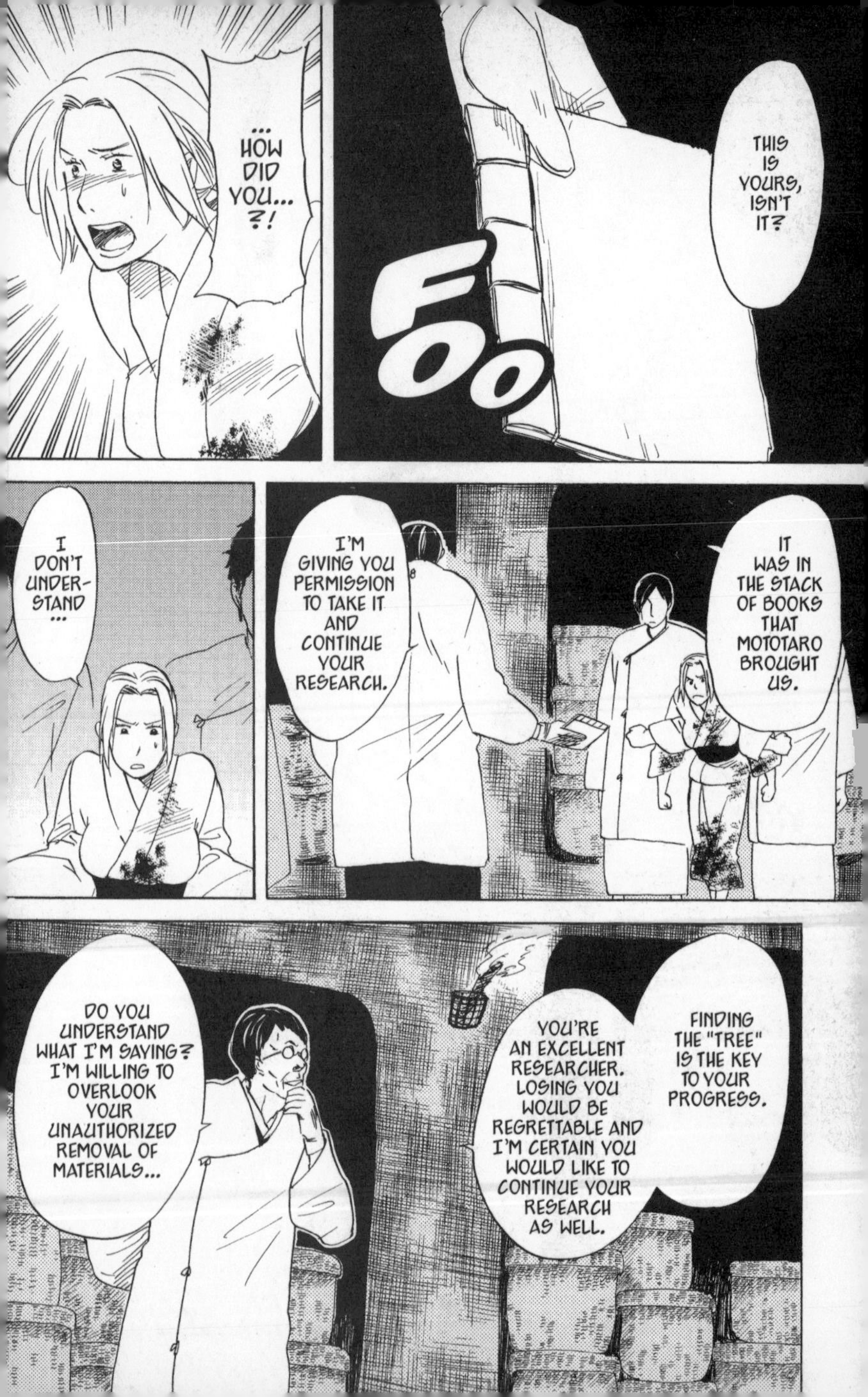
THIS IS YOURS, ISN'T IT?
FOO
... HOW DID YOU... ?!
IT WAS IN THE STACK OF BOOKS THAT MOTOTARO BROUGHT US.
I'M GIVING YOU PERMISSION TO TAKE IT AND CONTINUE YOUR RESEARCH.
I DON'T UNDER-STAND ...
FINDING THE "TREE" IS THE KEY TO YOUR PROGRESS.
YOU'RE AN EXCELLENT RESEARCHER. LOSING YOU WOULD BE REGRETTABLE AND I'M CERTAIN YOU WOULD LIKE TO CONTINUE YOUR RESEARCH AS WELL.
DO YOU UNDERSTAND WHAT I'M SAYING? I'M WILLING TO OVERLOOK YOUR UNAUTHORIZED REMOVAL OF MATERIALS...

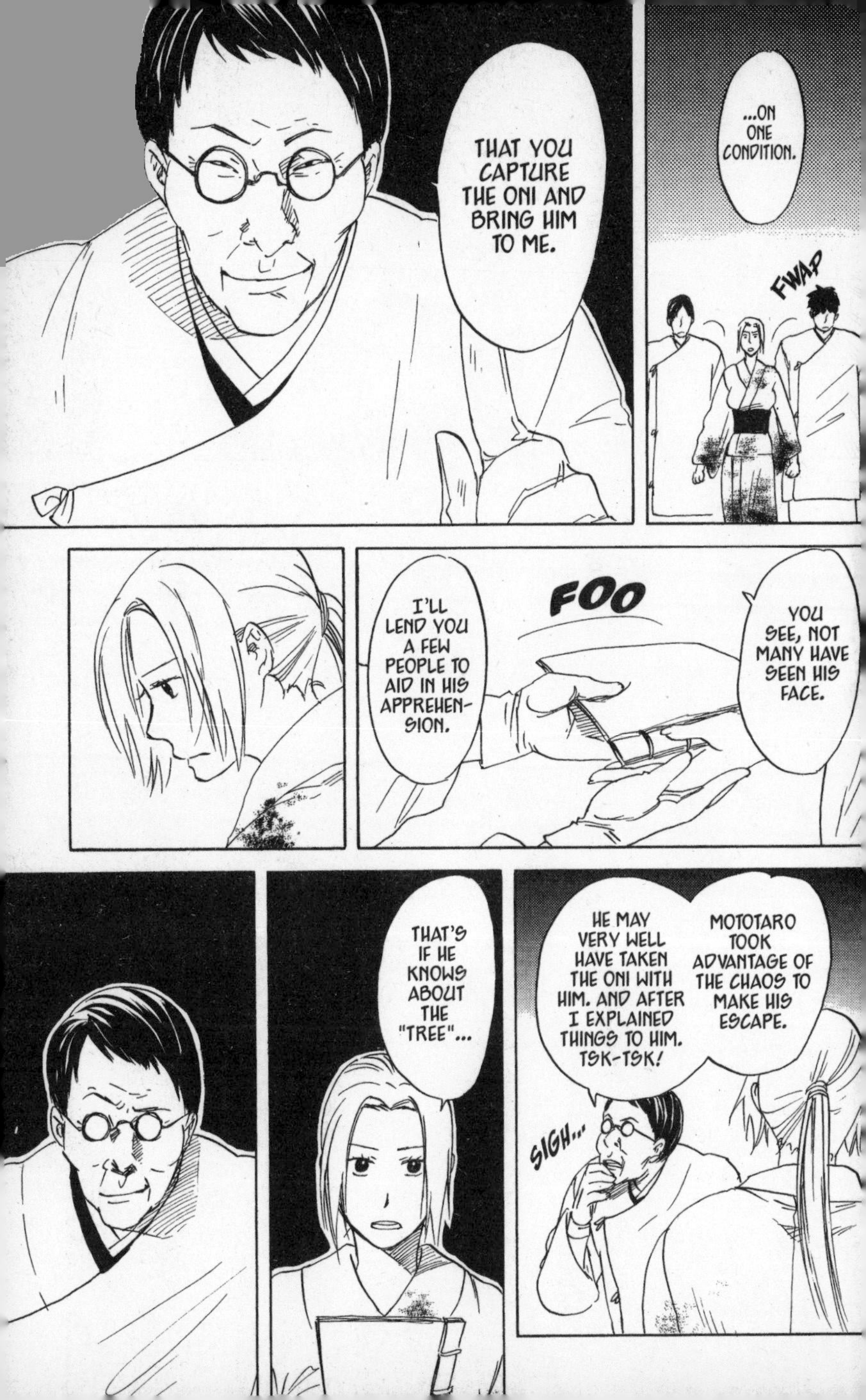
...ON ONE CONDITION.
FWAP
THAT YOU CAPTURE THE ONI AND BRING HIM TO ME.
YOU SEE, NOT MANY HAVE SEEN HIS FACE.
FOO
I'LL LEND YOU A FEW PEOPLE TO AID IN HIS APPREHEN-SION.
MOTOTARO TOOK ADVANTAGE OF THE CHAOS TO MAKE HIS ESCAPE.
HE MAY VERY WELL HAVE TAKEN THE ONI WITH HIM. AND AFTER I EXPLAINED THINGS TO HIM. TSK-TSK!
SIGH...
THAT'S IF HE KNOWS ABOUT THE "TREE"...

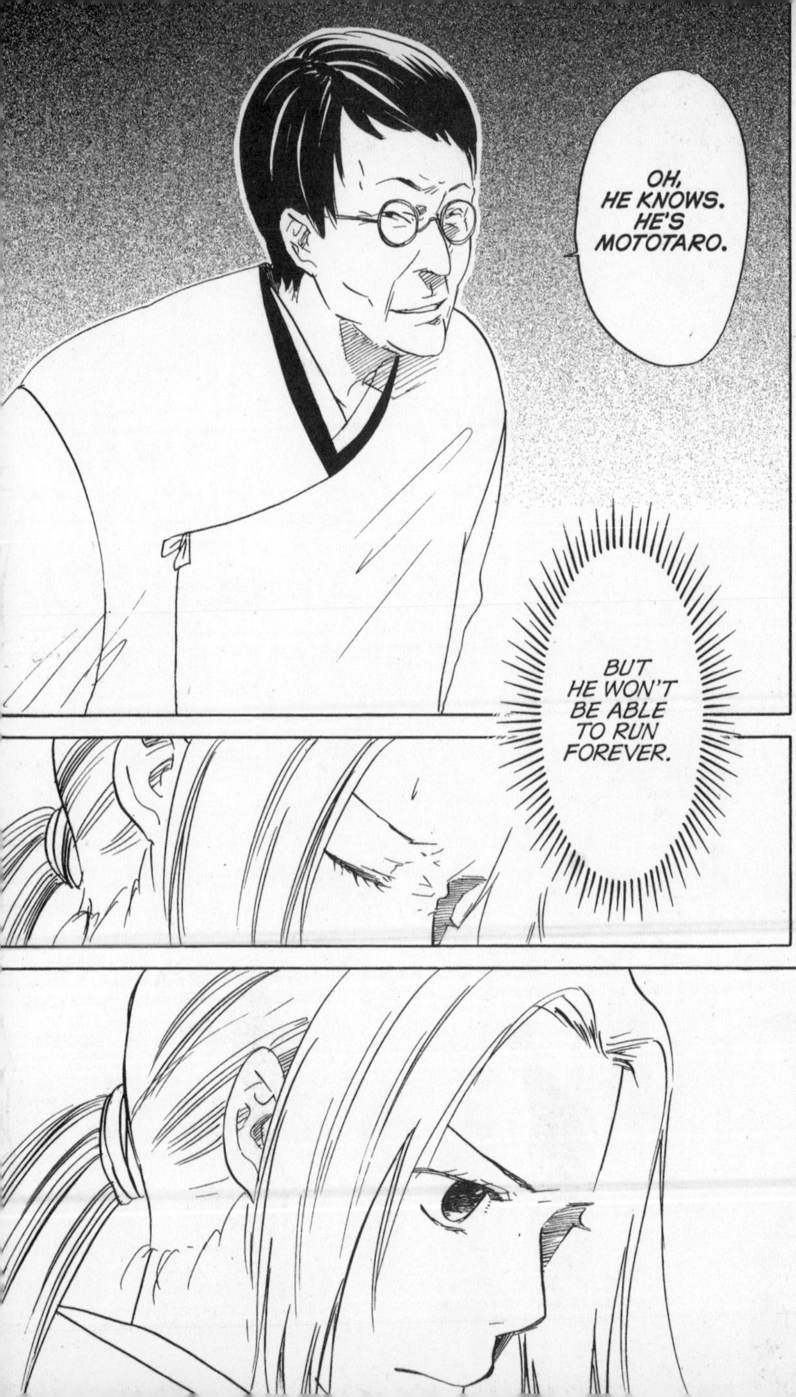
OH, HE KNOWS. HE'S MOTOTARO.
BUT HE WON'T BE ABLE TO RUN FOREVER.

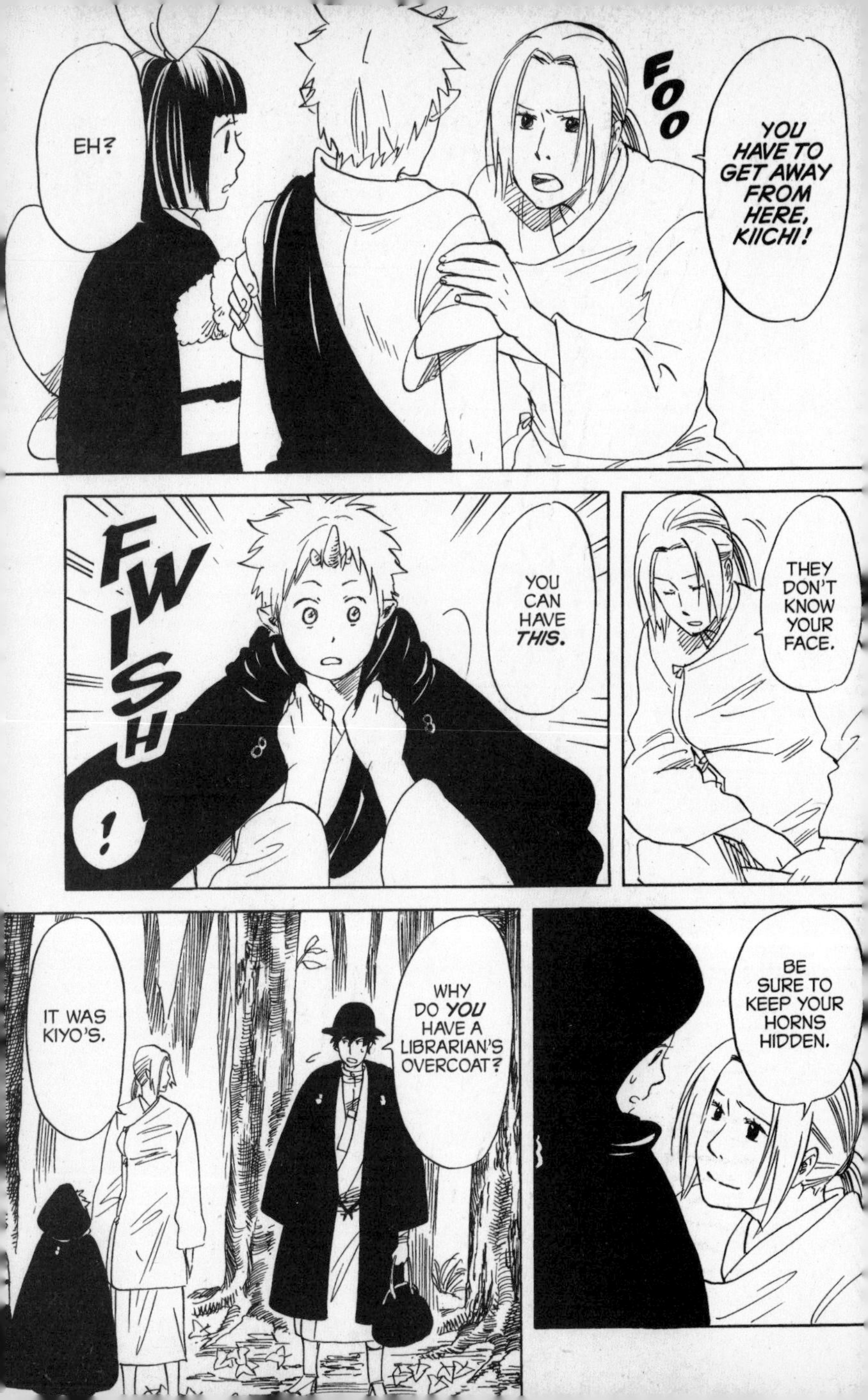

YOU HAVE TO GET AWAY FROM HERE, KIICHI!
FOO
EH?
THEY DON'T KNOW YOUR FACE.
YOU CAN HAVE THIS.
FWISH!
BE SURE TO KEEP YOUR HORNS HIDDEN.
WHY DO YOU HAVE A LIBRARIAN'S OVERCOAT?
IT WAS KIYO'S.

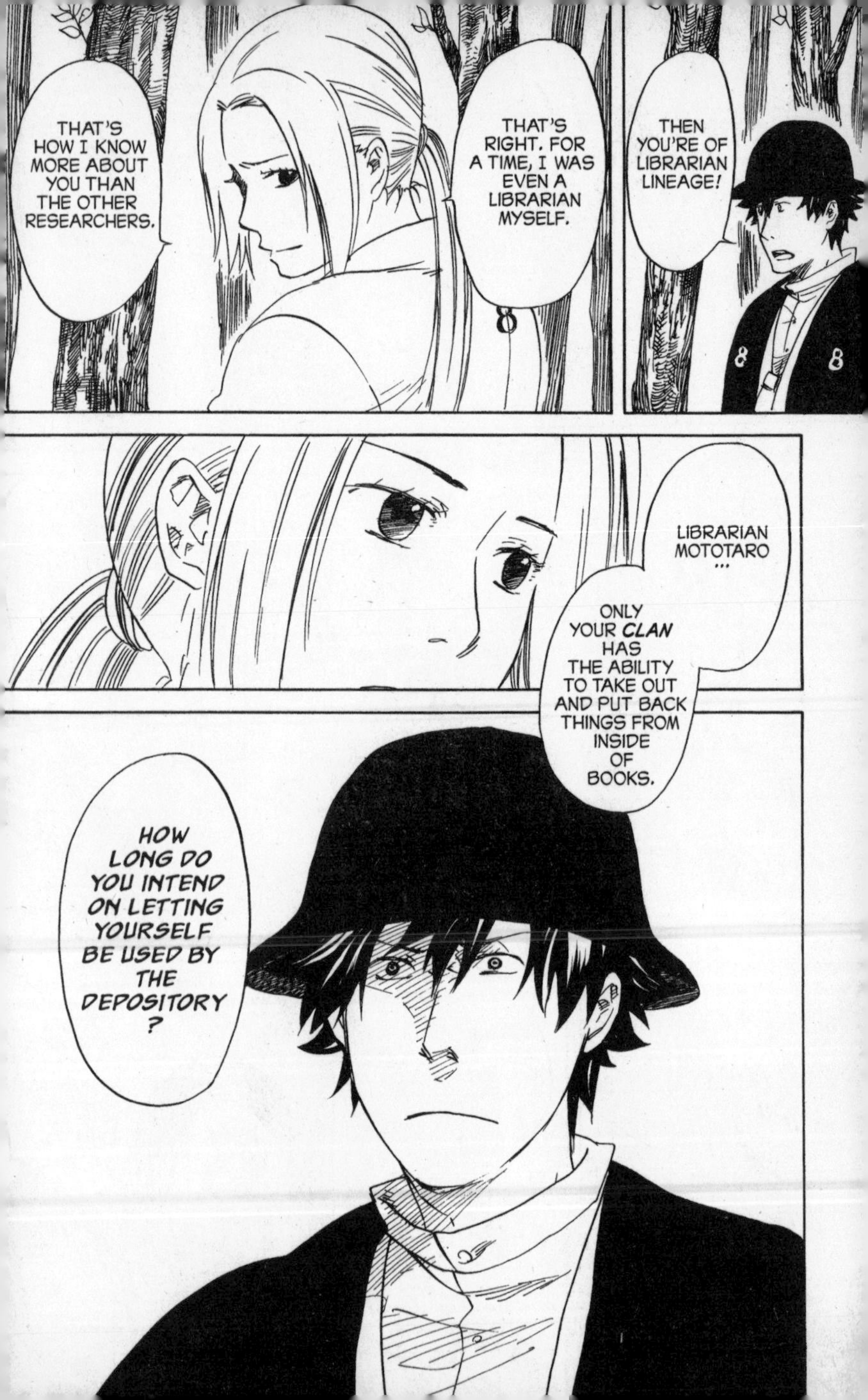
THEN YOU'RE OF LIBRARIAN LINEAGE!
THAT'S RIGHT. FOR A TIME, I WAS EVEN A LIBRARIAN MYSELF.
THAT'S HOW I KNOW MORE ABOUT YOU THAN THE OTHER RESEARCHERS.
LIBRARIAN MOTOTARO...
ONLY YOUR *CLAN* HAS THE ABILITY TO TAKE OUT AND PUT BACK THINGS FROM INSIDE OF BOOKS.
HOW LONG DO YOU INTEND ON LETTING YOURSELF BE USED BY THE DEPOSITORY?

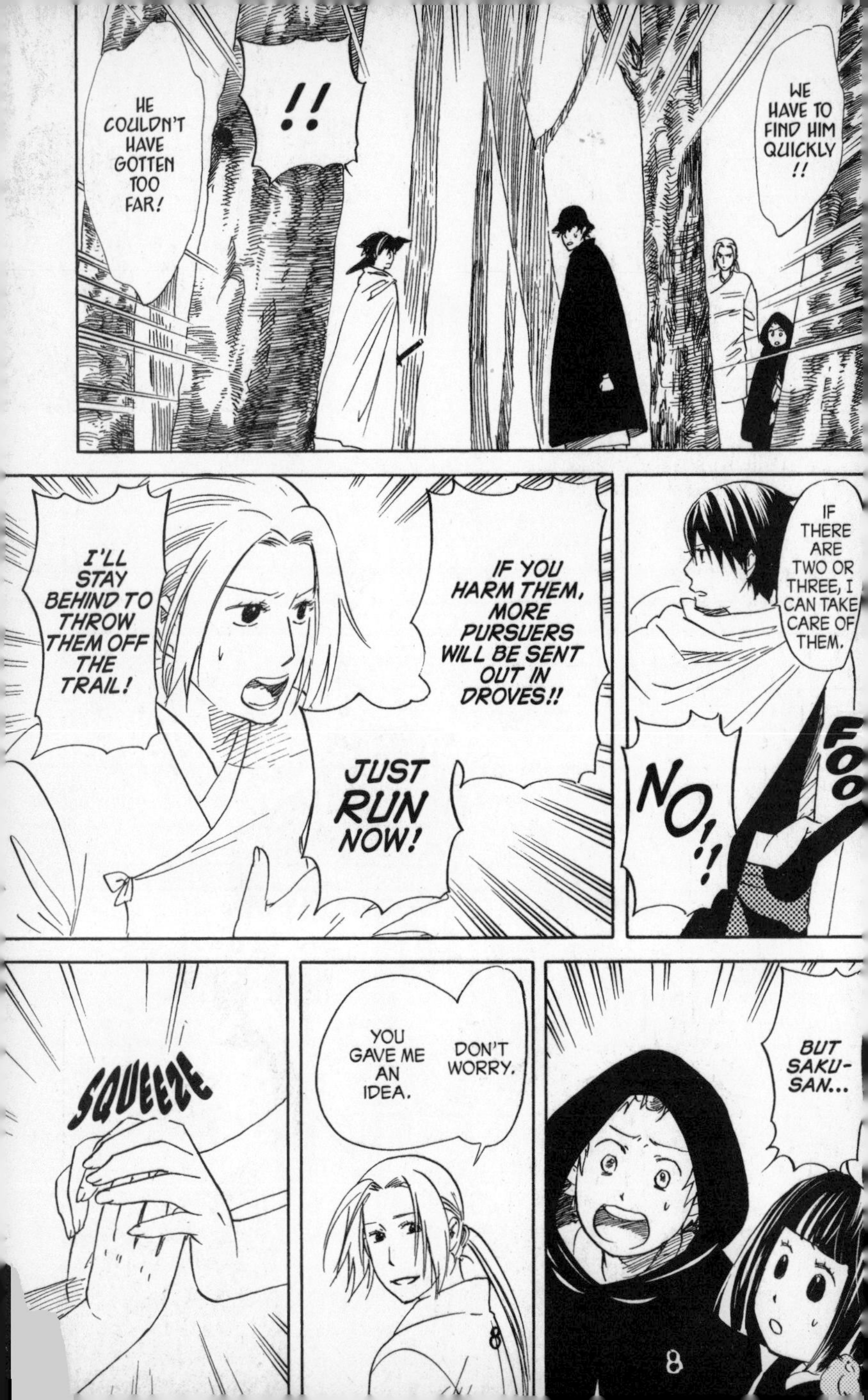
WE HAVE TO FIND HIM QUICKLY!!
!!
HE COULDN'T HAVE GOTTEN TOO FAR!
IF THERE ARE TWO OR THREE, I CAN TAKE CARE OF THEM.
FOO
NO!!
IF YOU HARM THEM, MORE PURSUERS WILL BE SENT OUT IN DROVES!!
I'LL STAY BEHIND TO THROW THEM OFF THE TRAIL!
JUST RUN NOW!
BUT SAKU-SAN...
DON'T WORRY.
YOU GAVE ME AN IDEA.
SQUEEZE

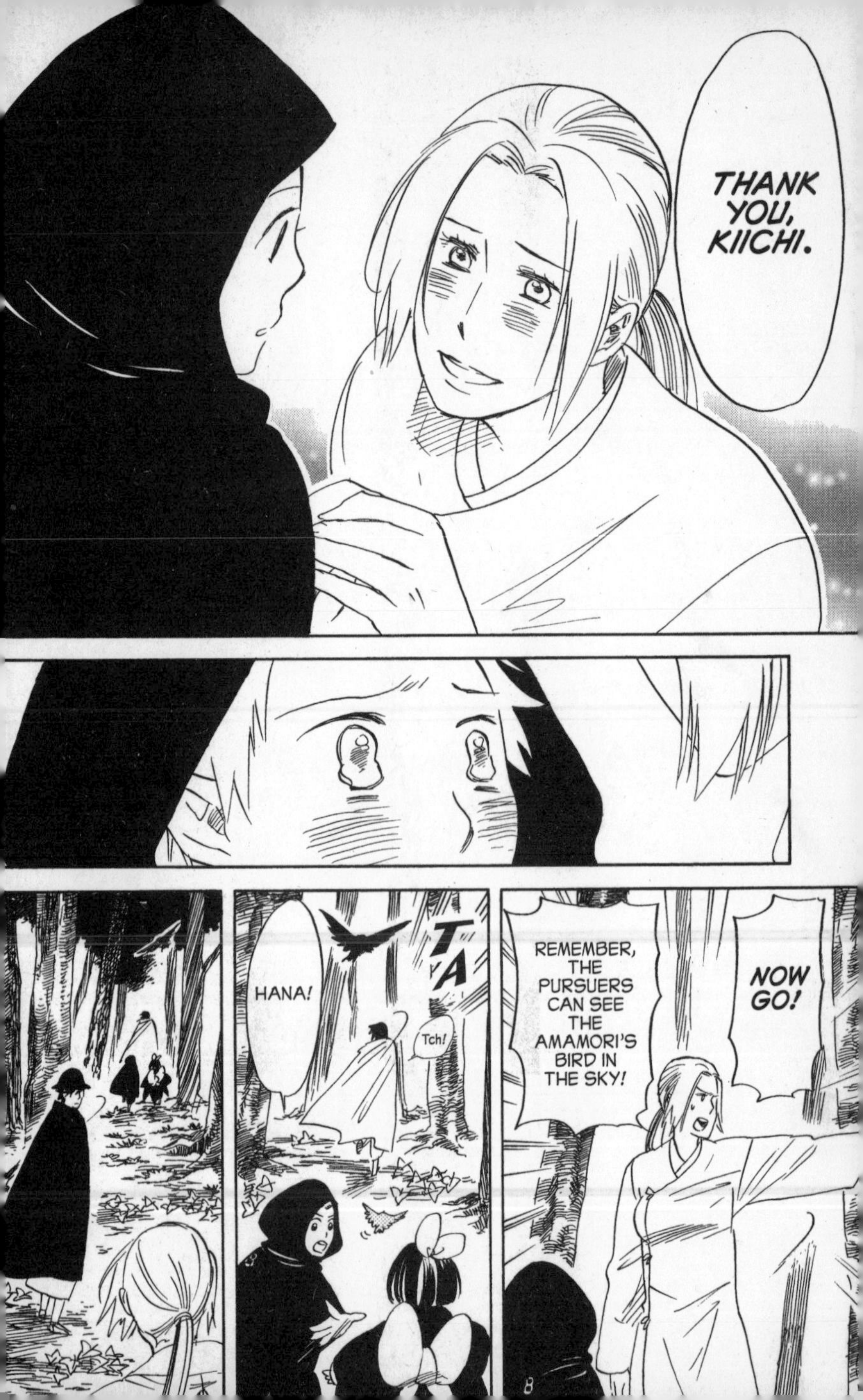
THANK YOU, KIICHI.
NOW GO!
REMEMBER, THE PURSUERS CAN SEE THE AMAMORI'S BIRD IN THE SKY!
TA
HANA!
Tch!

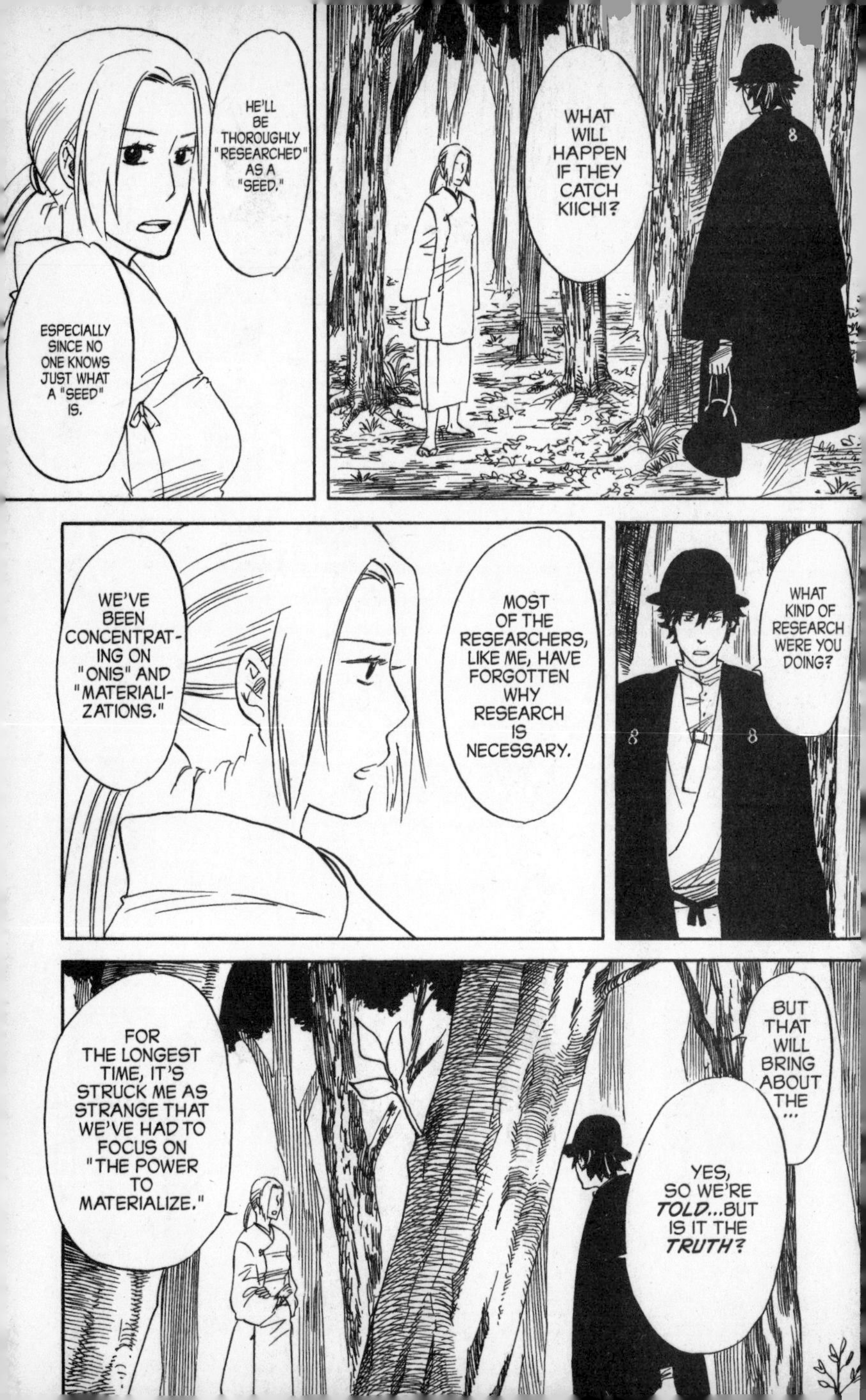
WHAT WILL HAPPEN IF THEY CATCH KIICHI?
HE'LL BE THOROUGHLY "RESEARCHED" AS A "SEED."
ESPECIALLY SINCE NO ONE KNOWS JUST WHAT A "SEED" IS.
WHAT KIND OF RESEARCH WERE YOU DOING?
MOST OF THE RESEARCHERS, LIKE ME, HAVE FORGOTTEN WHY RESEARCH IS NECESSARY.
WE'VE BEEN CONCENTRATING ON "ONIS" AND "MATERIALIZATIONS."
FOR THE LONGEST TIME, IT'S STRUCK ME AS STRANGE THAT WE'VE HAD TO FOCUS ON "THE POWER TO MATERIALIZE."
BUT THAT WILL BRING ABOUT THE...
YES, SO WE'RE *TOLD*...BUT IS IT THE *TRUTH*?

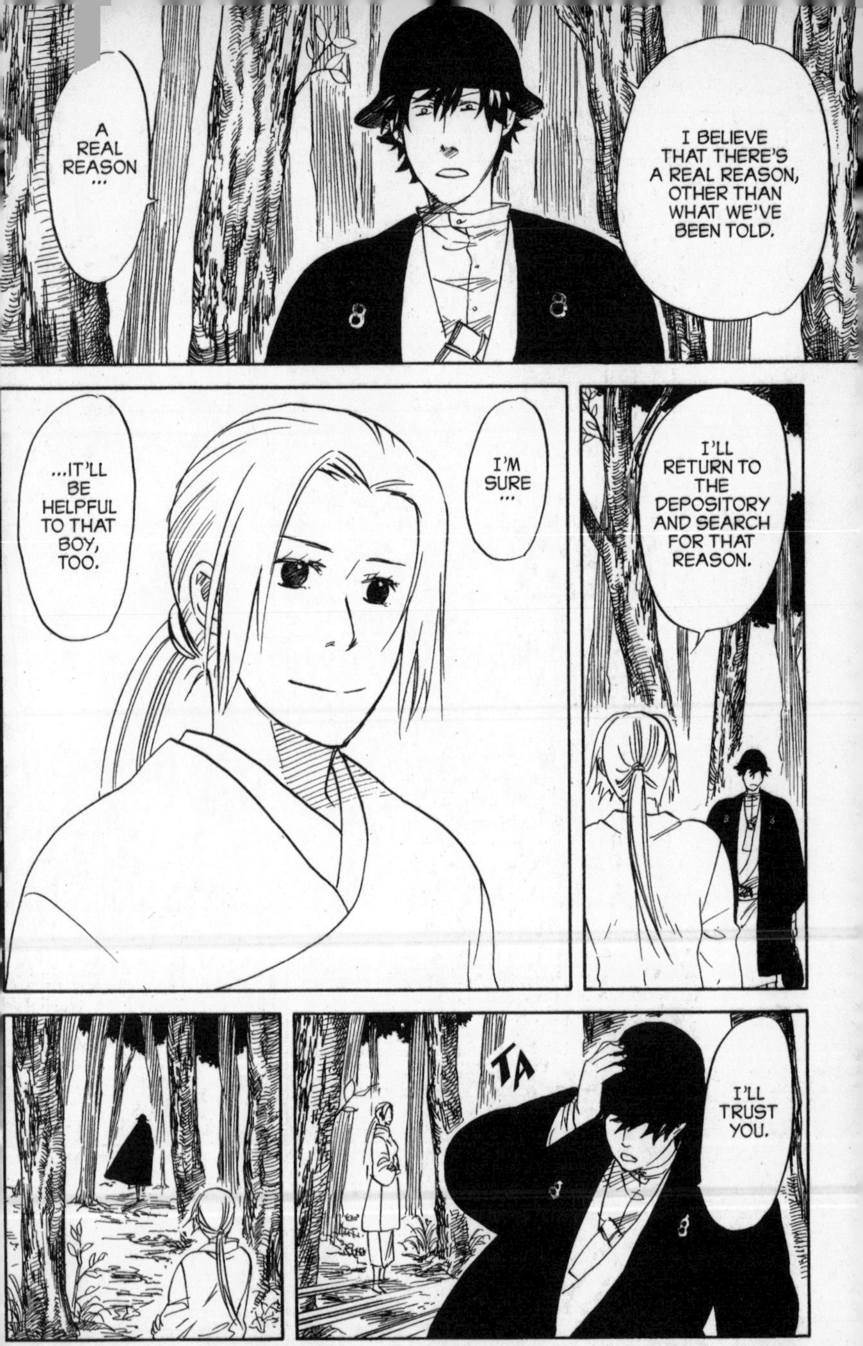
I BELIEVE THAT THERE'S A REAL REASON, OTHER THAN WHAT WE'VE BEEN TOLD.
A REAL REASON ...
I'LL RETURN TO THE DEPOSITORY AND SEARCH FOR THAT REASON.
I'M SURE ...
...IT'LL BE HELPFUL TO THAT BOY, TOO.
I'LL TRUST YOU.
TA

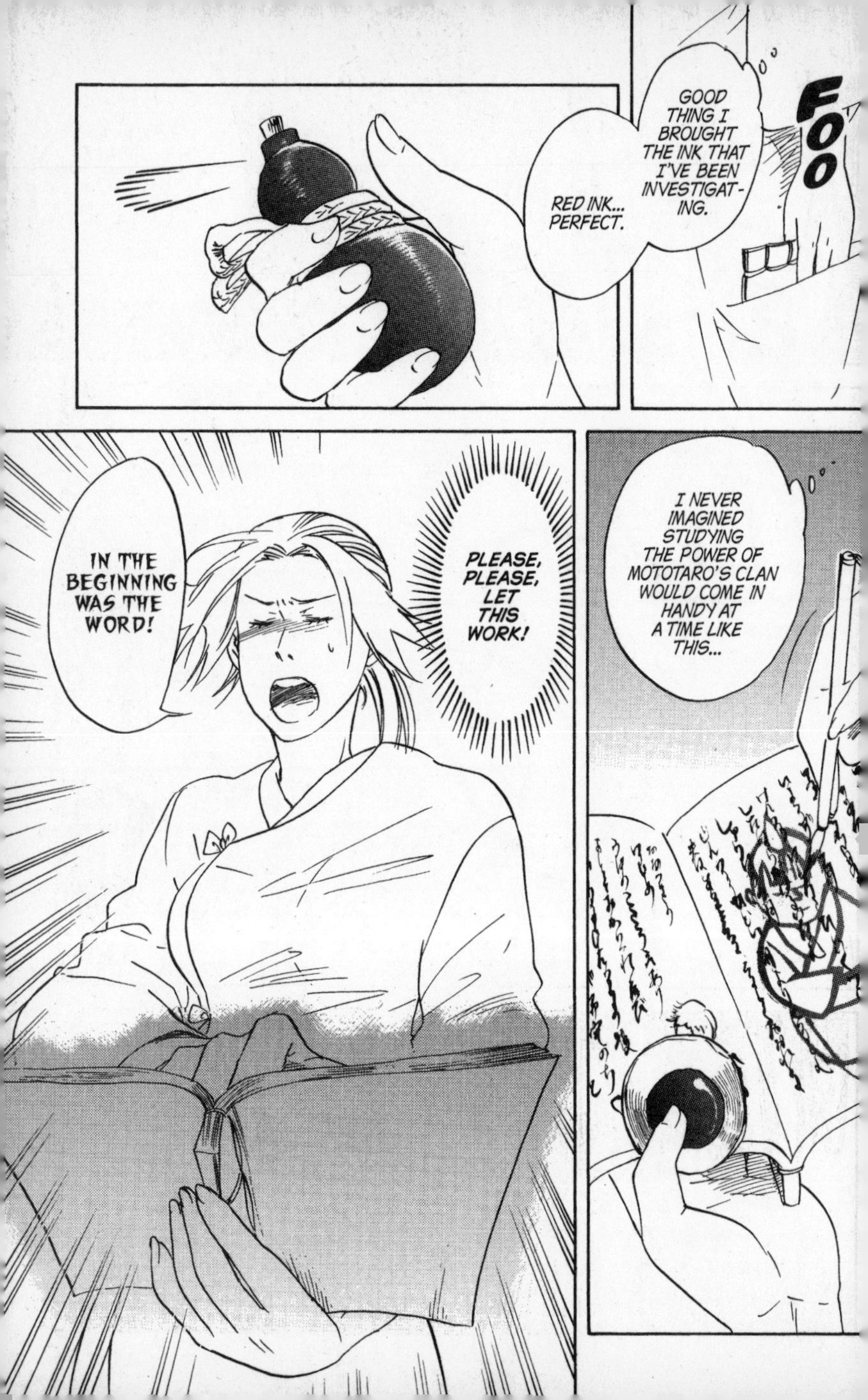
FOO
GOOD THING I BROUGHT THE INK THAT I'VE BEEN INVESTIGAT-ING.
RED INK... PERFECT.
I NEVER IMAGINED STUDYING THE POWER OF MOTOTARO'S CLAN WOULD COME IN HANDY AT A TIME LIKE THIS...
PLEASE, PLEASE, LET THIS WORK!
IN THE BEGINNING WAS THE WORD!

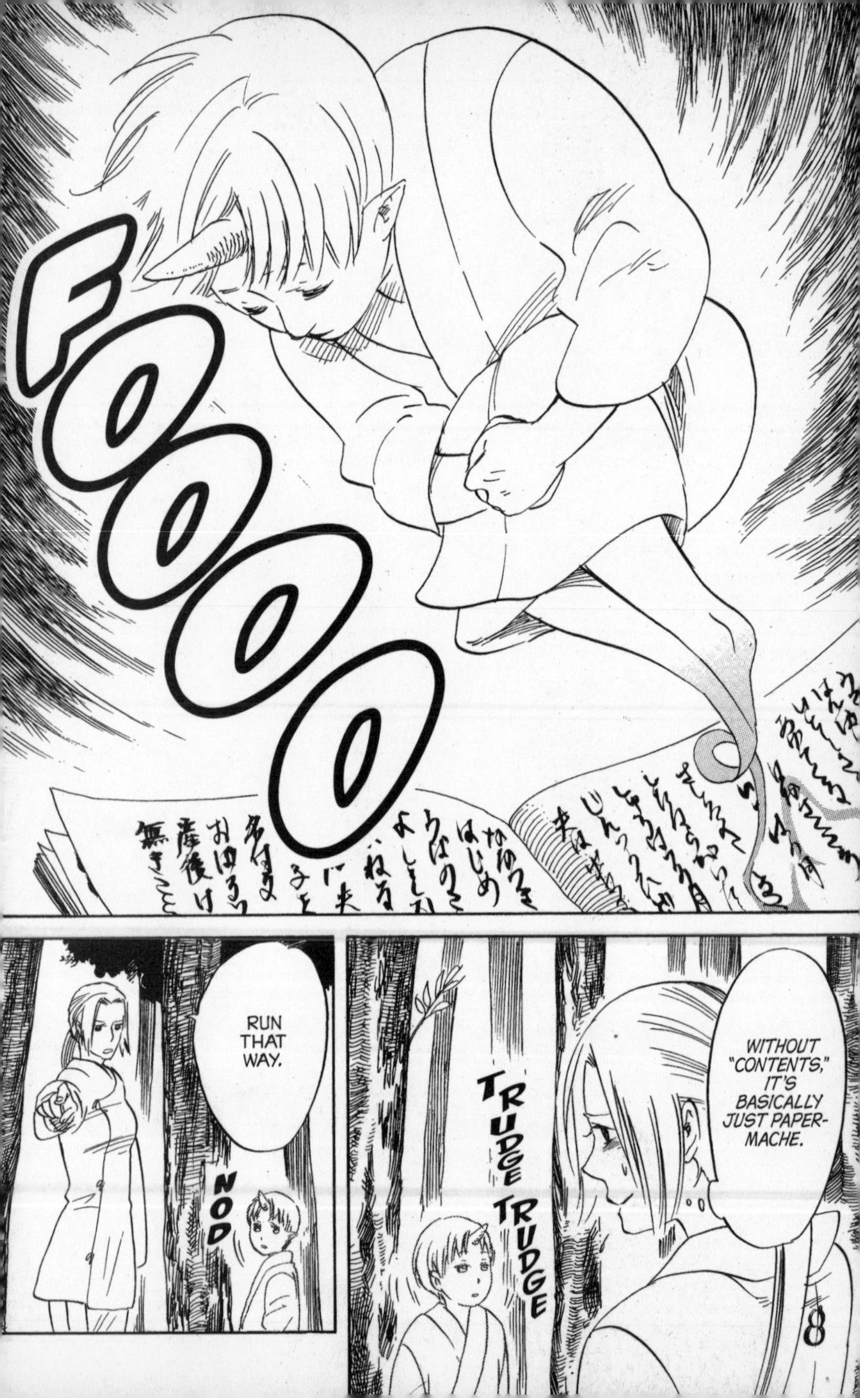
FOOOOO
WITHOUT "CONTENTS," IT'S BASICALLY JUST PAPER-MACHE.
TRUDGE TRUDGE
RUN THAT WAY.
NOD

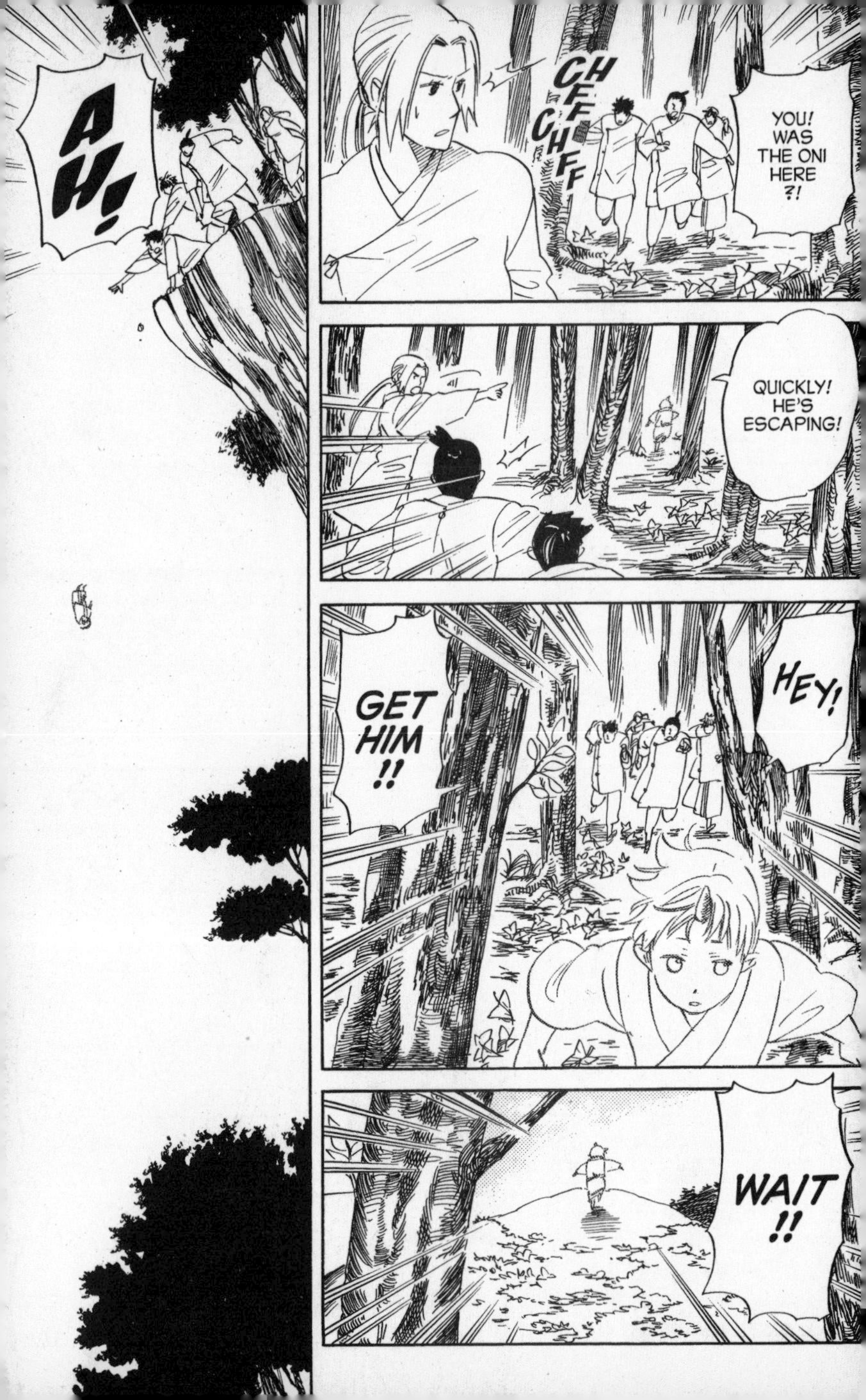
YOU! WAS THE ONI HERE ?!
CHFF CHFF
QUICKLY! HE'S ESCAPING!
HEY!
GET HIM !!
WAIT !!
AH!

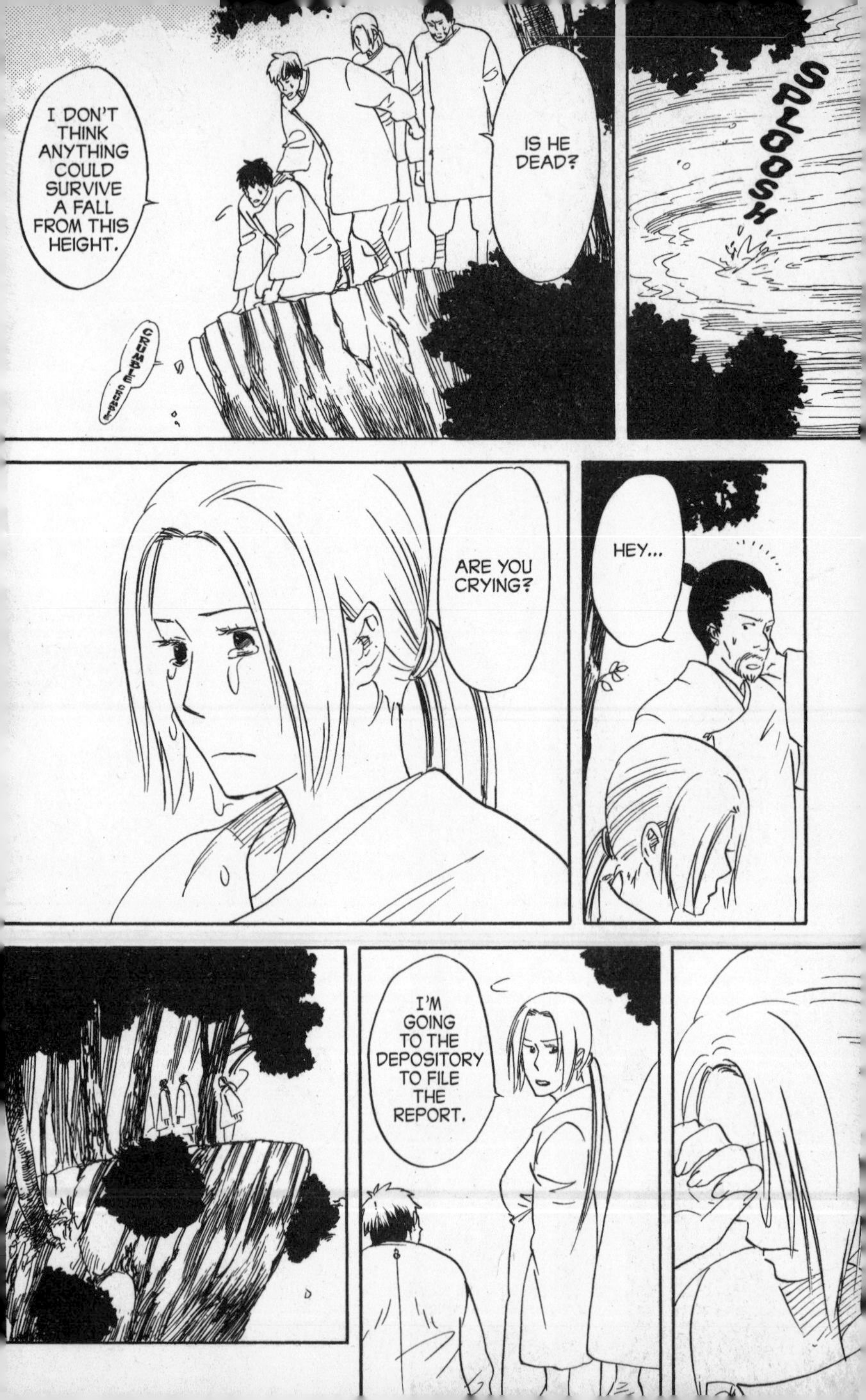
SPLOOOSH
IS HE DEAD?
I DON'T THINK ANYTHING COULD SURVIVE A FALL FROM THIS HEIGHT.
CRUMBLE CRUMBLE
HEY...
ARE YOU CRYING?
I'M GOING TO THE DEPOSITORY TO FILE THE REPORT.

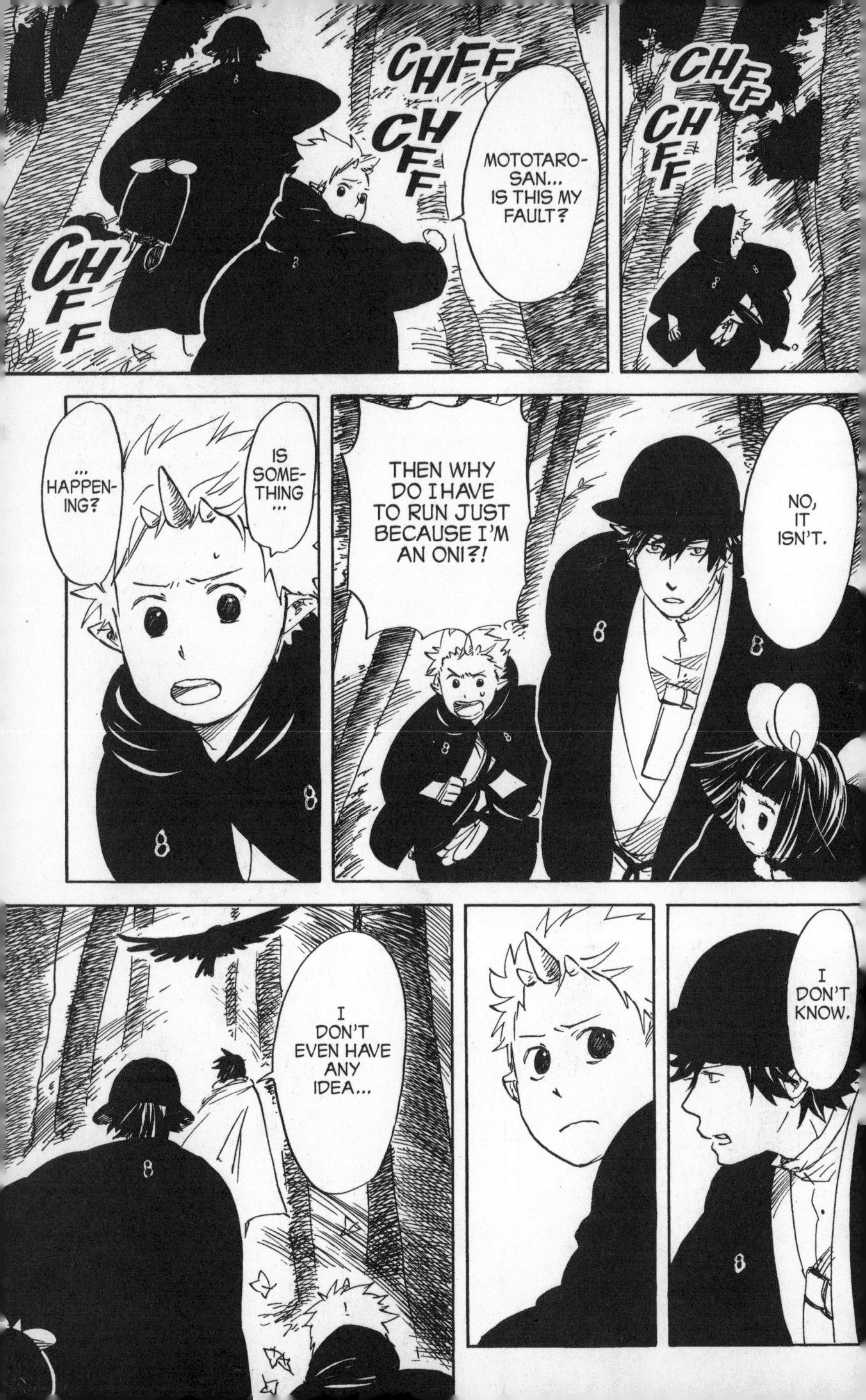
CHFF
CHFF
CHFF
MOTOTARO-SAN... IS THIS MY FAULT?
CHFF
CHFF
NO, IT ISN'T.
THEN WHY DO I HAVE TO RUN JUST BECAUSE I'M AN ONI?!
IS SOMETHING...
...HAPPENING?
I DON'T KNOW.
I DON'T EVEN HAVE ANY IDEA...

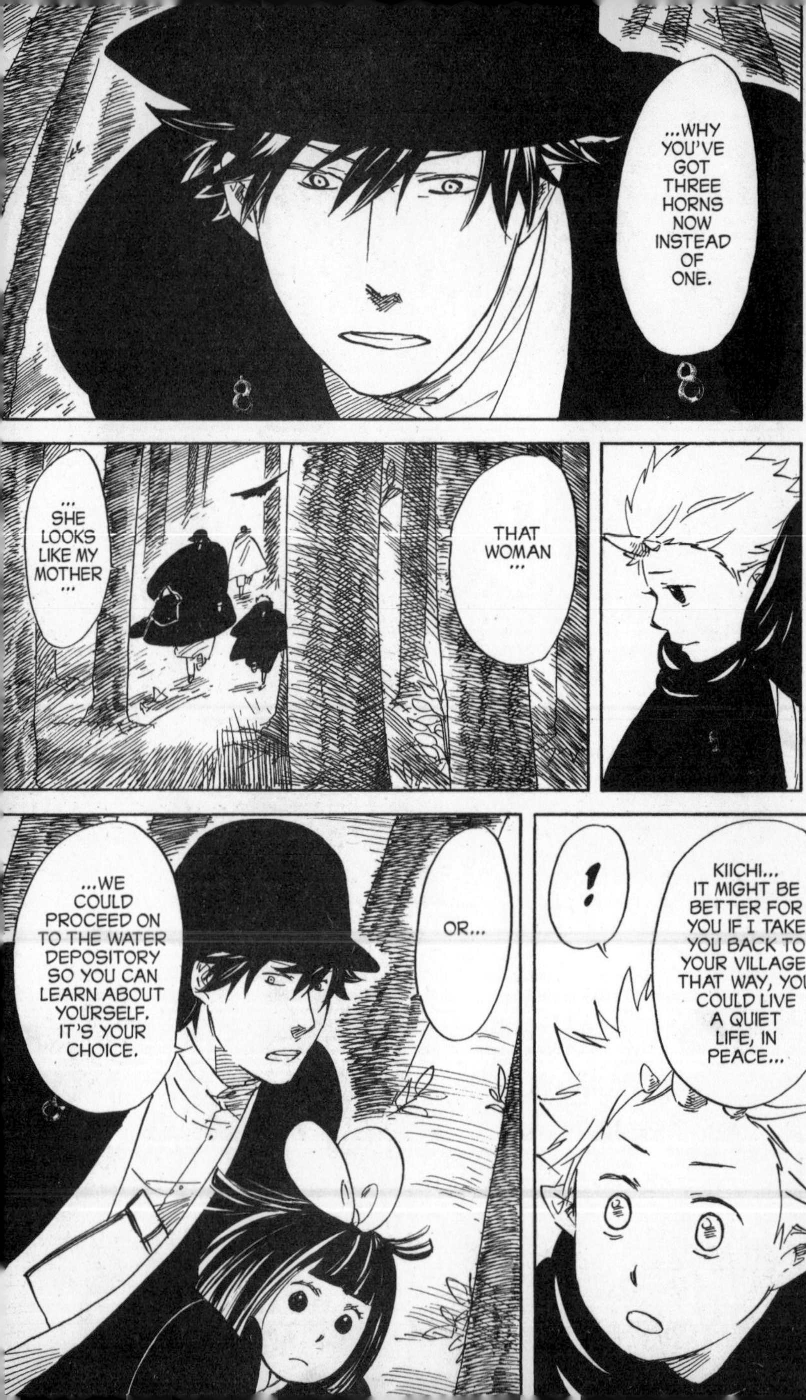
...WHY YOU'VE GOT THREE HORNS NOW INSTEAD OF ONE.
THAT WOMAN...
...SHE LOOKS LIKE MY MOTHER...
KIICHI... IT MIGHT BE BETTER FOR YOU IF I TAKE YOU BACK TO YOUR VILLAGE. THAT WAY, YOU COULD LIVE A QUIET LIFE, IN PEACE...
!
OR...
...WE COULD PROCEED ON TO THE WATER DEPOSITORY SO YOU CAN LEARN ABOUT YOURSELF. IT'S YOUR CHOICE.

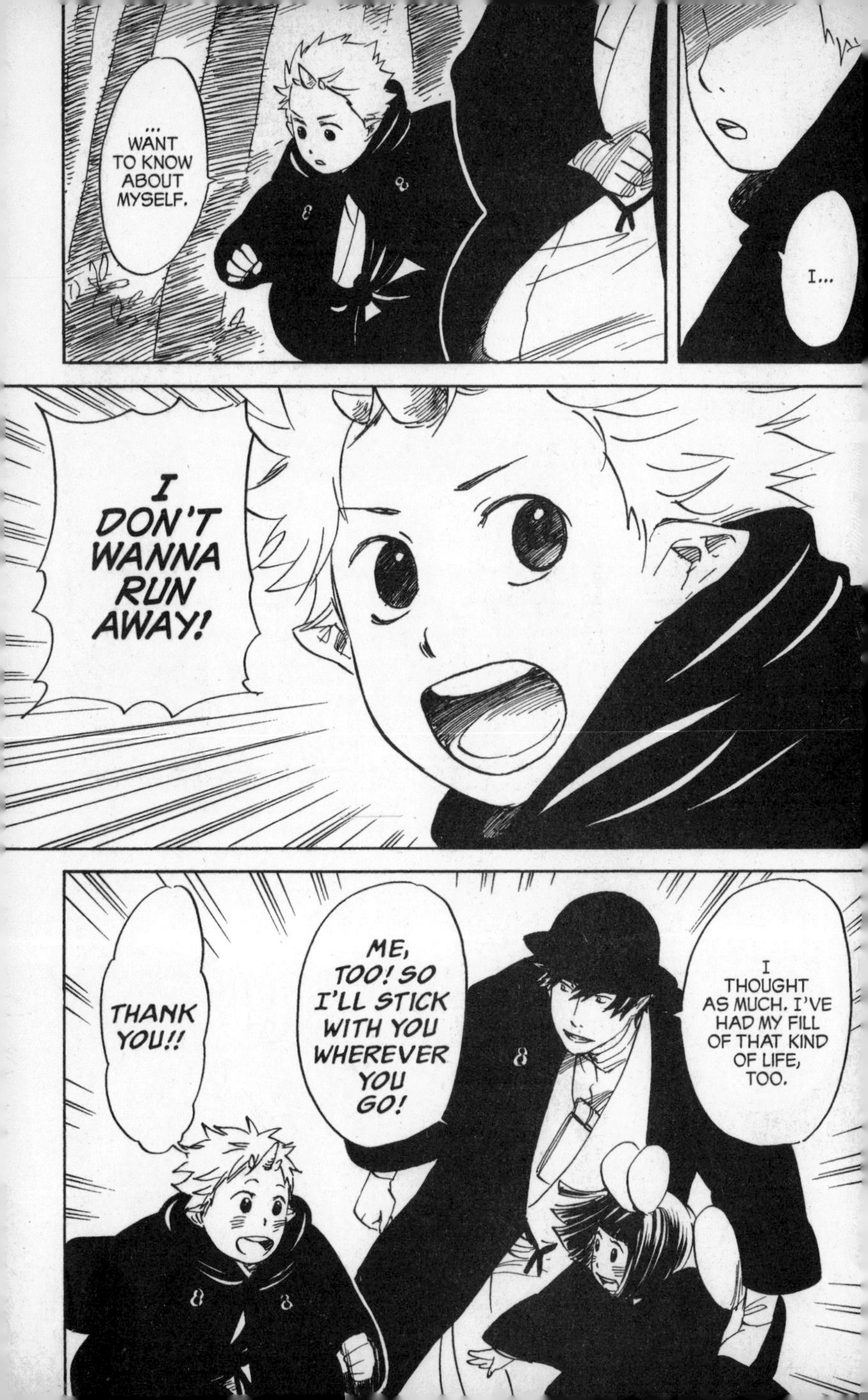
I...
... WANT TO KNOW ABOUT MYSELF.
I DON'T WANNA RUN AWAY!
I THOUGHT AS MUCH. I'VE HAD MY FILL OF THAT KIND OF LIFE, TOO.
ME, TOO! SO I'LL STICK WITH YOU WHEREVER YOU GO!
THANK YOU!!

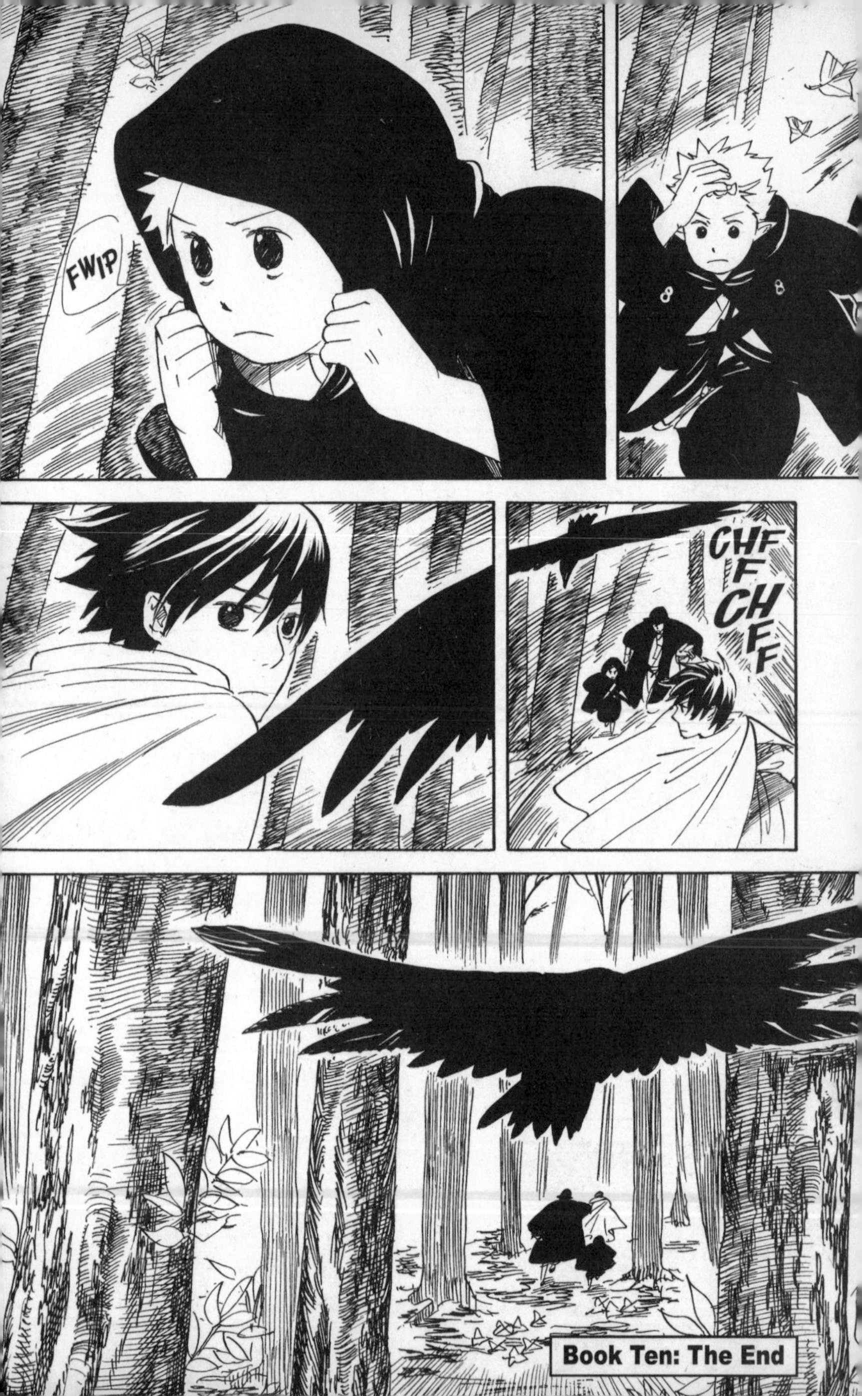
FWIP
CHF F CHFF
Book Ten: The End

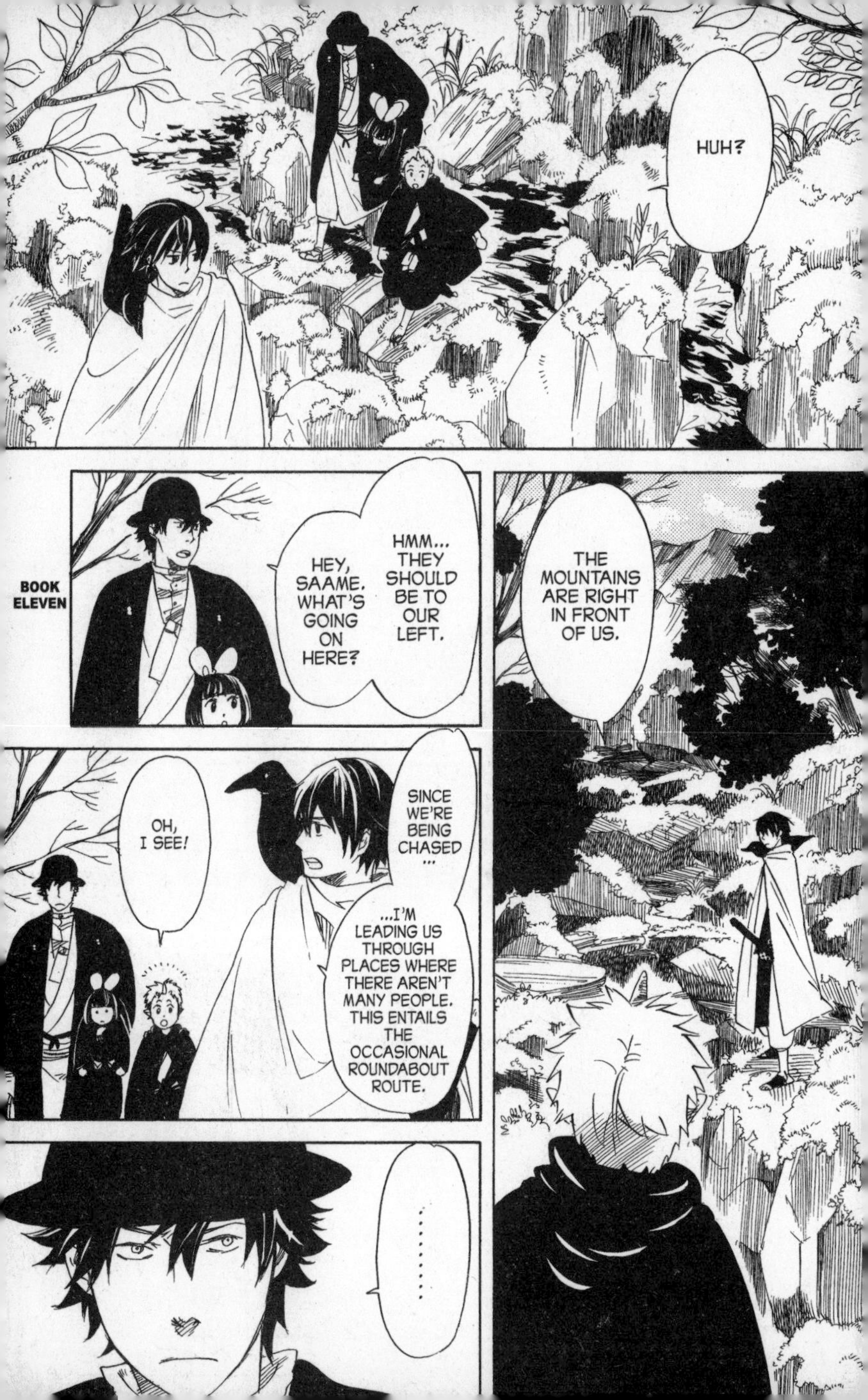
HUH?
THE MOUNTAINS ARE RIGHT IN FRONT OF US.
HMM... THEY SHOULD BE TO OUR LEFT.
HEY, SAAME. WHAT'S GOING ON HERE?
SINCE WE'RE BEING CHASED...
...I'M LEADING US THROUGH PLACES WHERE THERE AREN'T MANY PEOPLE. THIS ENTAILS THE OCCASIONAL ROUNDABOUT ROUTE.
OH, I SEE!
....

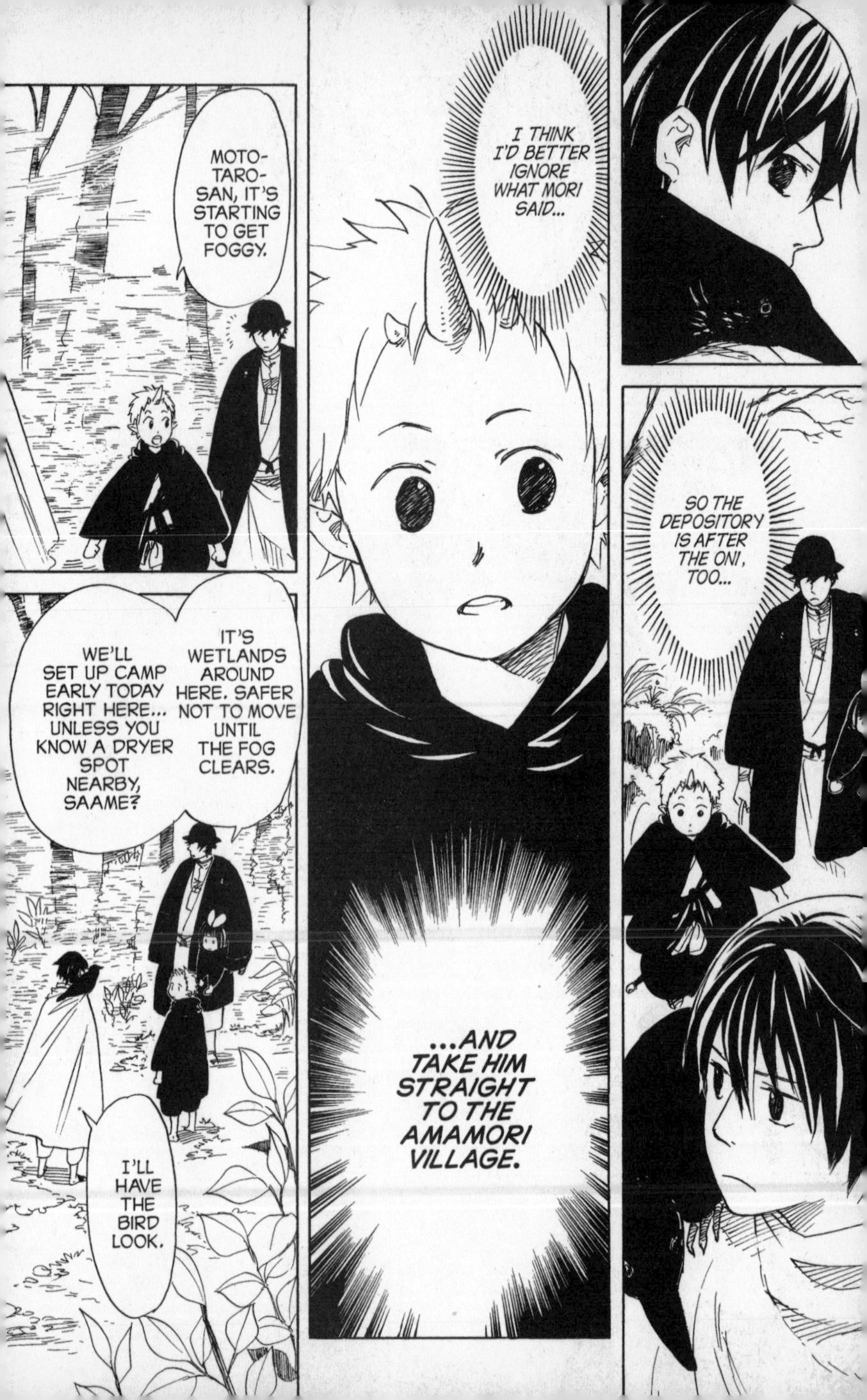
SO THE DEPOSITORY IS AFTER THE ONI, TOO...
I THINK I'D BETTER IGNORE WHAT MORI SAID...
...AND TAKE HIM STRAIGHT TO THE AMAMORI VILLAGE.
MOTO-TARO-SAN, IT'S STARTING TO GET FOGGY.
IT'S WETLANDS AROUND HERE. SAFER NOT TO MOVE UNTIL THE FOG CLEARS.
WE'LL SET UP CAMP EARLY TODAY RIGHT HERE... UNLESS YOU KNOW A DRYER SPOT NEARBY, SAAME?
I'LL HAVE THE BIRD LOOK.

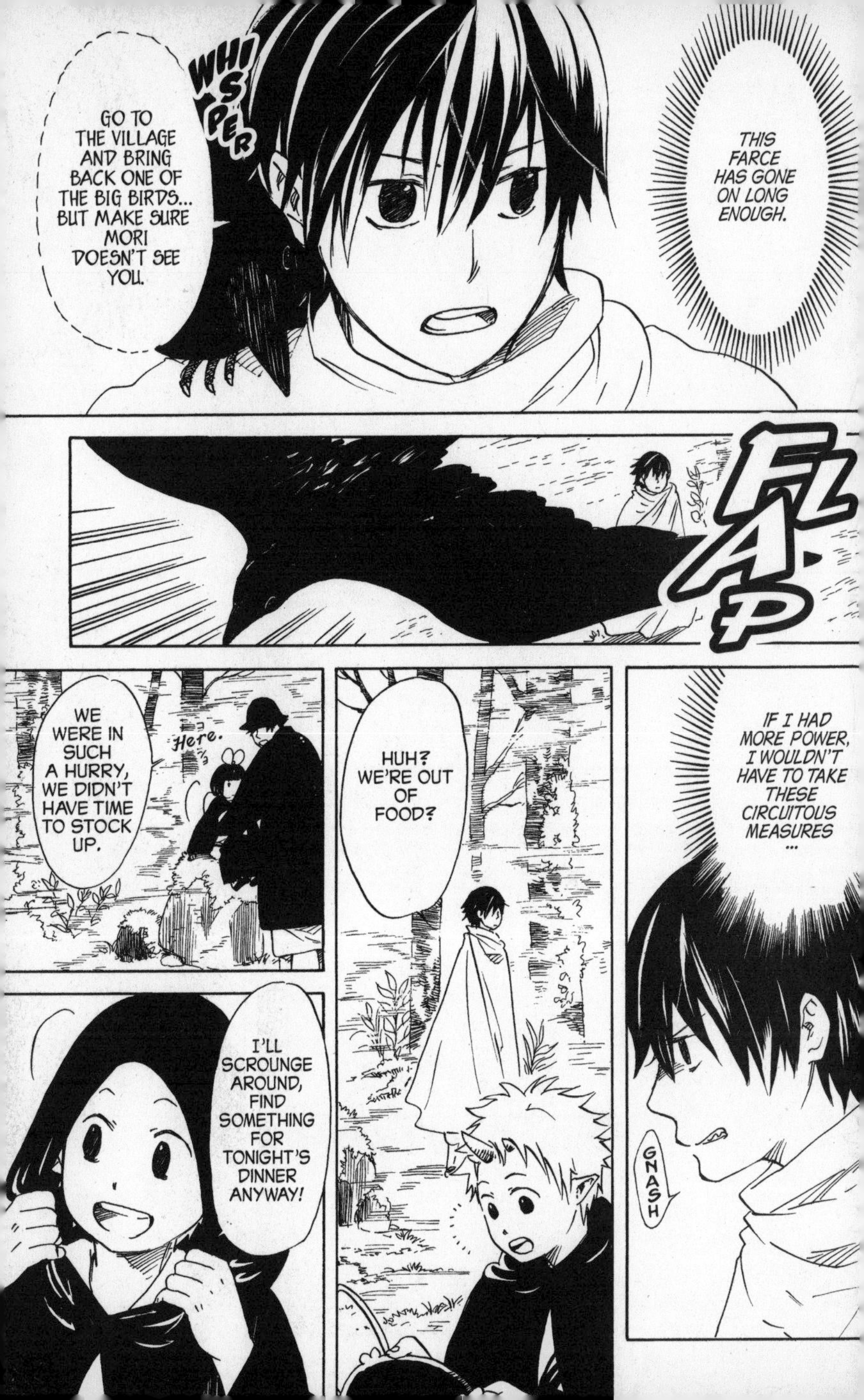
THIS FARCE HAS GONE ON LONG ENOUGH.
WHISPER
GO TO THE VILLAGE AND BRING BACK ONE OF THE BIG BIRDS... BUT MAKE SURE MORI DOESN'T SEE YOU.
FLAP
IF I HAD MORE POWER, I WOULDN'T HAVE TO TAKE THESE CIRCUITOUS MEASURES...
GNASH
HUH? WE'RE OUT OF FOOD?
Here.
WE WERE IN SUCH A HURRY, WE DIDN'T HAVE TIME TO STOCK UP.
I'LL SCROUNGE AROUND, FIND SOMETHING FOR TONIGHT'S DINNER ANYWAY!

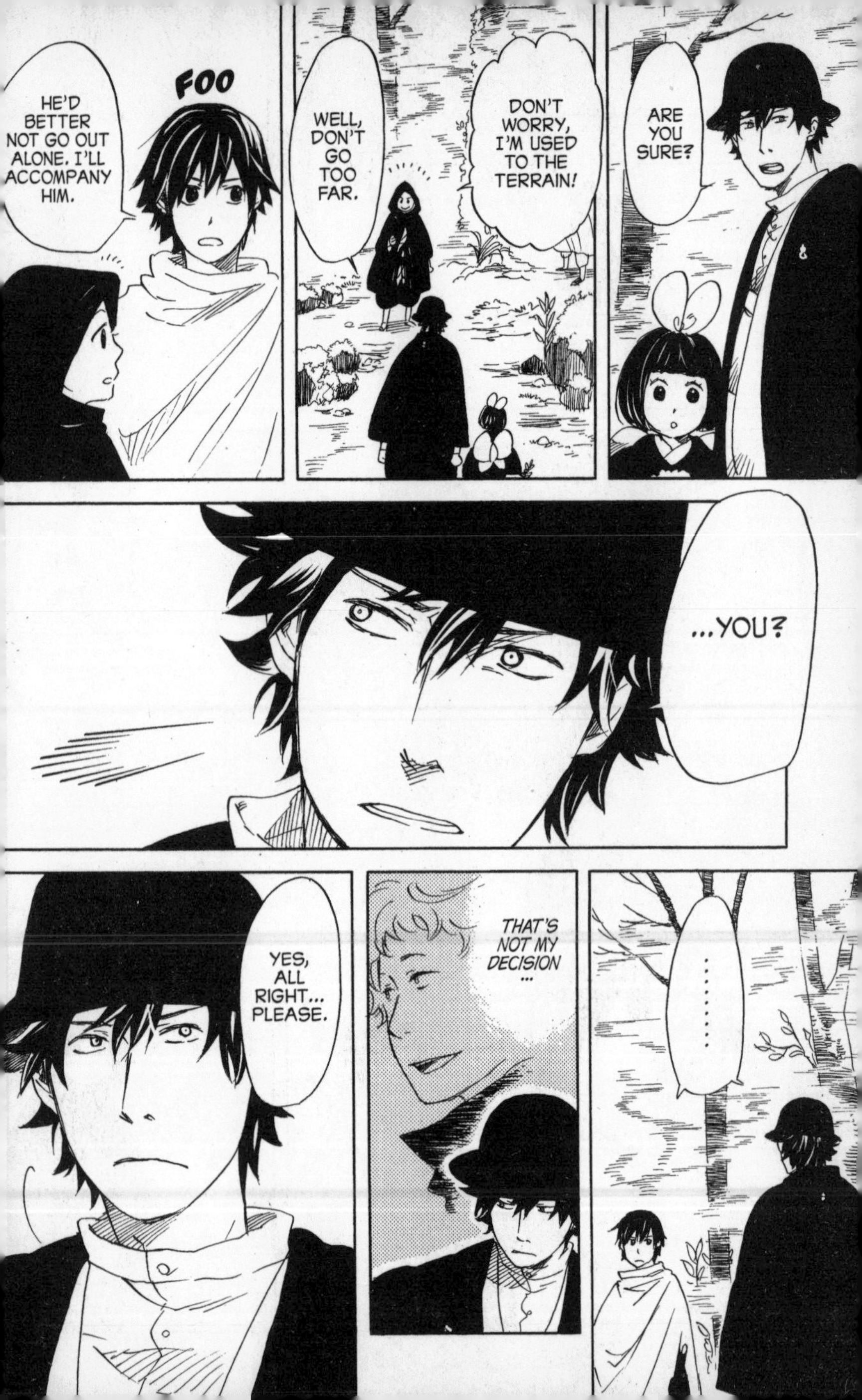
ARE YOU SURE?
DON'T WORRY, I'M USED TO THE TERRAIN!
WELL, DON'T GO TOO FAR.
FOO
HE'D BETTER NOT GO OUT ALONE. I'LL ACCOMPANY HIM.
...YOU?
......
THAT'S NOT MY DECISION ...
YES, ALL RIGHT... PLEASE.

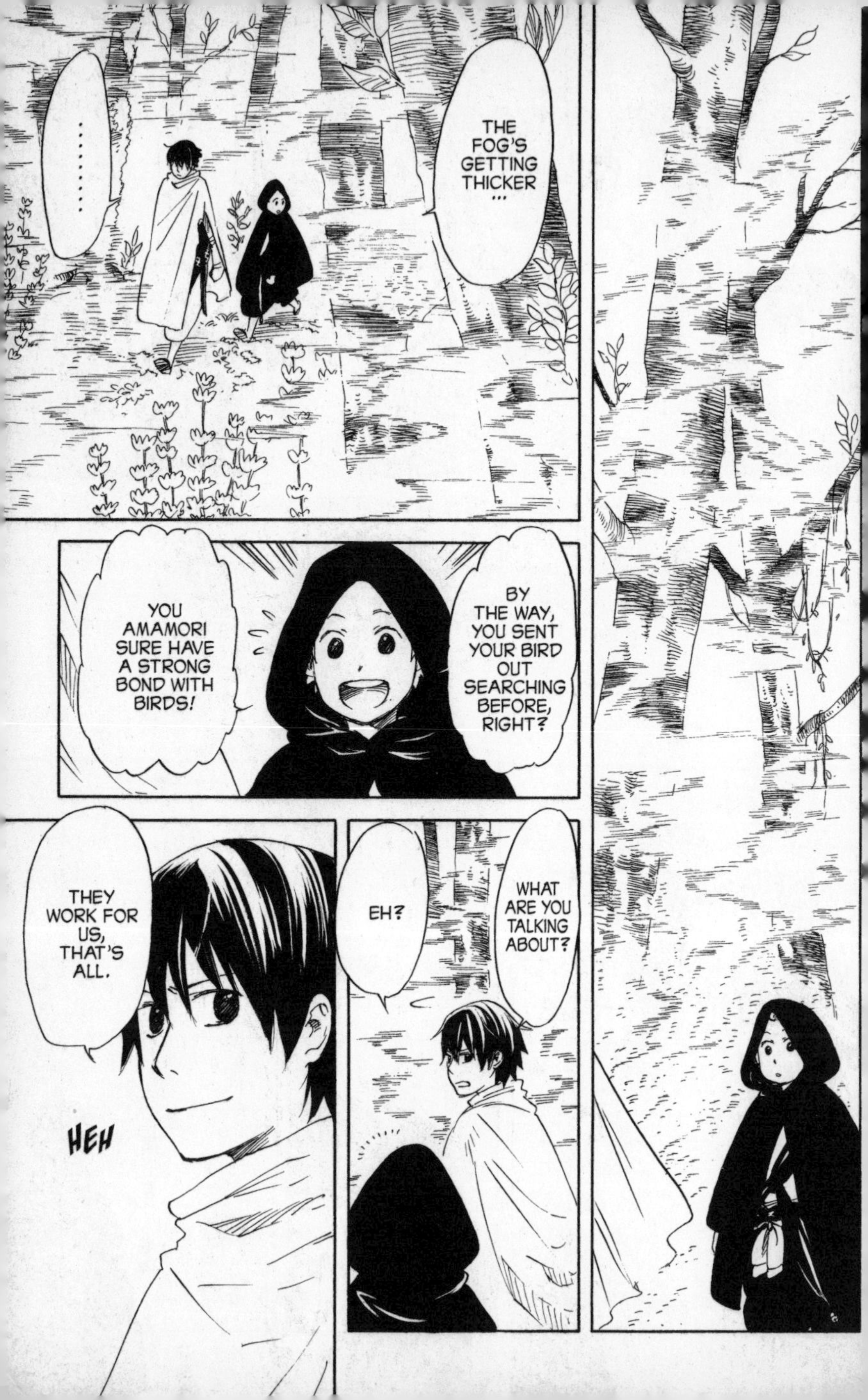
THE FOG'S GETTING THICKER...
......
BY THE WAY, YOU SENT YOUR BIRD OUT SEARCHING BEFORE, RIGHT?
YOU AMAMORI SURE HAVE A STRONG BOND WITH BIRDS!
WHAT ARE YOU TALKING ABOUT?
EH?
THEY WORK FOR US, THAT'S ALL.
HEH

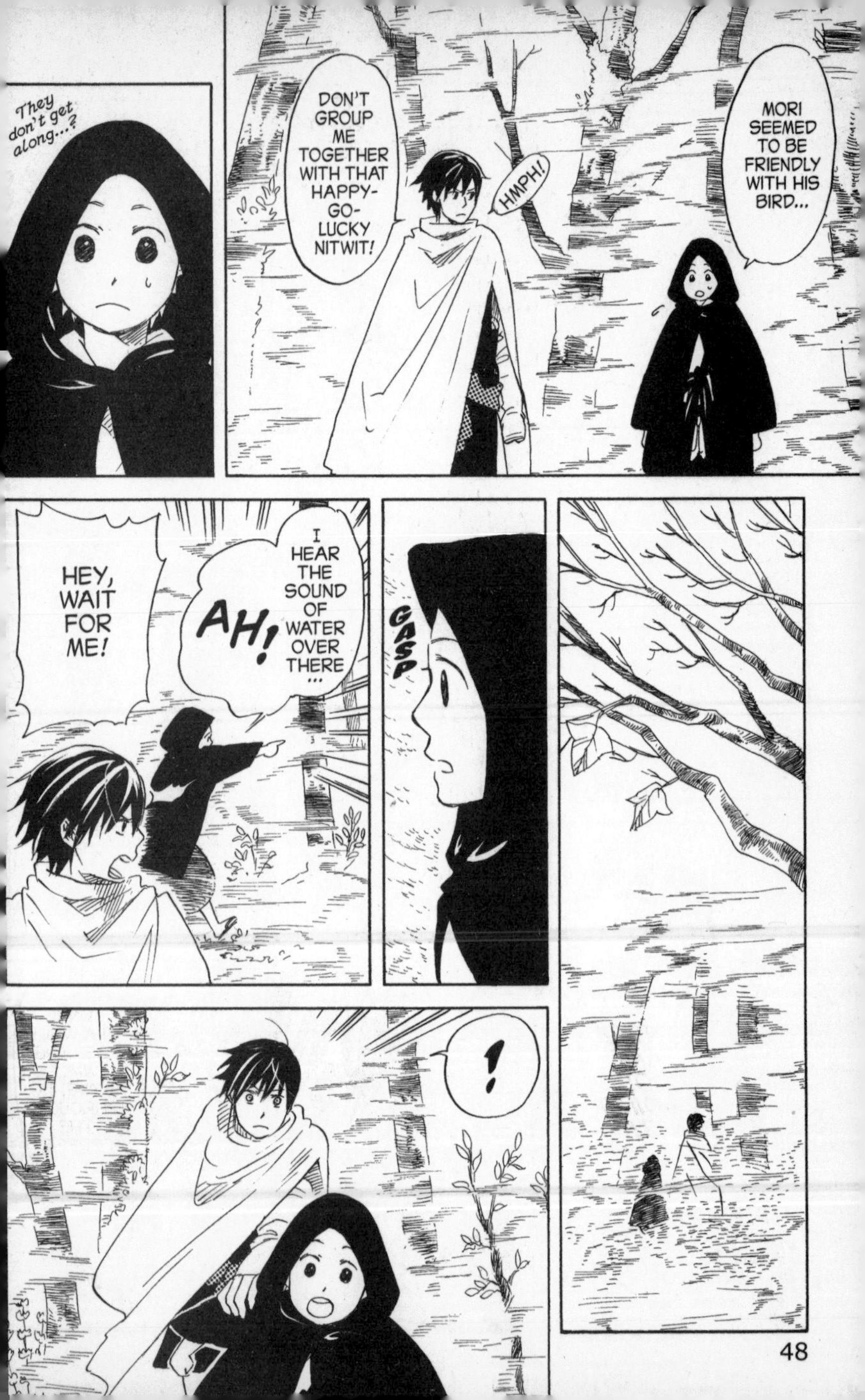
MORI SEEMED TO BE FRIENDLY WITH HIS BIRD...
HMPH!
DON'T GROUP ME TOGETHER WITH THAT HAPPY-GO-LUCKY NITWIT!
They don't get along...?
GASP
AH!
I HEAR THE SOUND OF WATER OVER THERE...
HEY, WAIT FOR ME!
!

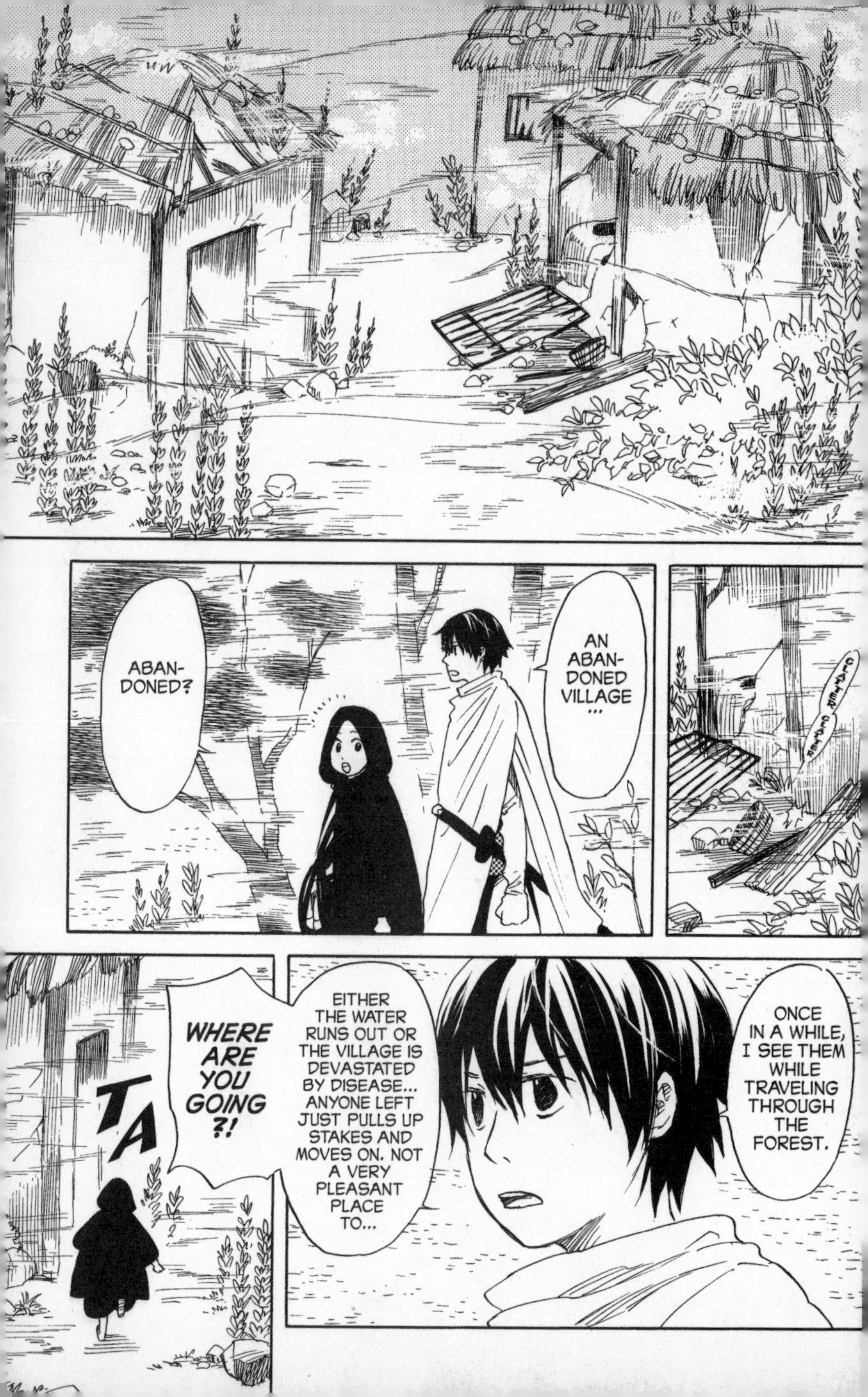
CLATTER CLATTER
AN ABAN-DONED VILLAGE...
ABAN-DONED?
ONCE IN A WHILE, I SEE THEM WHILE TRAVELING THROUGH THE FOREST.
EITHER THE WATER RUNS OUT OR THE VILLAGE IS DEVASTATED BY DISEASE... ANYONE LEFT JUST PULLS UP STAKES AND MOVES ON. NOT A VERY PLEASANT PLACE TO...
WHERE ARE YOU GOING?!
TA

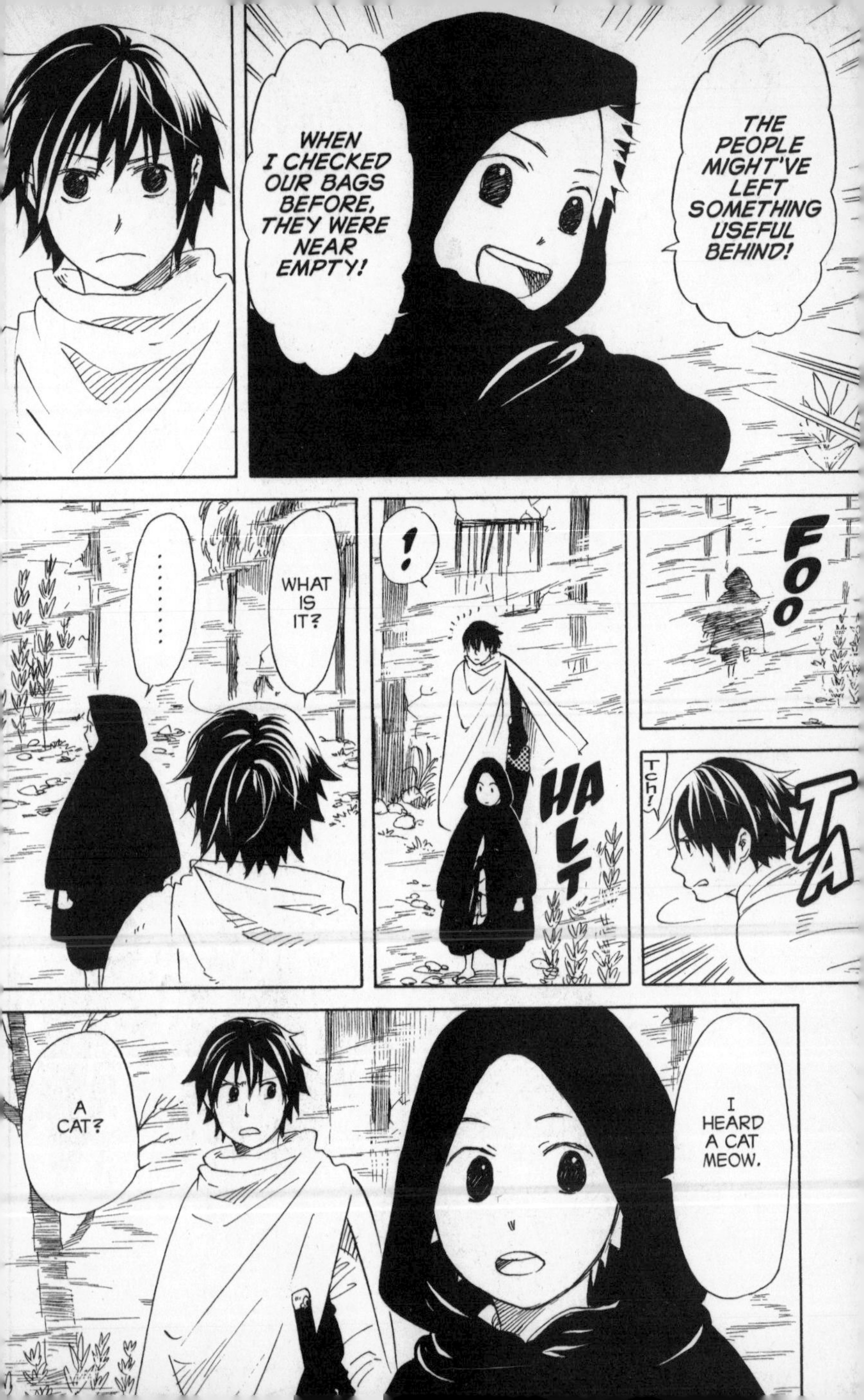
THE PEOPLE MIGHT'VE LEFT SOMETHING USEFUL BEHIND!
WHEN I CHECKED OUR BAGS BEFORE, THEY WERE NEAR EMPTY!
FOO
Tch!
TA
!
HALT
WHAT IS IT?
......
I HEARD A CAT MEOW.
A CAT?

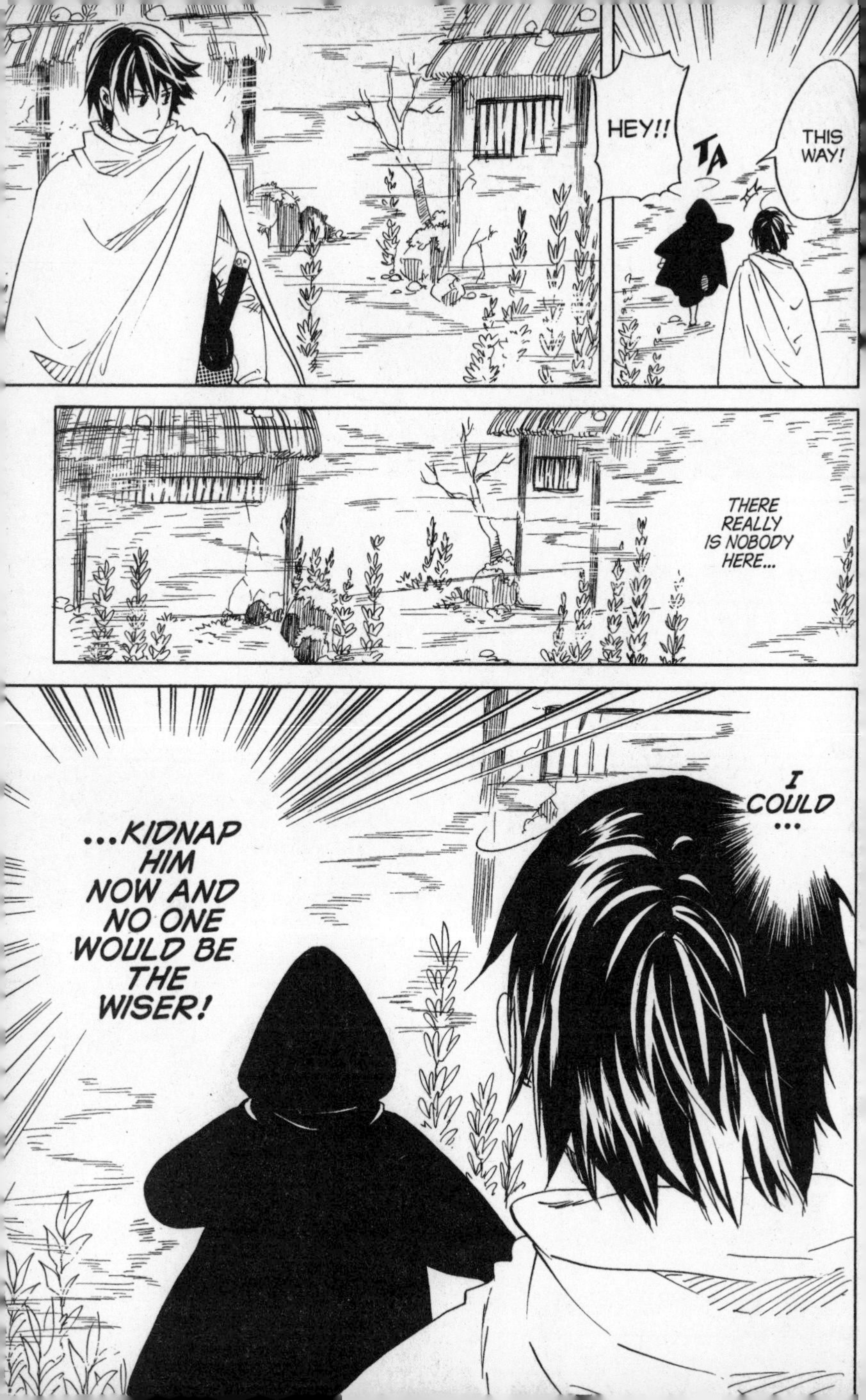
THIS WAY!
TA
HEY!!
THERE REALLY IS NOBODY HERE...
I COULD ...
...KIDNAP HIM NOW AND NO ONE WOULD BE THE WISER!

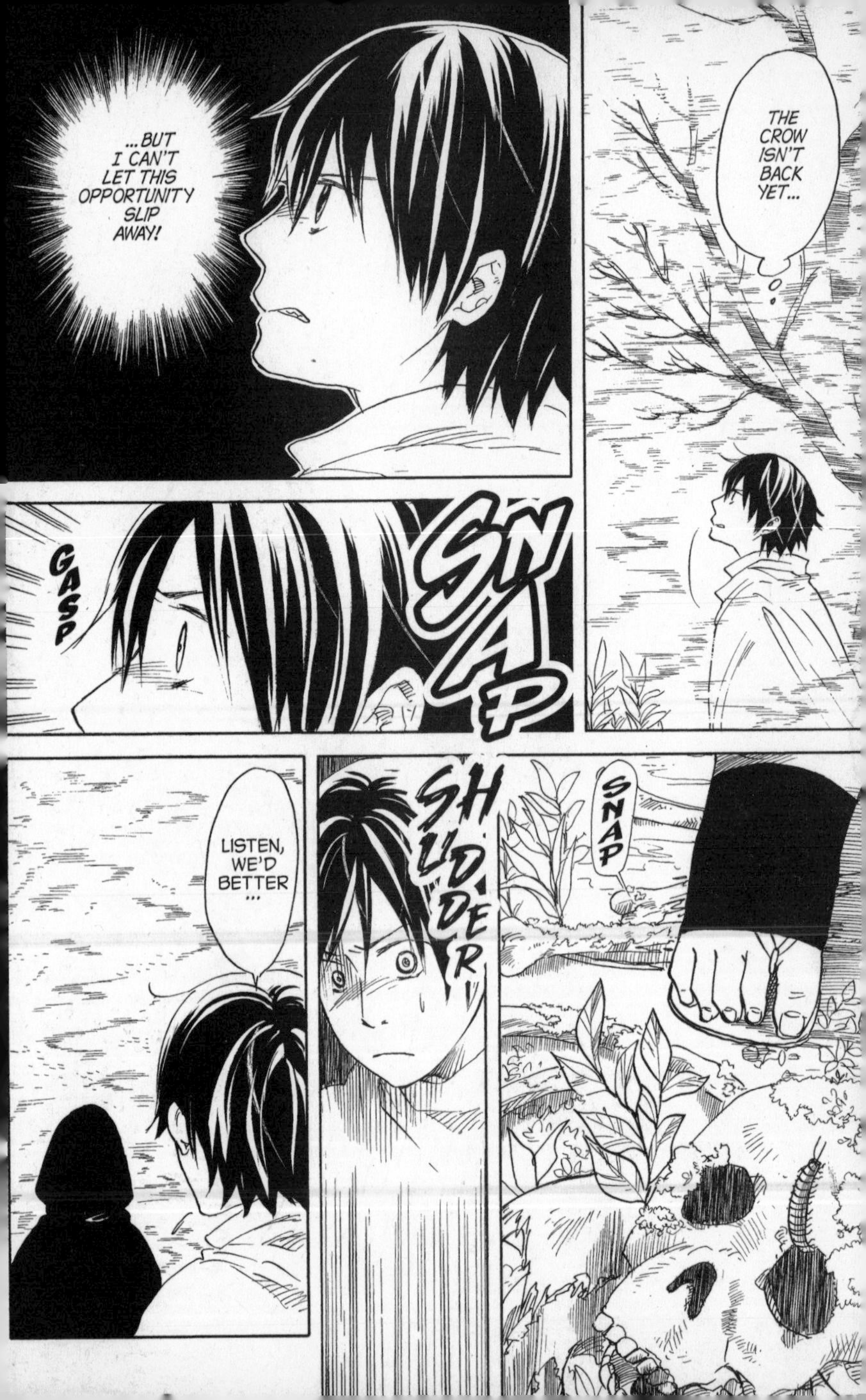
THE CROW ISN'T BACK YET...
...BUT I CAN'T LET THIS OPPORTUNITY SLIP AWAY!
SNAP
GASP
SNAP
SHUDDER
LISTEN, WE'D BETTER ...

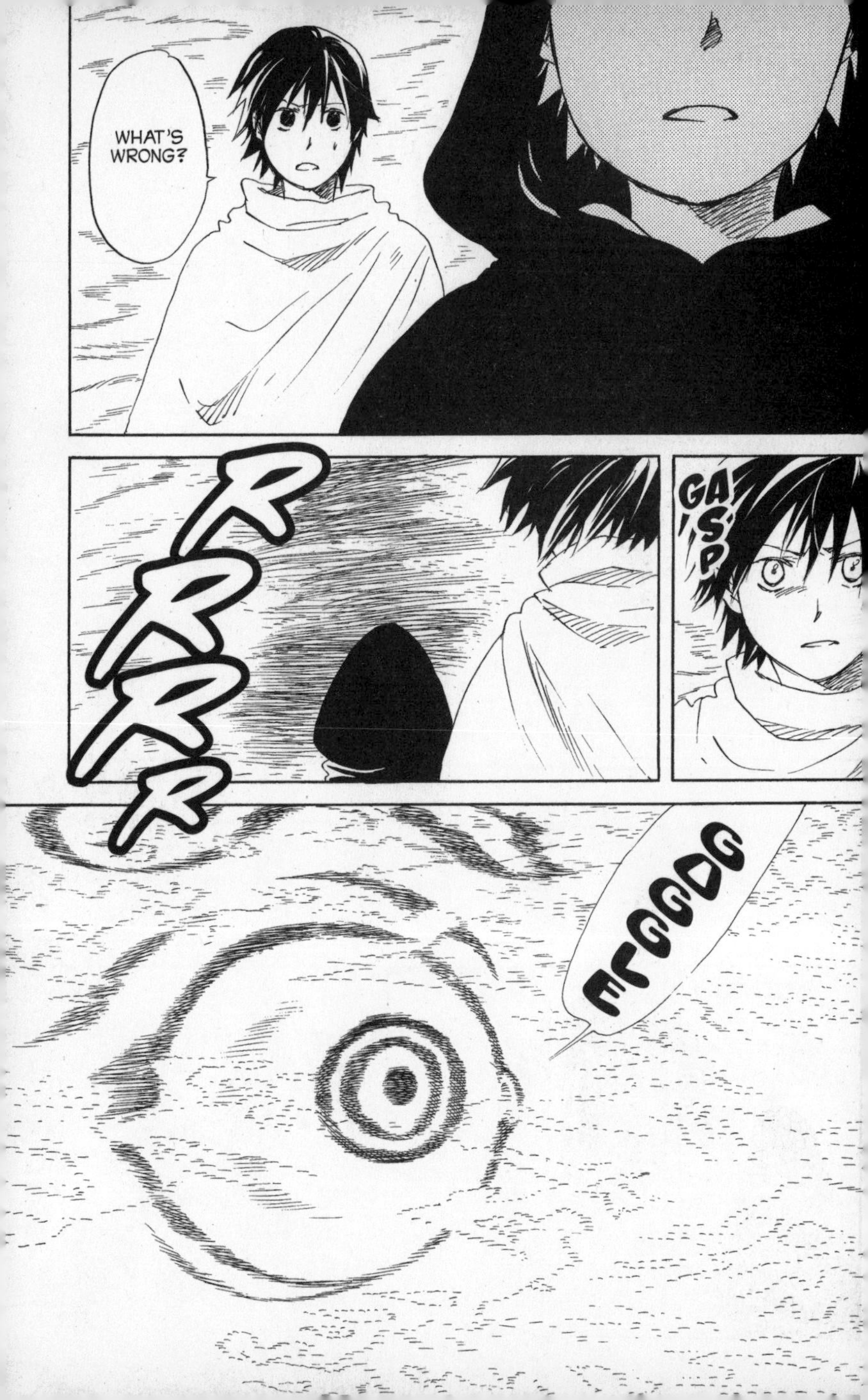
WHAT'S WRONG?
GASP
RRRRR

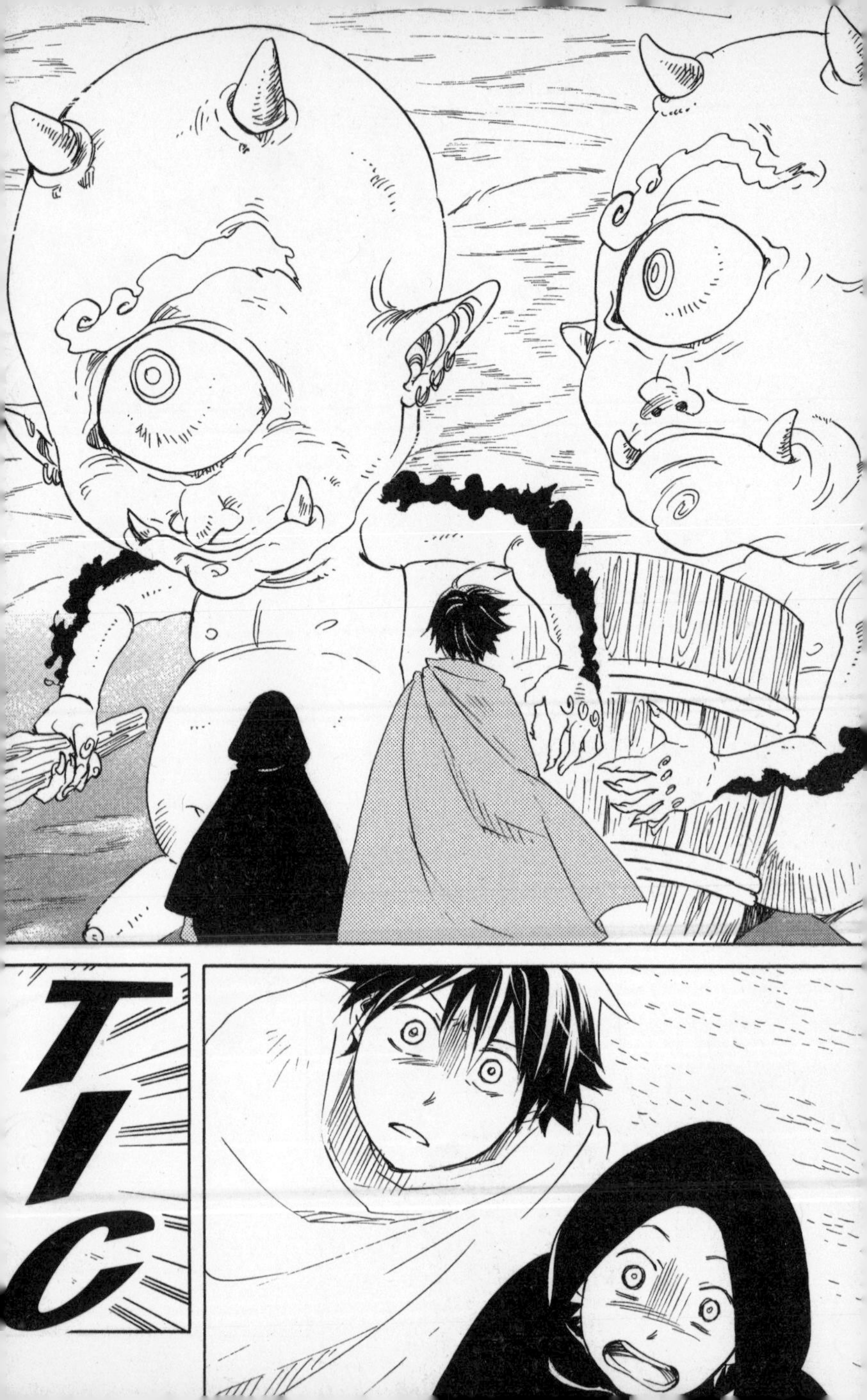
TIC

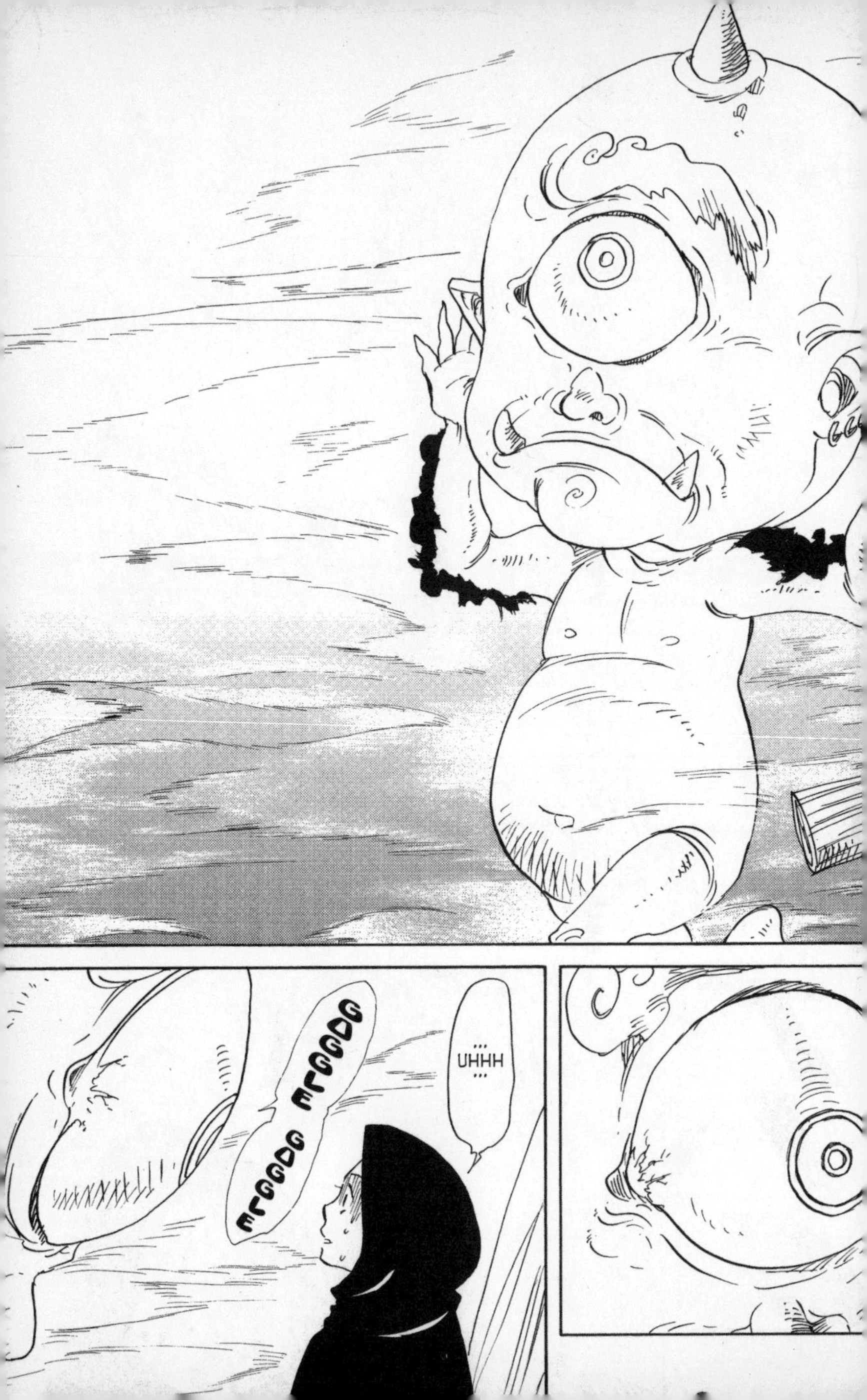
...UHHH...
GUGGLE GUGGLE

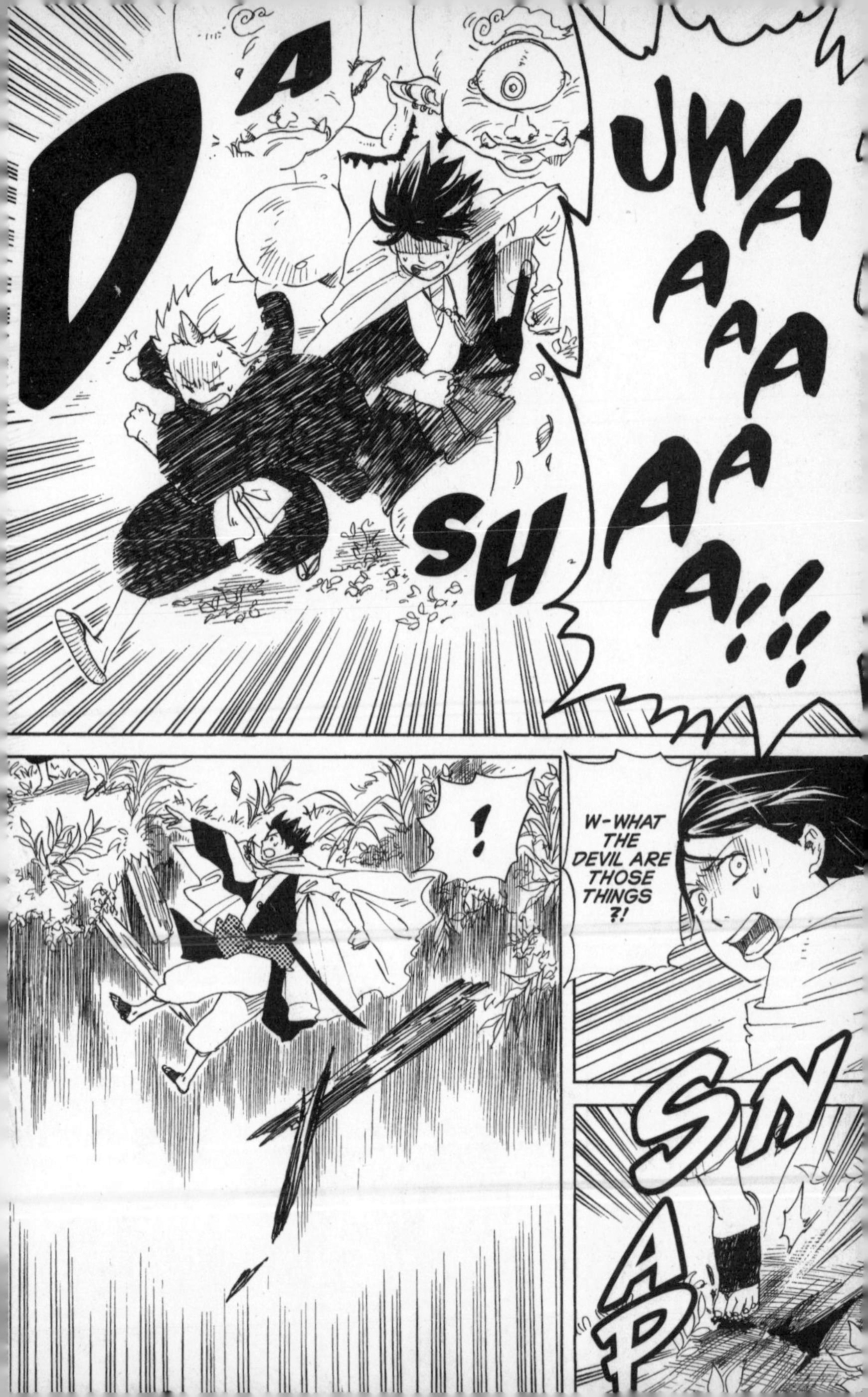
UWAAAAAAAAA!!
DA
SH
W-WHAT THE DEVIL ARE THOSE THINGS?!
SNAP
!

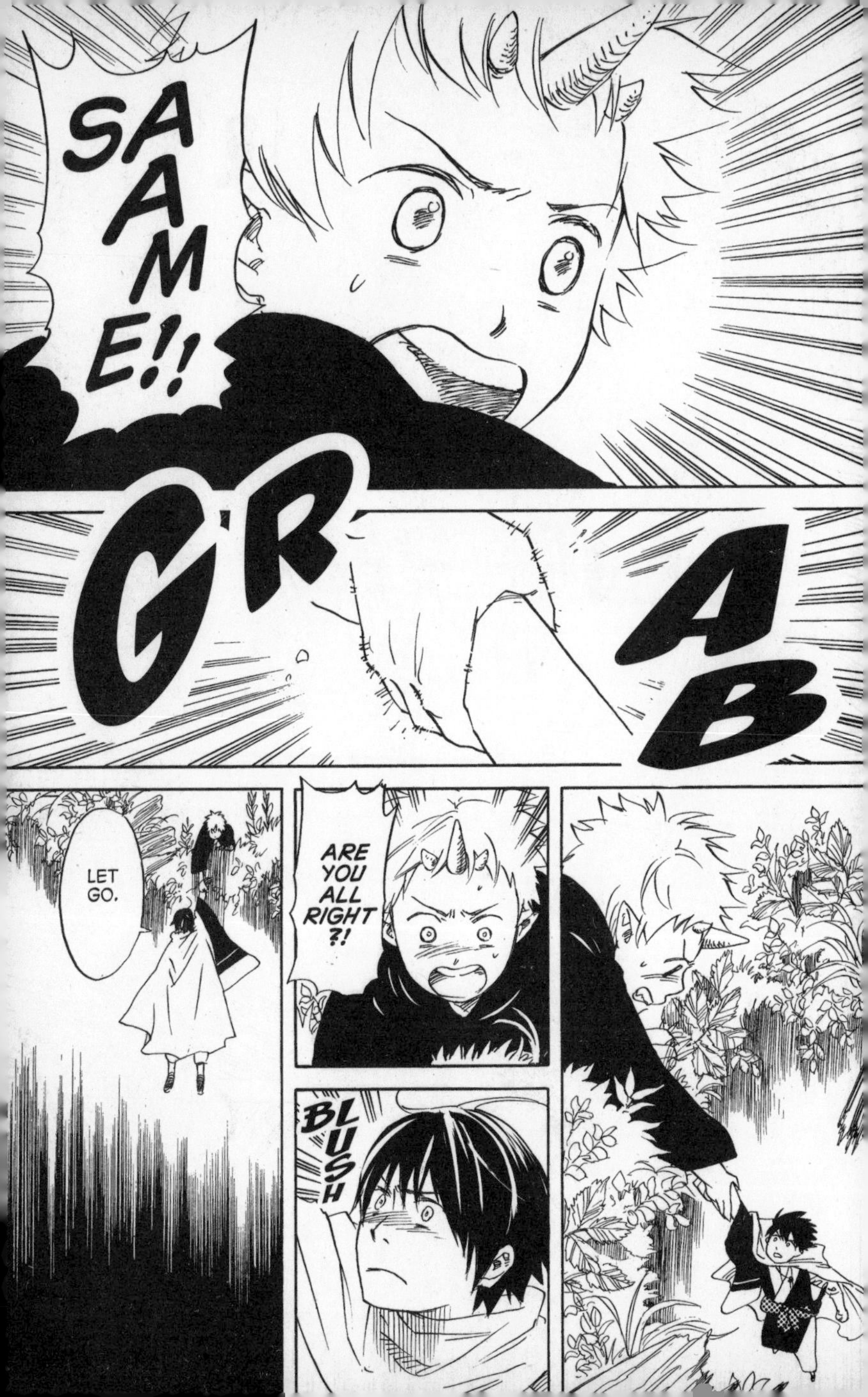
SAAME!!
GRAB
ARE YOU ALL RIGHT?!
BLUSH
LET GO.

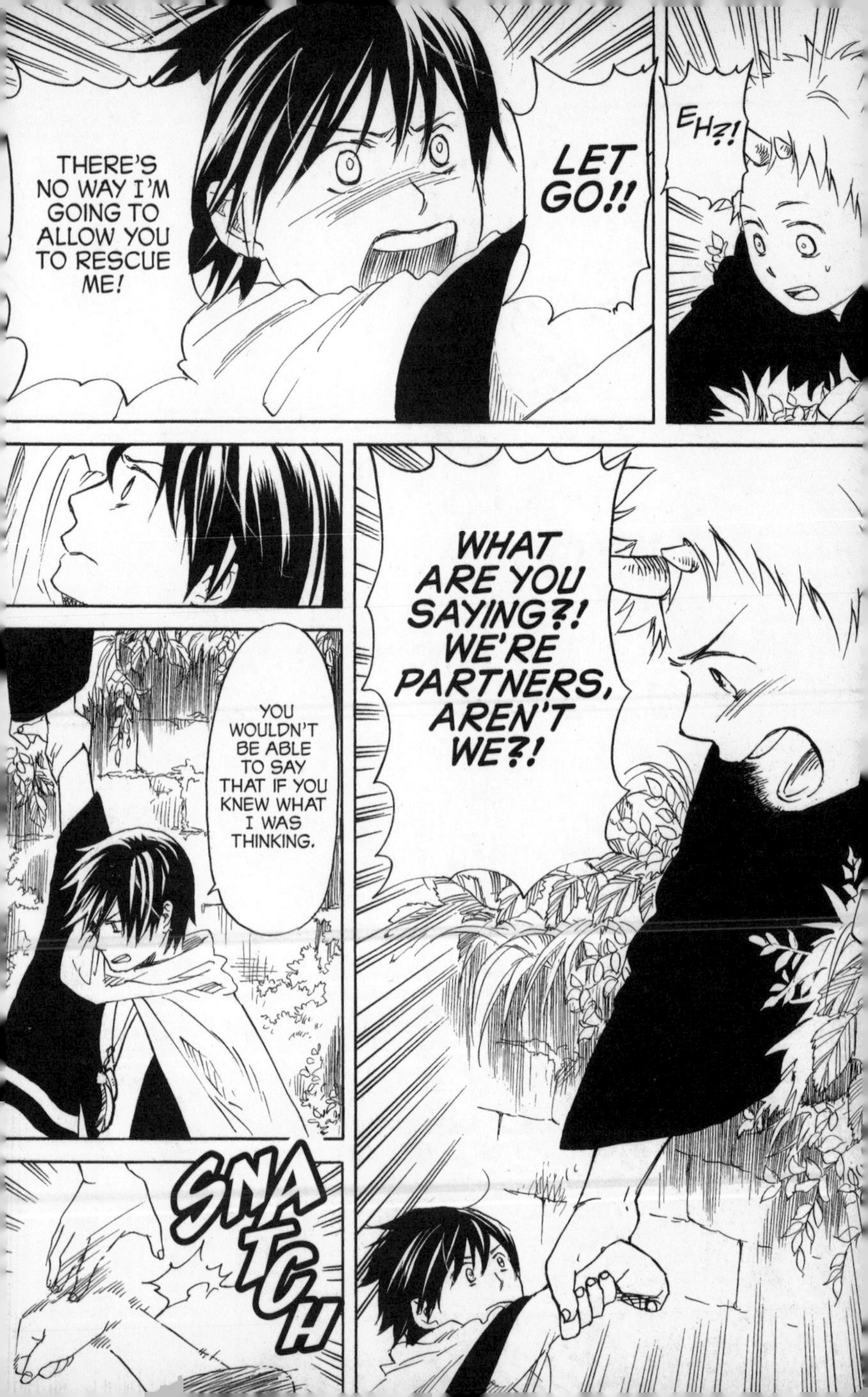
EH?!
LET GO!!
THERE'S NO WAY I'M GOING TO ALLOW YOU TO RESCUE ME!
WHAT ARE YOU SAYING?! WE'RE PARTNERS, AREN'T WE?!
YOU WOULDN'T BE ABLE TO SAY THAT IF YOU KNEW WHAT I WAS THINKING.
SNATCH

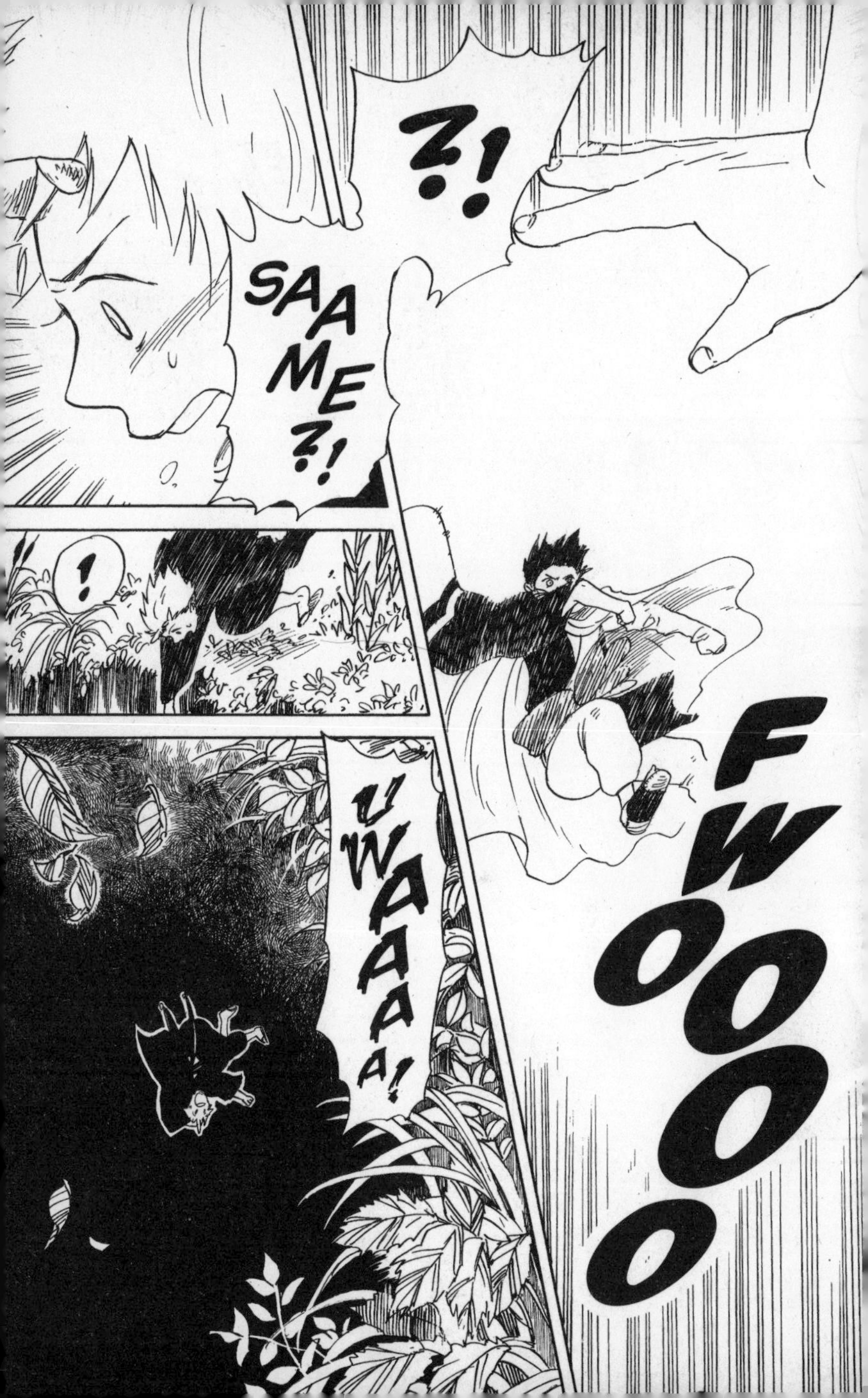
?!
SAAME?!
FWOOOO
!
UWAAAA!

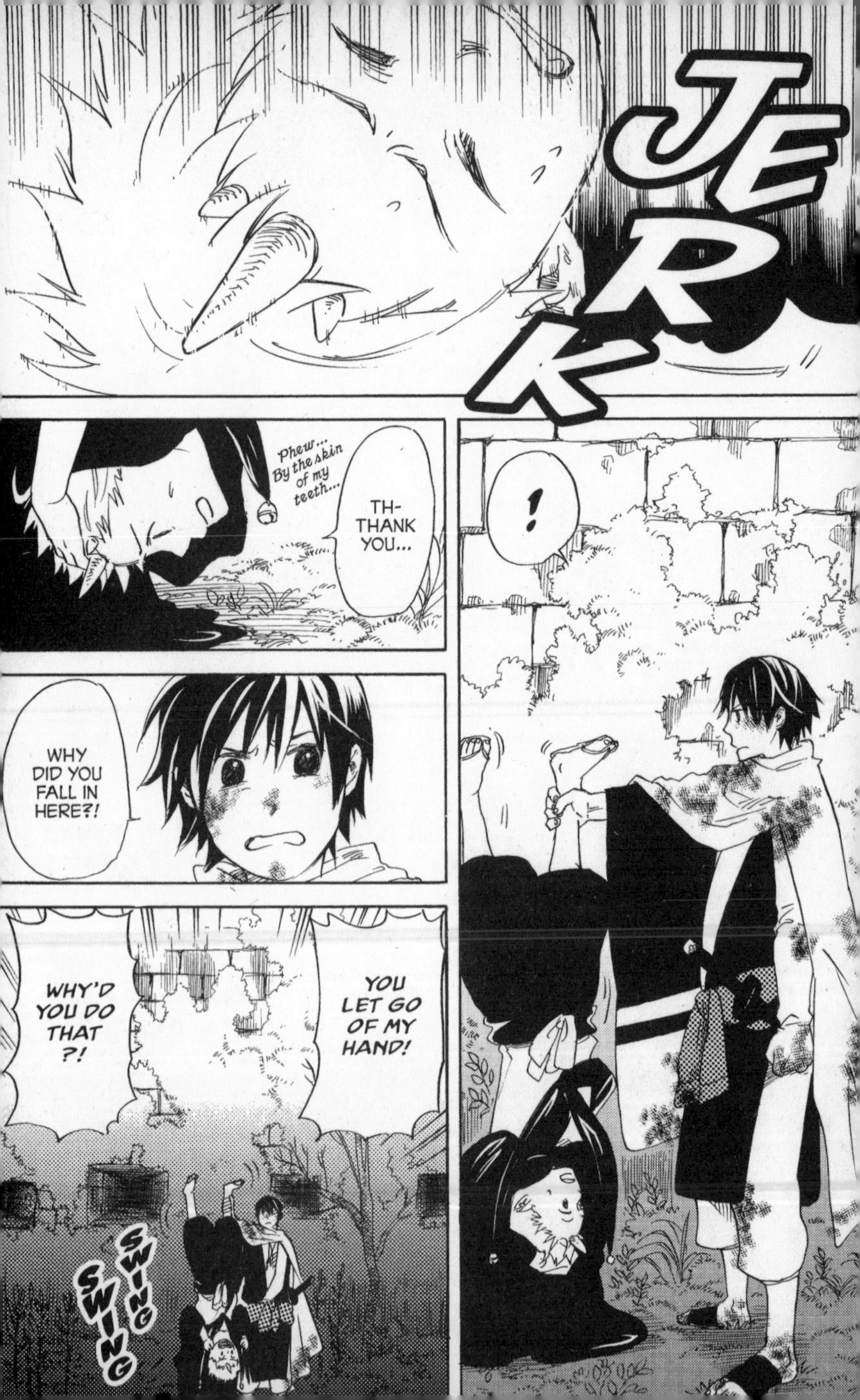
JERK
!
TH-THANK YOU...
Phew... By the skin of my teeth...
WHY DID YOU FALL IN HERE?!
YOU LET GO OF MY HAND!
WHY'D YOU DO THAT?!
SWING SWING

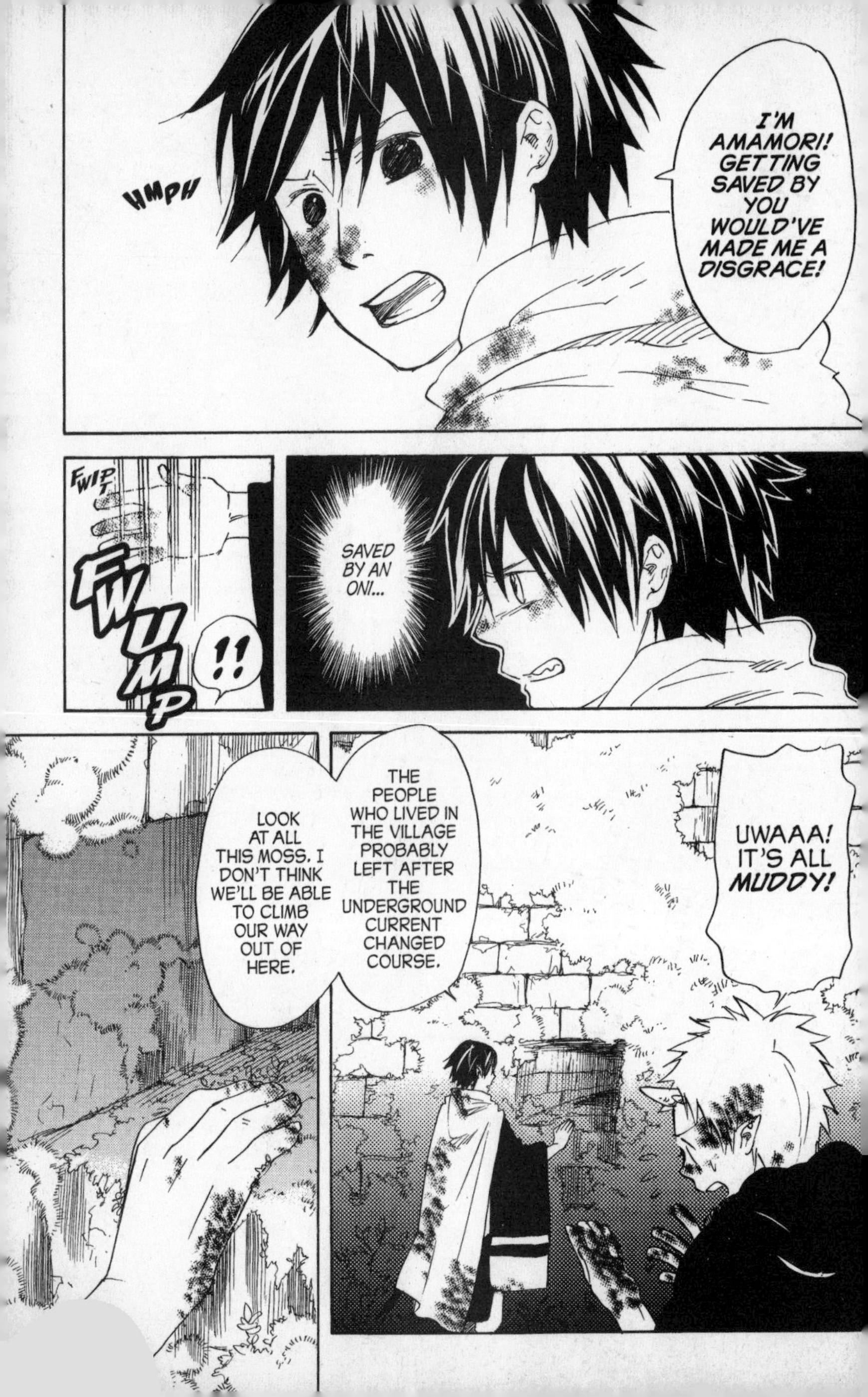
I'M AMAMORI! GETTING SAVED BY YOU WOULD'VE MADE ME A DISGRACE!
HMPH
SAVED BY AN ONI...
FWIPT
FWUMP
!!
UWAAA! IT'S ALL *MUDDY!*
THE PEOPLE WHO LIVED IN THE VILLAGE PROBABLY LEFT AFTER THE UNDERGROUND CURRENT CHANGED COURSE.
LOOK AT ALL THIS MOSS. I DON'T THINK WE'LL BE ABLE TO CLIMB OUR WAY OUT OF HERE.

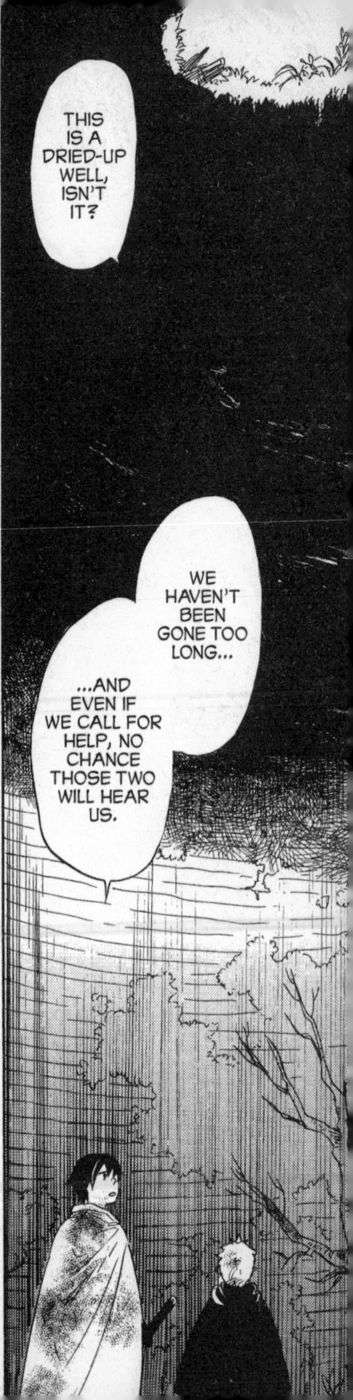
THIS IS A DRIED-UP WELL, ISN'T IT?
WE HAVEN'T BEEN GONE TOO LONG...
...AND EVEN IF WE CALL FOR HELP, NO CHANCE THOSE TWO WILL HEAR US.
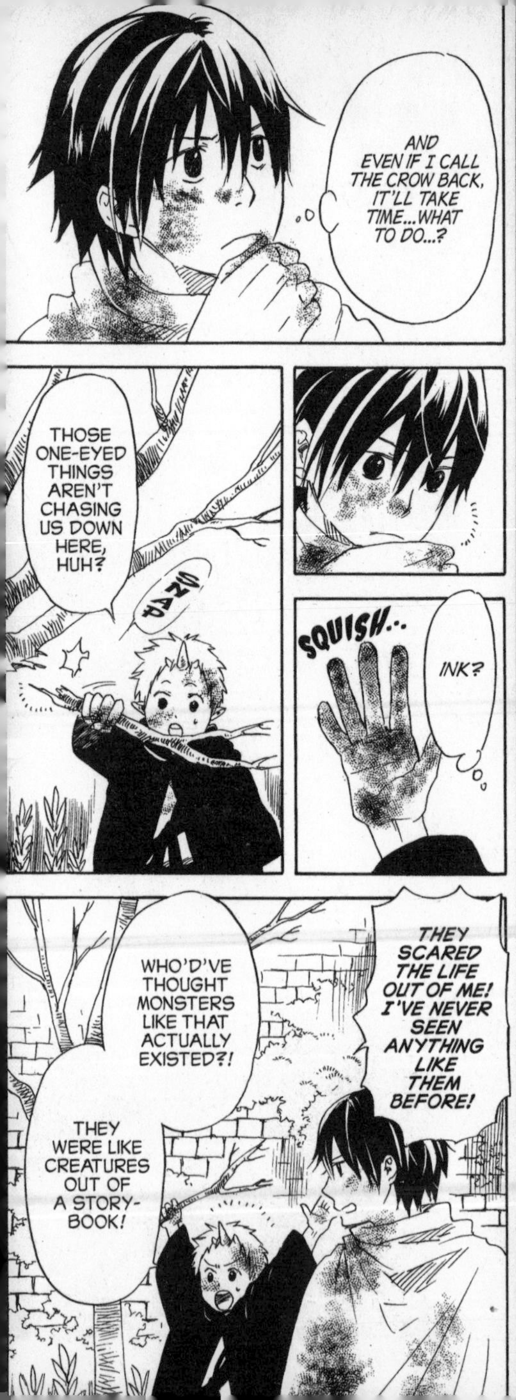
AND EVEN IF I CALL THE CROW BACK, IT'LL TAKE TIME...WHAT TO DO...?
SQUISH...
INK?
THOSE ONE-EYED THINGS AREN'T CHASING US DOWN HERE, HUH?
SNAP
THEY SCARED THE LIFE OUT OF ME! I'VE NEVER SEEN ANYTHING LIKE THEM BEFORE!
WHO'D'VE THOUGHT MONSTERS LIKE THAT ACTUALLY EXISTED?!
THEY WERE LIKE CREATURES OUT OF A STORY-BOOK!

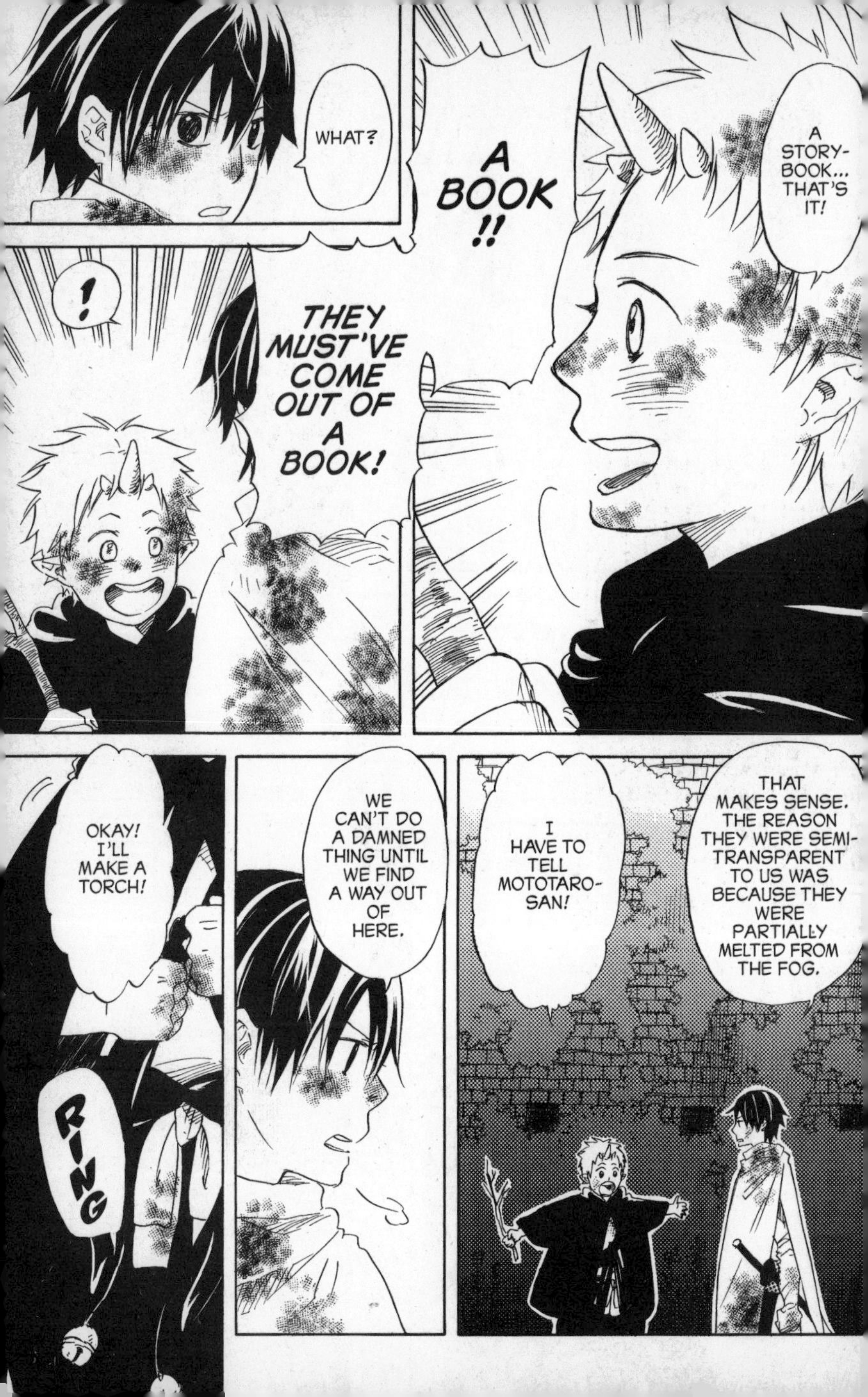
A STORY-BOOK... THAT'S IT!
A BOOK!!
WHAT?
THEY MUST'VE COME OUT OF A BOOK!
!
THAT MAKES SENSE. THE REASON THEY WERE SEMI-TRANSPARENT TO US WAS BECAUSE THEY WERE PARTIALLY MELTED FROM THE FOG.
I HAVE TO TELL MOTOTARO-SAN!
WE CAN'T DO A DAMNED THING UNTIL WE FIND A WAY OUT OF HERE.
OKAY! I'LL MAKE A TORCH!
RING

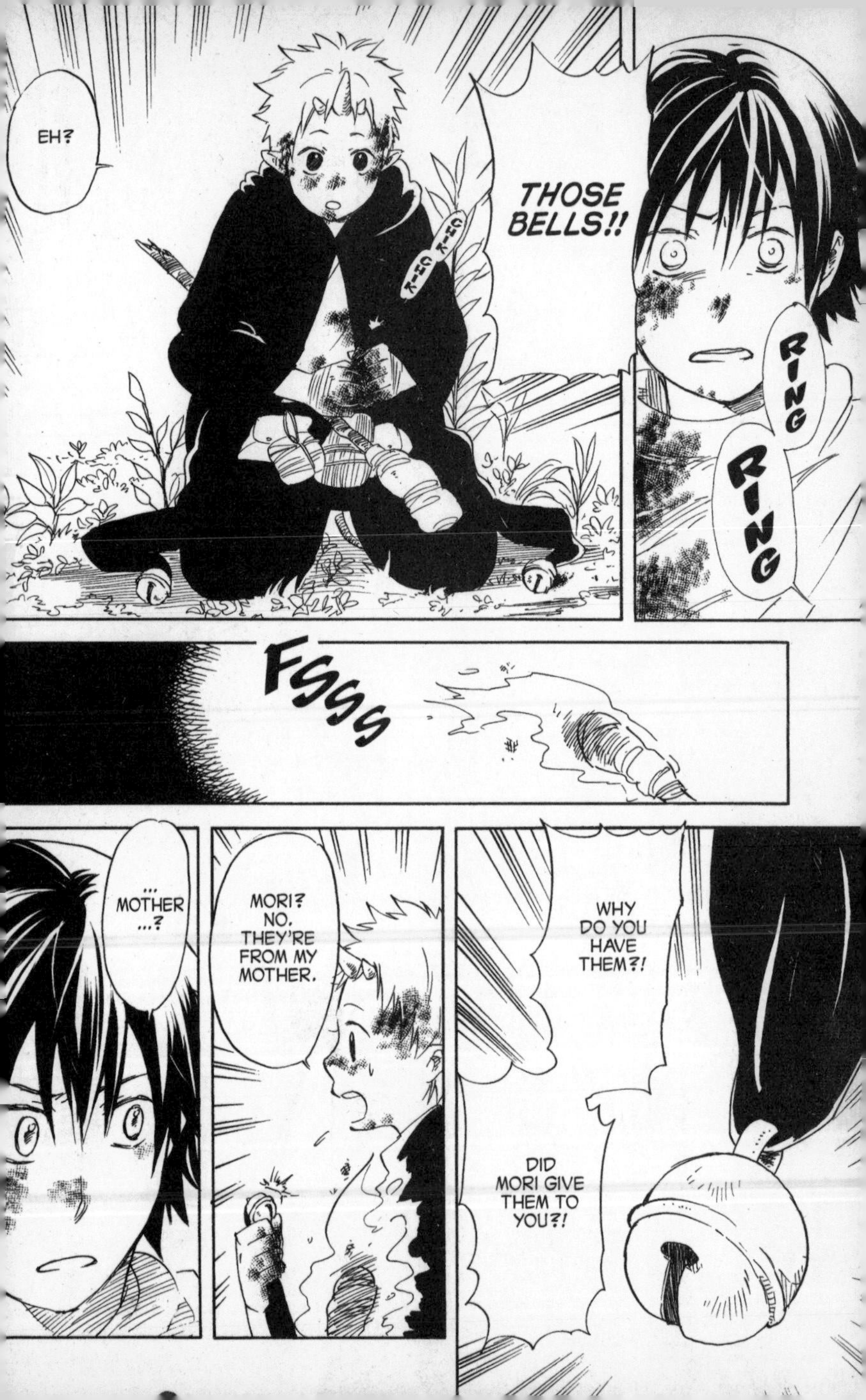
RING RING
THOSE BELLS!!
CHIK CHIK
EH?
FSSS
WHY DO YOU HAVE THEM?!
DID MORI GIVE THEM TO YOU?!
MORI? NO. THEY'RE FROM MY MOTHER.
... MOTHER ...?

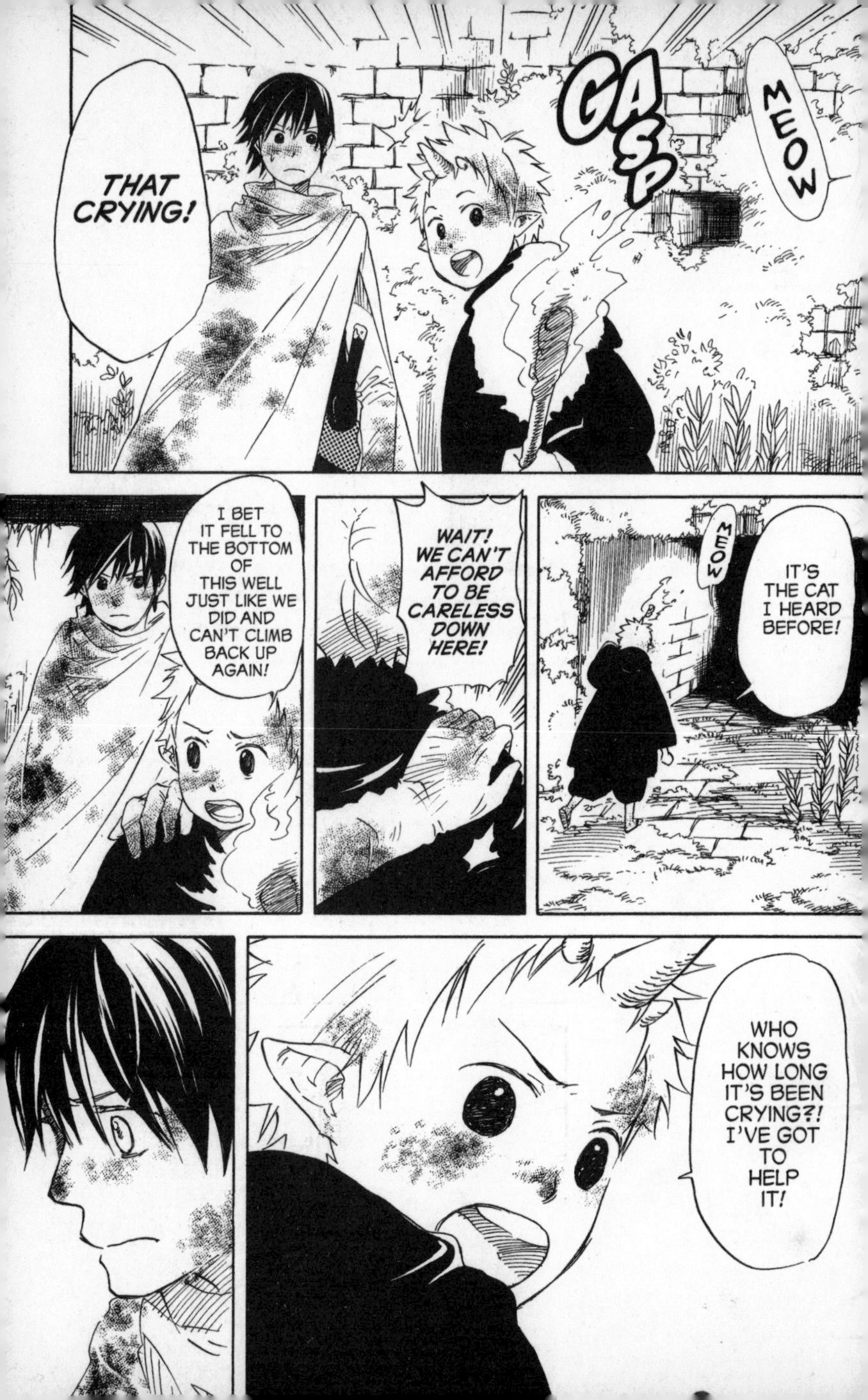
MEOW
GASP
THAT CRYING!
IT'S THE CAT I HEARD BEFORE!
MEOW
WAIT! WE CAN'T AFFORD TO BE CARELESS DOWN HERE!
I BET IT FELL TO THE BOTTOM OF THIS WELL JUST LIKE WE DID AND CAN'T CLIMB BACK UP AGAIN!
WHO KNOWS HOW LONG IT'S BEEN CRYING?! I'VE GOT TO HELP IT!

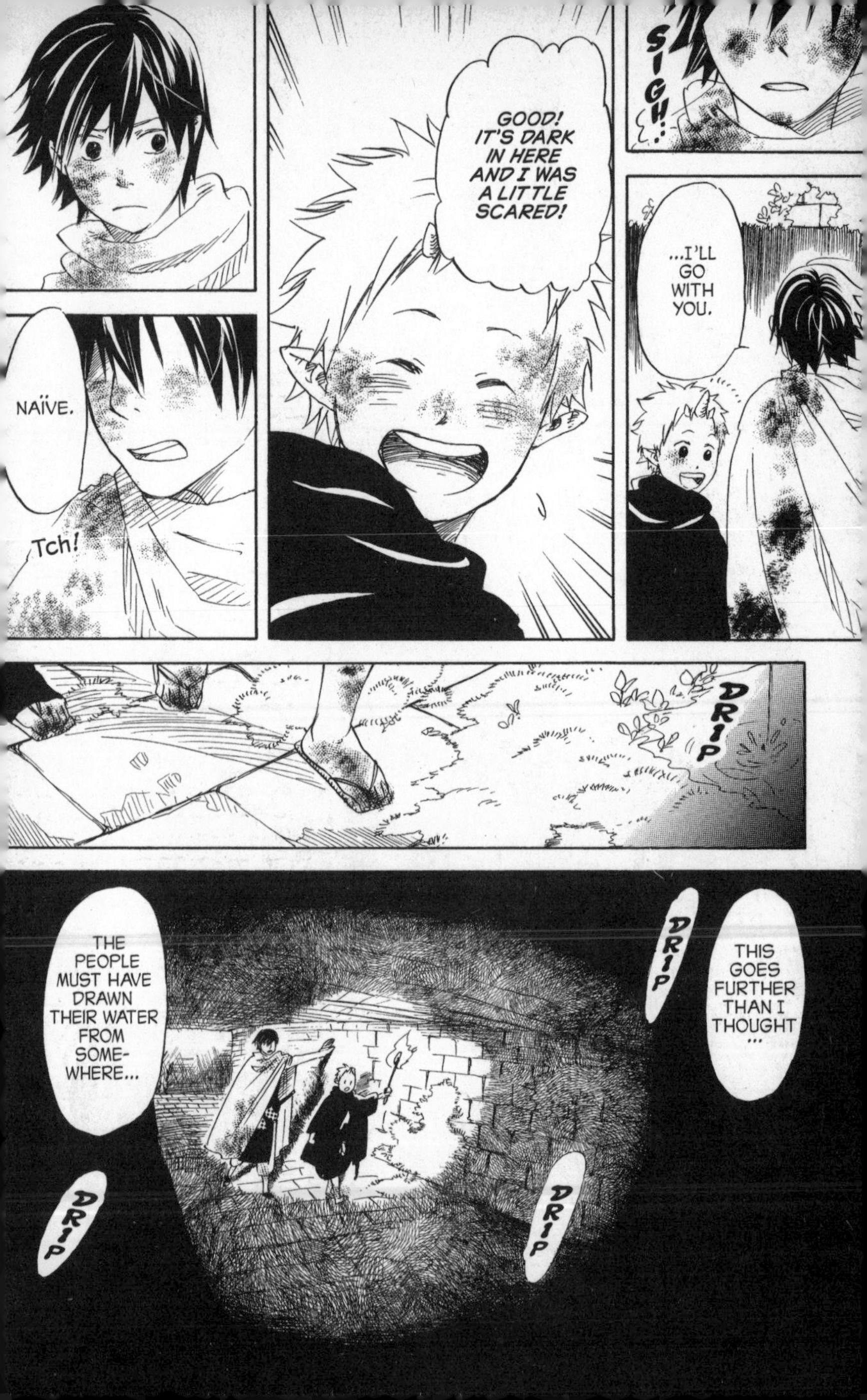
SIGH...
...I'LL GO WITH YOU.
GOOD! IT'S DARK IN HERE AND I WAS A LITTLE SCARED!
NAÏVE.
Tch!
DRIP
THIS GOES FURTHER THAN I THOUGHT...
DRIP
THE PEOPLE MUST HAVE DRAWN THEIR WATER FROM SOME-WHERE...
DRIP
DRIP

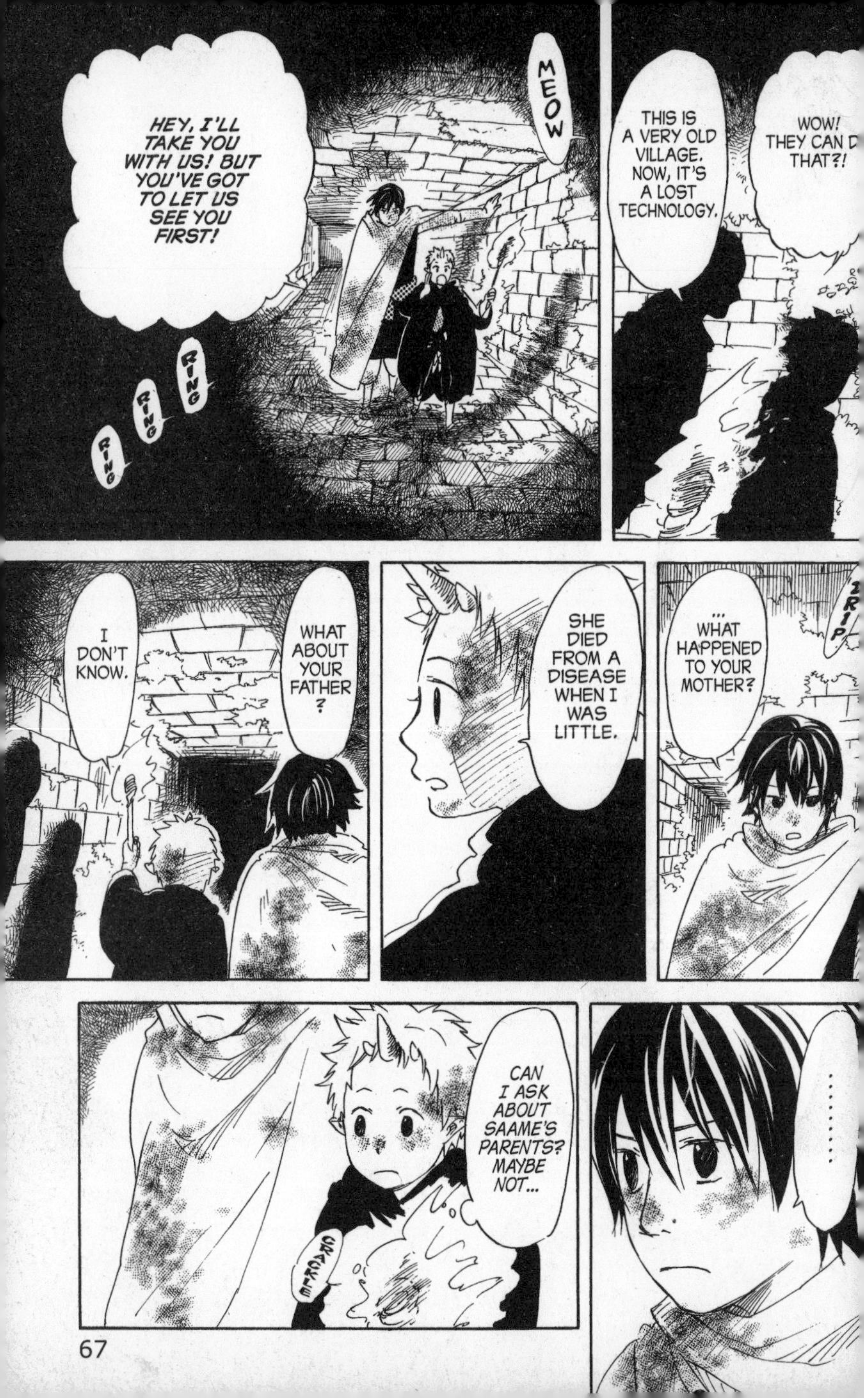
WOW! THEY CAN D THAT?!
THIS IS A VERY OLD VILLAGE. NOW, IT'S A LOST TECHNOLOGY.
MEOW
HEY, I'LL TAKE YOU WITH US! BUT YOU'VE GOT TO LET US SEE YOU FIRST!
RING
RING
RING
DRIP
... WHAT HAPPENED TO YOUR MOTHER?
SHE DIED FROM A DISEASE WHEN I WAS LITTLE.
WHAT ABOUT YOUR FATHER?
I DON'T KNOW.
......
CAN I ASK ABOUT SAAME'S PARENTS? MAYBE NOT...
CRACKLE

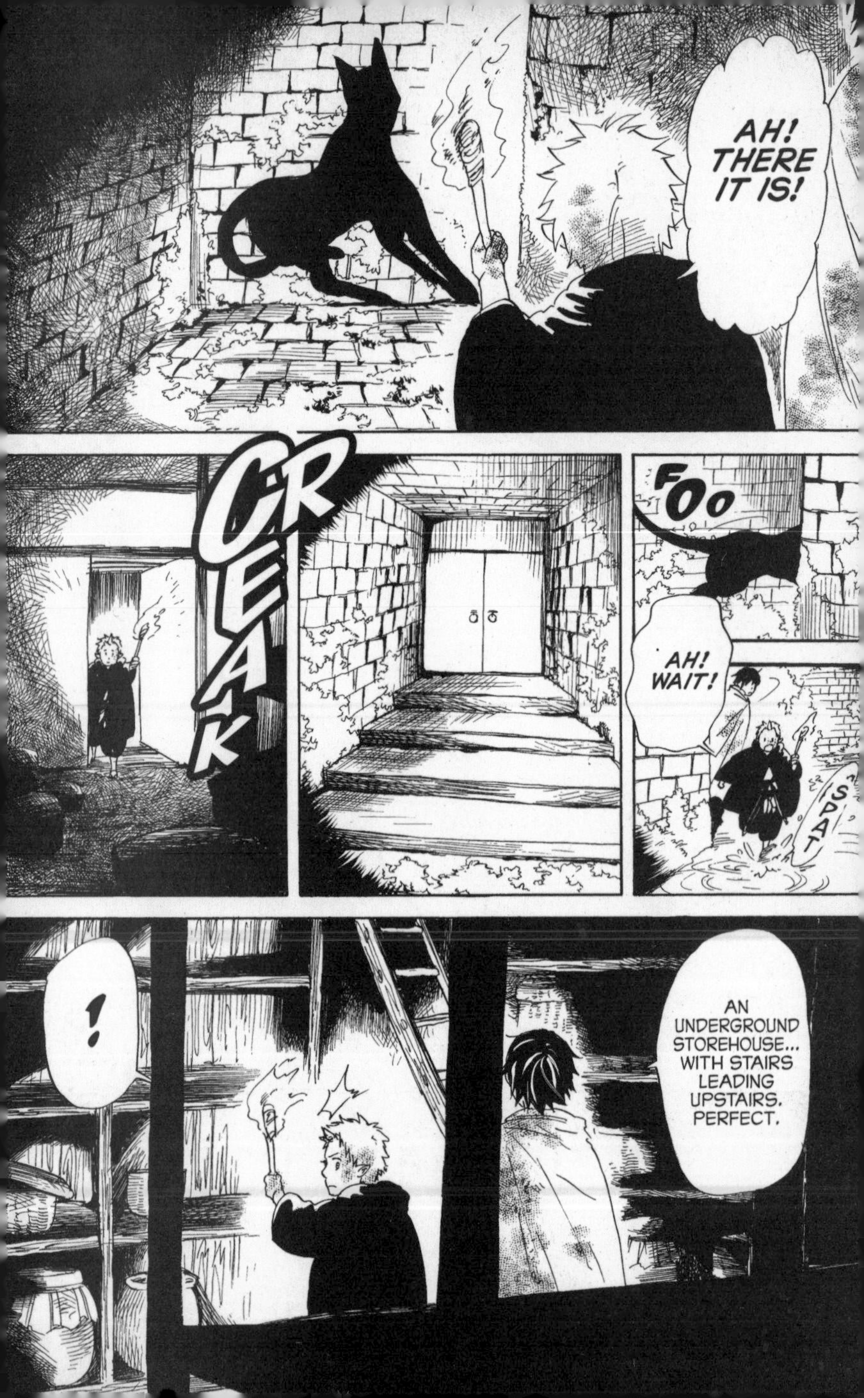
AH! THERE IT IS!
FOO
AH! WAIT!
SPAT
CREAK
AN UNDERGROUND STOREHOUSE... WITH STAIRS LEADING UPSTAIRS. PERFECT.
!

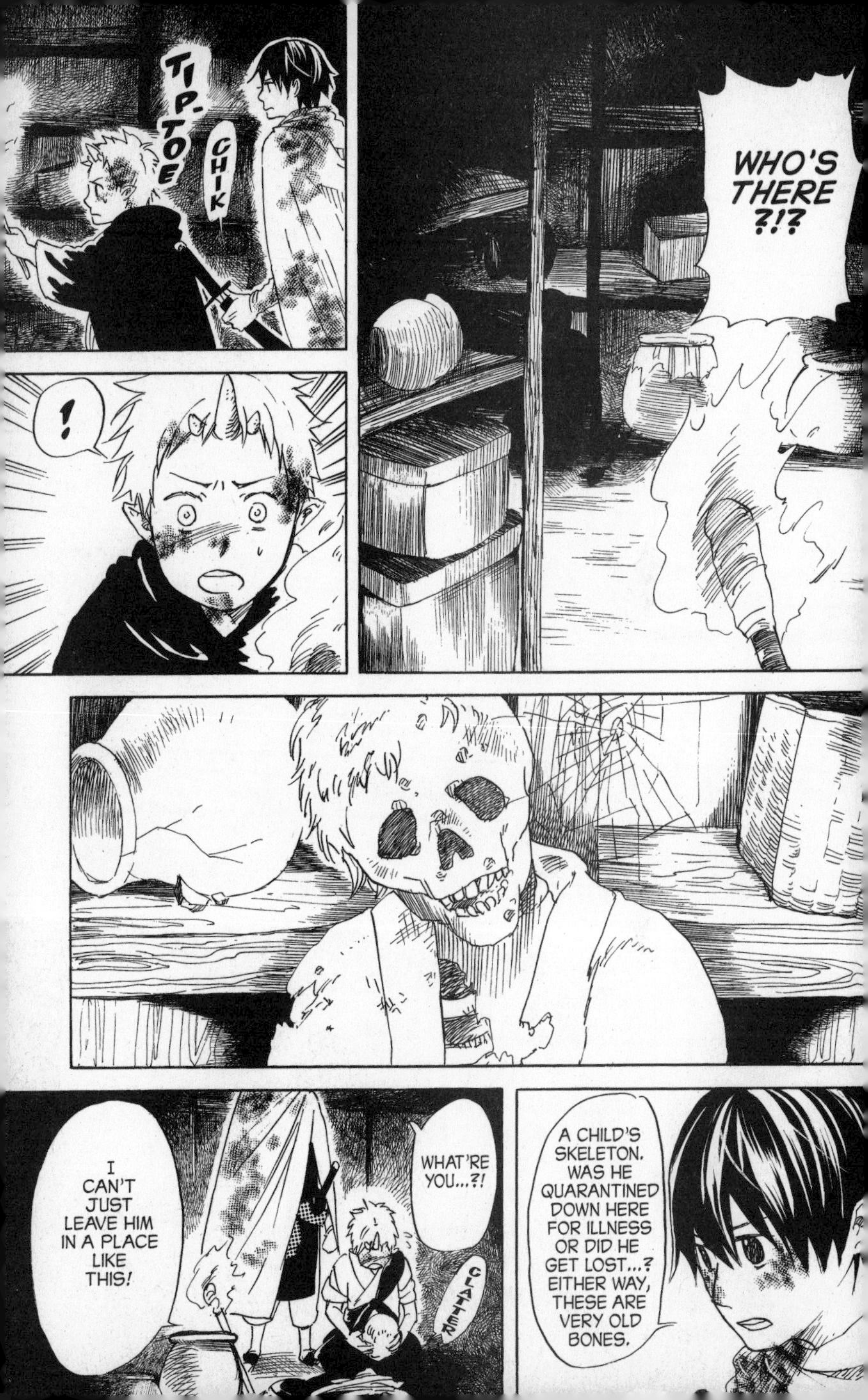
WHO'S THERE ?!?
TIP-TOE
CHIK
!
A CHILD'S SKELETON. WAS HE QUARANTINED DOWN HERE FOR ILLNESS OR DID HE GET LOST...? EITHER WAY, THESE ARE VERY OLD BONES.
WHAT'RE YOU...?!
I CAN'T JUST LEAVE HIM IN A PLACE LIKE THIS!
CLATTER

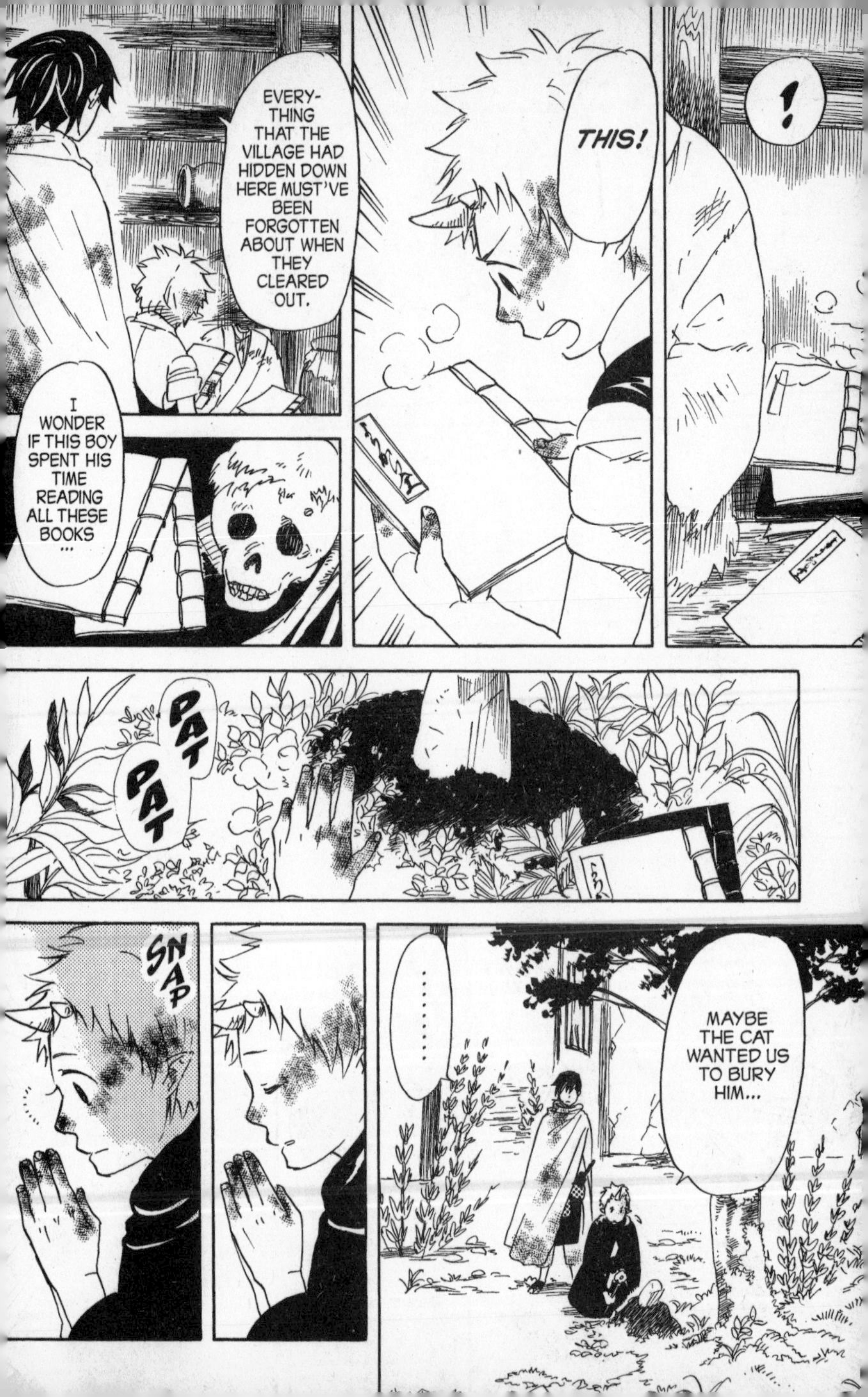
!
THIS!
EVERYTHING THAT THE VILLAGE HAD HIDDEN DOWN HERE MUST'VE BEEN FORGOTTEN ABOUT WHEN THEY CLEARED OUT.
I WONDER IF THIS BOY SPENT HIS TIME READING ALL THESE BOOKS...
PAT PAT
MAYBE THE CAT WANTED US TO BURY HIM...
......
SNAP

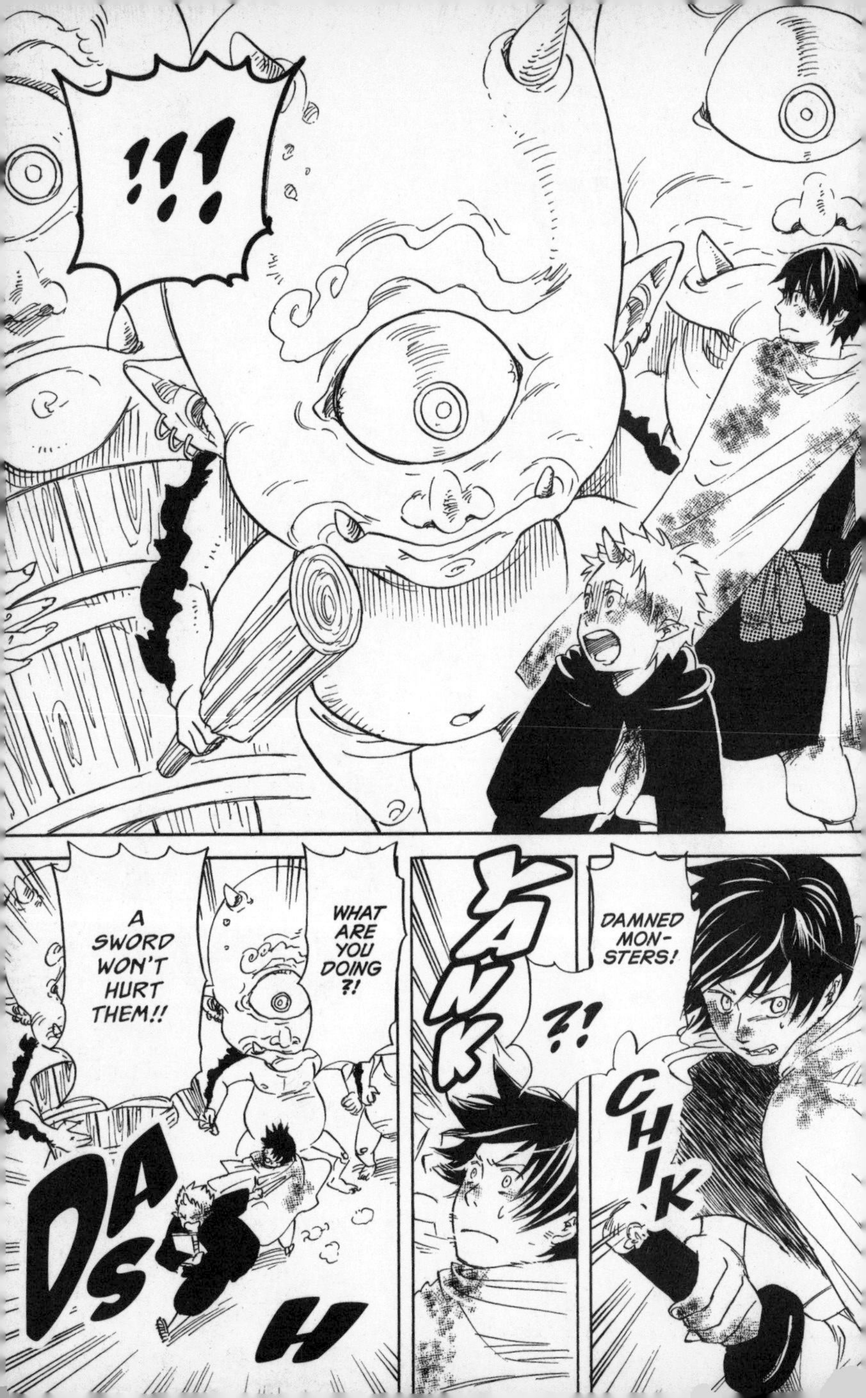
!!!
DAMNED MONSTERS!
CHIK
YANK
?!
WHAT ARE YOU DOING?!
A SWORD WON'T HURT THEM!!
DASH

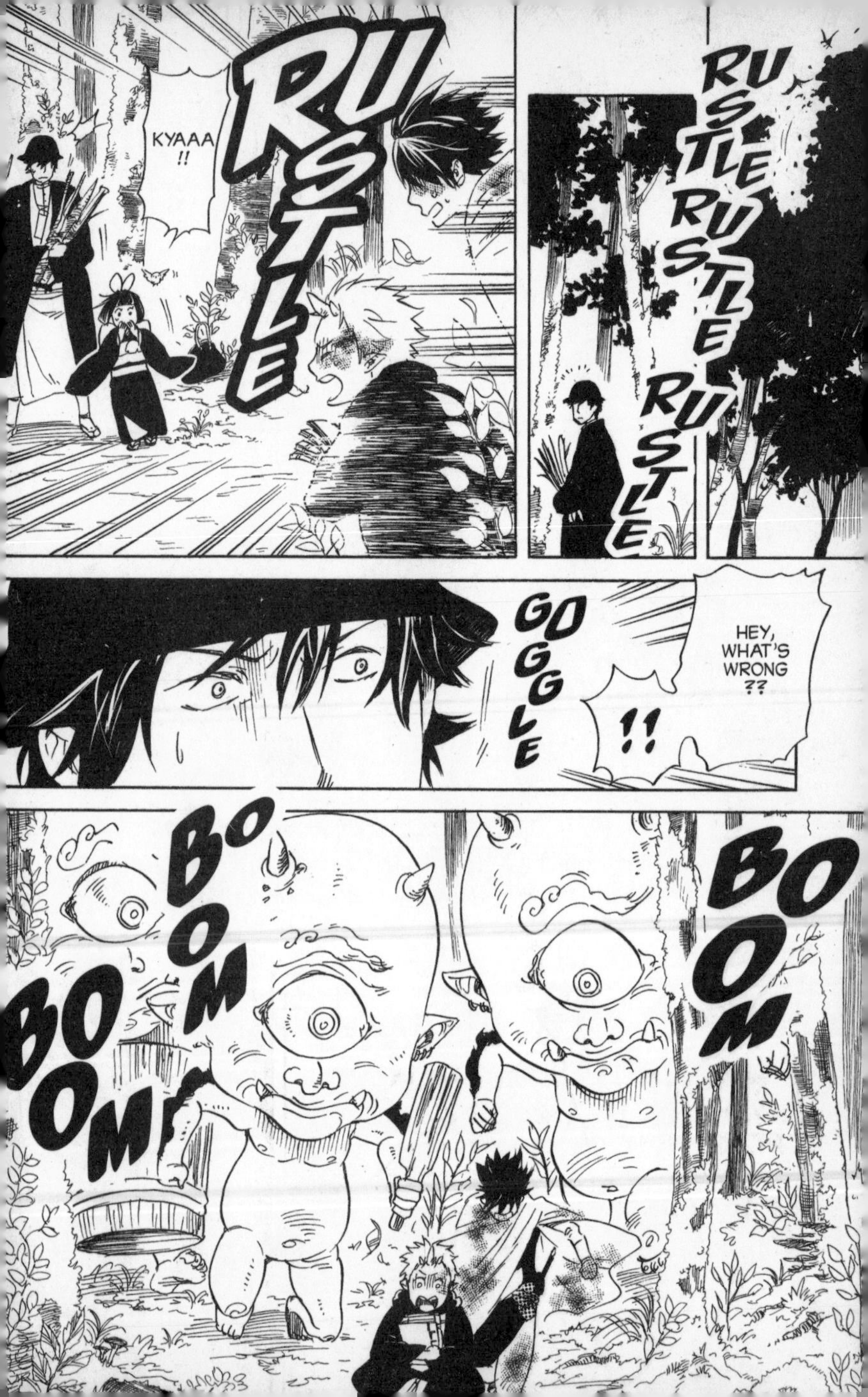
RUSTLE RUSTLE RUSTLE
RUSTLE
KYAAA!!
HEY, WHAT'S WRONG??
!!
GOGGLE
BOOM
BOOM
BOOM

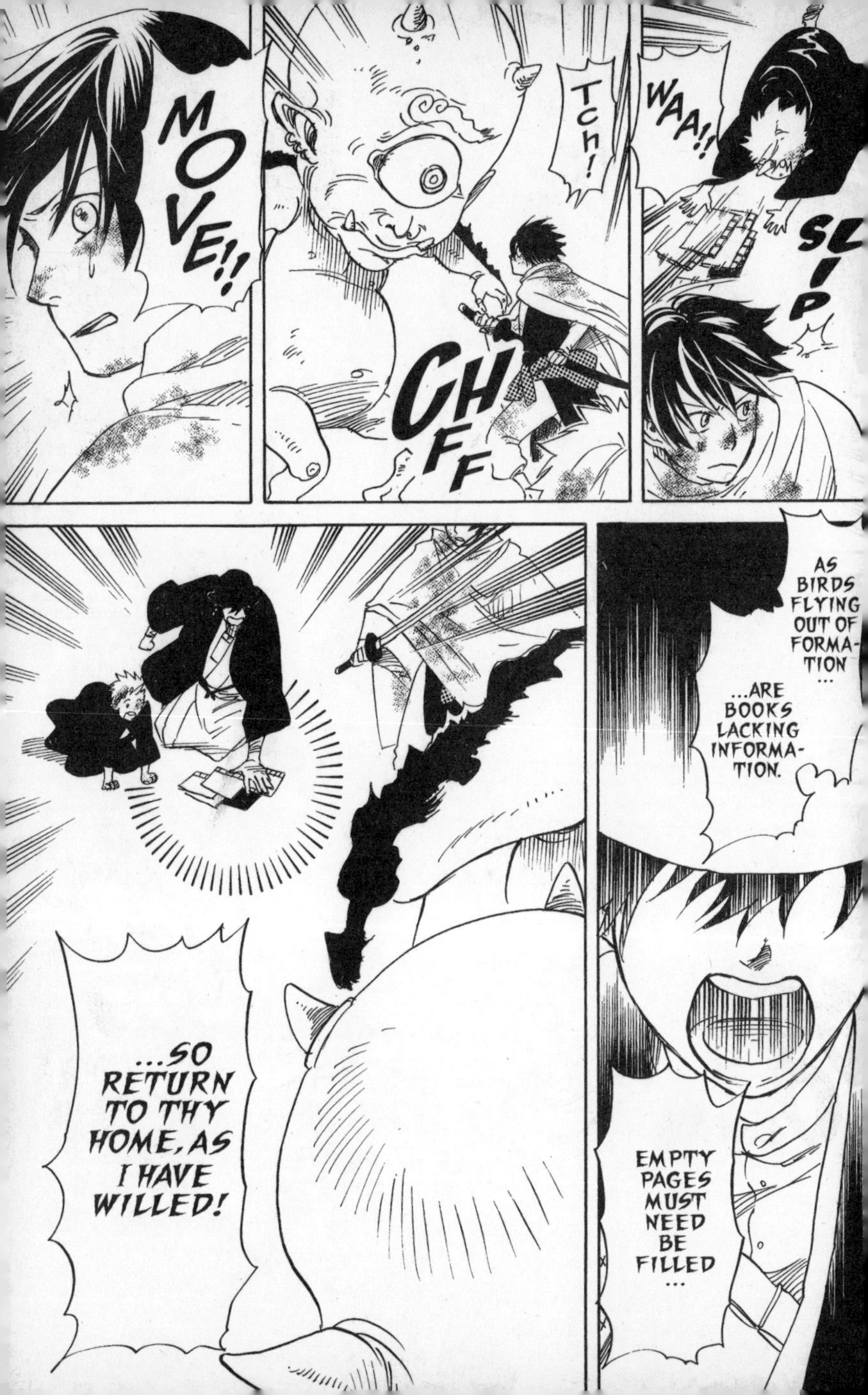
WAA!!
SLIP
Tch!
CHFF
MOVE!!
AS BIRDS FLYING OUT OF FORMATION...
...ARE BOOKS LACKING INFORMATION.
EMPTY PAGES MUST NEED BE FILLED...
...SO RETURN TO THY HOME, AS I HAVE WILLED!

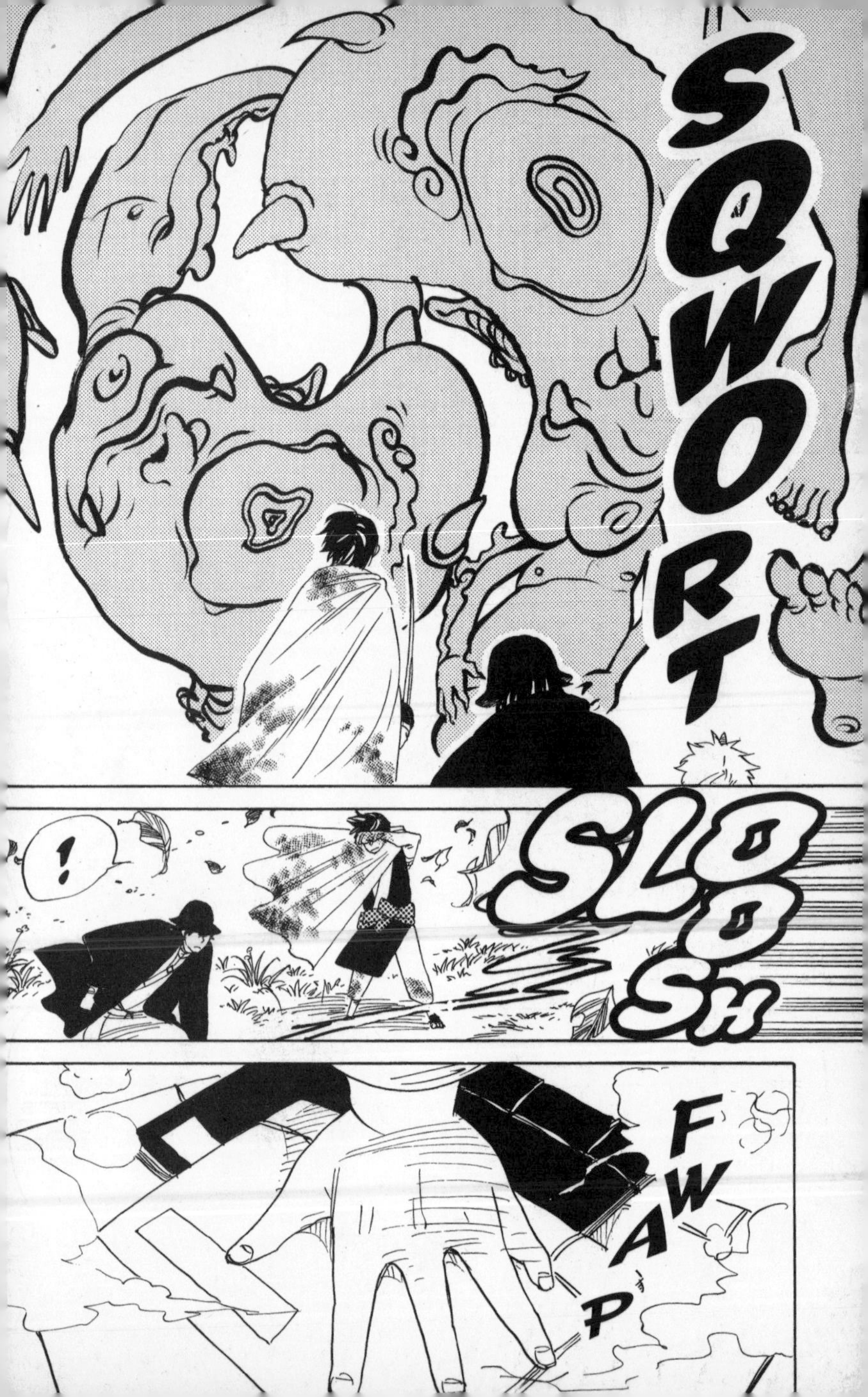
SQWORT
SLOOSH
!
FWAP

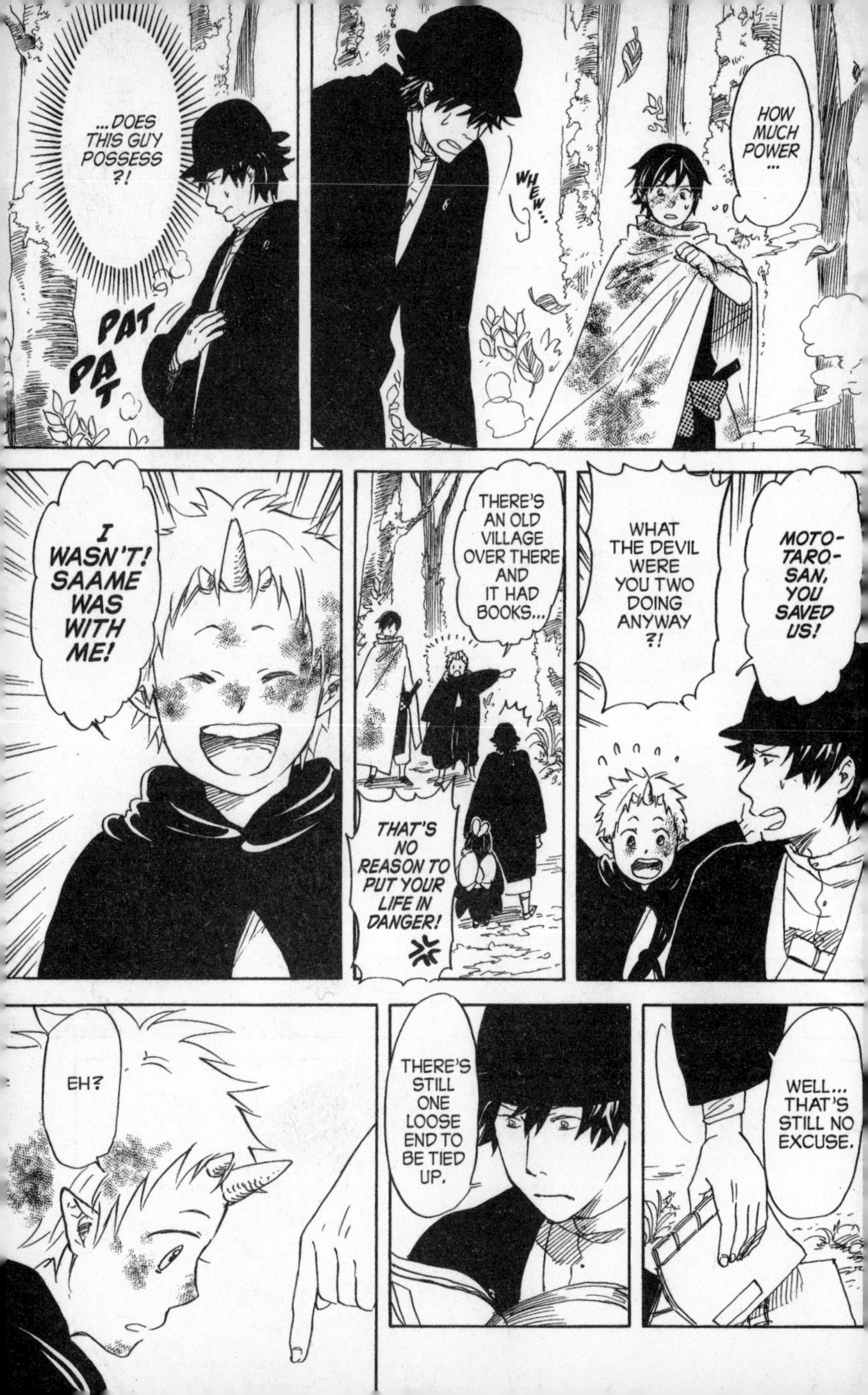
HOW MUCH POWER ...
WHEW...
...DOES THIS GUY POSSESS ?!
PAT PAT
MOTO-TARO-SAN, YOU SAVED US!
WHAT THE DEVIL WERE YOU TWO DOING ANYWAY ?!
THERE'S AN OLD VILLAGE OVER THERE AND IT HAD BOOKS...
THAT'S NO REASON TO PUT YOUR LIFE IN DANGER!
I WASN'T! SAAME WAS WITH ME!
WELL... THAT'S STILL NO EXCUSE.
THERE'S STILL ONE LOOSE END TO BE TIED UP.
EH?

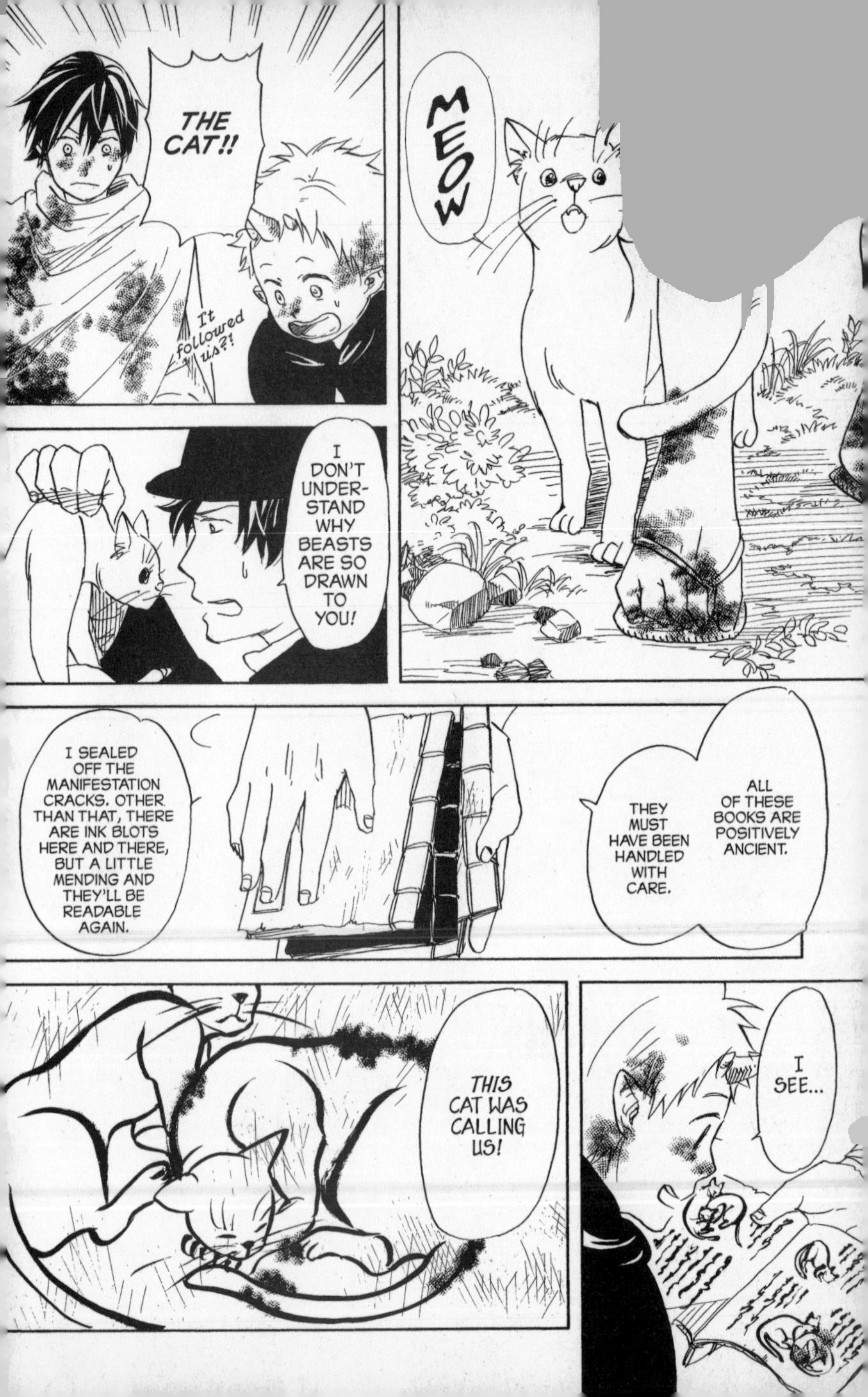
MEOW
THE CAT!!
It followed us?!
I DON'T UNDERSTAND WHY BEASTS ARE SO DRAWN TO YOU!
ALL OF THESE BOOKS ARE POSITIVELY ANCIENT.
THEY MUST HAVE BEEN HANDLED WITH CARE.
I SEALED OFF THE MANIFESTATION CRACKS. OTHER THAN THAT, THERE ARE INK BLOTS HERE AND THERE, BUT A LITTLE MENDING AND THEY'LL BE READABLE AGAIN.
I SEE...
THIS CAT WAS CALLING US!

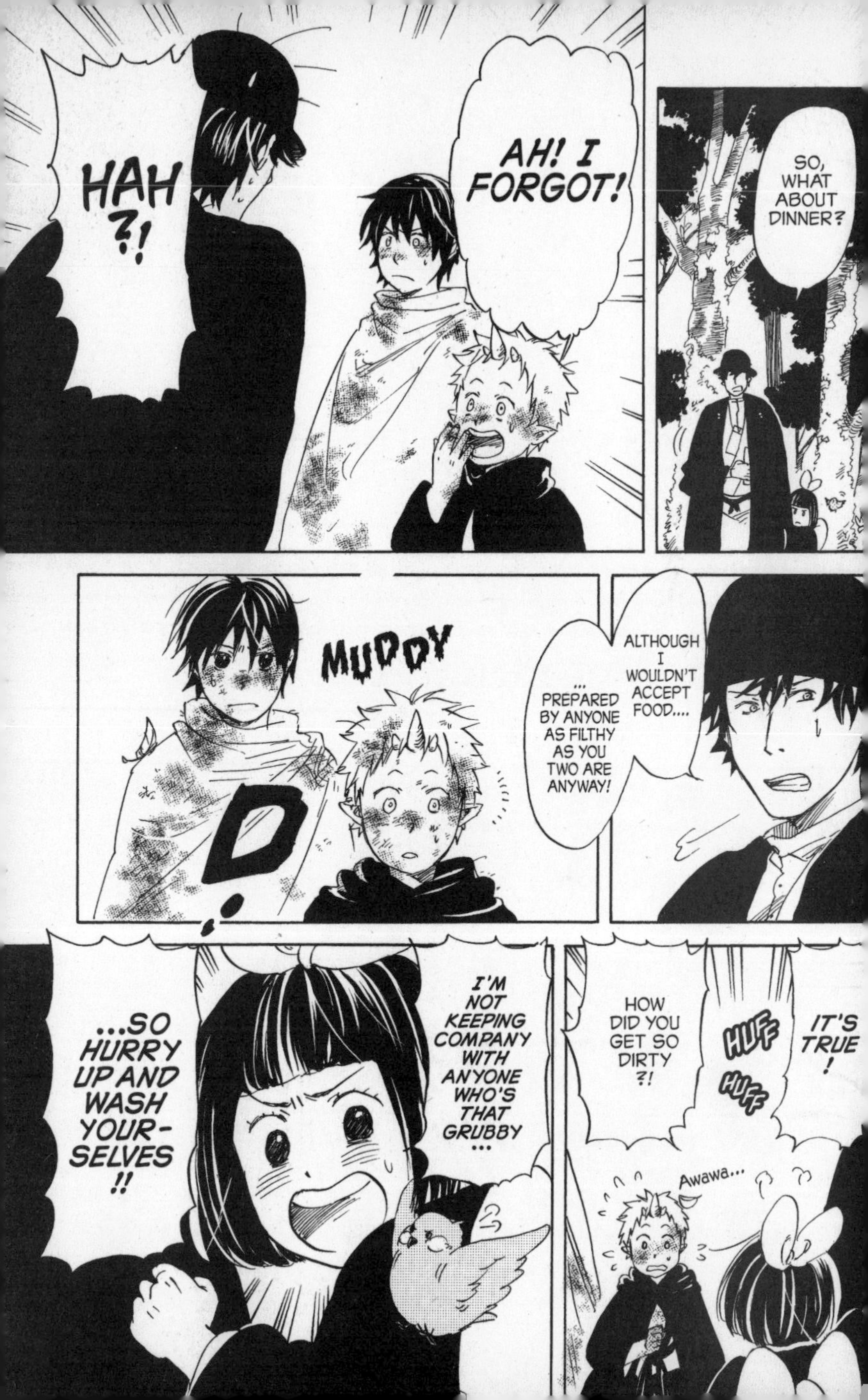
SO, WHAT ABOUT DINNER?
AH! I FORGOT!
HAH ?!
ALTHOUGH I WOULDN'T ACCEPT FOOD....
...PREPARED BY ANYONE AS FILTHY AS YOU TWO ARE ANYWAY!
MUDDY
D
IT'S TRUE!
HUFF
HUFF
HOW DID YOU GET SO DIRTY ?!
Awawa...
I'M NOT KEEPING COMPANY WITH ANYONE WHO'S THAT GRUBBY...
...SO HURRY UP AND WASH YOUR-SELVES !!

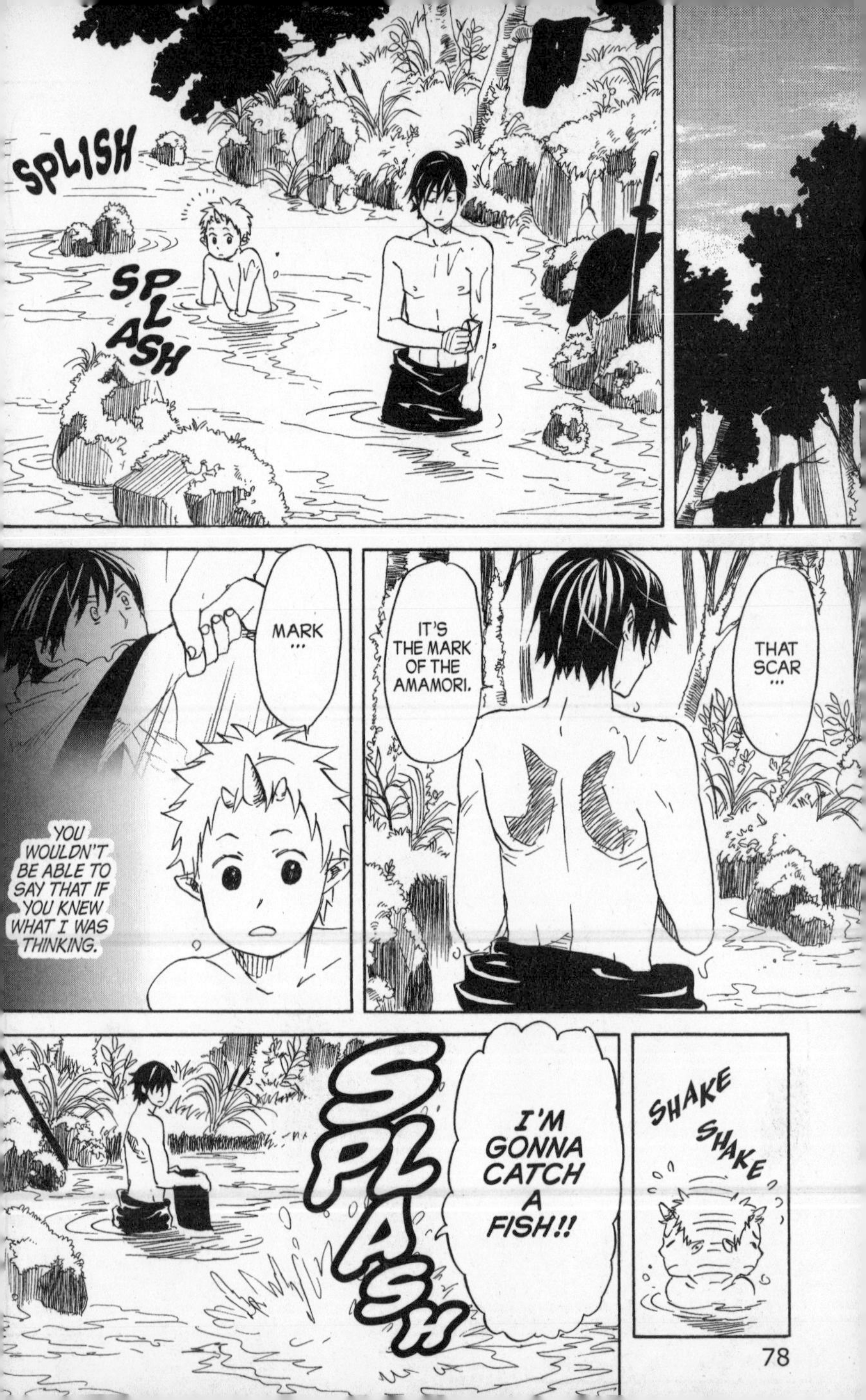
SPLISH
SPLASH
THAT SCAR...
IT'S THE MARK OF THE AMAMORI.
MARK...
YOU WOULDN'T BE ABLE TO SAY THAT IF YOU KNEW WHAT I WAS THINKING.
SHAKE SHAKE
I'M GONNA CATCH A FISH!!
SPLASH

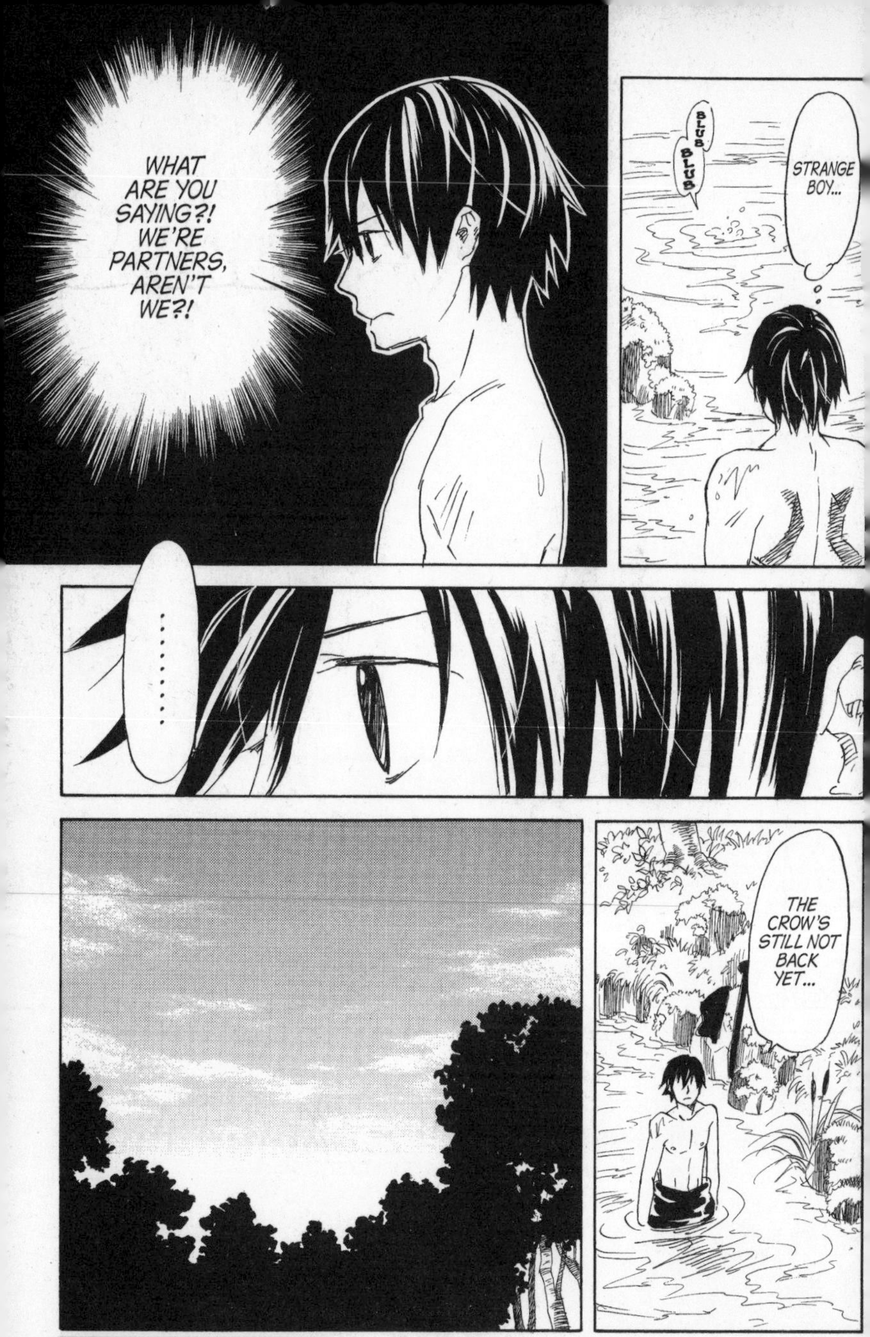
STRANGE BOY...
BLUB BLUB
WHAT ARE YOU SAYING?! WE'RE PARTNERS, AREN'T WE?!
......
THE CROW'S STILL NOT BACK YET...

Book Eleven: The End

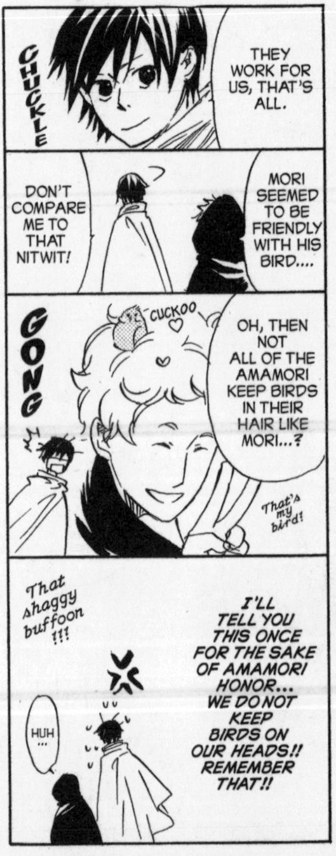
THEY WORK FOR US, THAT'S ALL.
CHUCKLE
MORI SEEMED TO BE FRIENDLY WITH HIS BIRD....
DON'T COMPARE ME TO THAT NITWIT!
OH, THEN NOT ALL OF THE AMAMORI KEEP BIRDS IN THEIR HAIR LIKE MORI...?
CUCKOO ♡
GONG
That's my bird!
I'LL TELL YOU THIS ONCE FOR THE SAKE OF AMAMORI HONOR... WE DO NOT KEEP BIRDS ON OUR HEADS!! REMEMBER THAT!!
That shaggy buffoon !!!
HUH ...

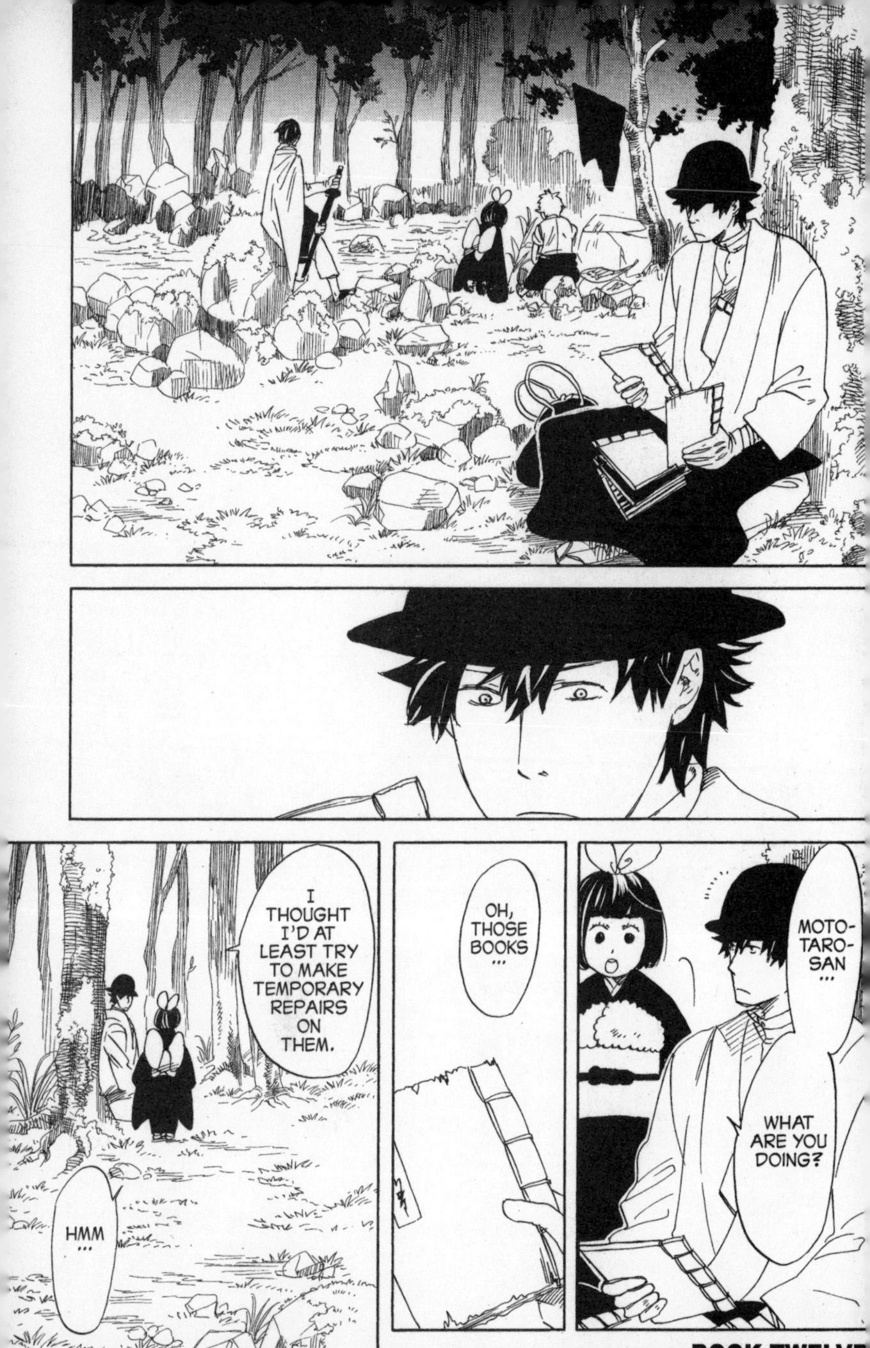
MOTO-TARO-SAN...
WHAT ARE YOU DOING?
OH, THOSE BOOKS...
I THOUGHT I'D AT LEAST TRY TO MAKE TEMPORARY REPAIRS ON THEM.
HMM...

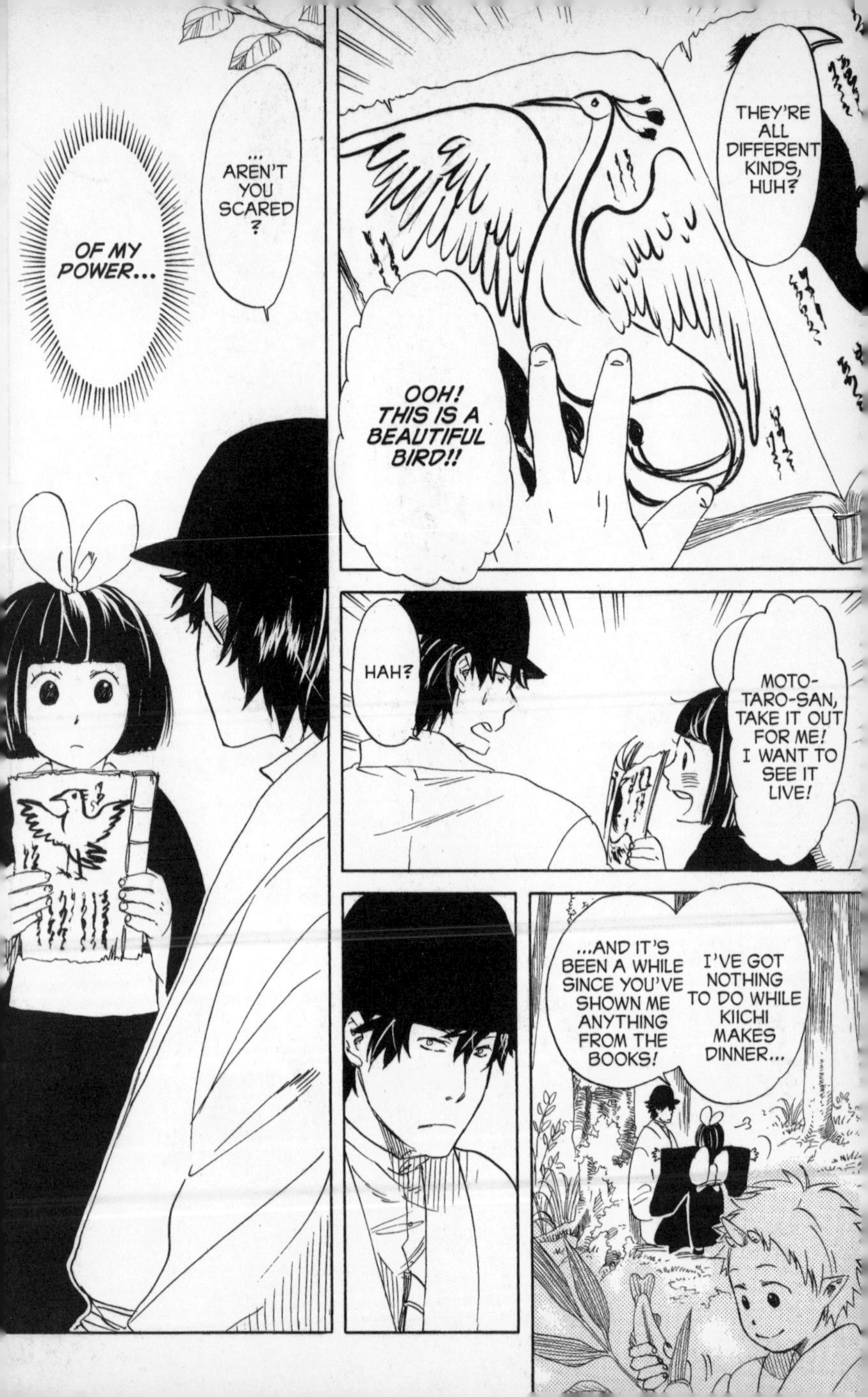
THEY'RE ALL DIFFERENT KINDS, HUH?
OOH! THIS IS A BEAUTIFUL BIRD!!
MOTO-TARO-SAN, TAKE IT OUT FOR ME! I WANT TO SEE IT LIVE!
HAH?
I'VE GOT NOTHING TO DO WHILE KIICHI MAKES DINNER...
...AND IT'S BEEN A WHILE SINCE YOU'VE SHOWN ME ANYTHING FROM THE BOOKS!
...AREN'T YOU SCARED?
OF MY POWER...

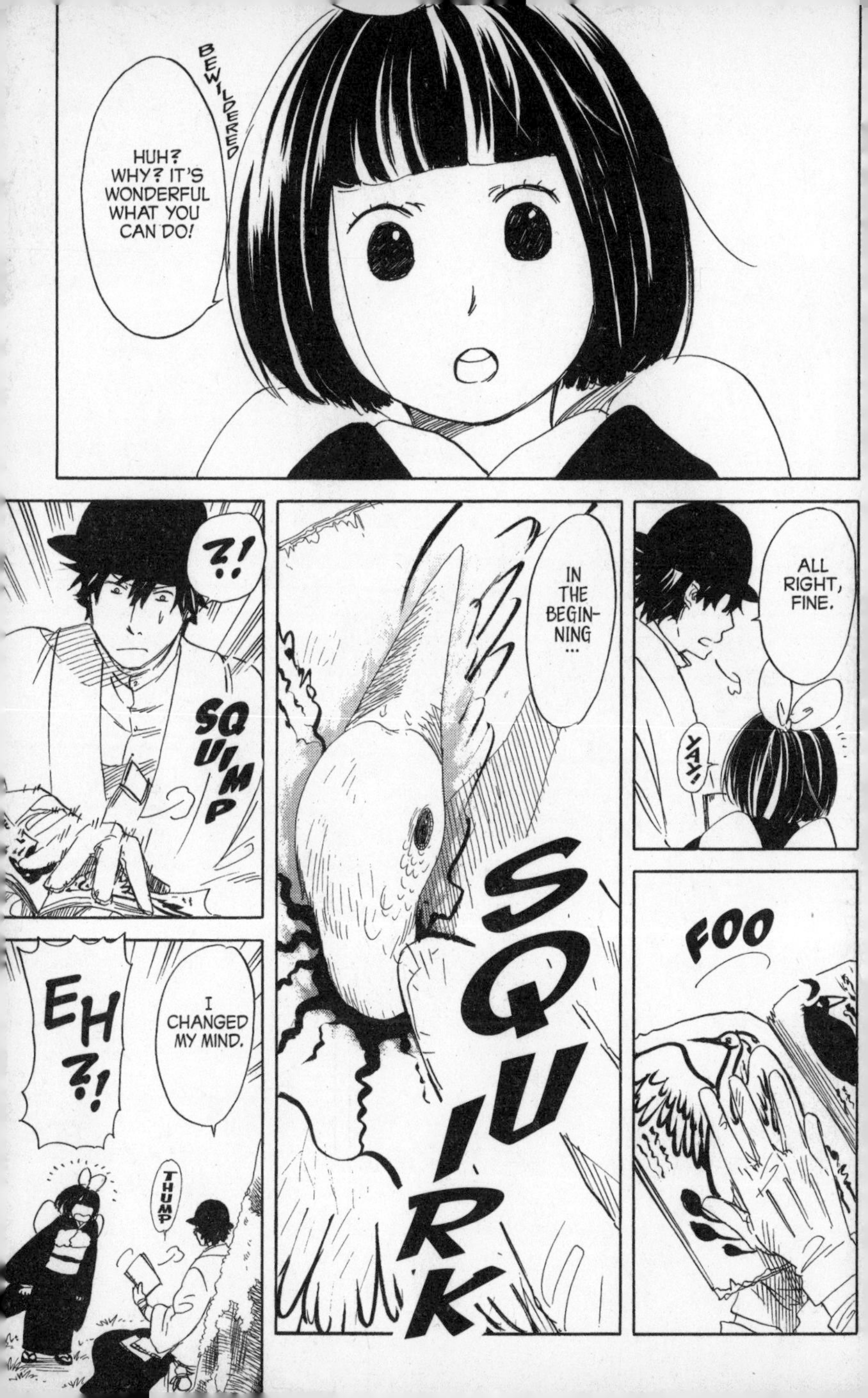
BEWILDERED
HUH? WHY? IT'S WONDERFUL WHAT YOU CAN DO!
ALL RIGHT, FINE.
YAY!
FOO
IN THE BEGIN-NING...
SQUIRK
?!
SQUIMP
I CHANGED MY MIND.
EH?!
THUMP

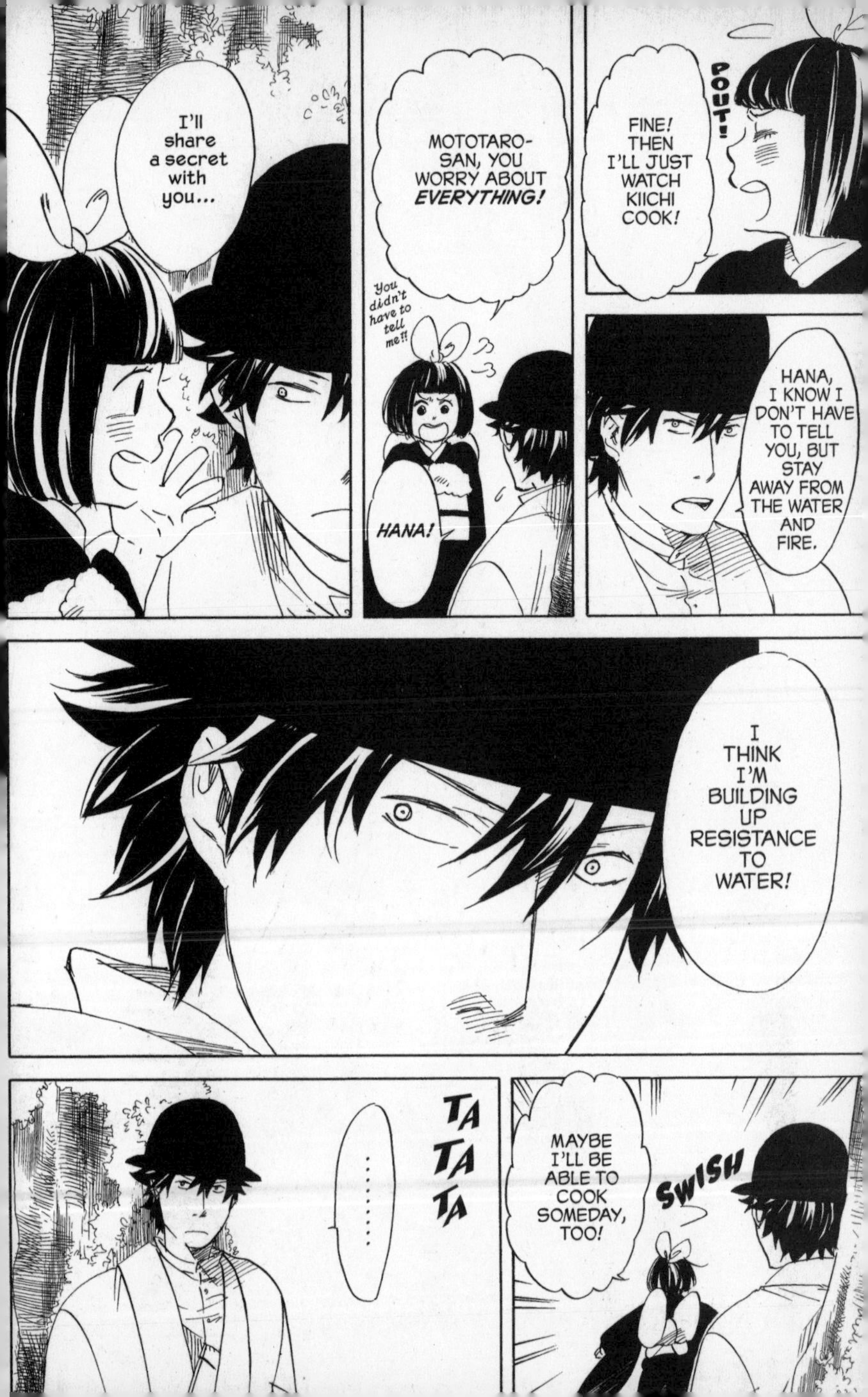
POUT!
FINE! THEN I'LL JUST WATCH KIICHI COOK!
HANA, I KNOW I DON'T HAVE TO TELL YOU, BUT STAY AWAY FROM THE WATER AND FIRE.
MOTOTARO-SAN, YOU WORRY ABOUT *EVERYTHING!*
You didn't have to tell me!!
HANA!
I'll share a secret with you...
I THINK I'M BUILDING UP RESISTANCE TO WATER!
MAYBE I'LL BE ABLE TO COOK SOMEDAY, TOO!
SWISH
TA TA TA TA
......

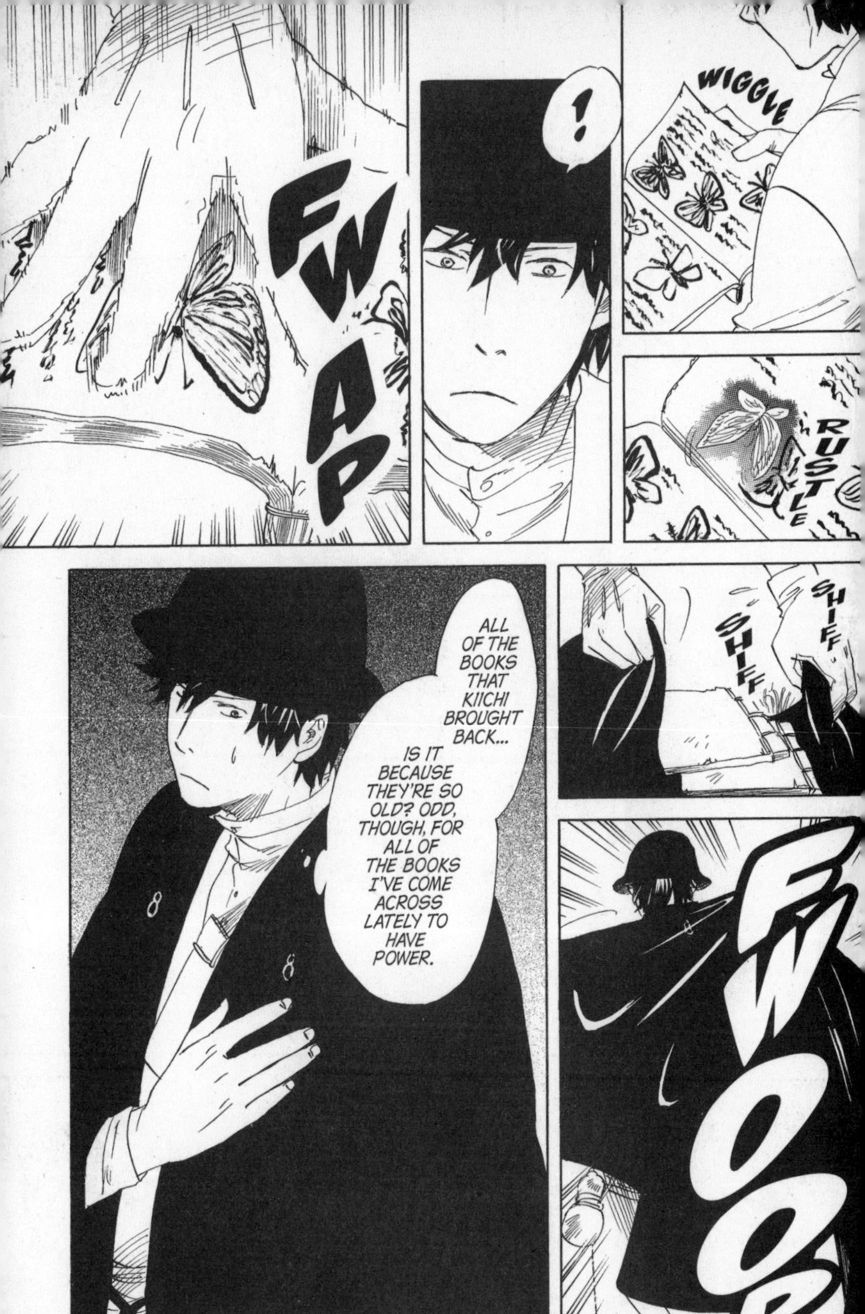
WIGGLE
RUSTLE
!
FWAP
SHIFF
SHIFF
FWOOP
ALL OF THE BOOKS THAT KIICHI BROUGHT BACK... IS IT BECAUSE THEY'RE SO OLD? ODD, THOUGH, FOR ALL OF THE BOOKS I'VE COME ACROSS LATELY TO HAVE POWER.

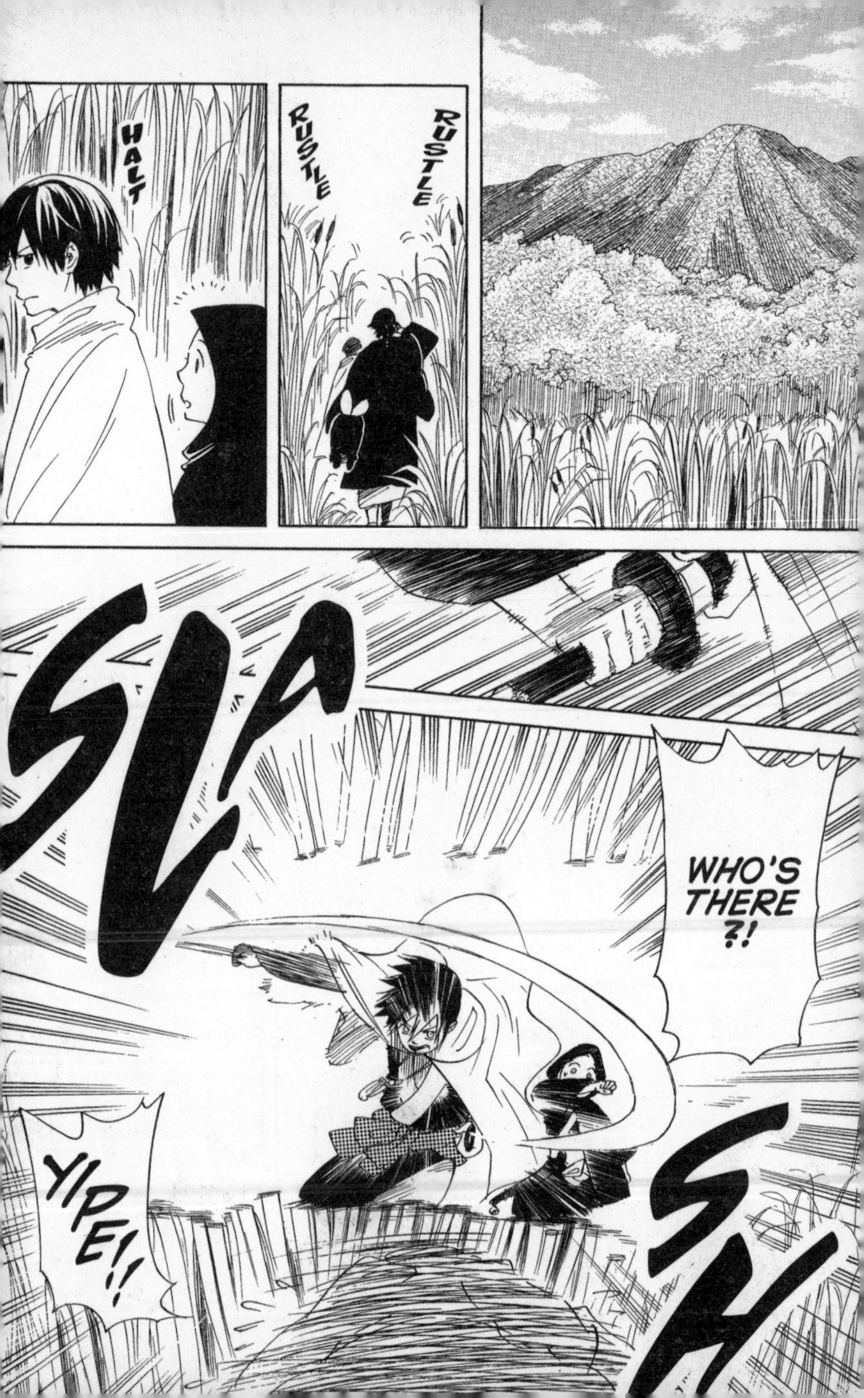
RUSTLE
RUSTLE
HALT
SLA
WHO'S THERE ?!
SH
YIPE!!

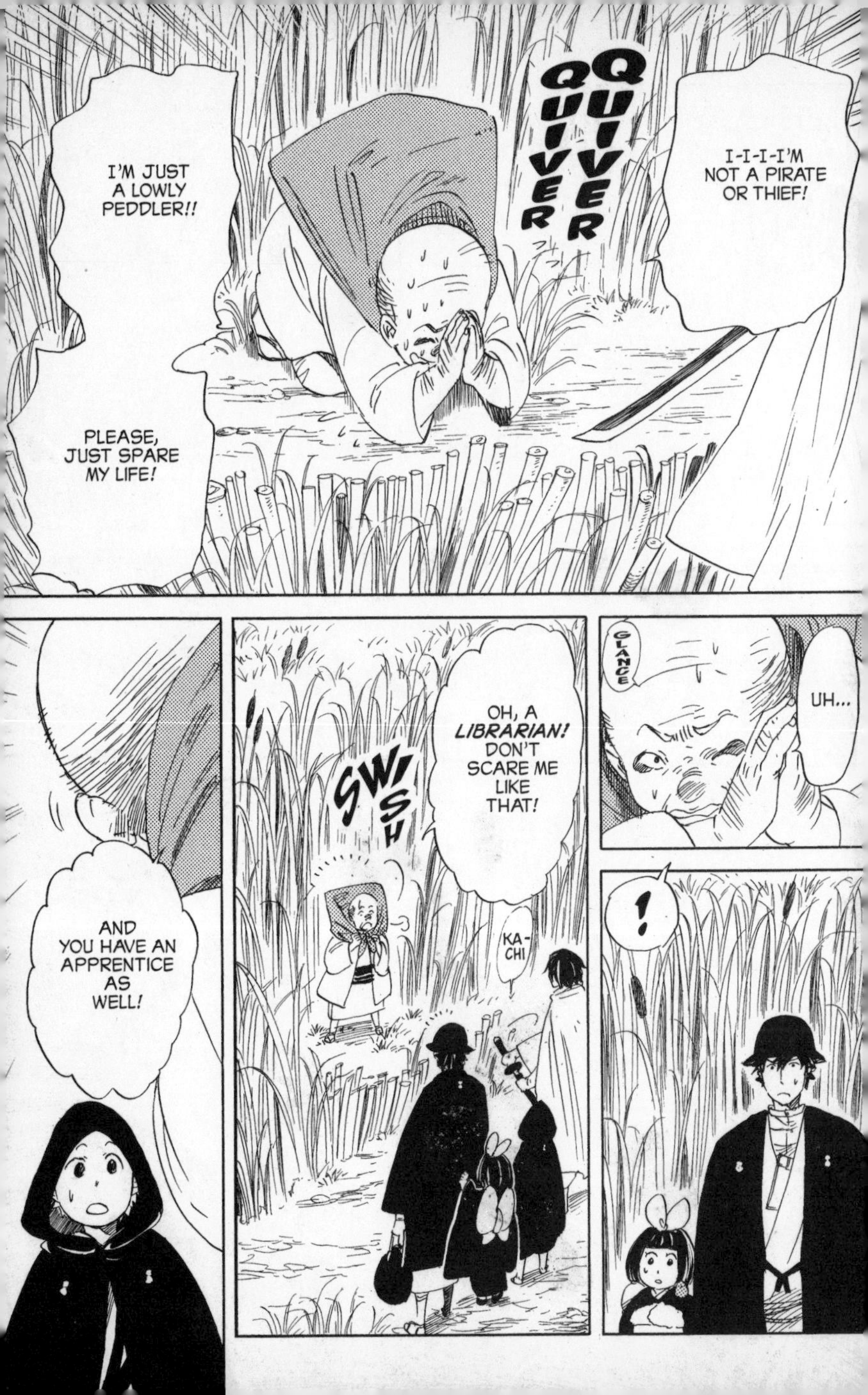

I-I-I-I'M NOT A PIRATE OR THIEF!
QUIVER QUIVER
I'M JUST A LOWLY PEDDLER!!
PLEASE, JUST SPARE MY LIFE!
GLANCE
UH...
!
OH, A *LIBRARIAN!* DON'T SCARE ME LIKE THAT!
SWISH
KA-CHI
AND YOU HAVE AN APPRENTICE AS WELL!

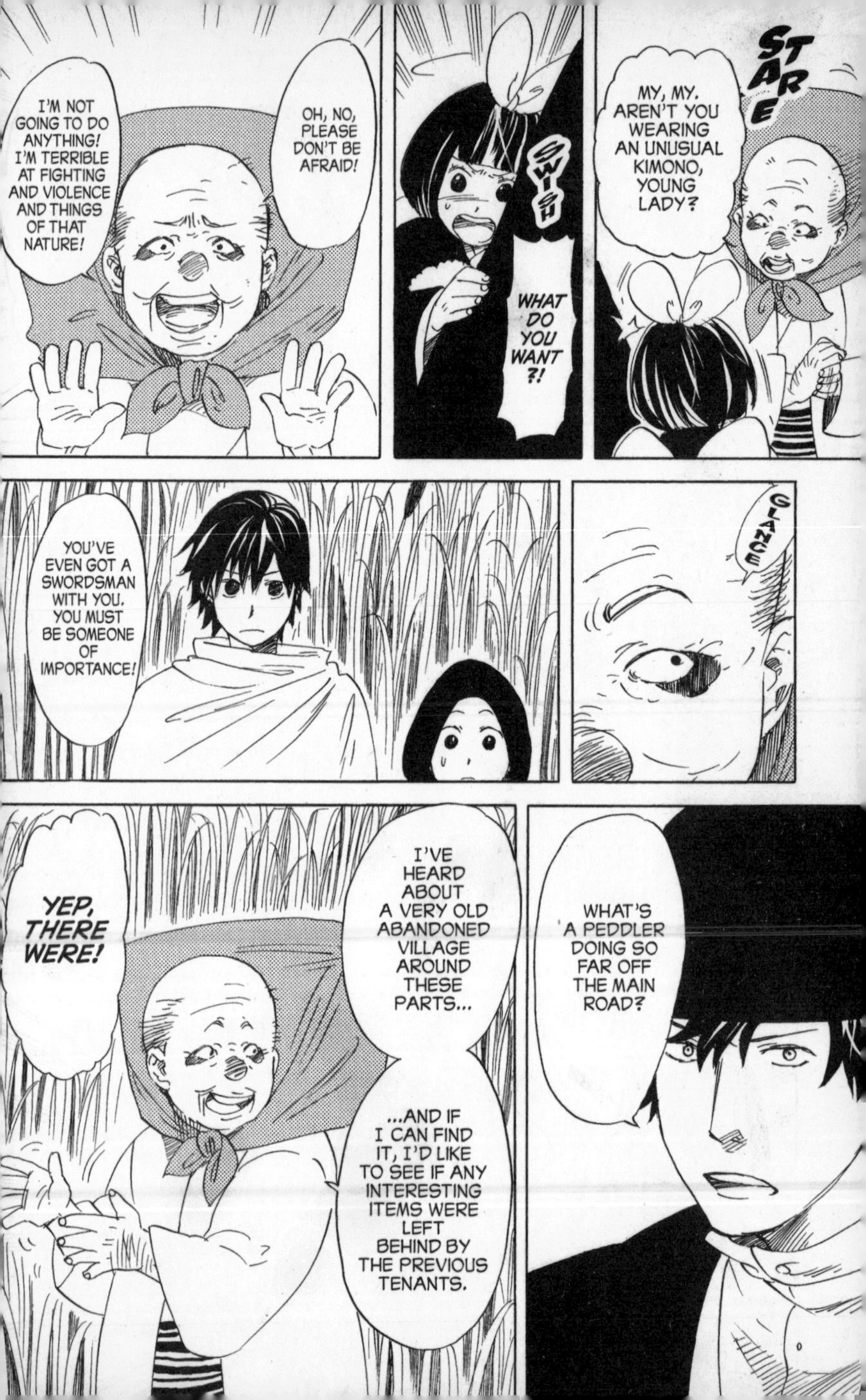
STARE
MY, MY. AREN'T YOU WEARING AN UNUSUAL KIMONO, YOUNG LADY?
SWISH
WHAT DO YOU WANT?!
OH, NO, PLEASE DON'T BE AFRAID!
I'M NOT GOING TO DO ANYTHING! I'M TERRIBLE AT FIGHTING AND VIOLENCE AND THINGS OF THAT NATURE!
GLANCE
YOU'VE EVEN GOT A SWORDSMAN WITH YOU. YOU MUST BE SOMEONE OF IMPORTANCE!
WHAT'S A PEDDLER DOING SO FAR OFF THE MAIN ROAD?
I'VE HEARD ABOUT A VERY OLD ABANDONED VILLAGE AROUND THESE PARTS...
...AND IF I CAN FIND IT, I'D LIKE TO SEE IF ANY INTERESTING ITEMS WERE LEFT BEHIND BY THE PREVIOUS TENANTS.
YEP, THERE WERE!

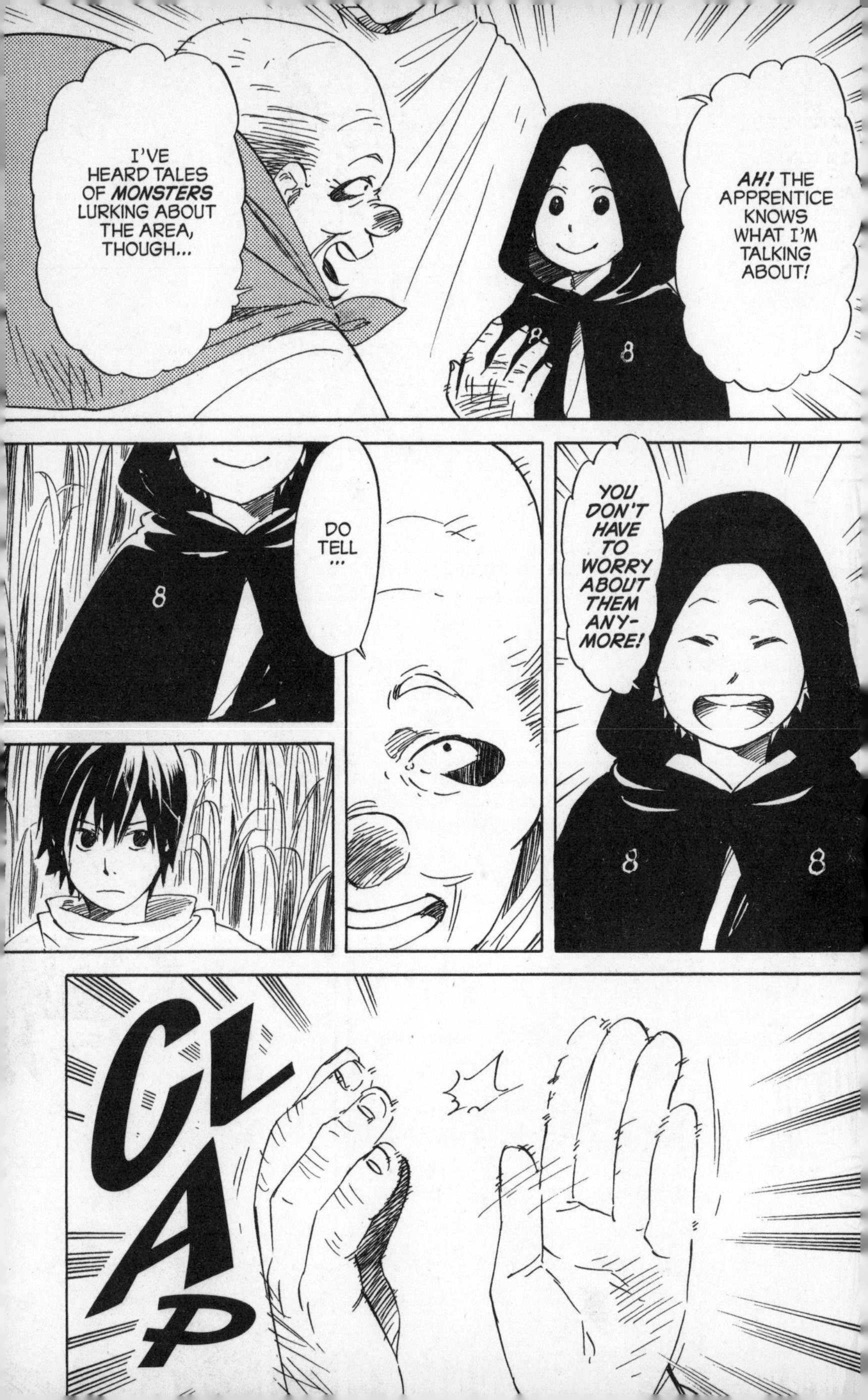
AH! THE APPRENTICE KNOWS WHAT I'M TALKING ABOUT!
I'VE HEARD TALES OF MONSTERS LURKING ABOUT THE AREA, THOUGH...
YOU DON'T HAVE TO WORRY ABOUT THEM ANY-MORE!
DO TELL...
CLAP

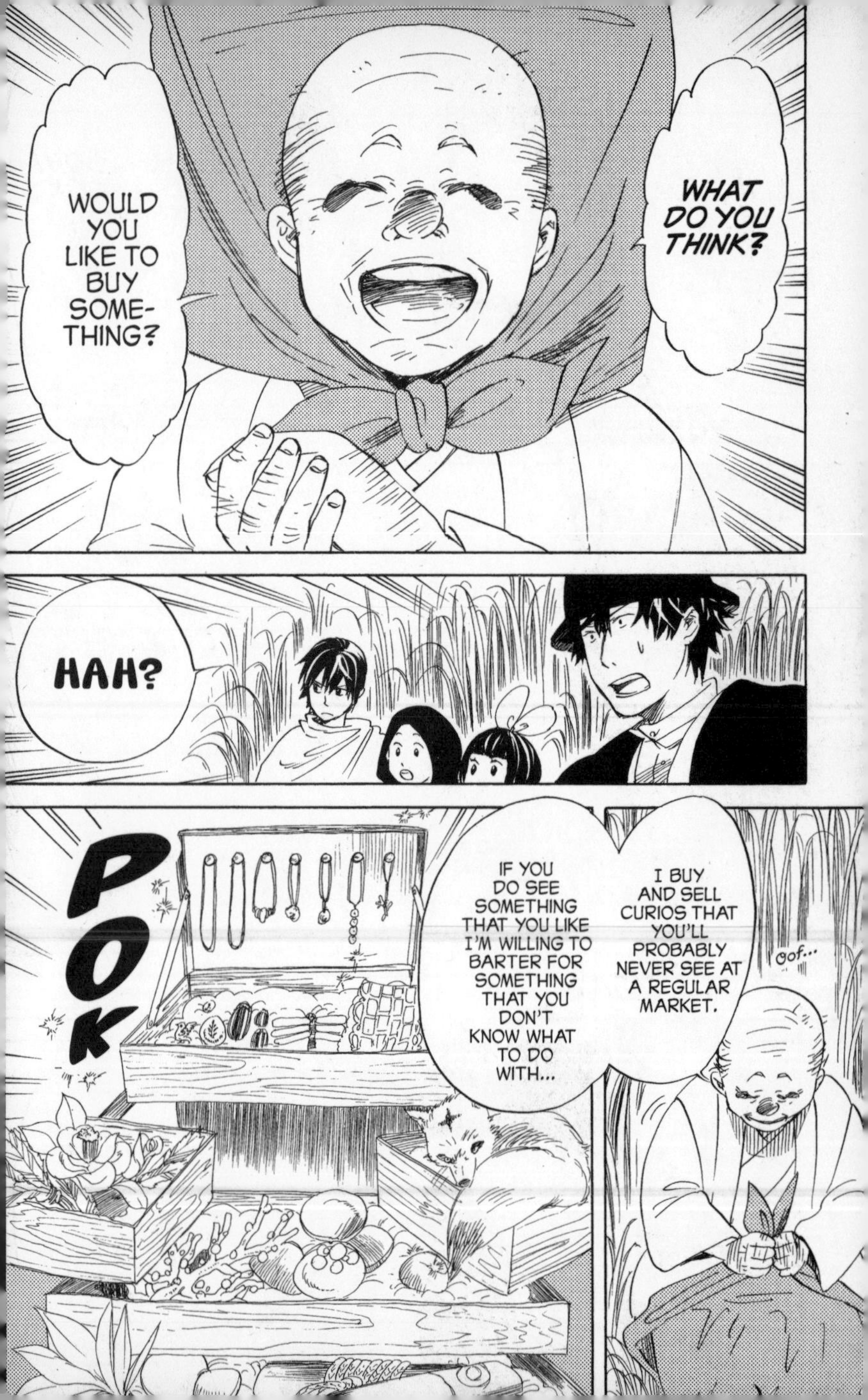
WHAT DO YOU THINK?
WOULD YOU LIKE TO BUY SOME-THING?
HAH?
I BUY AND SELL CURIOS THAT YOU'LL PROBABLY NEVER SEE AT A REGULAR MARKET.
IF YOU DO SEE SOMETHING THAT YOU LIKE I'M WILLING TO BARTER FOR SOMETHING THAT YOU DON'T KNOW WHAT TO DO WITH...
Oof...
POK

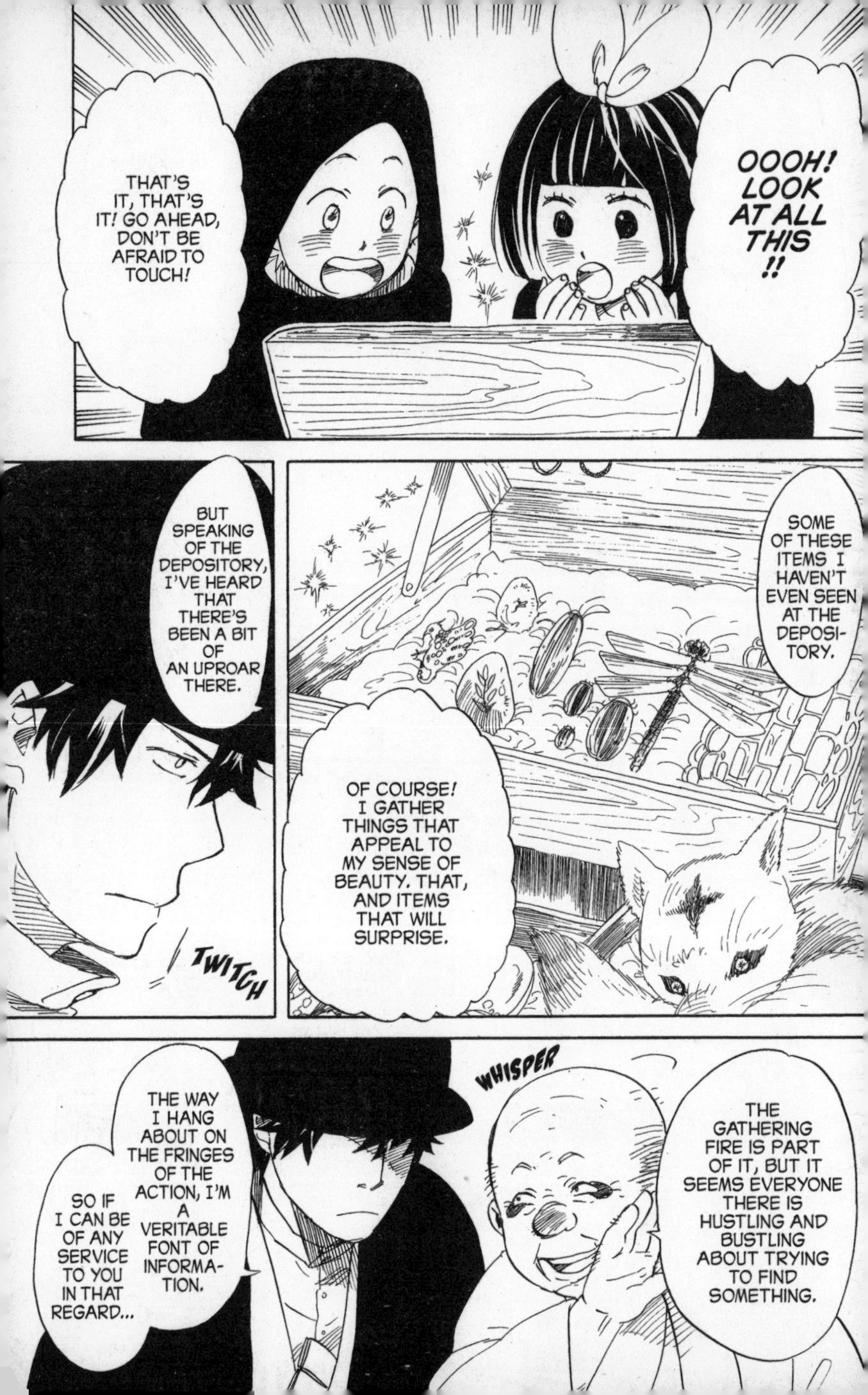
OOOH! LOOK AT ALL THIS !!
THAT'S IT, THAT'S IT! GO AHEAD, DON'T BE AFRAID TO TOUCH!
SOME OF THESE ITEMS I HAVEN'T EVEN SEEN AT THE DEPOSI-TORY.
OF COURSE! I GATHER THINGS THAT APPEAL TO MY SENSE OF BEAUTY. THAT, AND ITEMS THAT WILL SURPRISE.
BUT SPEAKING OF THE DEPOSITORY, I'VE HEARD THAT THERE'S BEEN A BIT OF AN UPROAR THERE.
TWITCH
WHISPER
THE GATHERING FIRE IS PART OF IT, BUT IT SEEMS EVERYONE THERE IS HUSTLING AND BUSTLING ABOUT TRYING TO FIND SOMETHING.
THE WAY I HANG ABOUT ON THE FRINGES OF THE ACTION, I'M A VERITABLE FONT OF INFORMA-TION.
SO IF I CAN BE OF ANY SERVICE TO YOU IN THAT REGARD...

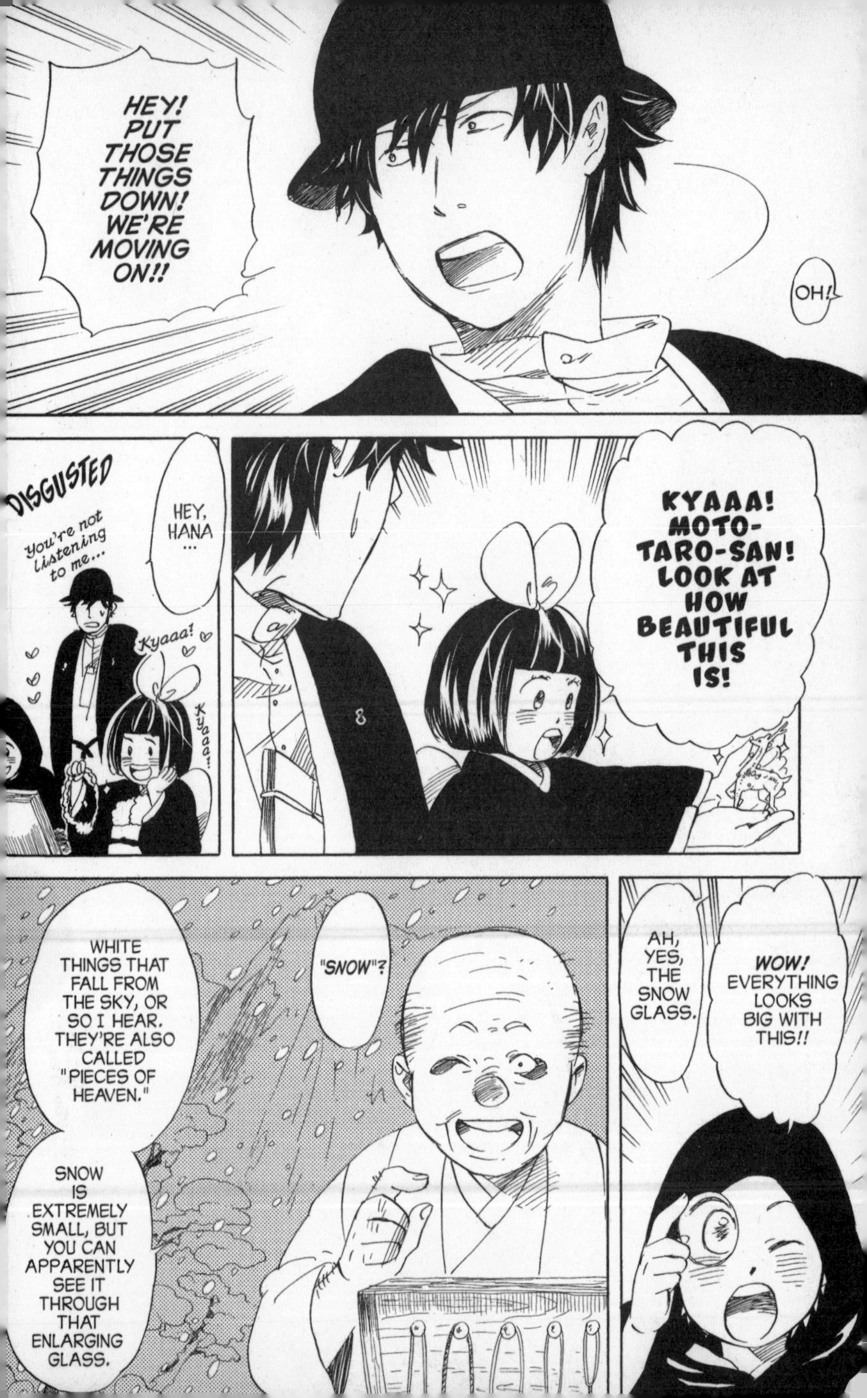
HEY! PUT THOSE THINGS DOWN! WE'RE MOVING ON!!
OH!
KYAAA! MOTO-TARO-SAN! LOOK AT HOW BEAUTIFUL THIS IS!
HEY, HANA...
DISGUSTED
You're not listening to me...
Kyaaa!
Kyaaa!
WOW! EVERYTHING LOOKS BIG WITH THIS!!
AH, YES, THE SNOW GLASS.
"SNOW"?
WHITE THINGS THAT FALL FROM THE SKY, OR SO I HEAR. THEY'RE ALSO CALLED "PIECES OF HEAVEN."
SNOW IS EXTREMELY SMALL, BUT YOU CAN APPARENTLY SEE IT THROUGH THAT ENLARGING GLASS.

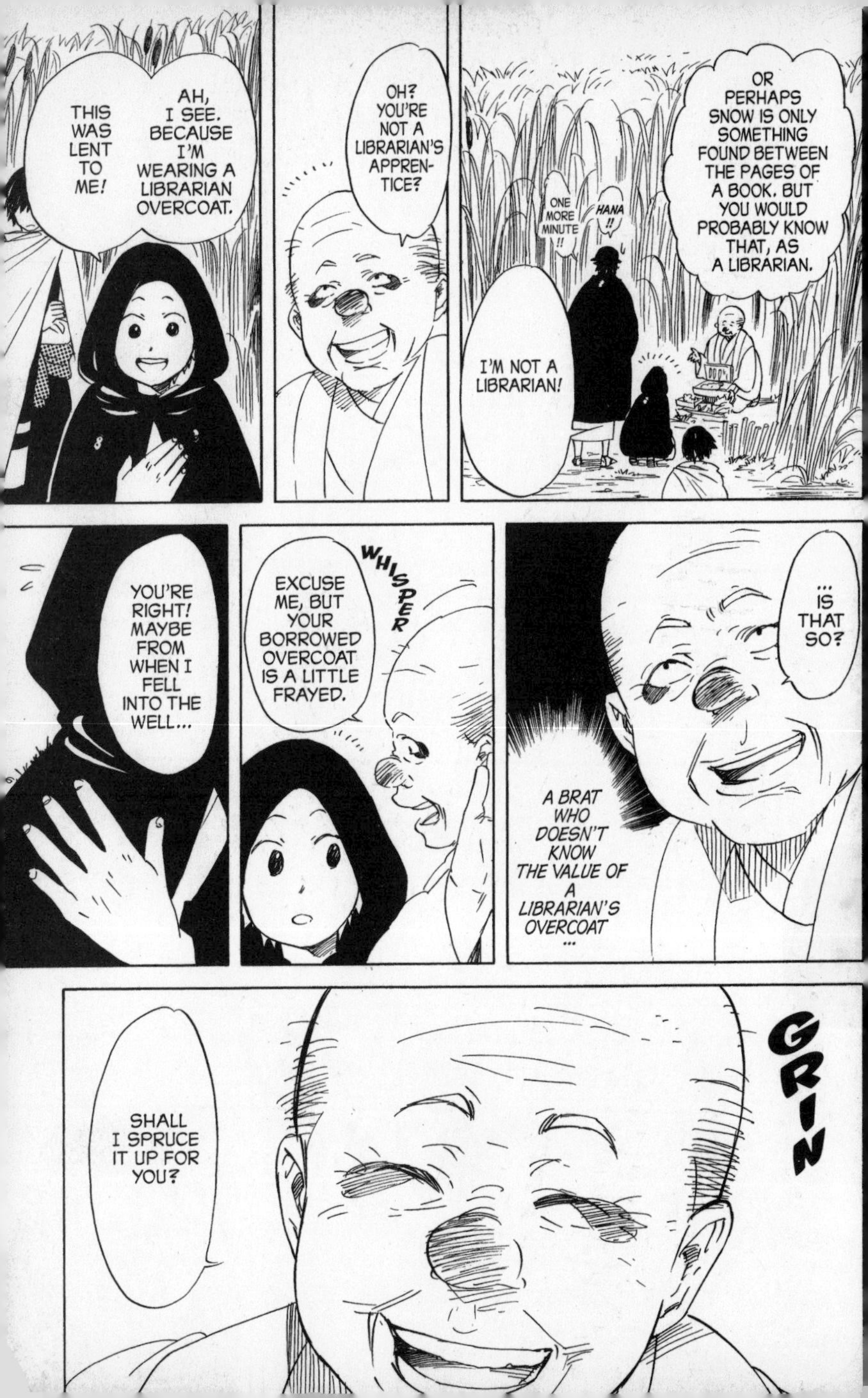
OR PERHAPS SNOW IS ONLY SOMETHING FOUND BETWEEN THE PAGES OF A BOOK. BUT YOU WOULD PROBABLY KNOW THAT, AS A LIBRARIAN.
HANA!!
ONE MORE MINUTE!!
I'M NOT A LIBRARIAN!
OH? YOU'RE NOT A LIBRARIAN'S APPREN-TICE?
AH, I SEE. BECAUSE I'M WEARING A LIBRARIAN OVERCOAT.
THIS WAS LENT TO ME!
...IS THAT SO?
A BRAT WHO DOESN'T KNOW THE VALUE OF A LIBRARIAN'S OVERCOAT...
WHISPER
EXCUSE ME, BUT YOUR BORROWED OVERCOAT IS A LITTLE FRAYED.
YOU'RE RIGHT! MAYBE FROM WHEN I FELL INTO THE WELL...
GRIN
SHALL I SPRUCE IT UP FOR YOU?

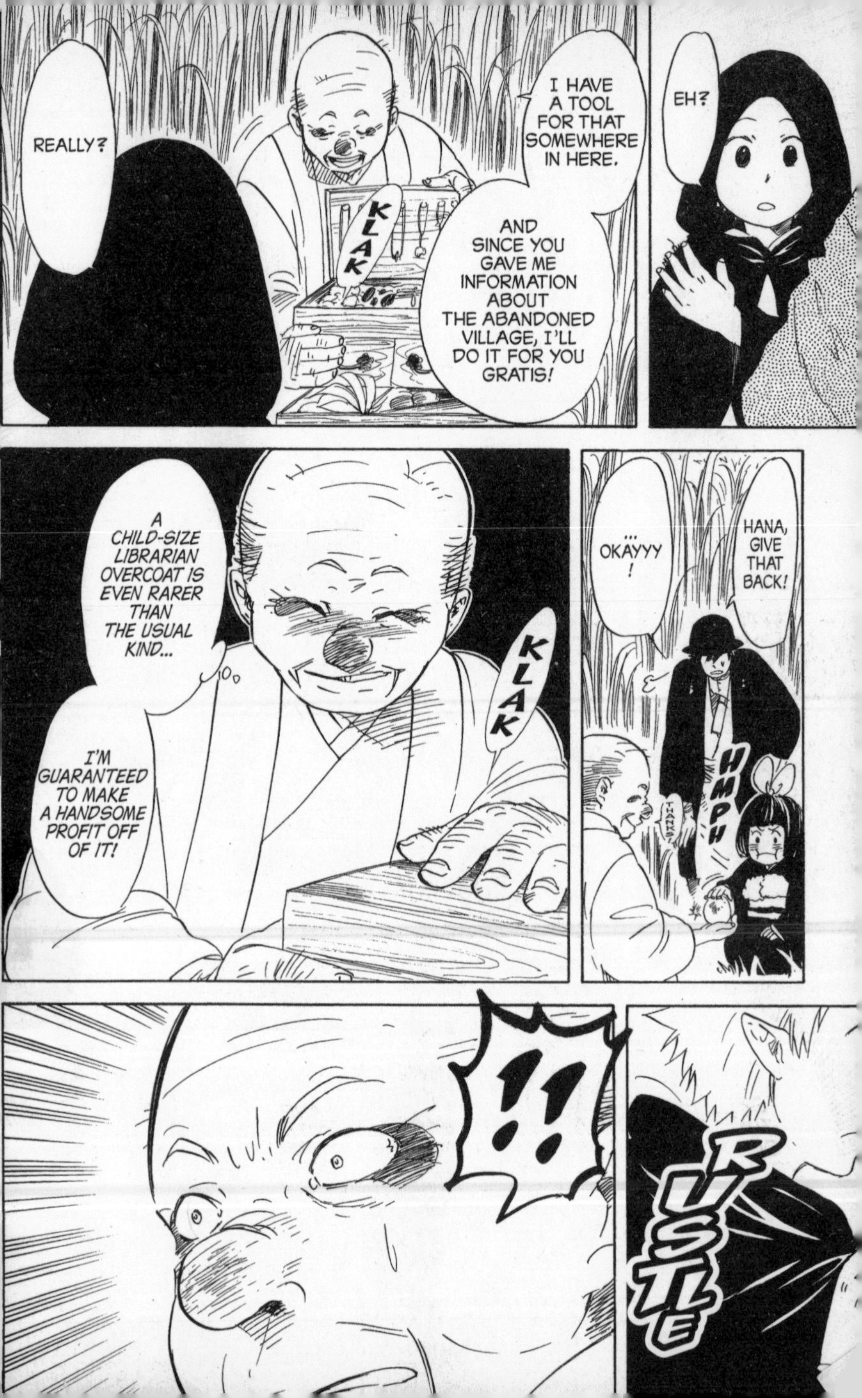
EH?
I HAVE A TOOL FOR THAT SOMEWHERE IN HERE.
AND SINCE YOU GAVE ME INFORMATION ABOUT THE ABANDONED VILLAGE, I'LL DO IT FOR YOU GRATIS!
KLAK
REALLY?
HANA, GIVE THAT BACK!
...OKAYYY!
HMPH
THANKS
KLAK
A CHILD-SIZE LIBRARIAN OVERCOAT IS EVEN RARER THAN THE USUAL KIND...
I'M GUARANTEED TO MAKE A HANDSOME PROFIT OFF OF IT!
RUSTLE
!!

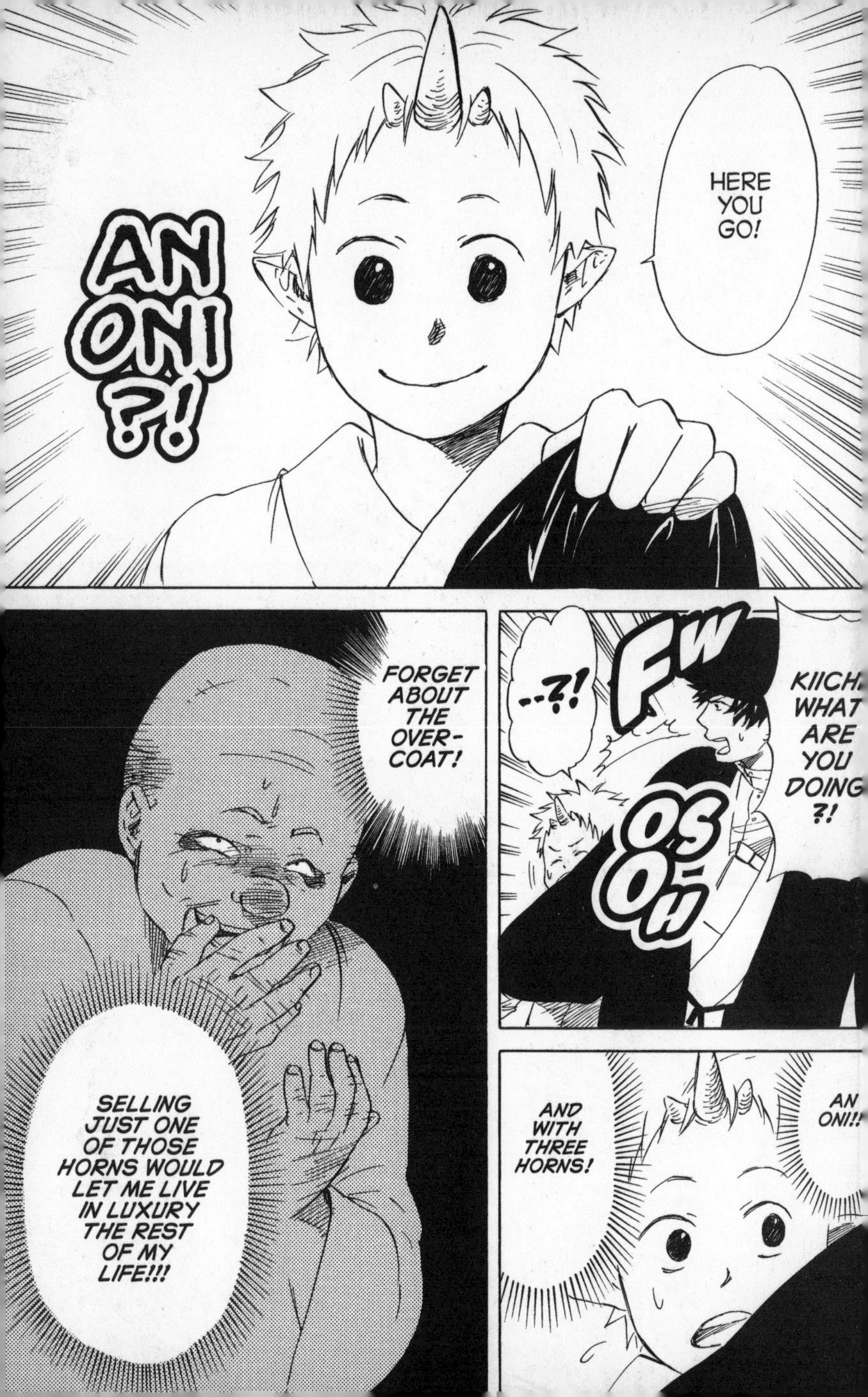
HERE YOU GO!
AN ONI ?!
KIICH WHAT ARE YOU DOING ?!
FW
OOSH
--?!
AN ONI!!
AND WITH THREE HORNS!
FORGET ABOUT THE OVER-COAT!
SELLING JUST ONE OF THOSE HORNS WOULD LET ME LIVE IN LUXURY THE REST OF MY LIFE!!!

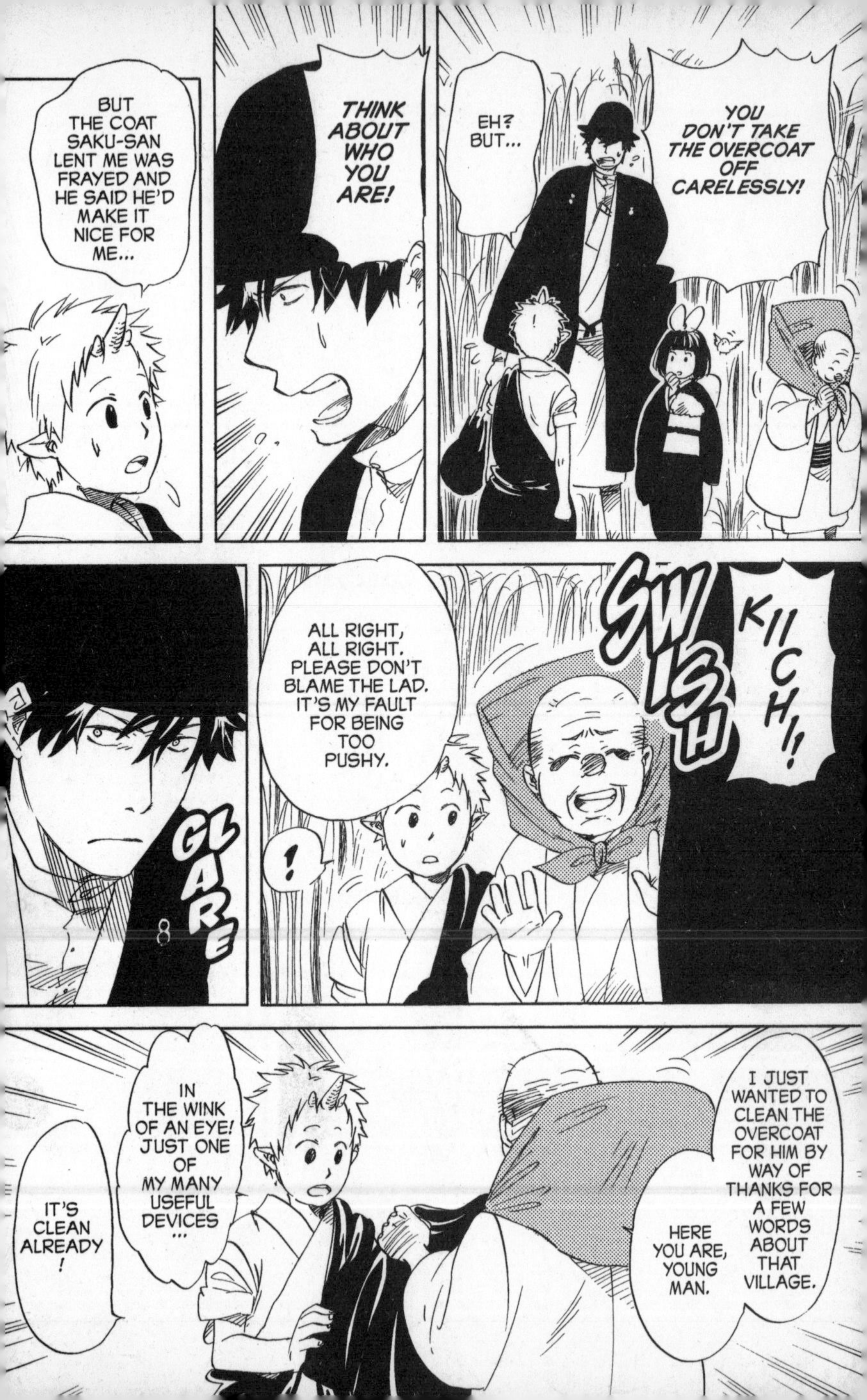
YOU DON'T TAKE THE OVERCOAT OFF CARELESSLY!
EH? BUT...
THINK ABOUT WHO YOU ARE!
BUT THE COAT SAKU-SAN LENT ME WAS FRAYED AND HE SAID HE'D MAKE IT NICE FOR ME...
KIICH!!
SWISH
ALL RIGHT, ALL RIGHT. PLEASE DON'T BLAME THE LAD. IT'S MY FAULT FOR BEING TOO PUSHY.
!
GLARE
I JUST WANTED TO CLEAN THE OVERCOAT FOR HIM BY WAY OF THANKS FOR A FEW WORDS ABOUT THAT VILLAGE.
HERE YOU ARE, YOUNG MAN.
IN THE WINK OF AN EYE! JUST ONE OF MY MANY USEFUL DEVICES...
IT'S CLEAN ALREADY!

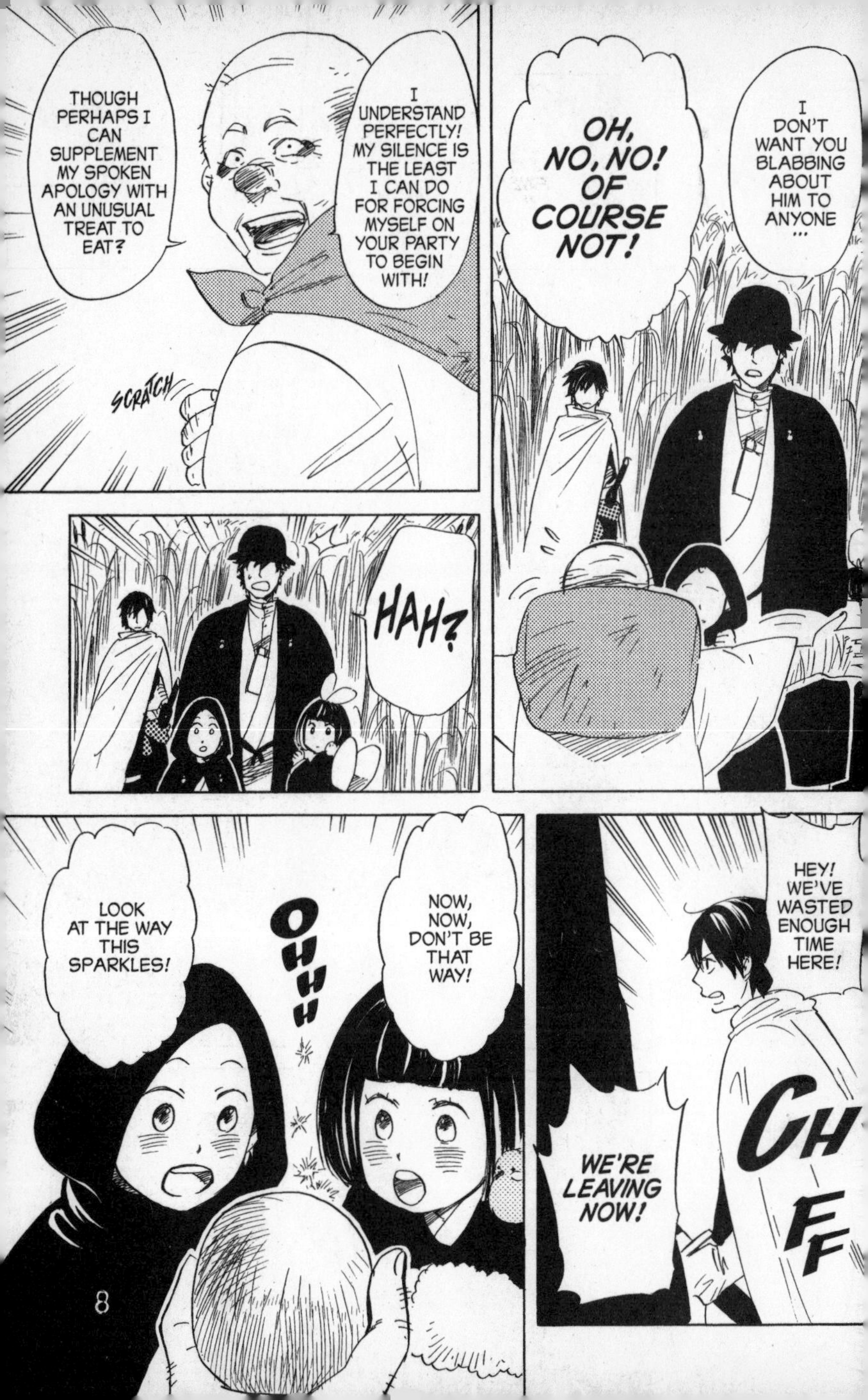
I DON'T WANT YOU BLABBING ABOUT HIM TO ANYONE...
OH, NO, NO! OF COURSE NOT!
I UNDERSTAND PERFECTLY! MY SILENCE IS THE LEAST I CAN DO FOR FORCING MYSELF ON YOUR PARTY TO BEGIN WITH!
THOUGH PERHAPS I CAN SUPPLEMENT MY SPOKEN APOLOGY WITH AN UNUSUAL TREAT TO EAT?
SCRATCH
HAH?
HEY! WE'VE WASTED ENOUGH TIME HERE!
CHFF
WE'RE LEAVING NOW!
NOW, NOW, DON'T BE THAT WAY!
OHHH
LOOK AT THE WAY THIS SPARKLES!

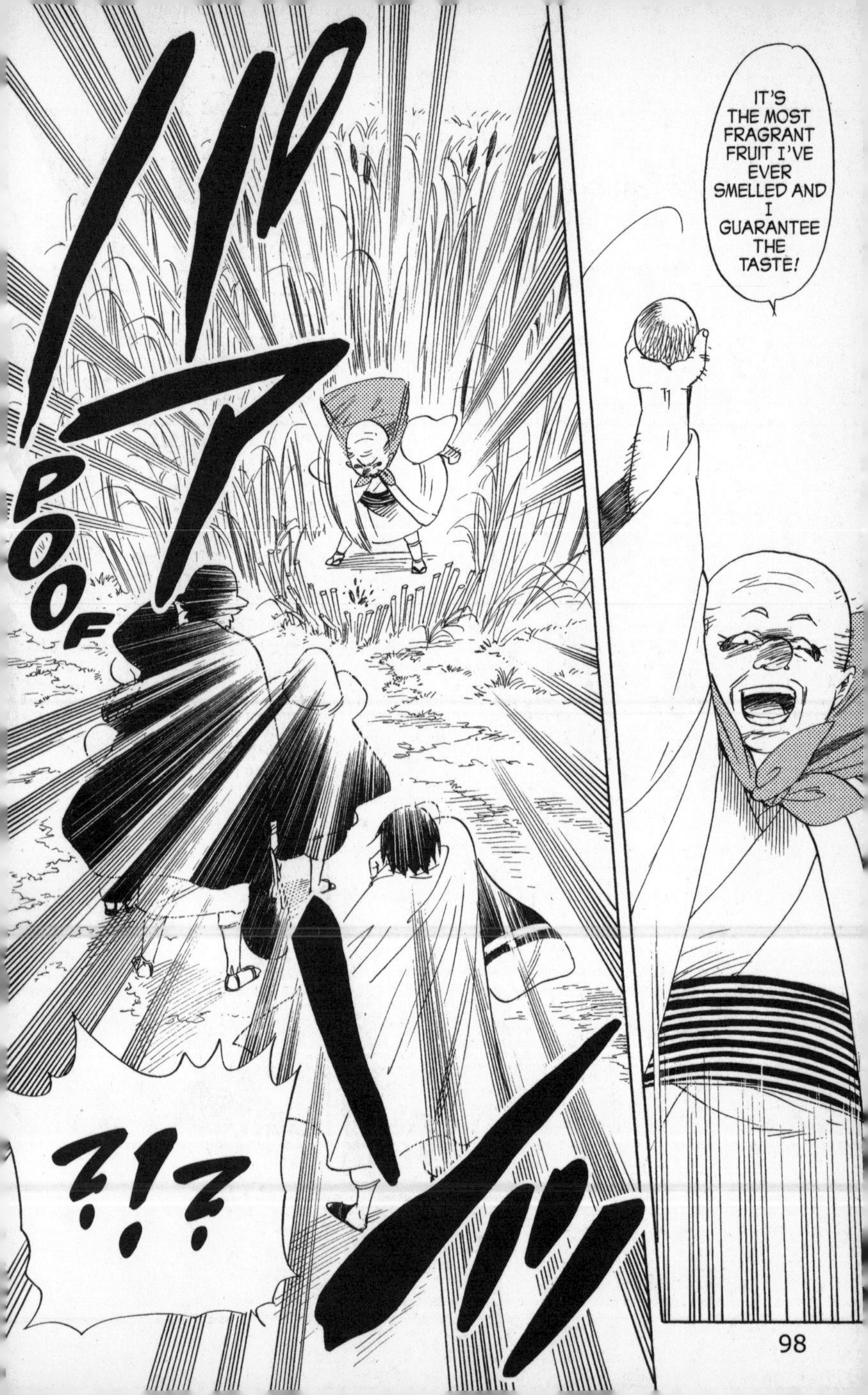
IT'S THE MOST FRAGRANT FRUIT I'VE EVER SMELLED AND I GUARANTEE THE TASTE!
POOF
?!?

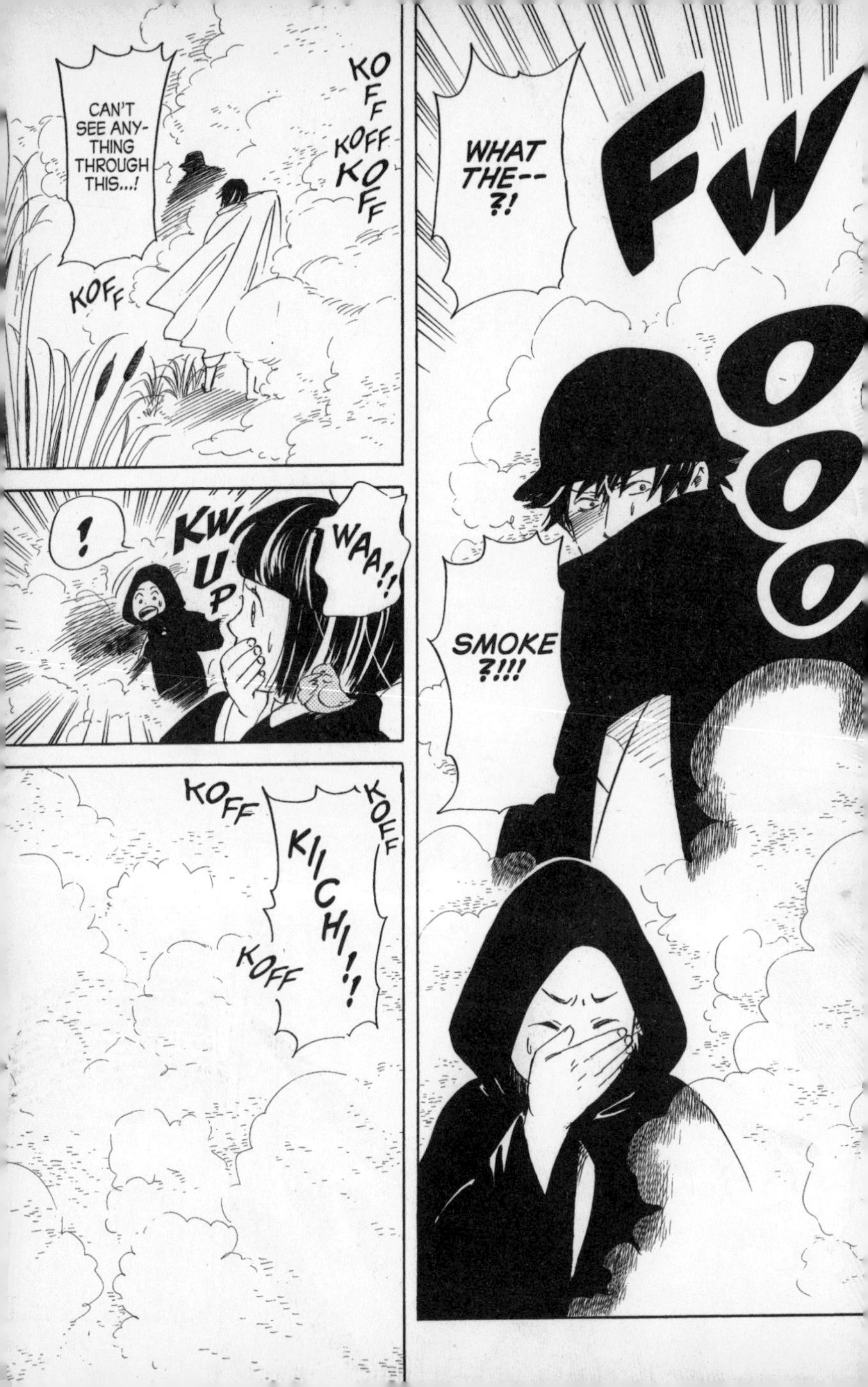
WHAT THE--?!
FWOOO
SMOKE?!!!
KOFF KOFF KOFF KOFF
CAN'T SEE ANYTHING THROUGH THIS...!
KOFF
WAA!!
KWUP
!
KOFF
KIICHI!!
KOFF
KOFF

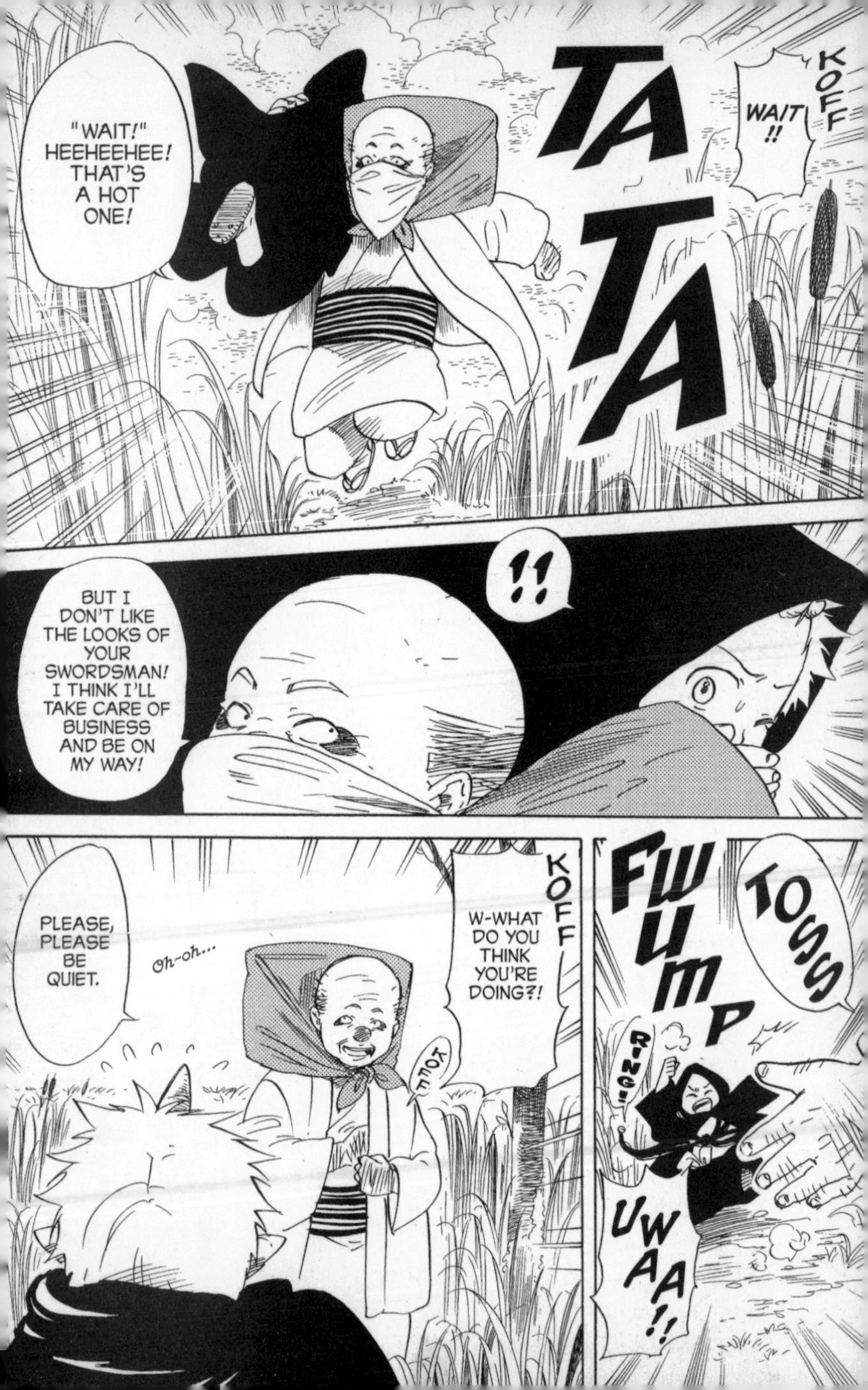
KOFF
WAIT!!
TATA
"WAIT!" HEEHEEHEE! THAT'S A HOT ONE!
!!
BUT I DON'T LIKE THE LOOKS OF YOUR SWORDSMAN! I THINK I'LL TAKE CARE OF BUSINESS AND BE ON MY WAY!
TOSS
FWUMP
RING!
UWAA!!
KOFF
W-WHAT DO YOU THINK YOU'RE DOING?!
KOFF
Oh-oh...
PLEASE, PLEASE BE QUIET.

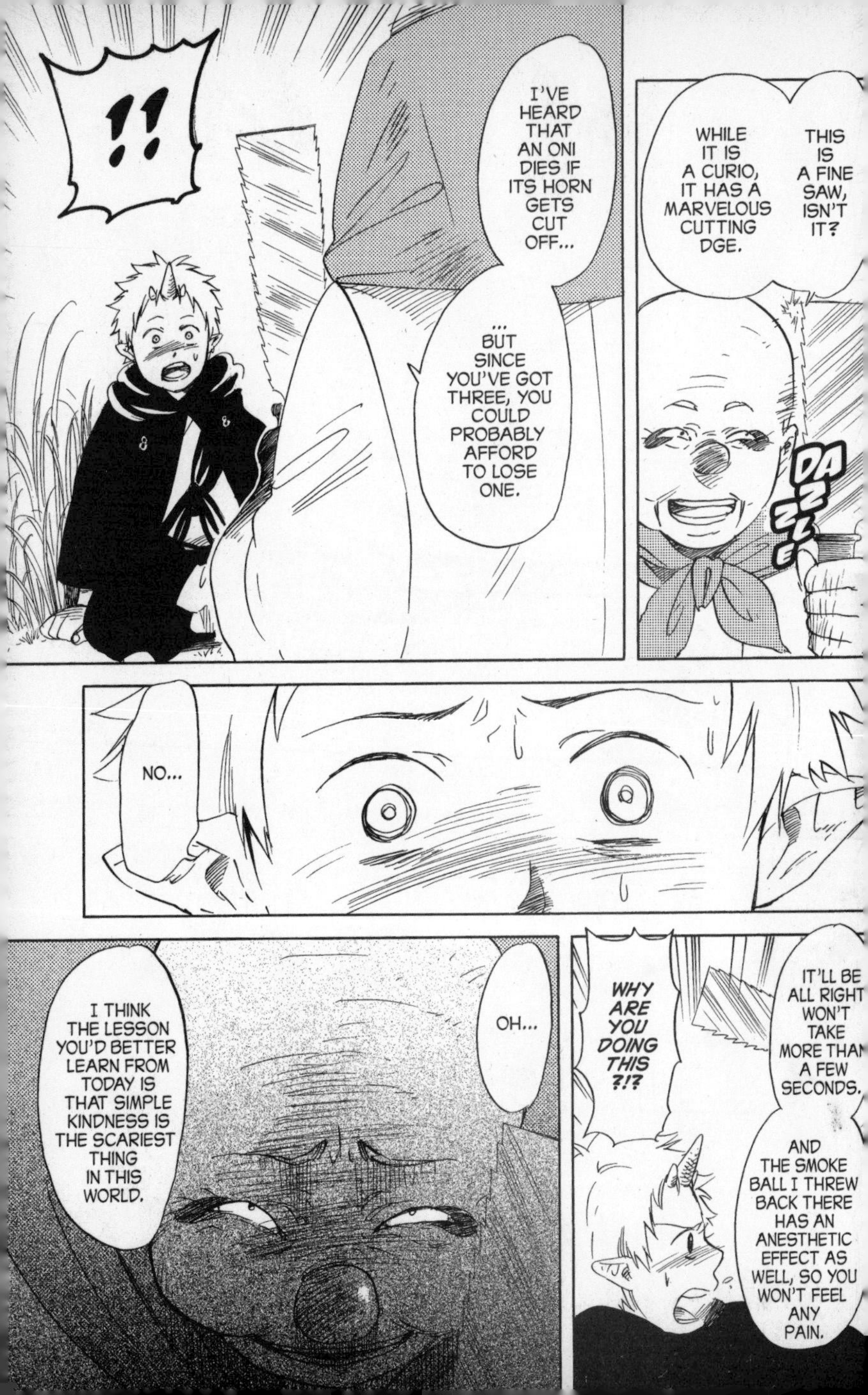
THIS IS A FINE SAW, ISN'T IT?
WHILE IT IS A CURIO, IT HAS A MARVELOUS CUTTING DGE.
DAZZLE
I'VE HEARD THAT AN ONI DIES IF ITS HORN GETS CUT OFF...
...BUT SINCE YOU'VE GOT THREE, YOU COULD PROBABLY AFFORD TO LOSE ONE.
!!
NO...
IT'LL BE ALL RIGHT WON'T TAKE MORE THAN A FEW SECONDS.
AND THE SMOKE BALL I THREW BACK THERE HAS AN ANESTHETIC EFFECT AS WELL, SO YOU WON'T FEEL ANY PAIN.
WHY ARE YOU DOING THIS?!?
OH...
I THINK THE LESSON YOU'D BETTER LEARN FROM TODAY IS THAT SIMPLE KINDNESS IS THE SCARIEST THING IN THIS WORLD.

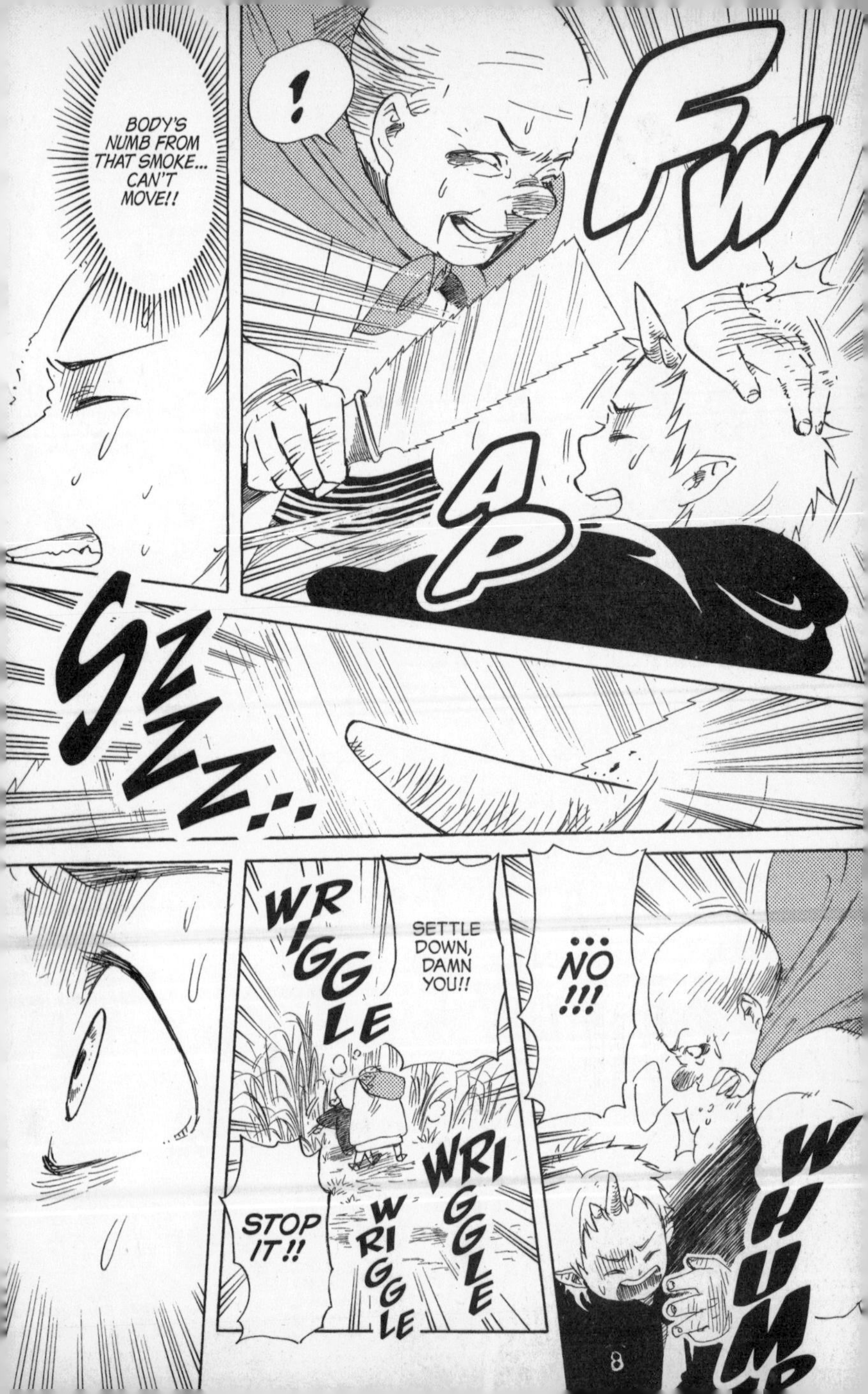
!
FW
AP
BODY'S NUMB FROM THAT SMOKE... CAN'T MOVE!!
SZZZ...
...NO!!!
WHUMP
SETTLE DOWN, DAMN YOU!!
WRIGGLE
WRIGGLE
WRIGGLE
STOP IT!!

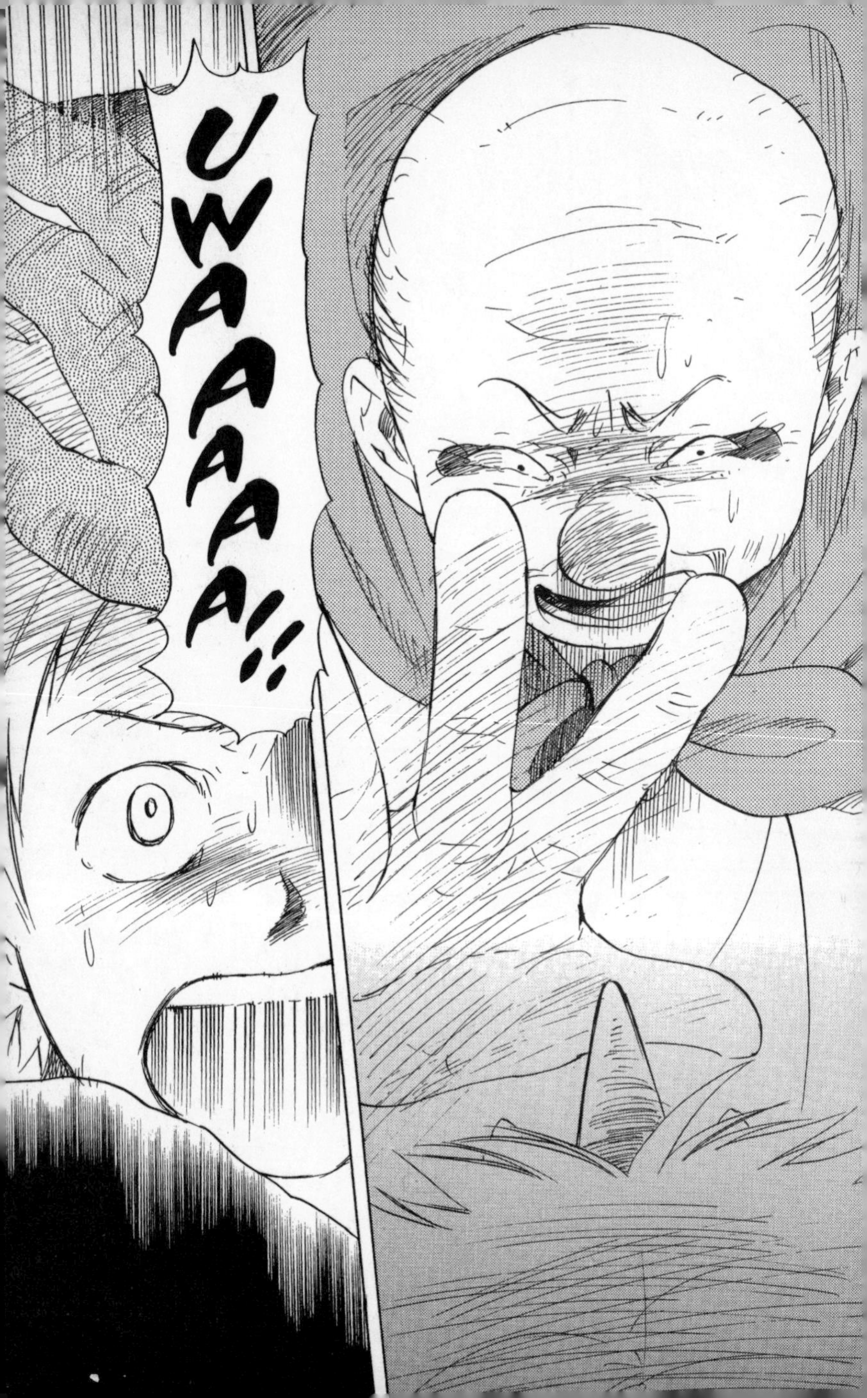
UWAAAAA!!

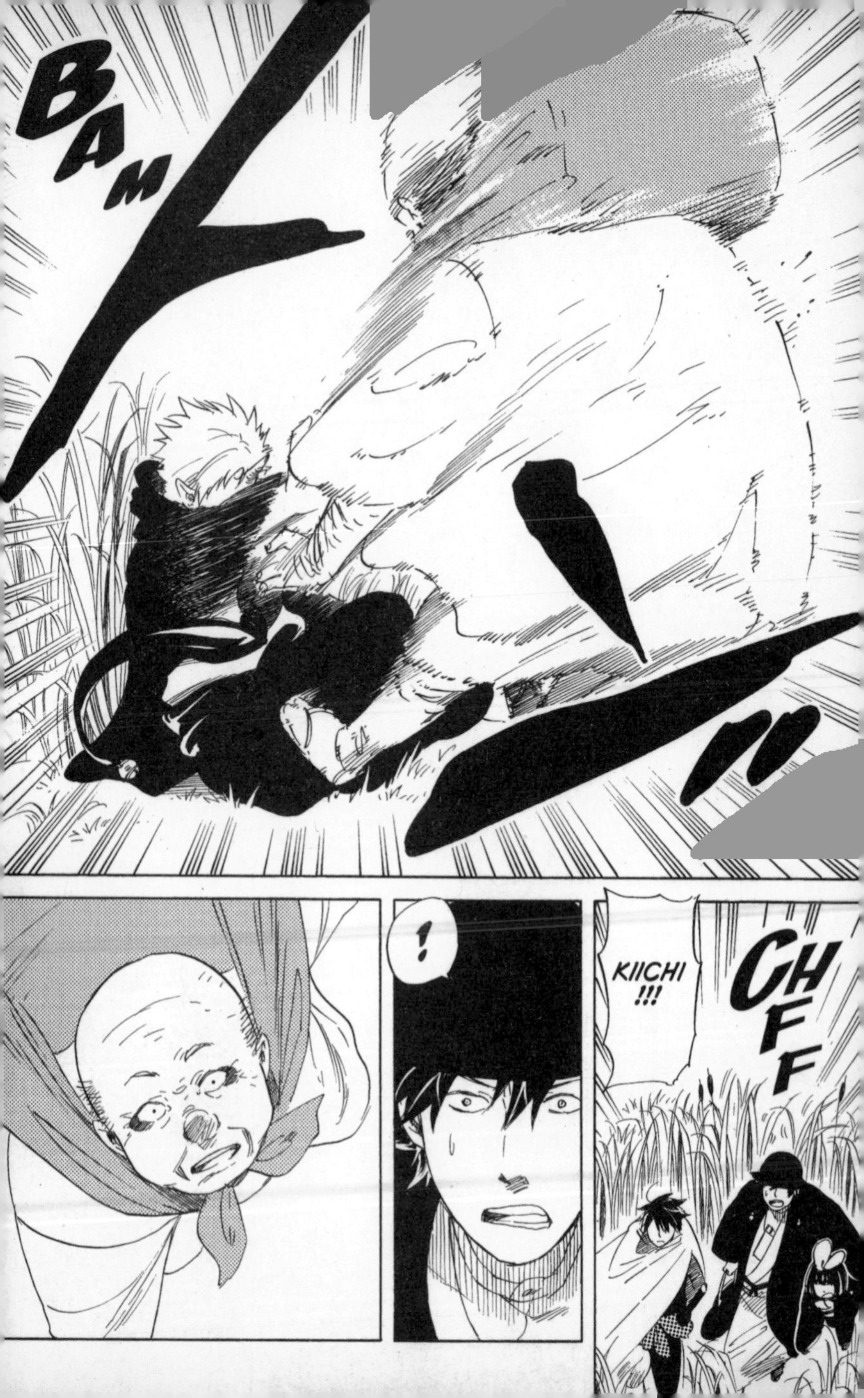
BAM
KIICHI !!!
CHFF
!

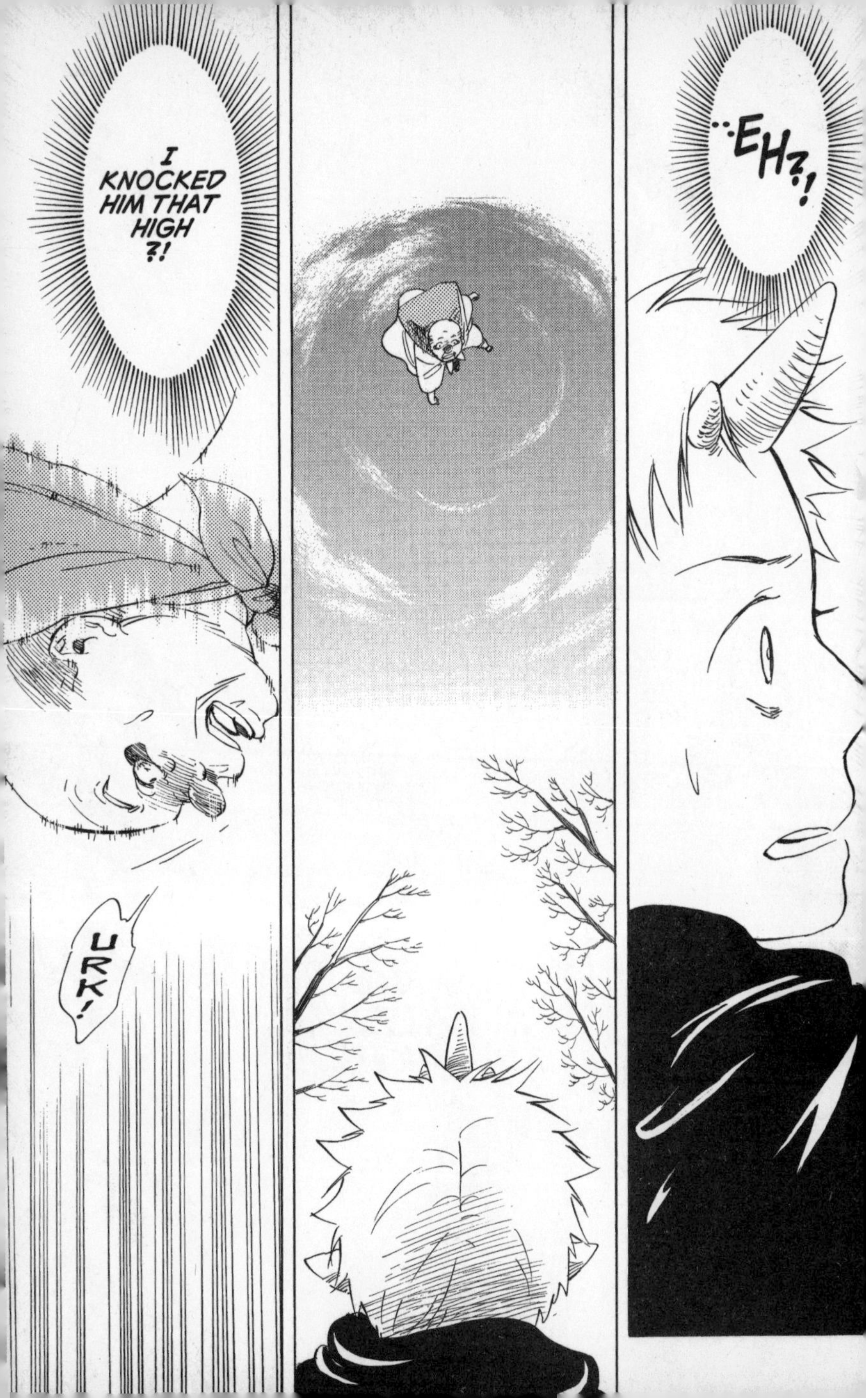
...EH?!
I KNOCKED HIM THAT HIGH?!
URK!

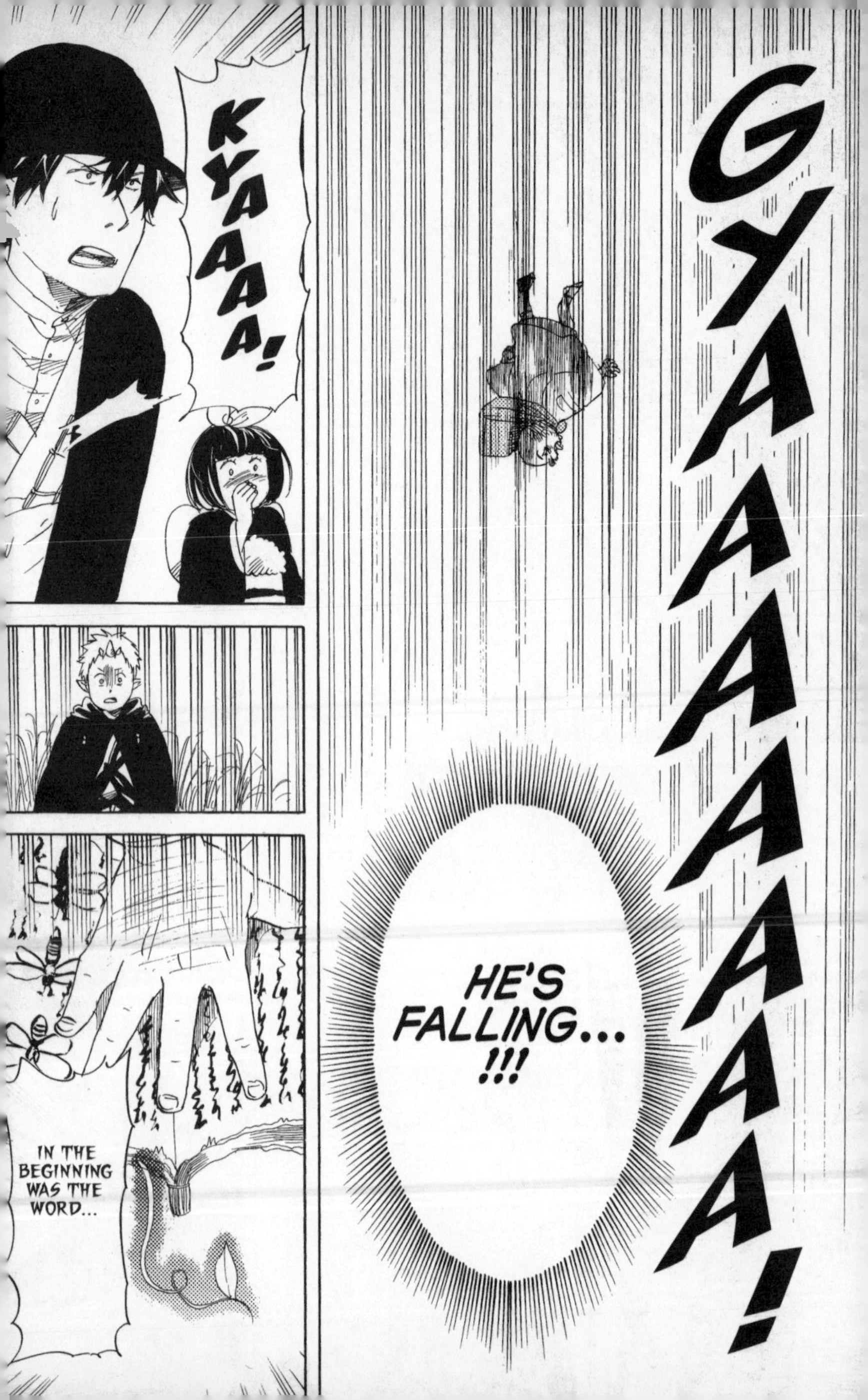
GYAAAAAAA!
HE'S FALLING... !!!
KYAAAA!
IN THE BEGINNING WAS THE WORD...

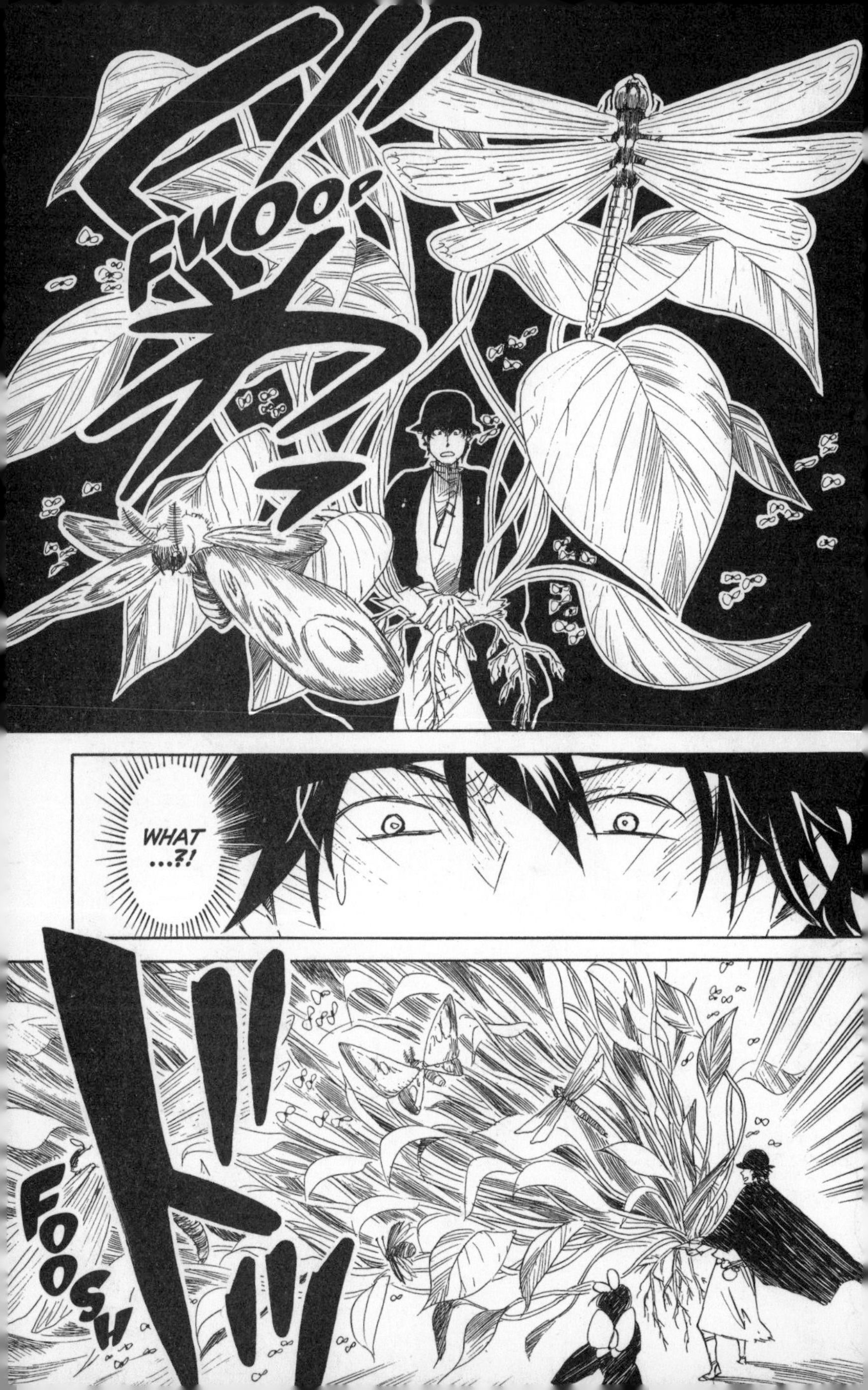
FWOOP
WHAT ...?!
FOOSH

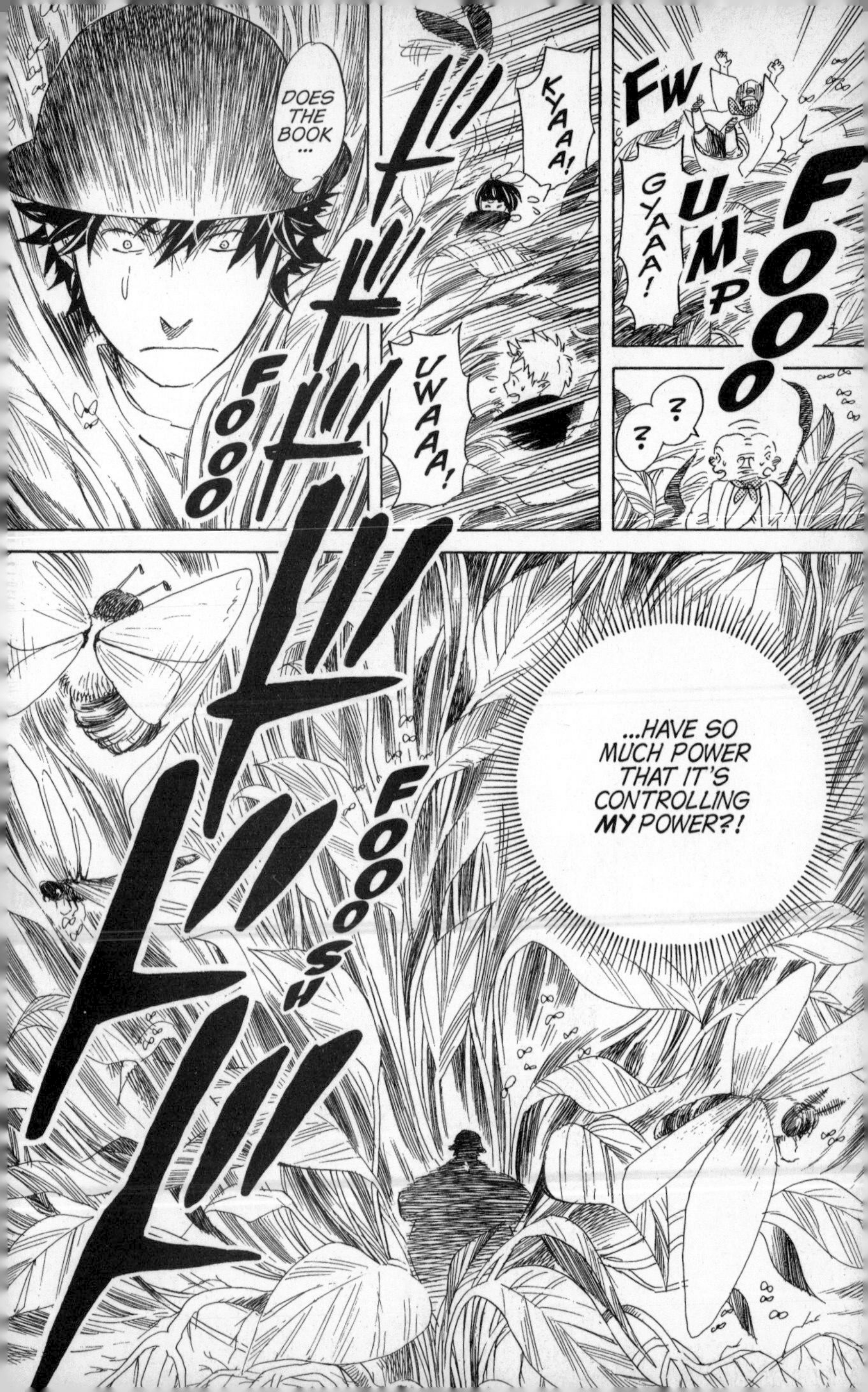
FW
GYAAA!
FUMP
FOOOO
?
?
KYAAA!
UWAAAA!
DOES THE BOOK ...
FOOOO
...HAVE SO MUCH POWER THAT IT'S CONTROLLING MY POWER?!
FOOOOSH

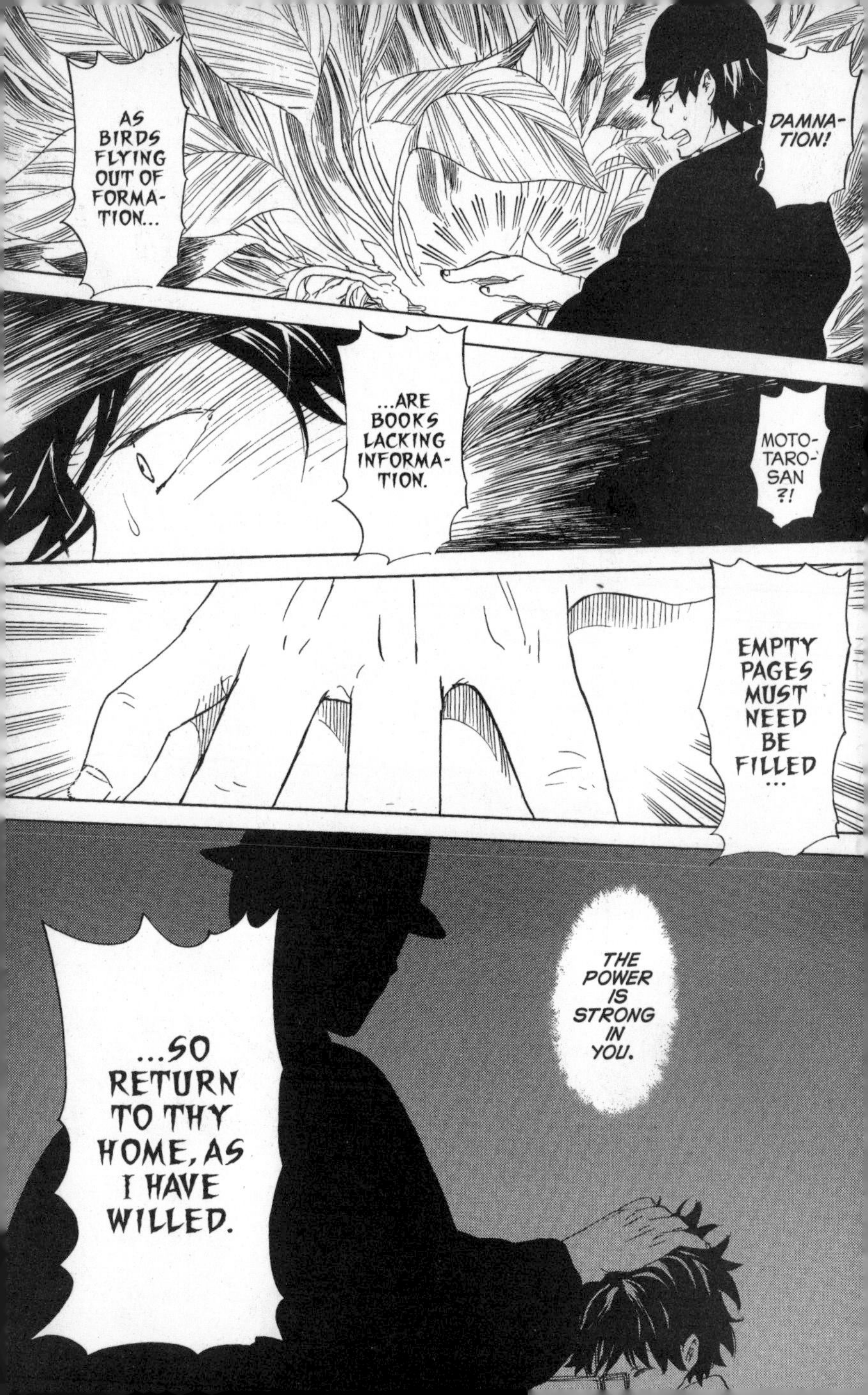
DAMNATION!
AS BIRDS FLYING OUT OF FORMATION...
MOTOTARO-SAN?!
...ARE BOOKS LACKING INFORMATION.
EMPTY PAGES MUST NEED BE FILLED...
THE POWER IS STRONG IN YOU.
...SO RETURN TO THY HOME, AS I HAVE WILLED.

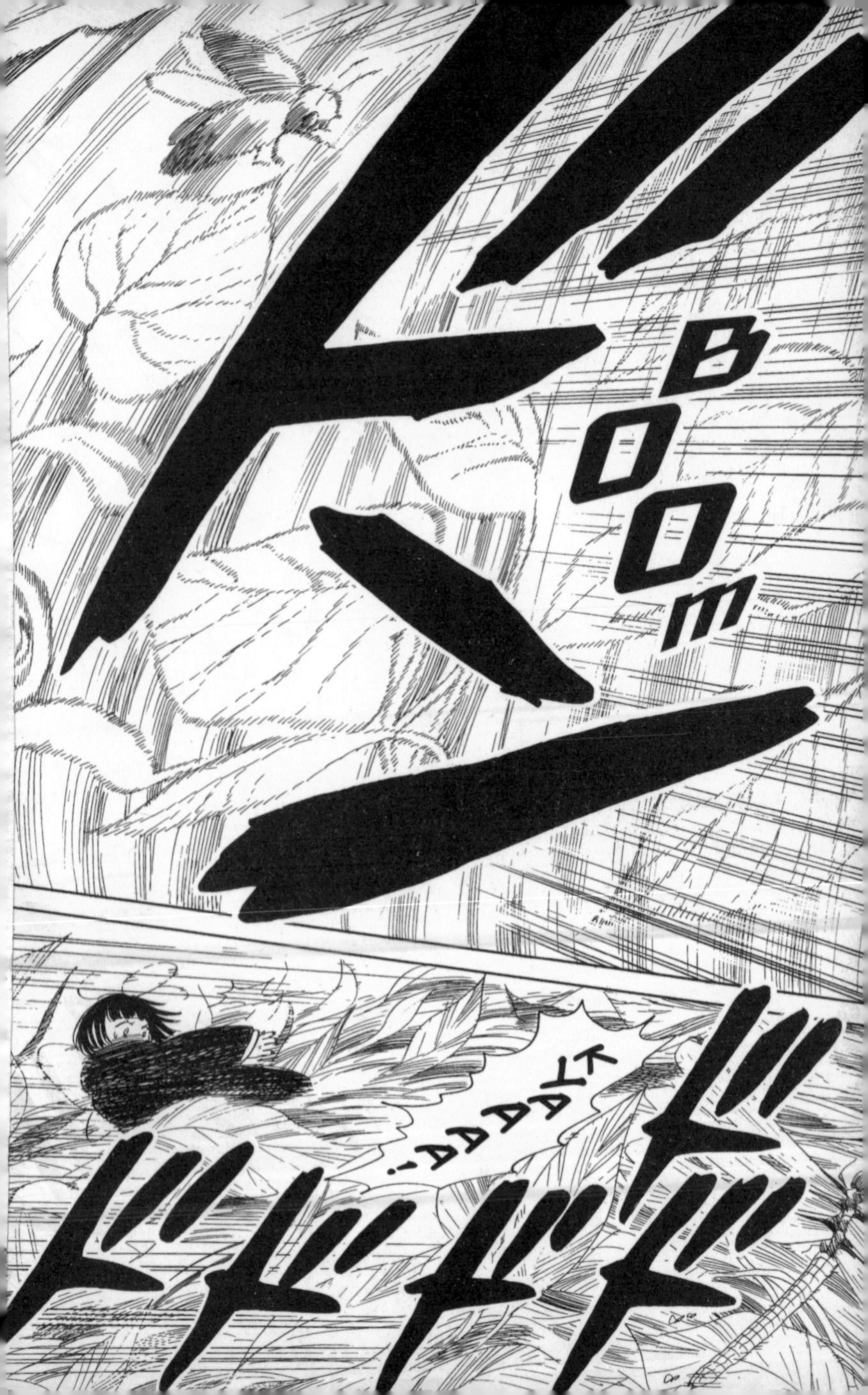
BOOM
KYAAAA!

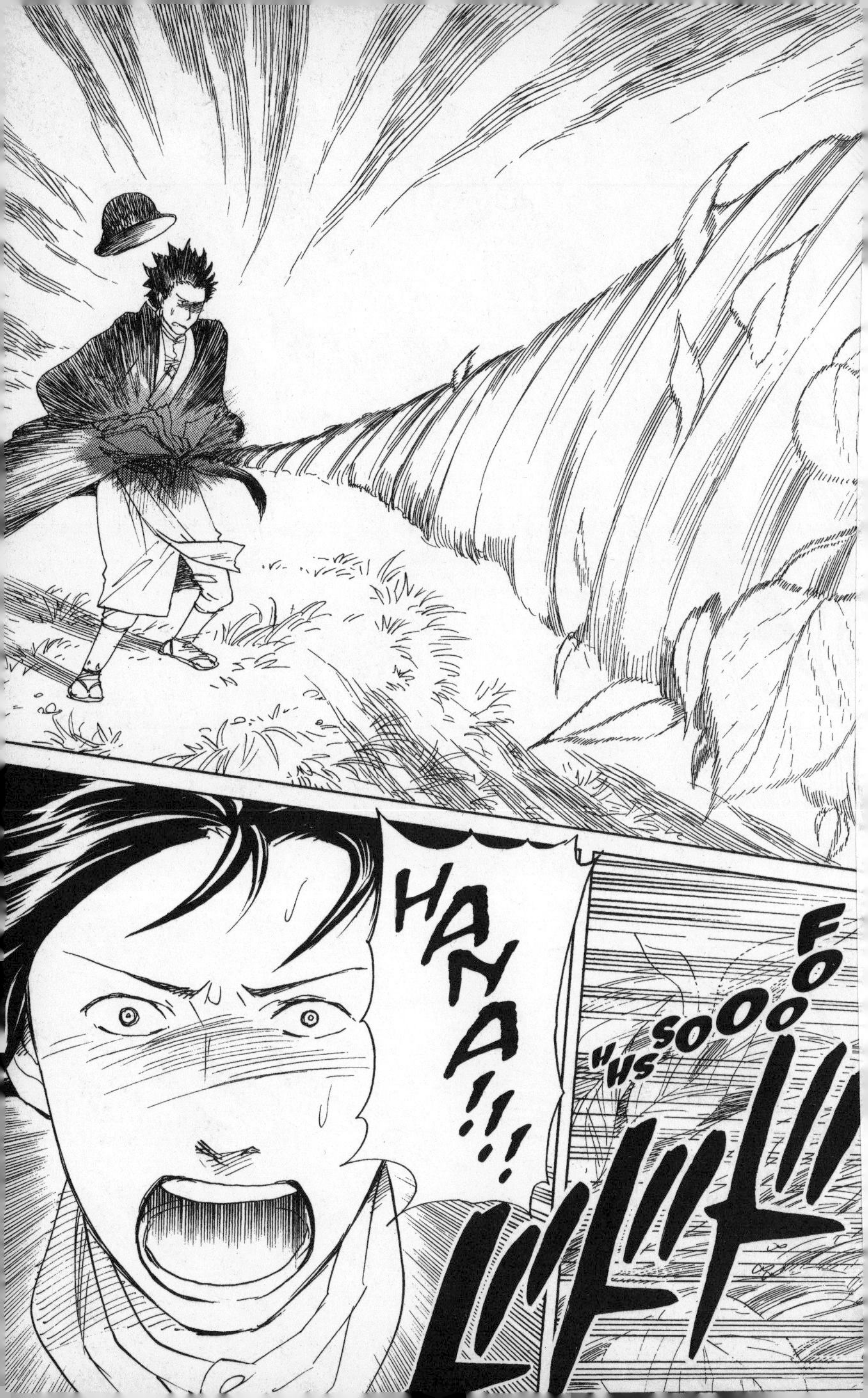
FOOOOSHH
HANA!!!!

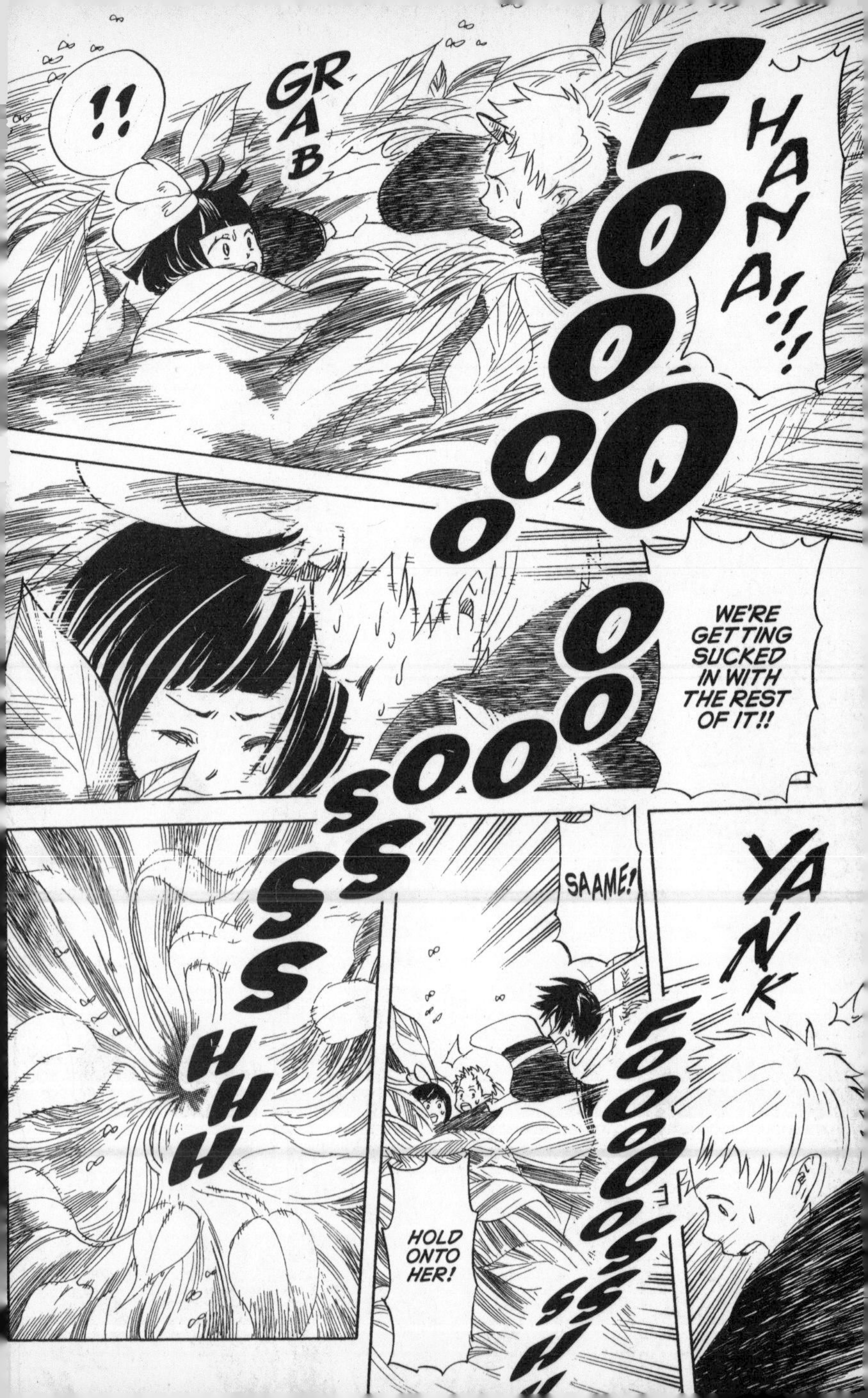
HANA!!!
GRAB
!!
FOOOOOOOOOOOSSSSSHHH
WE'RE GETTING SUCKED IN WITH THE REST OF IT!!
YANK
SAAME!
FOOOOOSSSHH
HOLD ONTO HER!

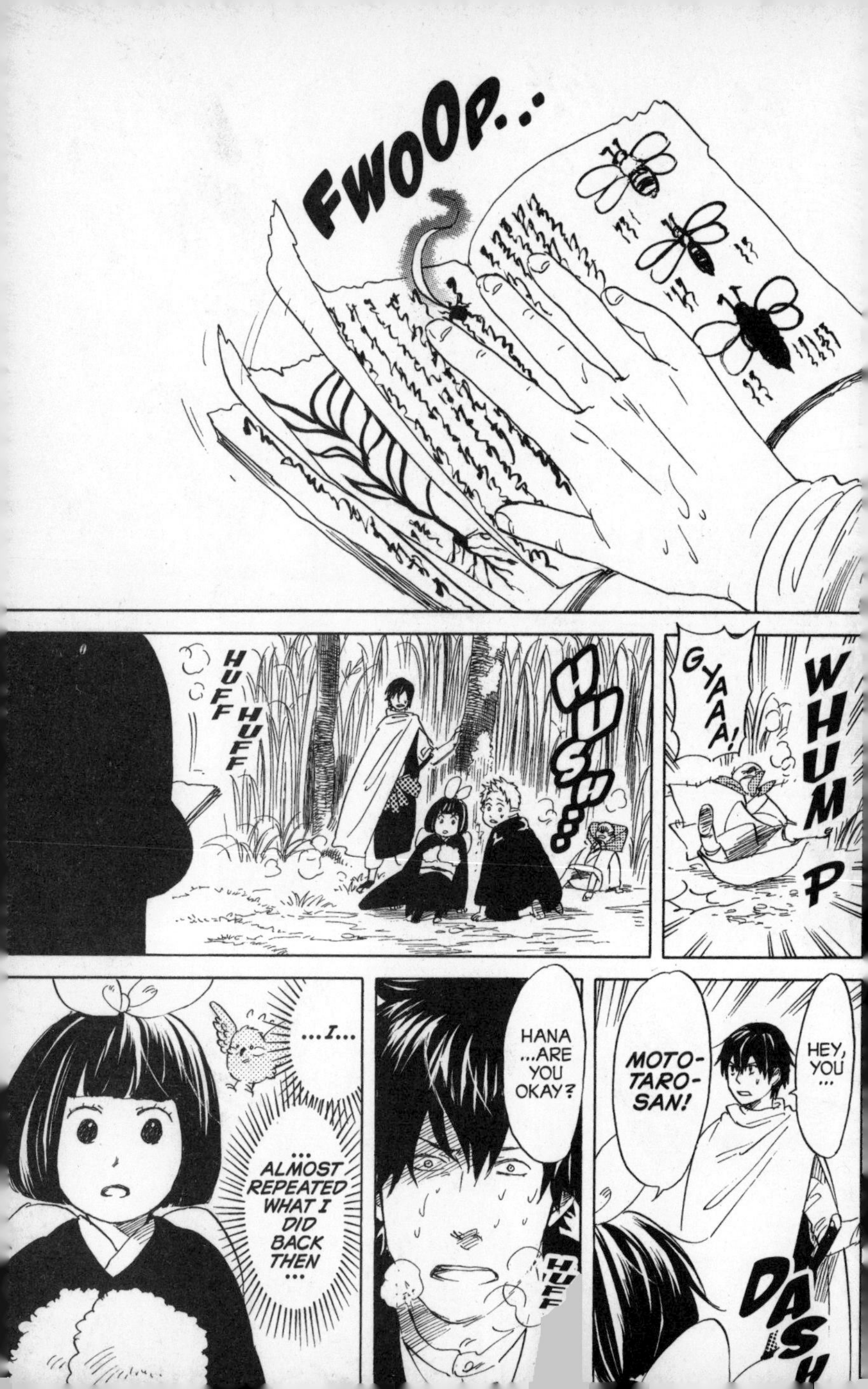
FWOOP...
WHUMP
GYAAA!
WHUSH...
HUFF HUFF
HEY, YOU...
MOTO-TARO-SAN!
DASH
HANA ...ARE YOU OKAY?
HUFF
...I...
...ALMOST REPEATED WHAT I DID BACK THEN...

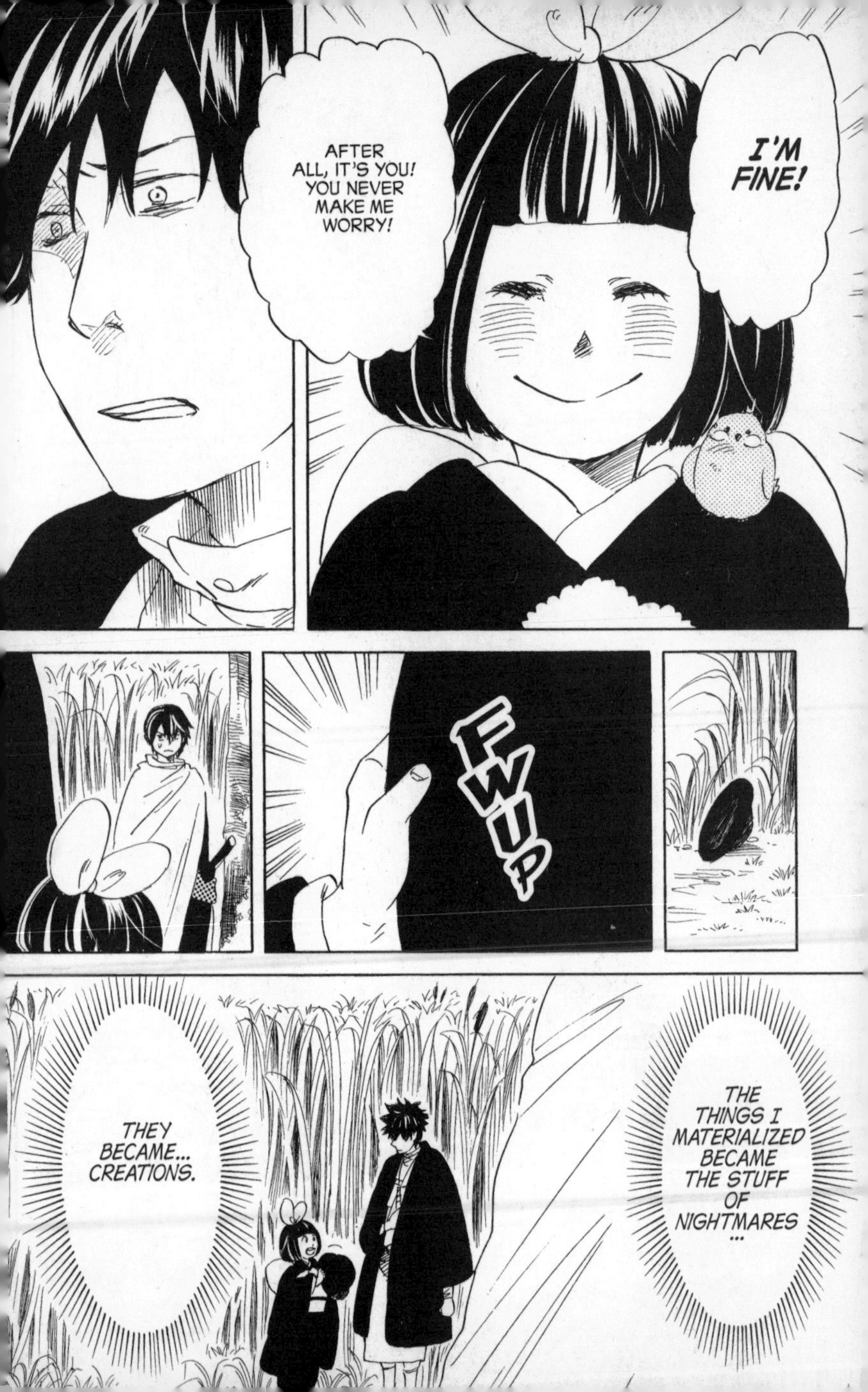
I'M FINE!
AFTER ALL, IT'S YOU! YOU NEVER MAKE ME WORRY!
FWUP
THE THINGS I MATERIALIZED BECAME THE STUFF OF NIGHTMARES...
THEY BECAME... CREATIONS.

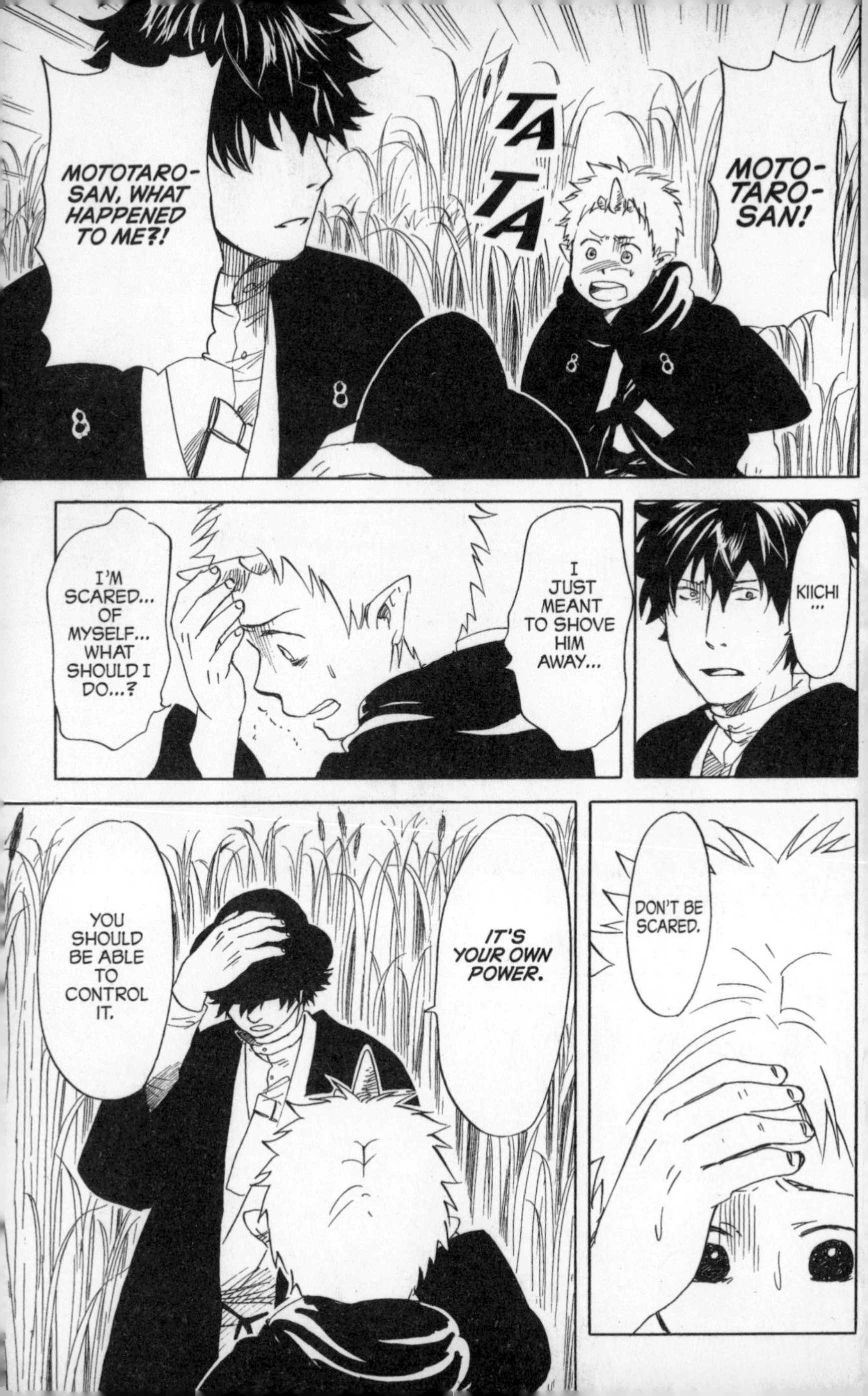
MOTO-TARO-SAN!
TA TA
MOTOTARO-SAN, WHAT HAPPENED TO ME?!
KIICHI ...
I JUST MEANT TO SHOVE HIM AWAY...
I'M SCARED... OF MYSELF... WHAT SHOULD I DO...?
DON'T BE SCARED.
IT'S YOUR OWN POWER.
YOU SHOULD BE ABLE TO CONTROL IT.

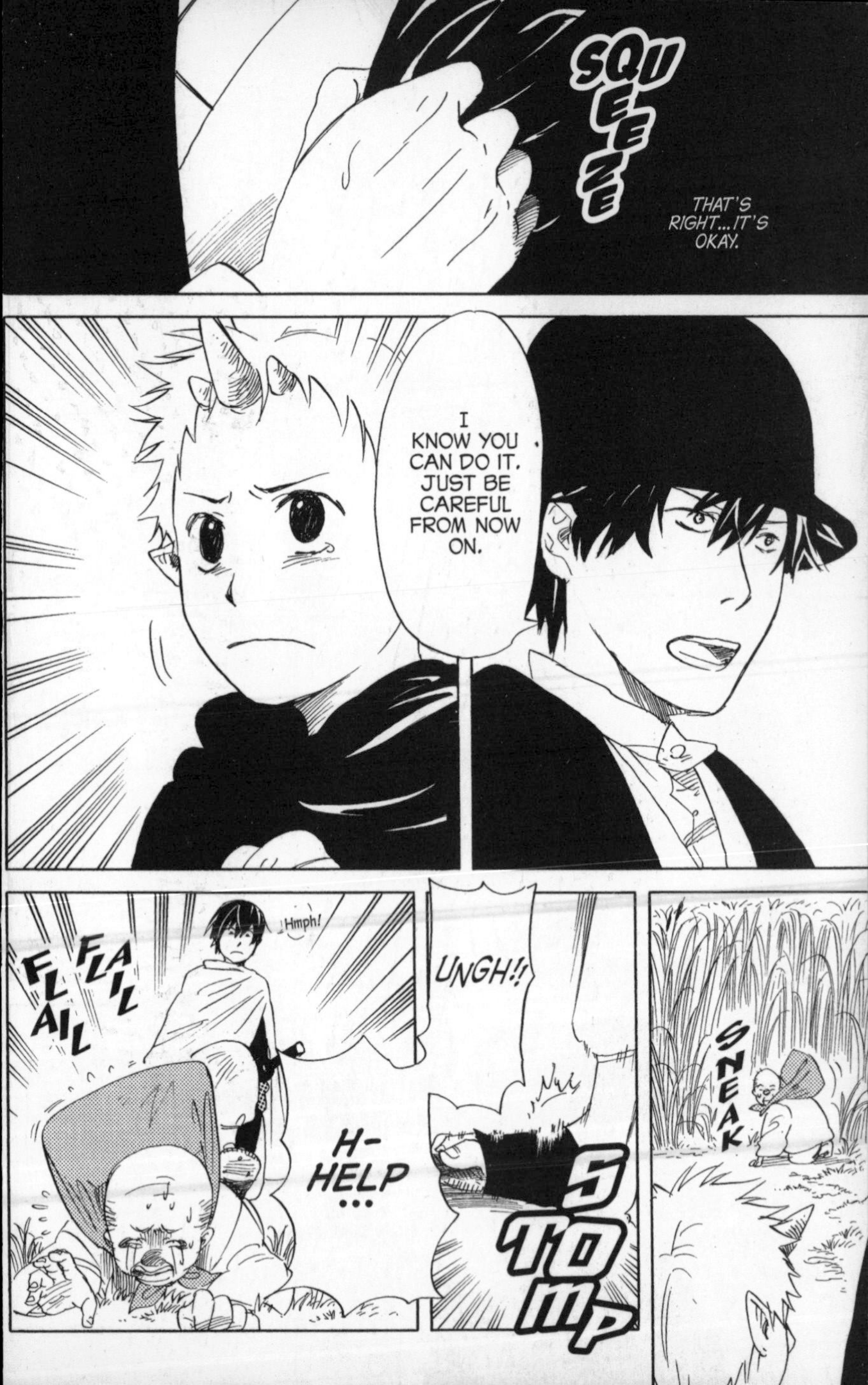
SQUEEZE
THAT'S RIGHT...IT'S OKAY.
I KNOW YOU CAN DO IT. JUST BE CAREFUL FROM NOW ON.
SNEAK
UNGH!!
STOMP
Hmph!
FLAIL FLAIL
H-HELP...

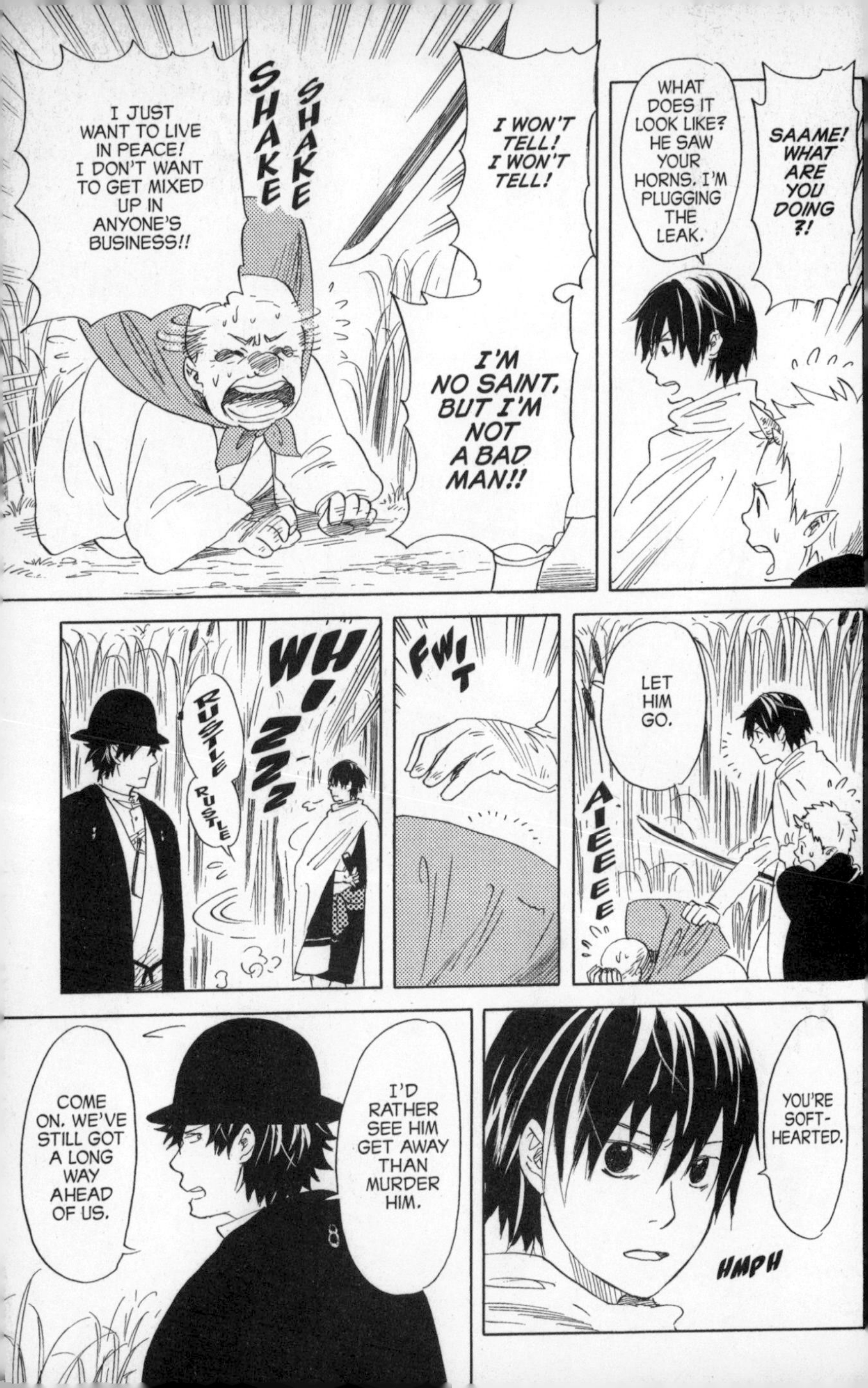
SAAME! WHAT ARE YOU DOING?!
WHAT DOES IT LOOK LIKE? HE SAW YOUR HORNS. I'M PLUGGING THE LEAK.
I WON'T TELL! I WON'T TELL!
SHAKE SHAKE
I JUST WANT TO LIVE IN PEACE! I DON'T WANT TO GET MIXED UP IN ANYONE'S BUSINESS!!
I'M NO SAINT, BUT I'M NOT A BAD MAN!!
LET HIM GO.
AIEEEEE
FWIT
WHIZZZ
RUSTLE RUSTLE
YOU'RE SOFT-HEARTED.
HMPH
I'D RATHER SEE HIM GET AWAY THAN MURDER HIM.
COME ON. WE'VE STILL GOT A LONG WAY AHEAD OF US.

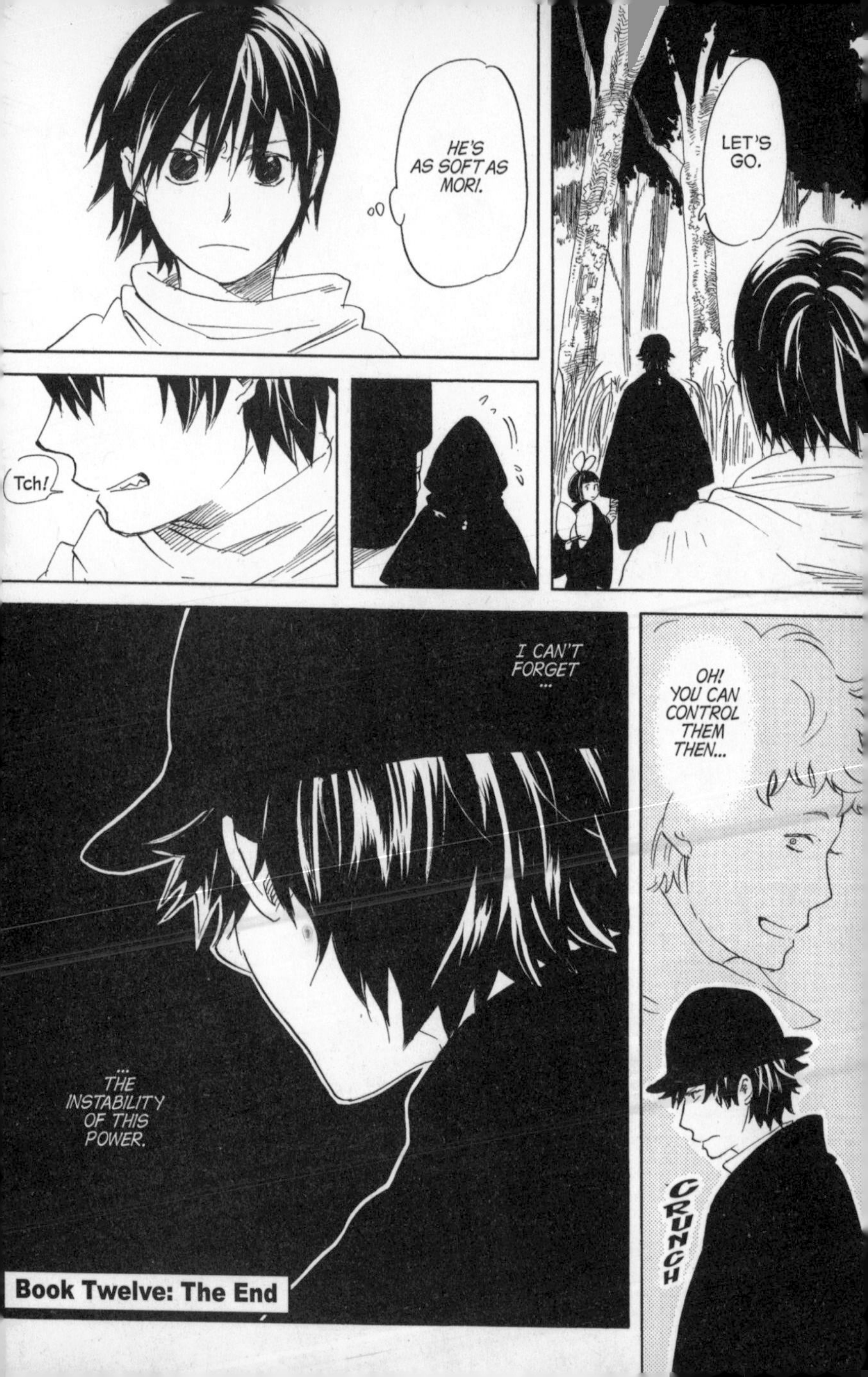
LET'S GO.
HE'S AS SOFT AS MORI.
Tch!
OH! YOU CAN CONTROL THEM THEN...
CRUNCH
I CAN'T FORGET ...
... THE INSTABILITY OF THIS POWER.
Book Twelve: The End

BOOK THIRTEEN

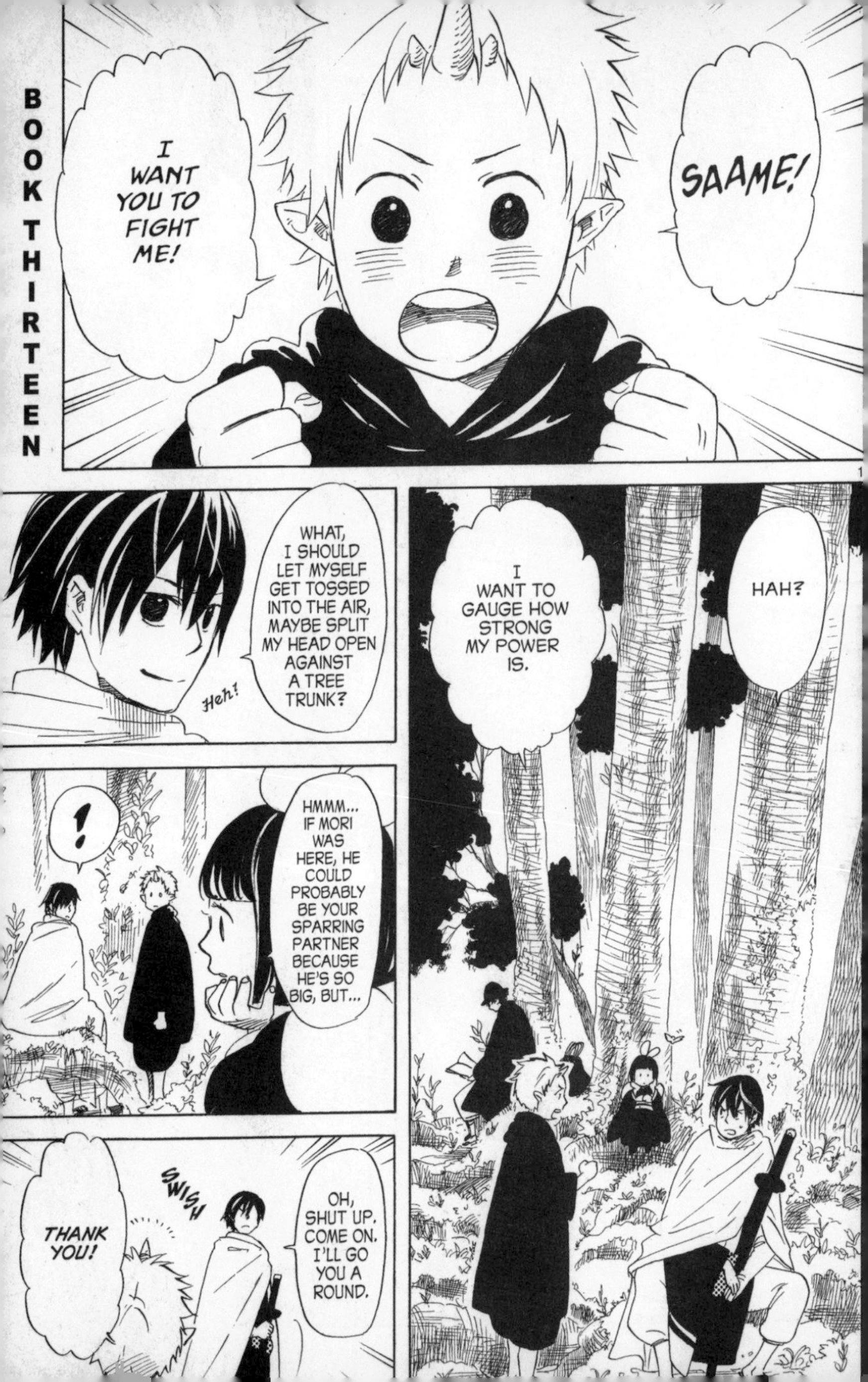
SAAME!
I WANT YOU TO FIGHT ME!
HAH?
I WANT TO GAUGE HOW STRONG MY POWER IS.
WHAT, I SHOULD LET MYSELF GET TOSSED INTO THE AIR, MAYBE SPLIT MY HEAD OPEN AGAINST A TREE TRUNK?
Heh!
HMMM... IF MORI WAS HERE, HE COULD PROBABLY BE YOUR SPARRING PARTNER BECAUSE HE'S SO BIG, BUT...
!
OH, SHUT UP. COME ON. I'LL GO YOU A ROUND.
SWISH
THANK YOU!

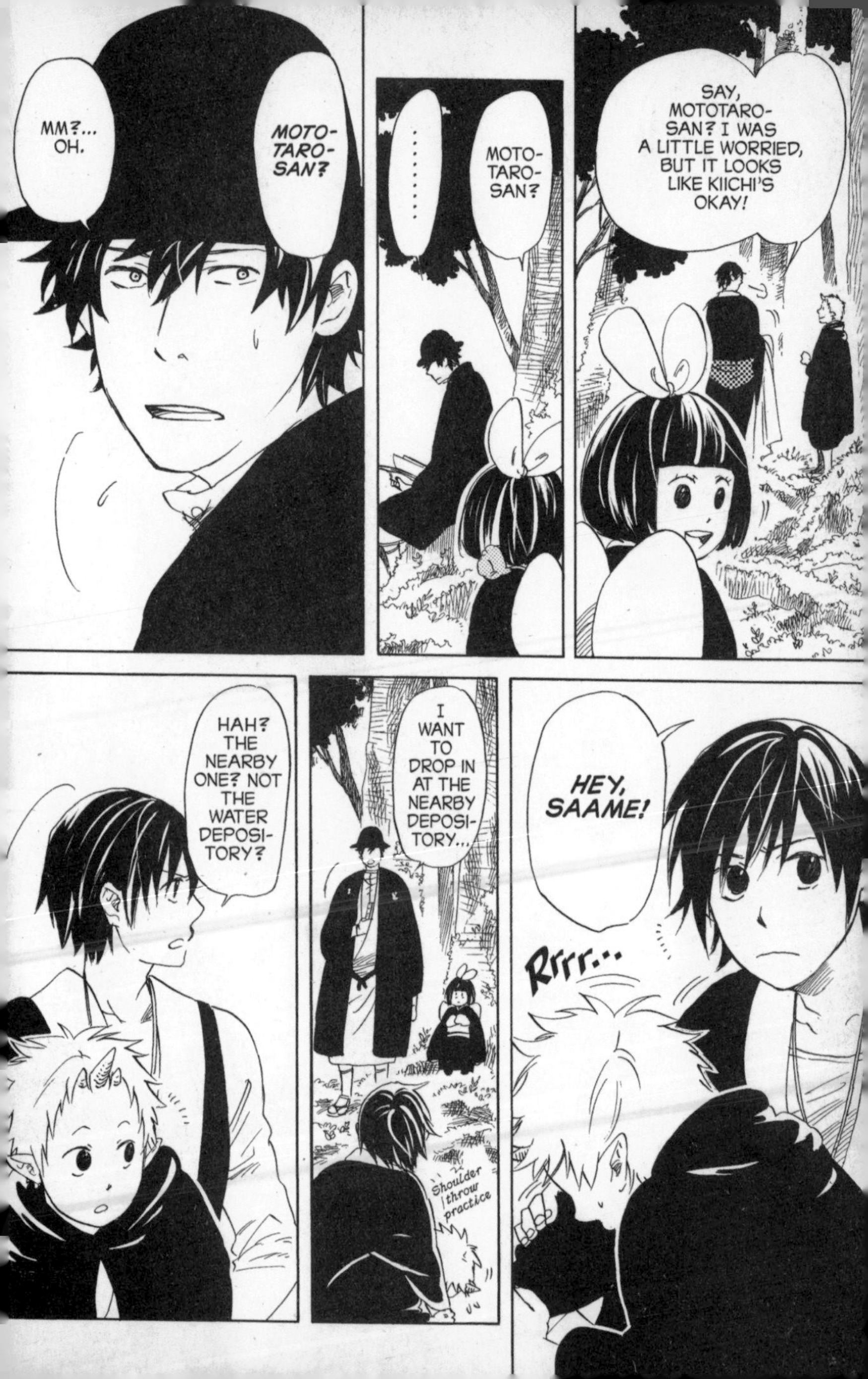
SAY, MOTOTARO-SAN? I WAS A LITTLE WORRIED, BUT IT LOOKS LIKE KIICHI'S OKAY!
MOTO-TARO-SAN?
....
MOTO-TARO-SAN?
MM?... OH.
HEY, SAAME!
Rrrr...
I WANT TO DROP IN AT THE NEARBY DEPOSITORY...
Shoulder throw practice
HAH? THE NEARBY ONE? NOT THE WATER DEPOSITORY?

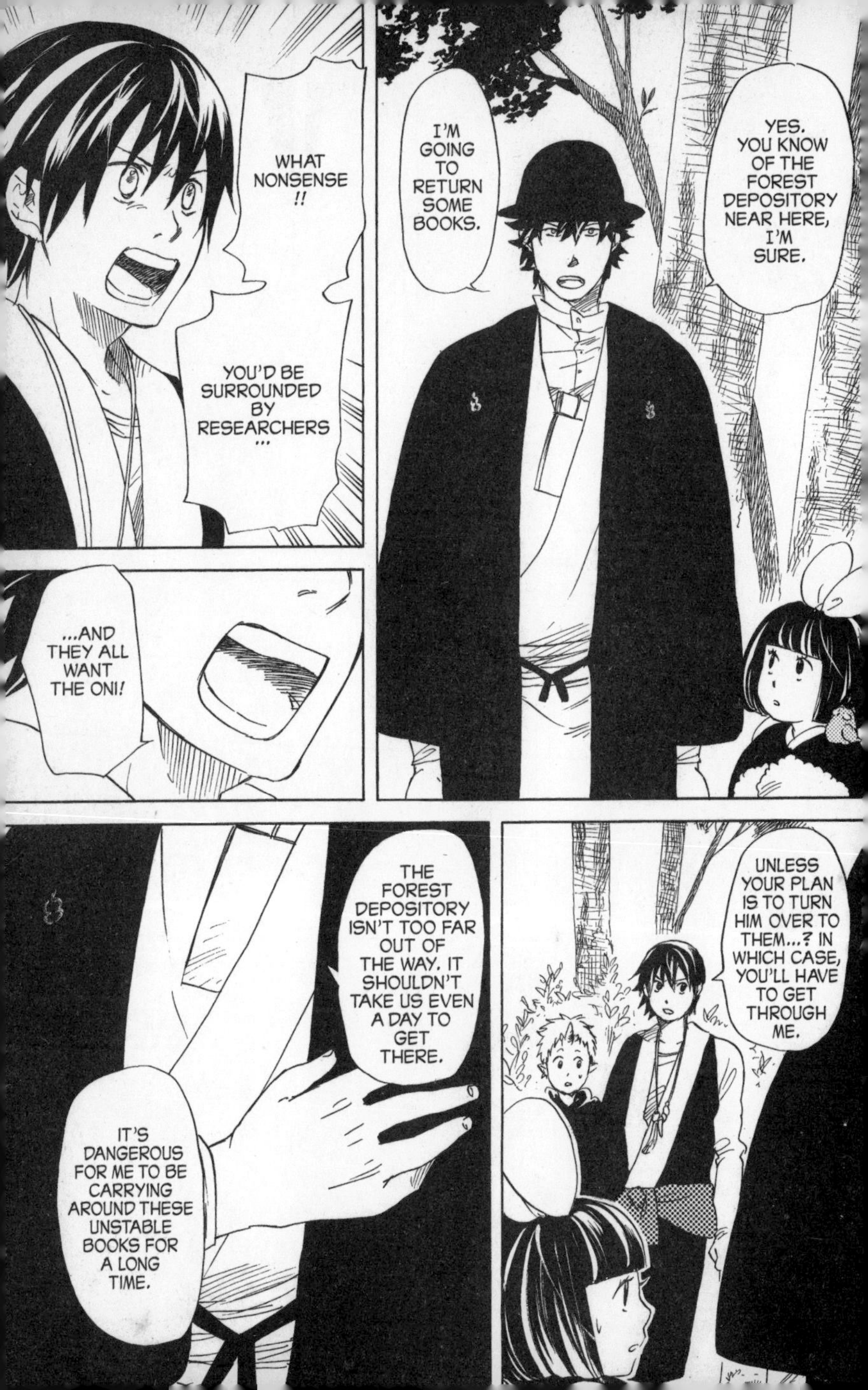
YES. YOU KNOW OF THE FOREST DEPOSITORY NEAR HERE, I'M SURE.
I'M GOING TO RETURN SOME BOOKS.
WHAT NONSENSE!!
YOU'D BE SURROUNDED BY RESEARCHERS...
...AND THEY ALL WANT THE ONI!
UNLESS YOUR PLAN IS TO TURN HIM OVER TO THEM...? IN WHICH CASE, YOU'LL HAVE TO GET THROUGH ME.
THE FOREST DEPOSITORY ISN'T TOO FAR OUT OF THE WAY. IT SHOULDN'T TAKE US EVEN A DAY TO GET THERE.
IT'S DANGEROUS FOR ME TO BE CARRYING AROUND THESE UNSTABLE BOOKS FOR A LONG TIME.

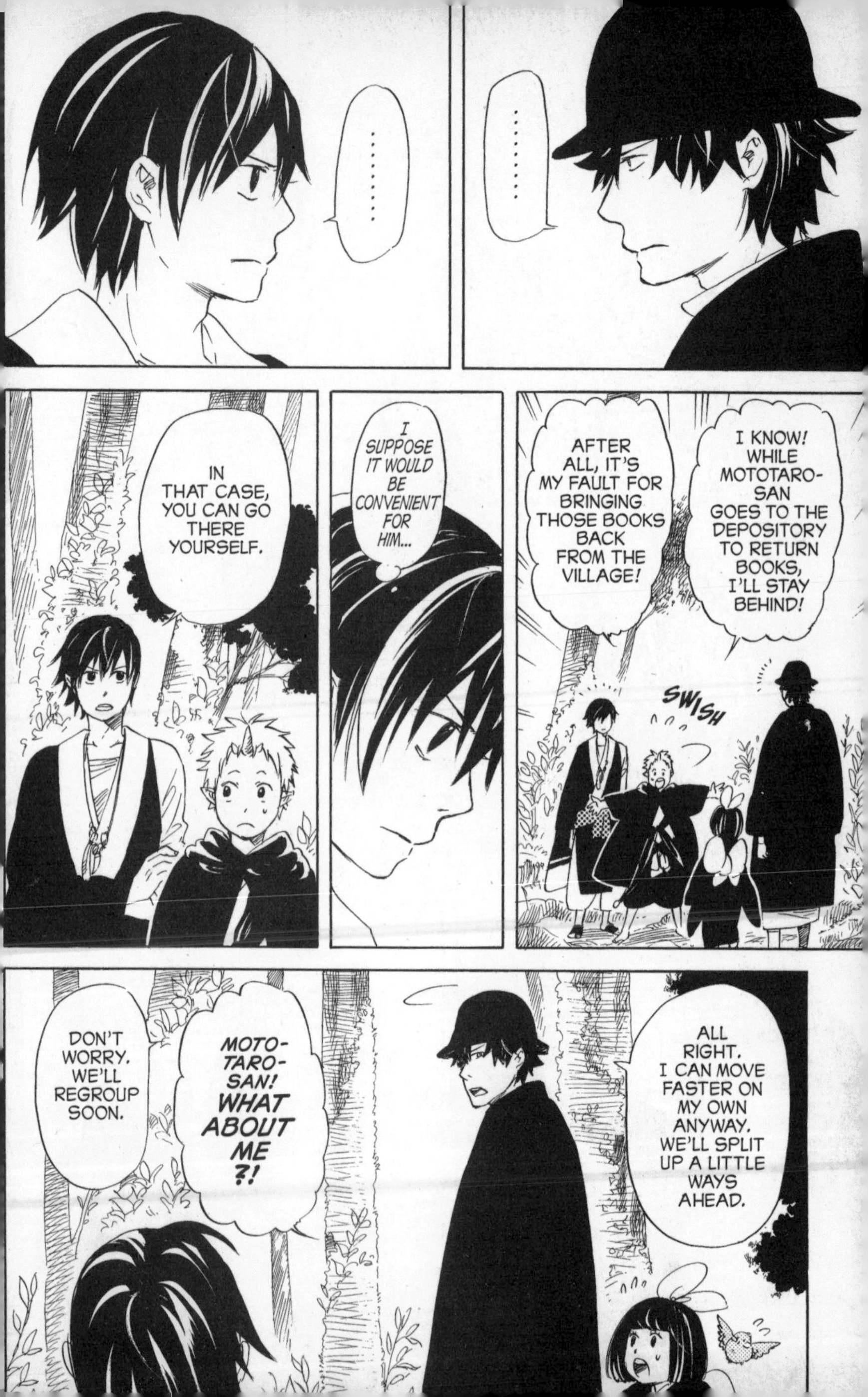
......
......
I KNOW! WHILE MOTOTARO-SAN GOES TO THE DEPOSITORY TO RETURN BOOKS, I'LL STAY BEHIND!
AFTER ALL, IT'S MY FAULT FOR BRINGING THOSE BOOKS BACK FROM THE VILLAGE!
SWISH
I SUPPOSE IT WOULD BE CONVENIENT FOR HIM...
IN THAT CASE, YOU CAN GO THERE YOURSELF.
ALL RIGHT. I CAN MOVE FASTER ON MY OWN ANYWAY. WE'LL SPLIT UP A LITTLE WAYS AHEAD.
MOTOTARO-SAN! WHAT ABOUT ME?!
DON'T WORRY. WE'LL REGROUP SOON.

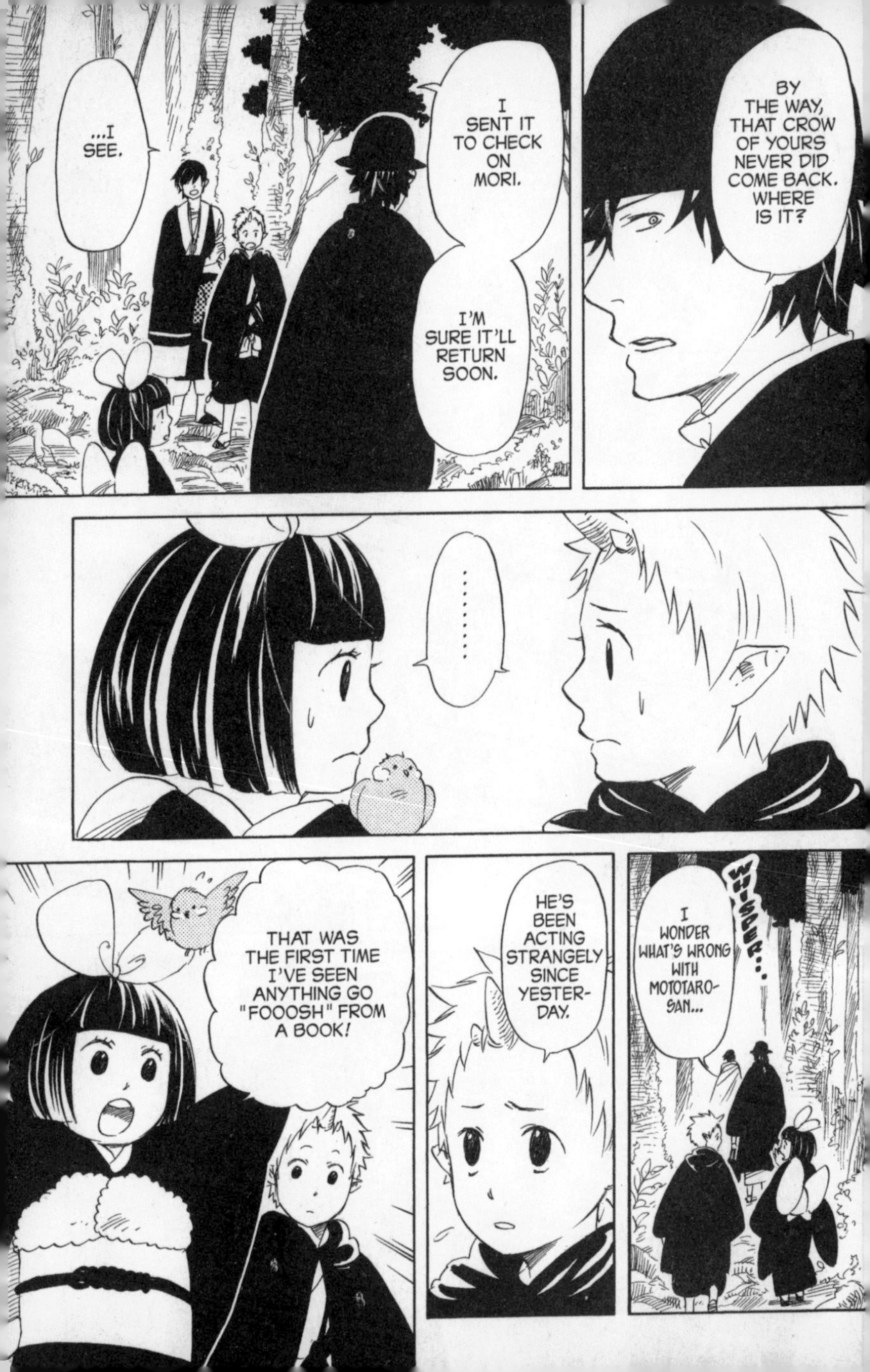
BY THE WAY, THAT CROW OF YOURS NEVER DID COME BACK. WHERE IS IT?
I SENT IT TO CHECK ON MORI.
I'M SURE IT'LL RETURN SOON.
...I SEE.
......
WHISPER...
I WONDER WHAT'S WRONG WITH MOTOTARO-SAN...
HE'S BEEN ACTING STRANGELY SINCE YESTER-DAY.
THAT WAS THE FIRST TIME I'VE SEEN ANYTHING GO "FOOOSH" FROM A BOOK!

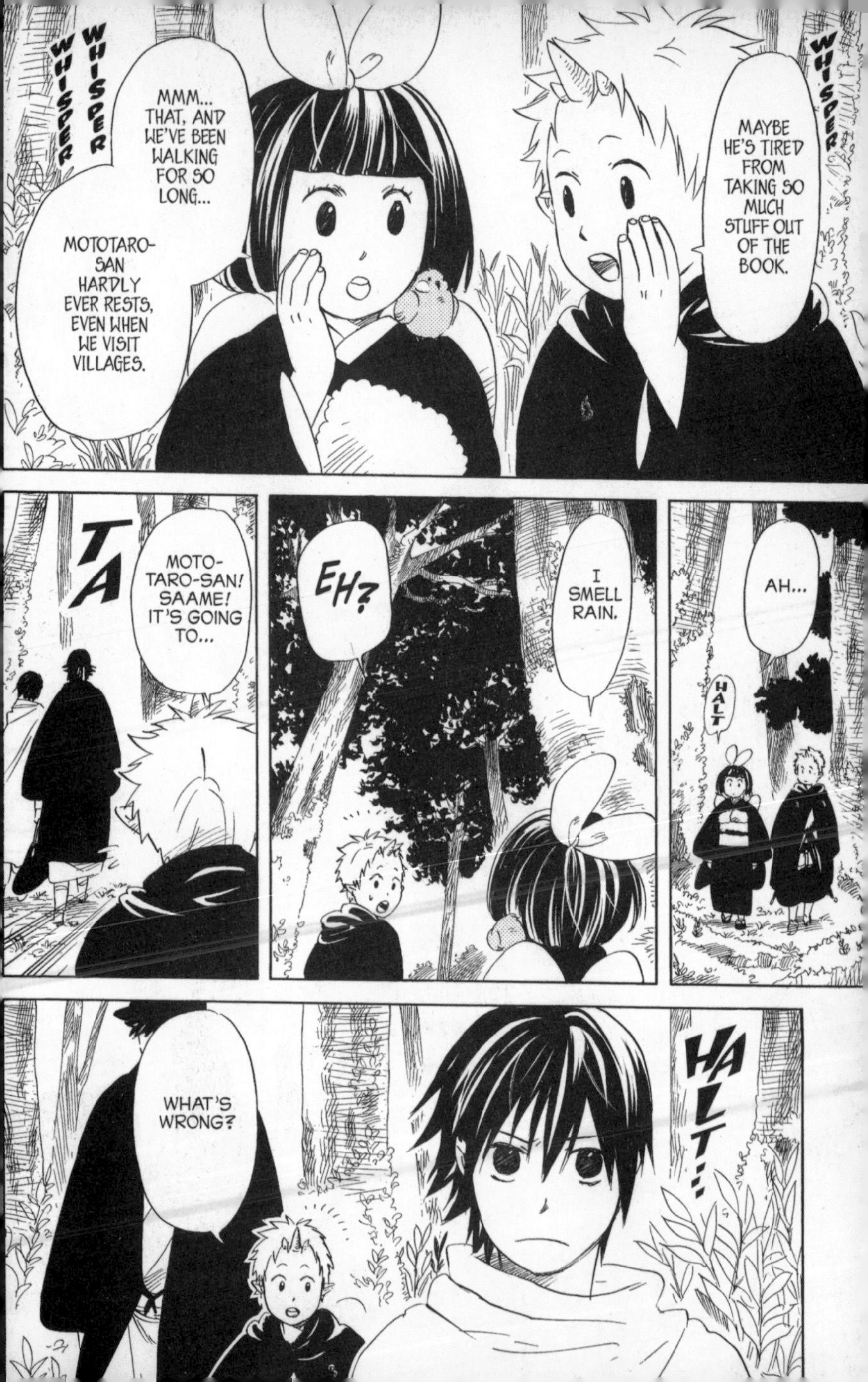
WHISPER
MAYBE HE'S TIRED FROM TAKING SO MUCH STUFF OUT OF THE BOOK.
MMM... THAT, AND WE'VE BEEN WALKING FOR SO LONG...
MOTOTARO-SAN HARDLY EVER RESTS, EVEN WHEN WE VISIT VILLAGES.
WHISPER WHISPER
AH...
HALT
I SMELL RAIN.
EH?
TA
MOTO-TARO-SAN! SAAME! IT'S GOING TO...
HALT!!
WHAT'S WRONG?

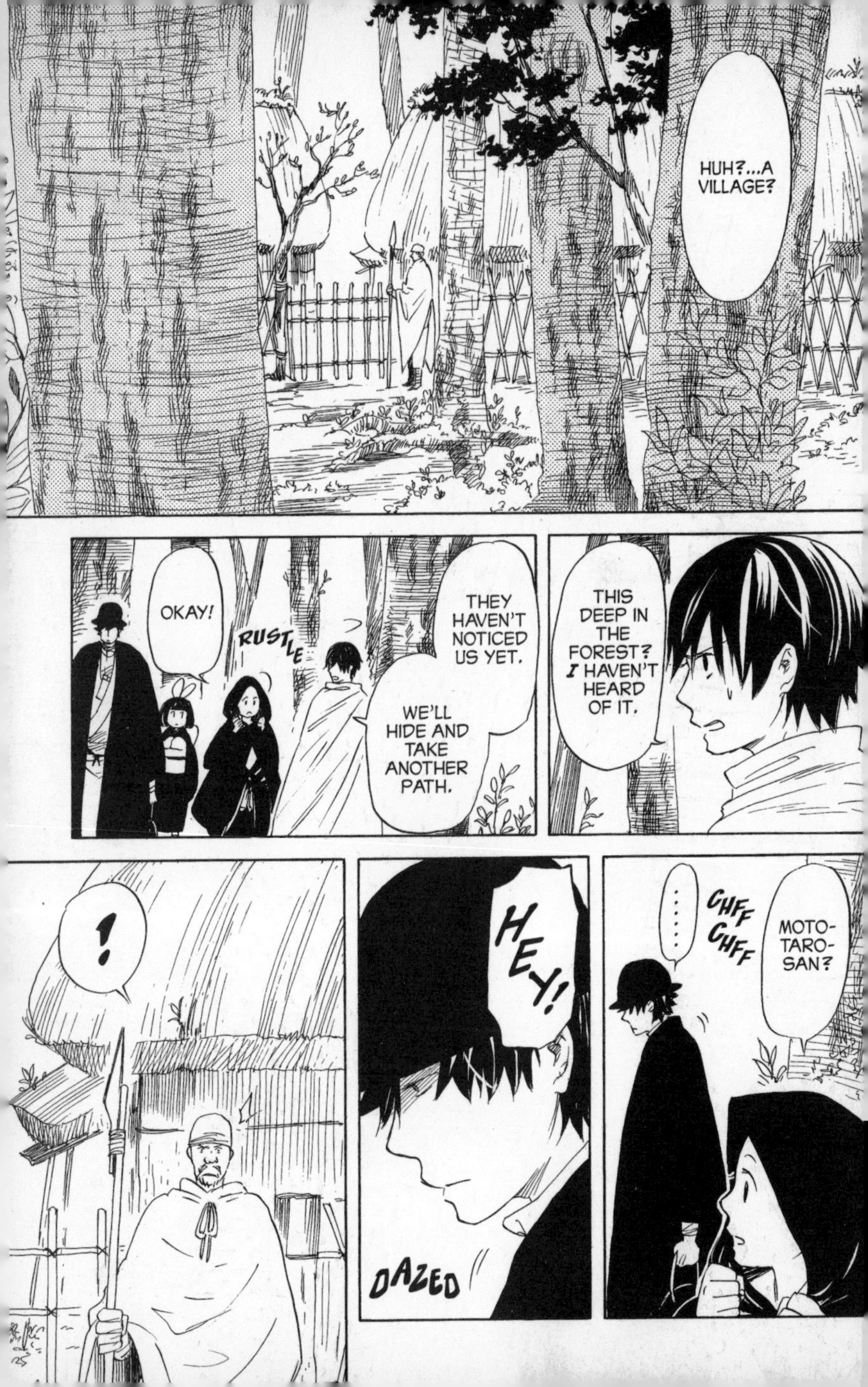
HUH?...A VILLAGE?
THIS DEEP IN THE FOREST? I HAVEN'T HEARD OF IT.
THEY HAVEN'T NOTICED US YET.
WE'LL HIDE AND TAKE ANOTHER PATH.
RUSTLE
OKAY!
MOTO-TARO-SAN?
CHFF CHFF
......
HEY!
DAZED
!

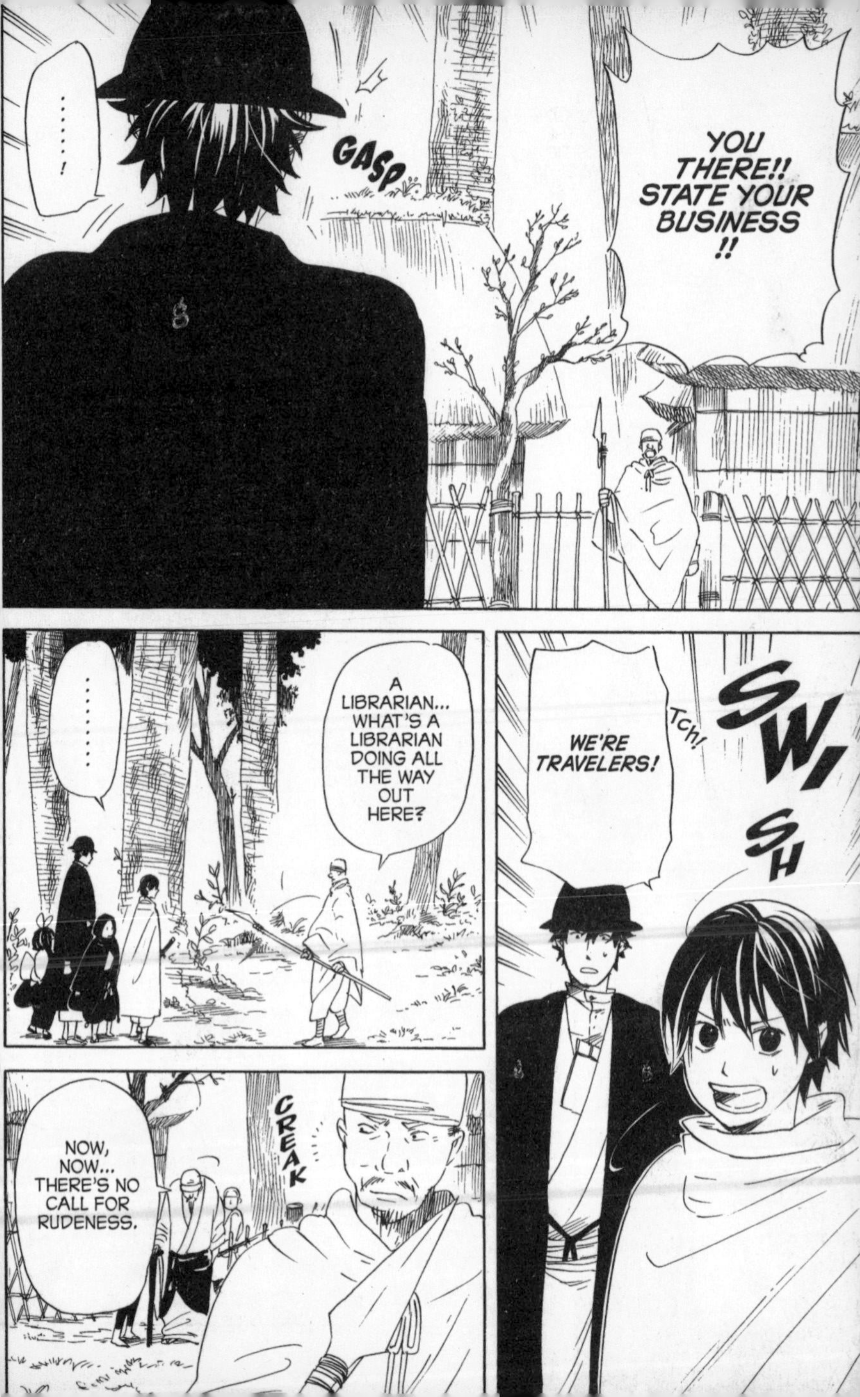
YOU THERE!! STATE YOUR BUSINESS !!
GASP
......!
WE'RE TRAVELERS!
Tch!
SWISH
A LIBRARIAN... WHAT'S A LIBRARIAN DOING ALL THE WAY OUT HERE?
......
CREAK
NOW, NOW... THERE'S NO CALL FOR RUDENESS.

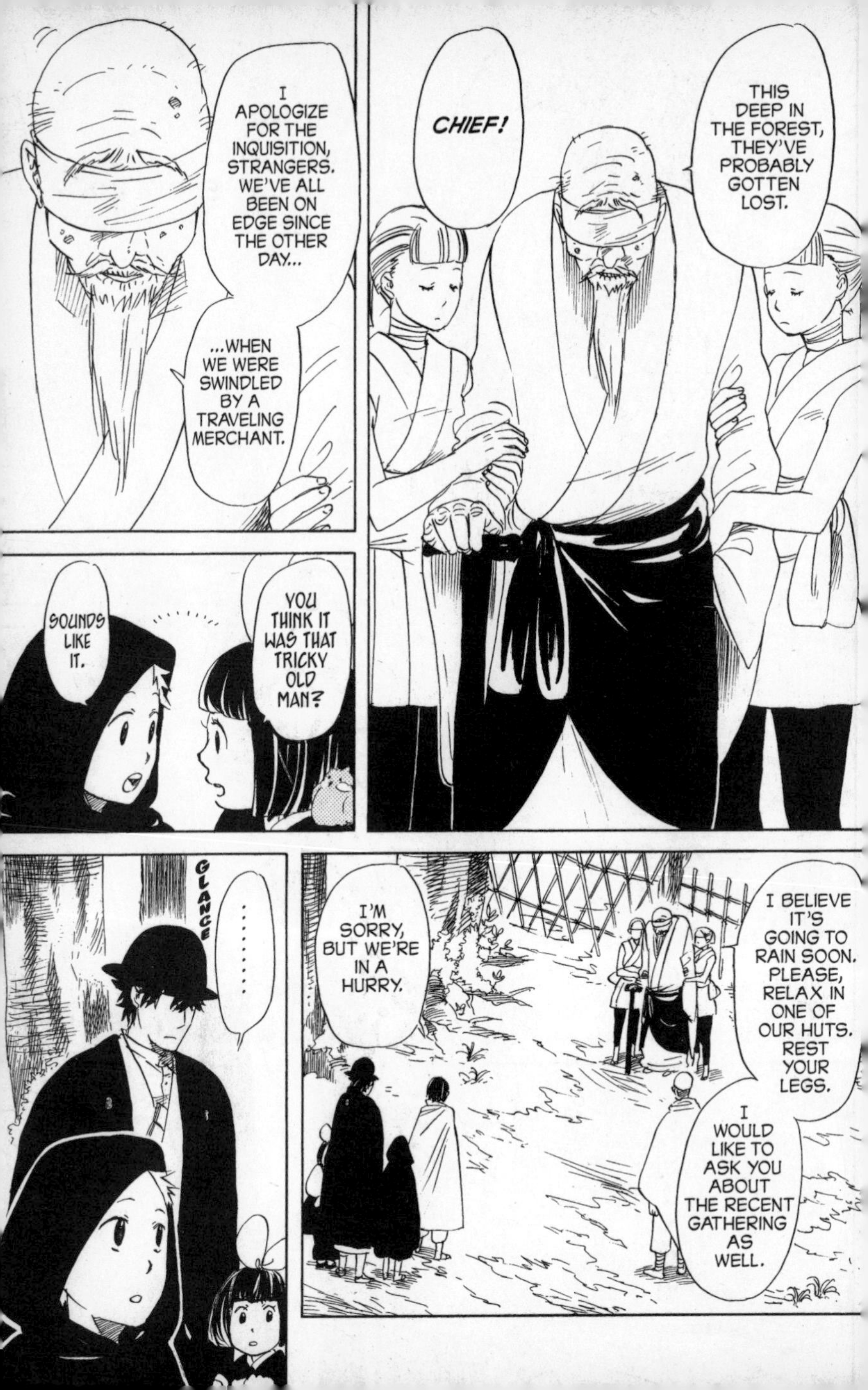
THIS DEEP IN THE FOREST, THEY'VE PROBABLY GOTTEN LOST.
CHIEF!
I APOLOGIZE FOR THE INQUISITION, STRANGERS. WE'VE ALL BEEN ON EDGE SINCE THE OTHER DAY...
...WHEN WE WERE SWINDLED BY A TRAVELING MERCHANT.
YOU THINK IT WAS THAT TRICKY OLD MAN?
SOUNDS LIKE IT.
I BELIEVE IT'S GOING TO RAIN SOON. PLEASE, RELAX IN ONE OF OUR HUTS. REST YOUR LEGS.
I WOULD LIKE TO ASK YOU ABOUT THE RECENT GATHERING AS WELL.
I'M SORRY, BUT WE'RE IN A HURRY.
GLANCE
......

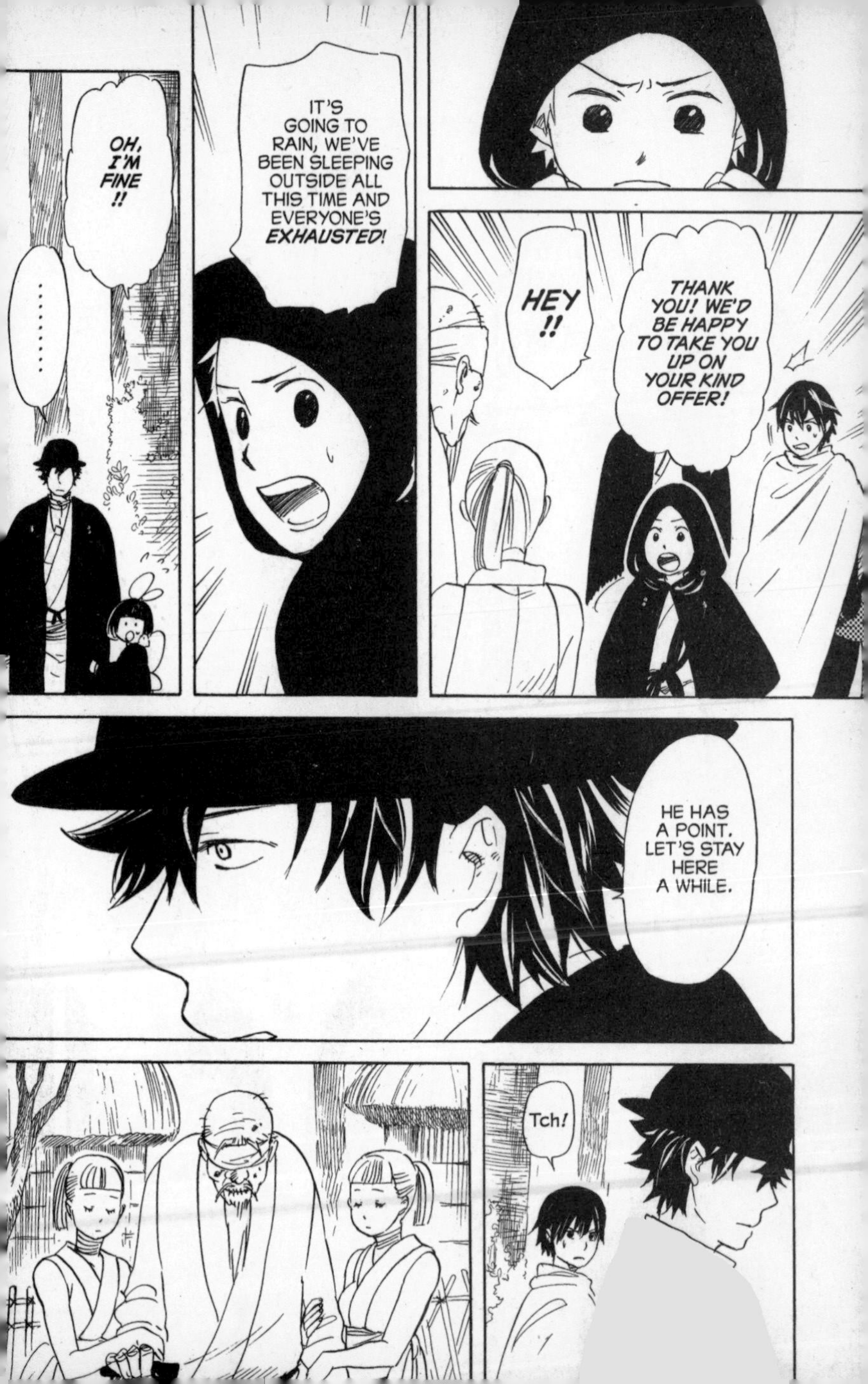
THANK YOU! WE'D BE HAPPY TO TAKE YOU UP ON YOUR KIND OFFER!
HEY !!
IT'S GOING TO RAIN, WE'VE BEEN SLEEPING OUTSIDE ALL THIS TIME AND EVERYONE'S *EXHAUSTED!*
OH, I'M FINE !!
....
HE HAS A POINT. LET'S STAY HERE A WHILE.
Tch!

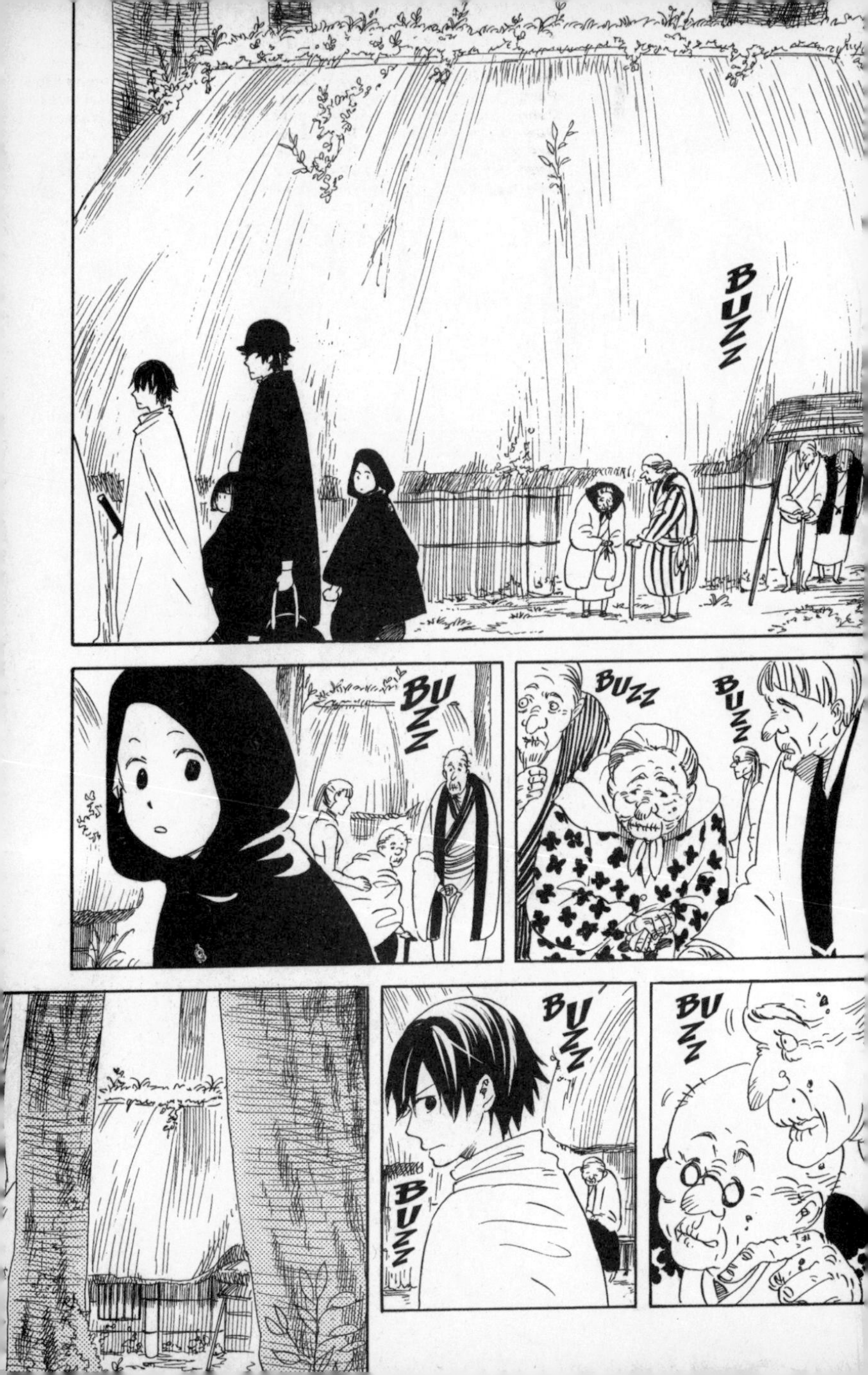
BUZZ
BUZZ
BUZZ
BUZZ
BUZZ
BUZZ
BUZZ

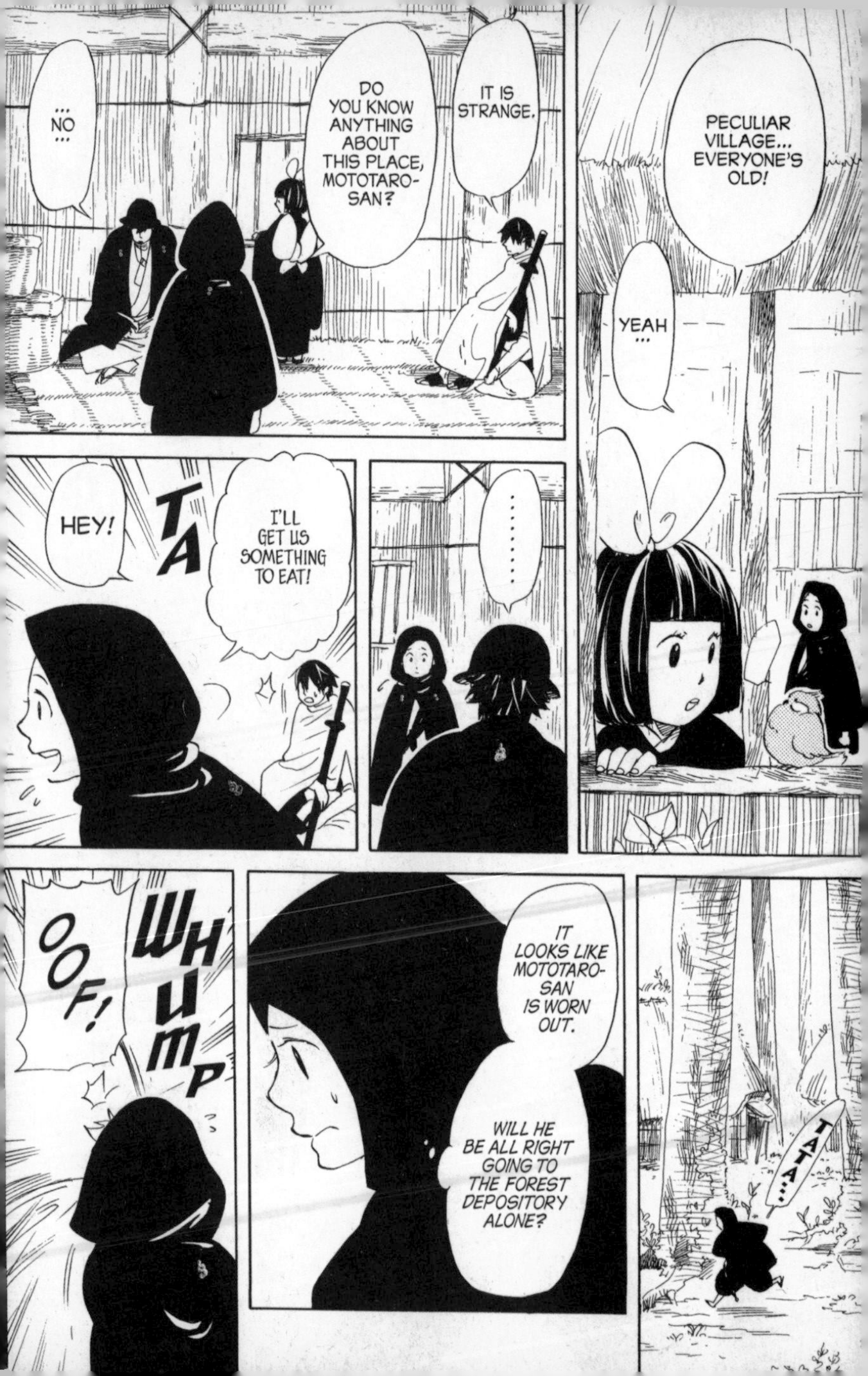
PECULIAR VILLAGE... EVERYONE'S OLD!
YEAH ...
IT IS STRANGE.
DO YOU KNOW ANYTHING ABOUT THIS PLACE, MOTOTARO-SAN?
... NO ...
....
I'LL GET US SOMETHING TO EAT!
TA
HEY!
TATA...
IT LOOKS LIKE MOTOTARO-SAN IS WORN OUT.
WILL HE BE ALL RIGHT GOING TO THE FOREST DEPOSITORY ALONE?
WHUMP
OOF!

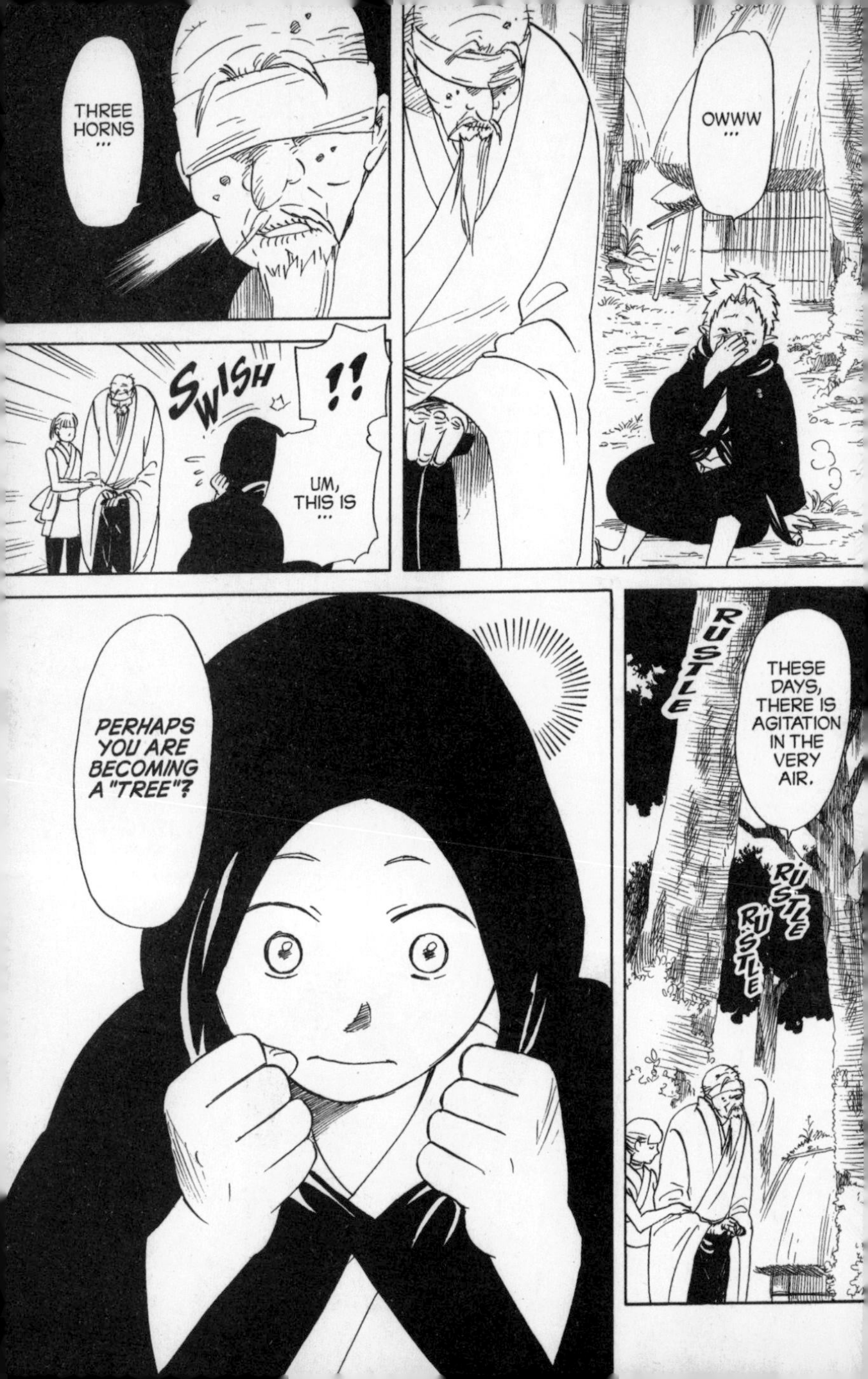
OWWW ...
THREE HORNS ...
SWISH
!!
UM, THIS IS ...
RUSTLE
THESE DAYS, THERE IS AGITATION IN THE VERY AIR.
RUSTLE
RUSTLE
PERHAPS YOU ARE BECOMING A "TREE"?

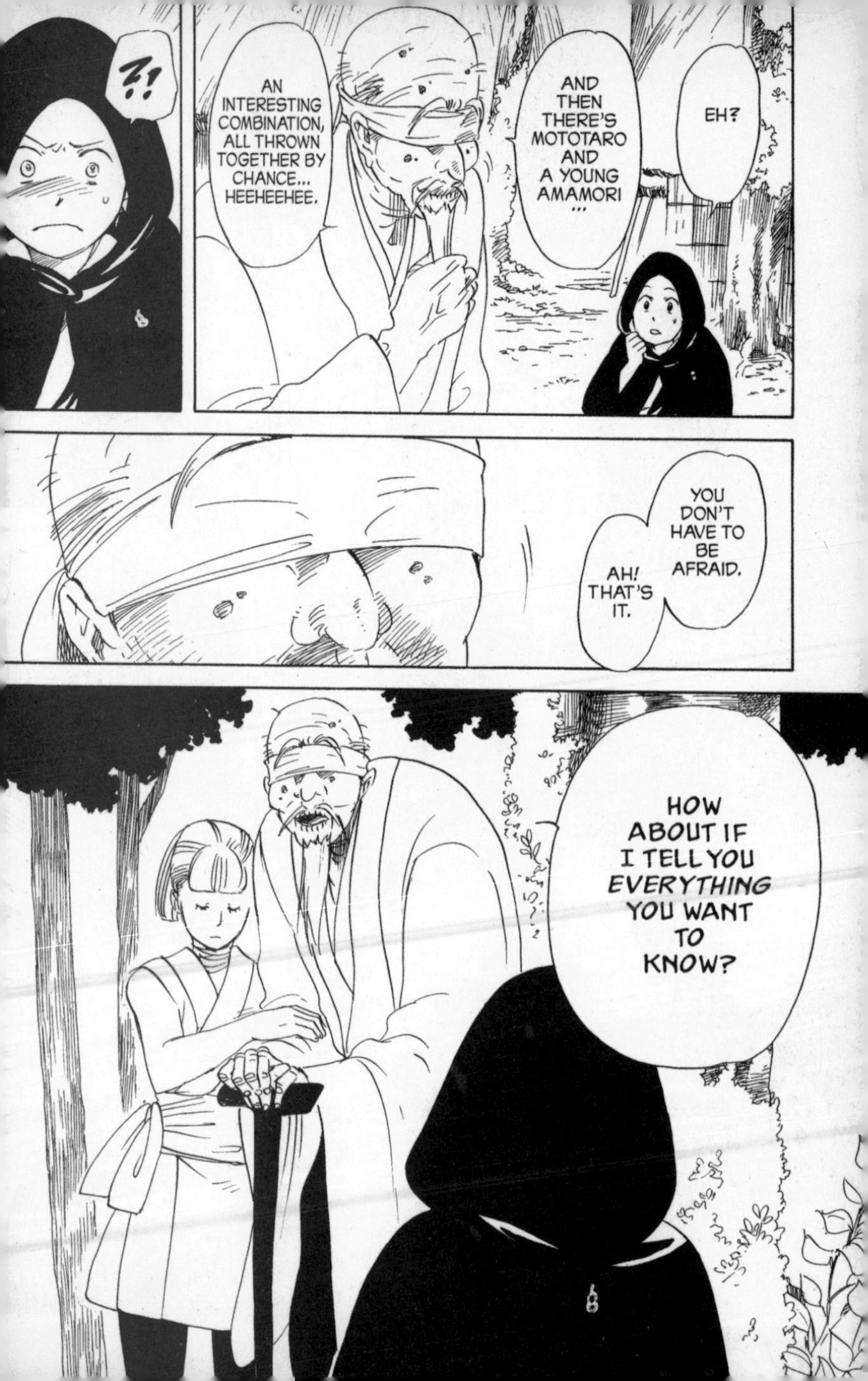
EH?
AND THEN THERE'S MOTOTARO AND A YOUNG AMAMORI...
AN INTERESTING COMBINATION, ALL THROWN TOGETHER BY CHANCE... HEEHEEHEE.
?!
YOU DON'T HAVE TO BE AFRAID.
AH! THAT'S IT.
HOW ABOUT IF I TELL YOU *EVERYTHING* YOU WANT TO KNOW?

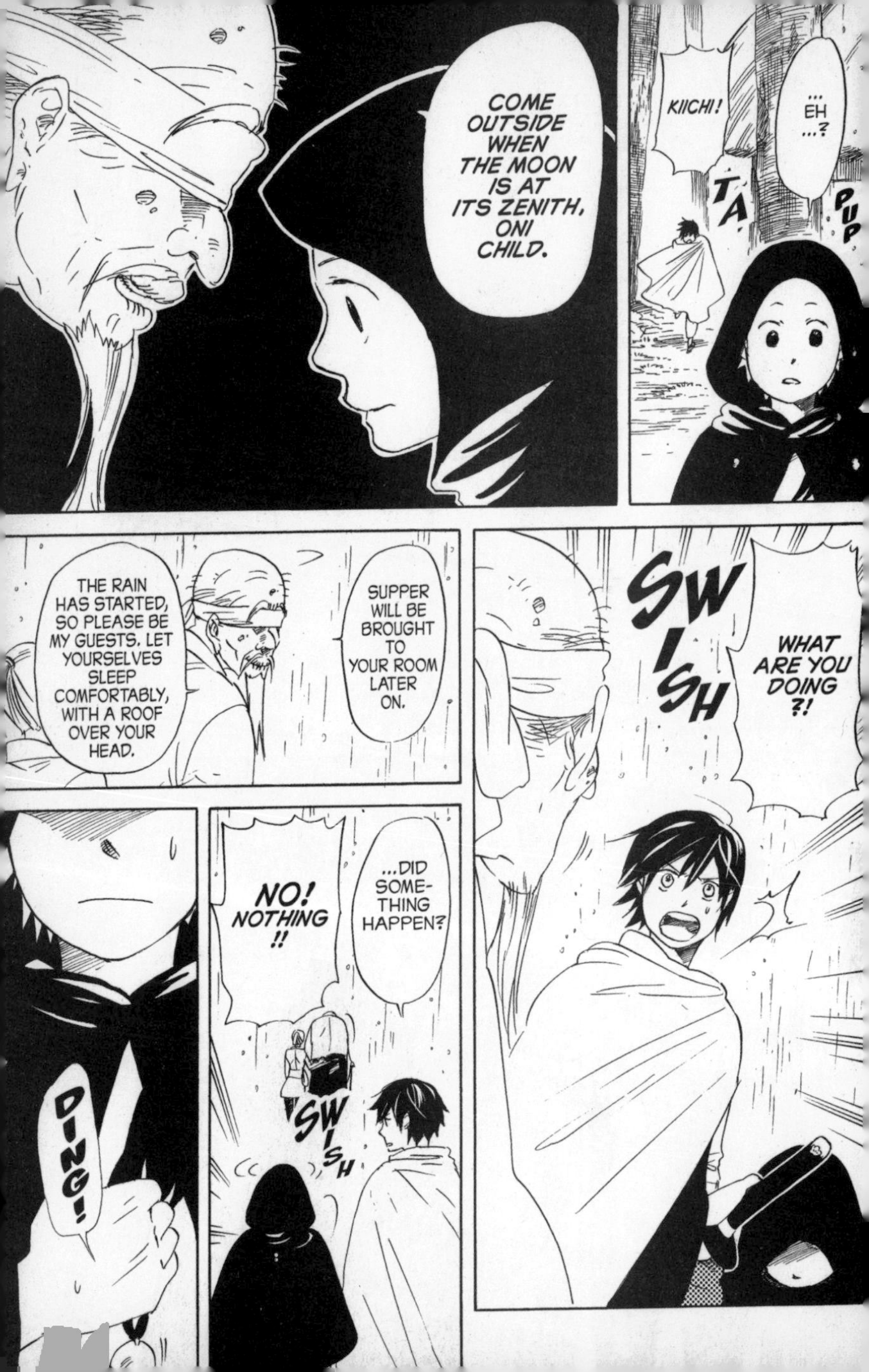
...EH ...?
KIICHI!
TA
PUP
COME OUTSIDE WHEN THE MOON IS AT ITS ZENITH, ONI CHILD.
WHAT ARE YOU DOING?!
SWISH
SUPPER WILL BE BROUGHT TO YOUR ROOM LATER ON.
THE RAIN HAS STARTED, SO PLEASE BE MY GUESTS. LET YOURSELVES SLEEP COMFORTABLY, WITH A ROOF OVER YOUR HEAD.
...DID SOME-THING HAPPEN?
NO! NOTHING!!
SWISH
DING!

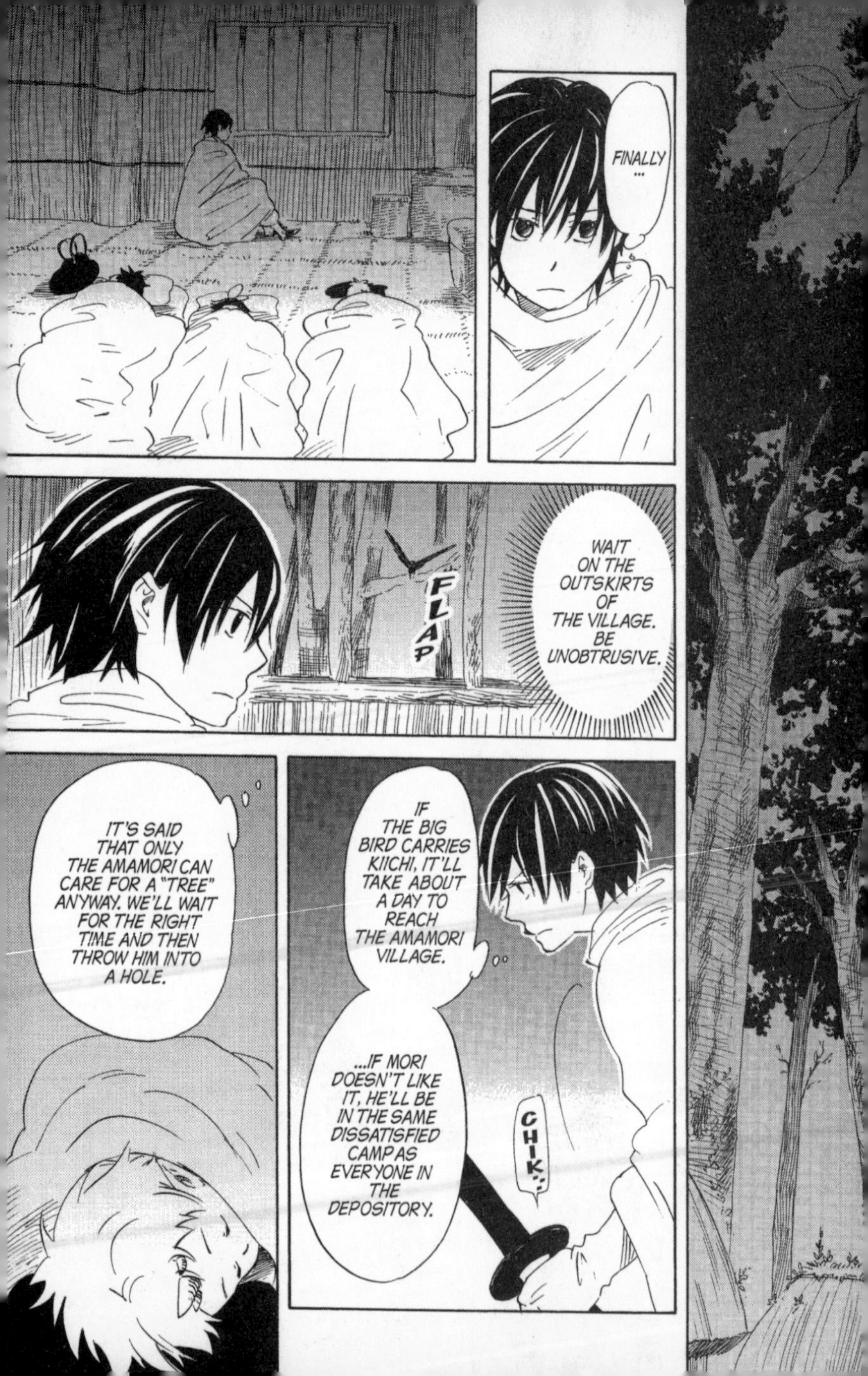
FINALLY ...
WAIT ON THE OUTSKIRTS OF THE VILLAGE. BE UNOBTRUSIVE.
FLAP
IF THE BIG BIRD CARRIES KIICHI, IT'LL TAKE ABOUT A DAY TO REACH THE AMAMORI VILLAGE.
...IF MORI DOESN'T LIKE IT, HE'LL BE IN THE SAME DISSATISFIED CAMP AS EVERYONE IN THE DEPOSITORY.
CHIK
IT'S SAID THAT ONLY THE AMAMORI CAN CARE FOR A "TREE" ANYWAY. WE'LL WAIT FOR THE RIGHT TIME AND THEN THROW HIM INTO A HOLE.

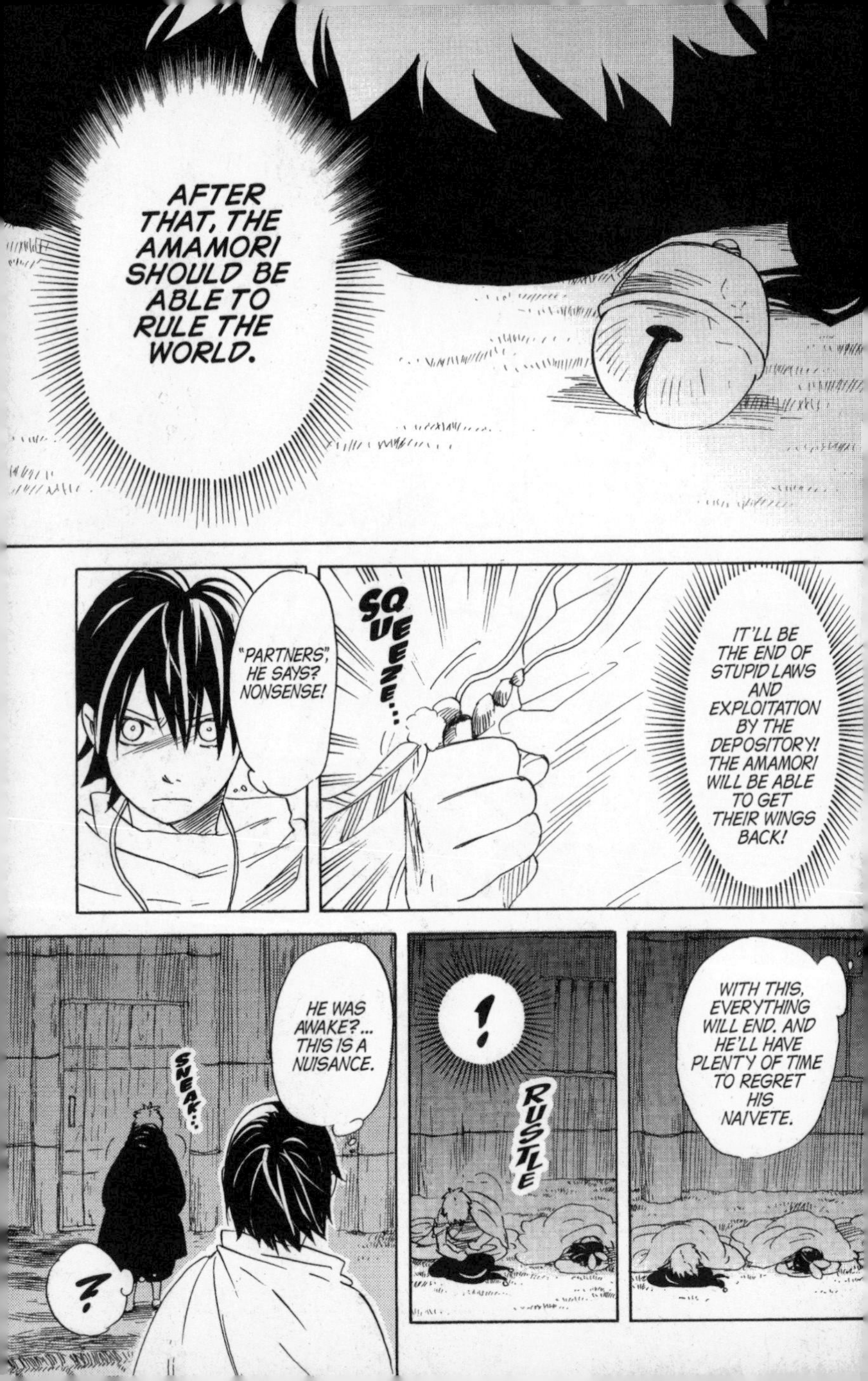
AFTER THAT, THE AMAMORI SHOULD BE ABLE TO RULE THE WORLD.
IT'LL BE THE END OF STUPID LAWS AND EXPLOITATION BY THE DEPOSITORY! THE AMAMORI WILL BE ABLE TO GET THEIR WINGS BACK!
SQUEEZE...
"PARTNERS", HE SAYS? NONSENSE!
WITH THIS, EVERYTHING WILL END. AND HE'LL HAVE PLENTY OF TIME TO REGRET HIS NAIVETE.
!
RUSTLE
HE WAS AWAKE?... THIS IS A NUISANCE.
SNEAK...
?

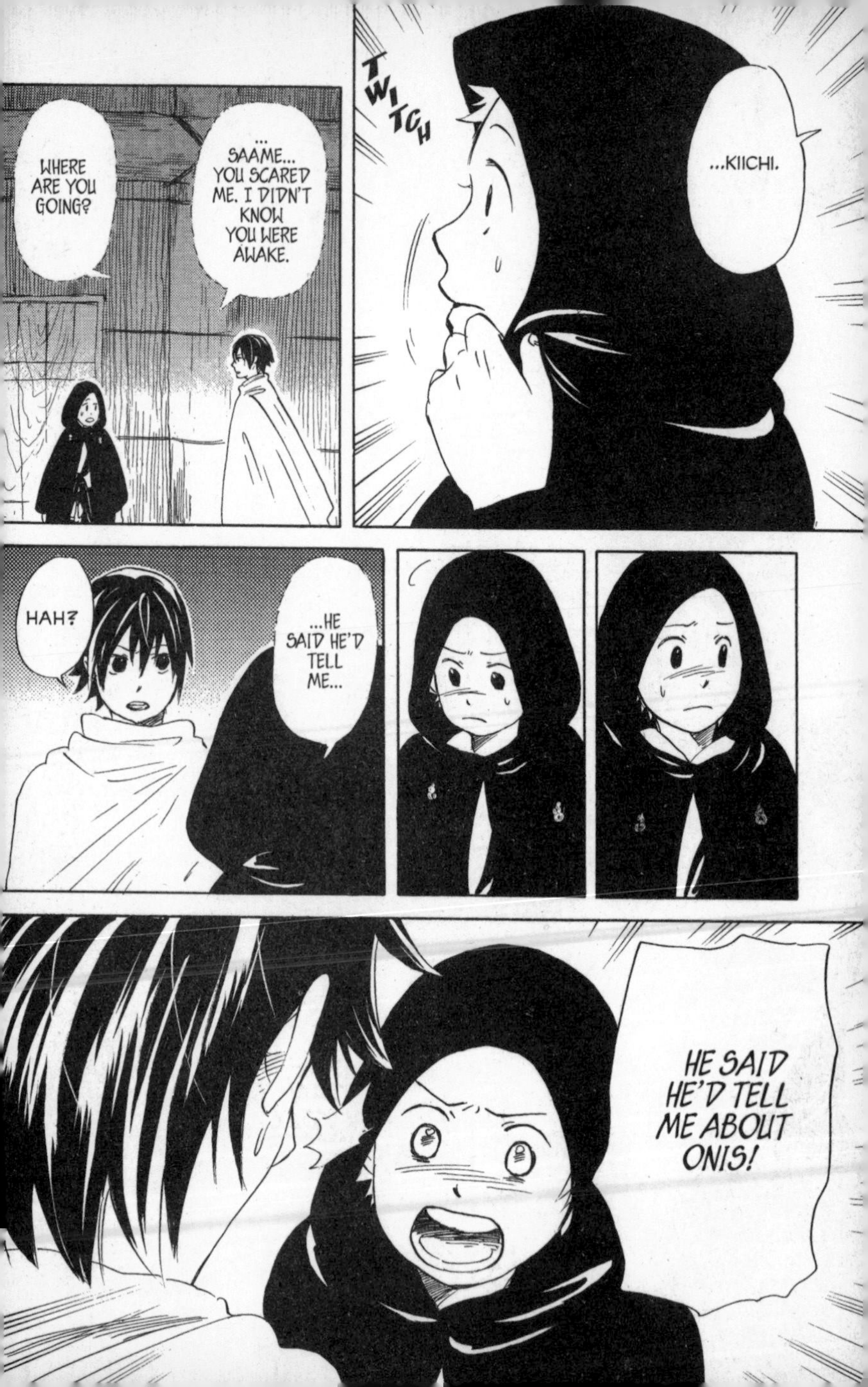
...KIICHI.
TWITCH
... SAAME... YOU SCARED ME. I DIDN'T KNOW YOU WERE AWAKE.
WHERE ARE YOU GOING?
...HE SAID HE'D TELL ME...
HAH?
HE SAID HE'D TELL ME ABOUT ONIS!

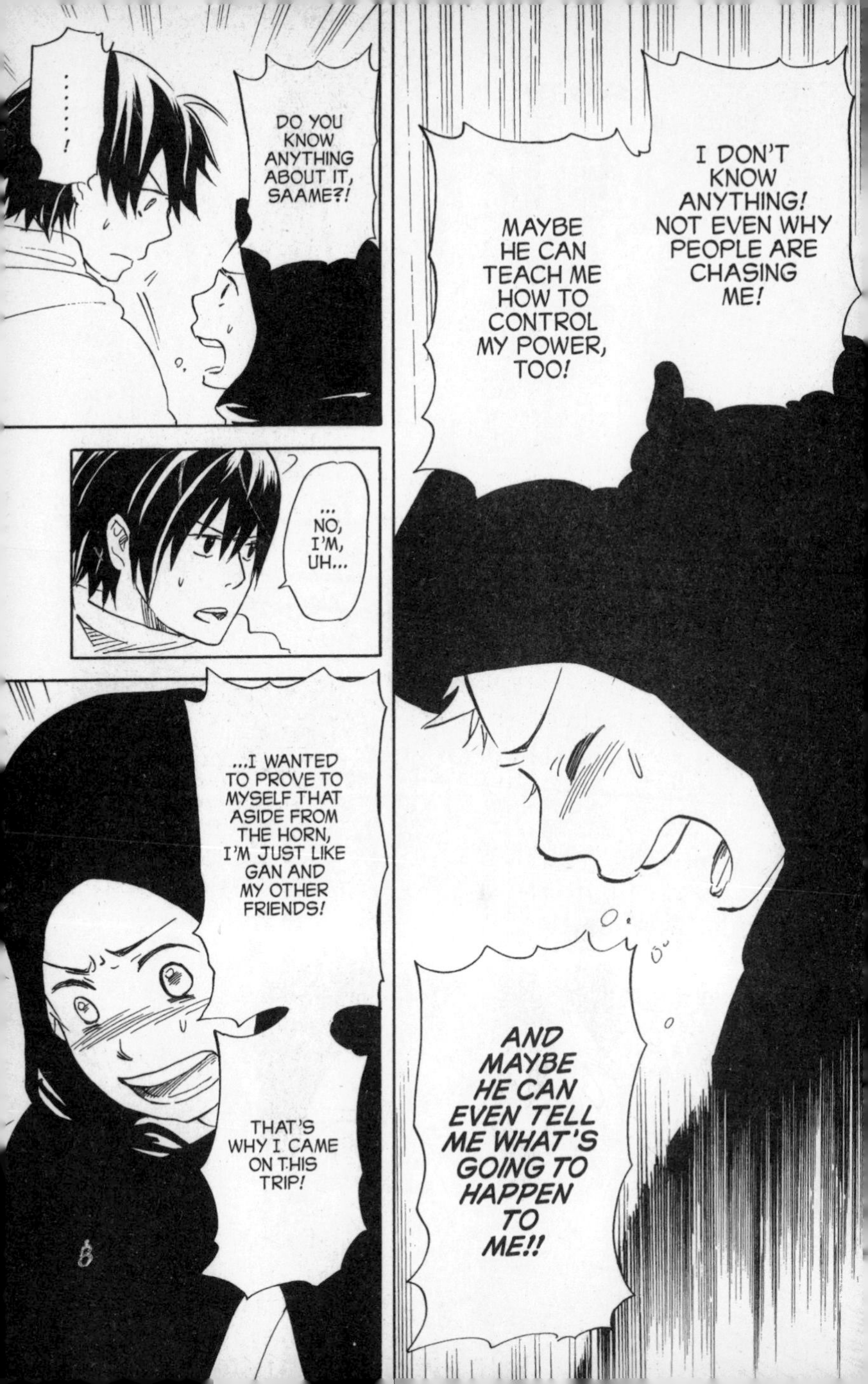
I DON'T KNOW ANYTHING! NOT EVEN WHY PEOPLE ARE CHASING ME!
MAYBE HE CAN TEACH ME HOW TO CONTROL MY POWER, TOO!
AND MAYBE HE CAN EVEN TELL ME WHAT'S GOING TO HAPPEN TO ME!!
DO YOU KNOW ANYTHING ABOUT IT, SAAME?!
......!
... NO, I'M, UH...
...I WANTED TO PROVE TO MYSELF THAT ASIDE FROM THE HORN, I'M JUST LIKE GAN AND MY OTHER FRIENDS!
THAT'S WHY I CAME ON THIS TRIP!

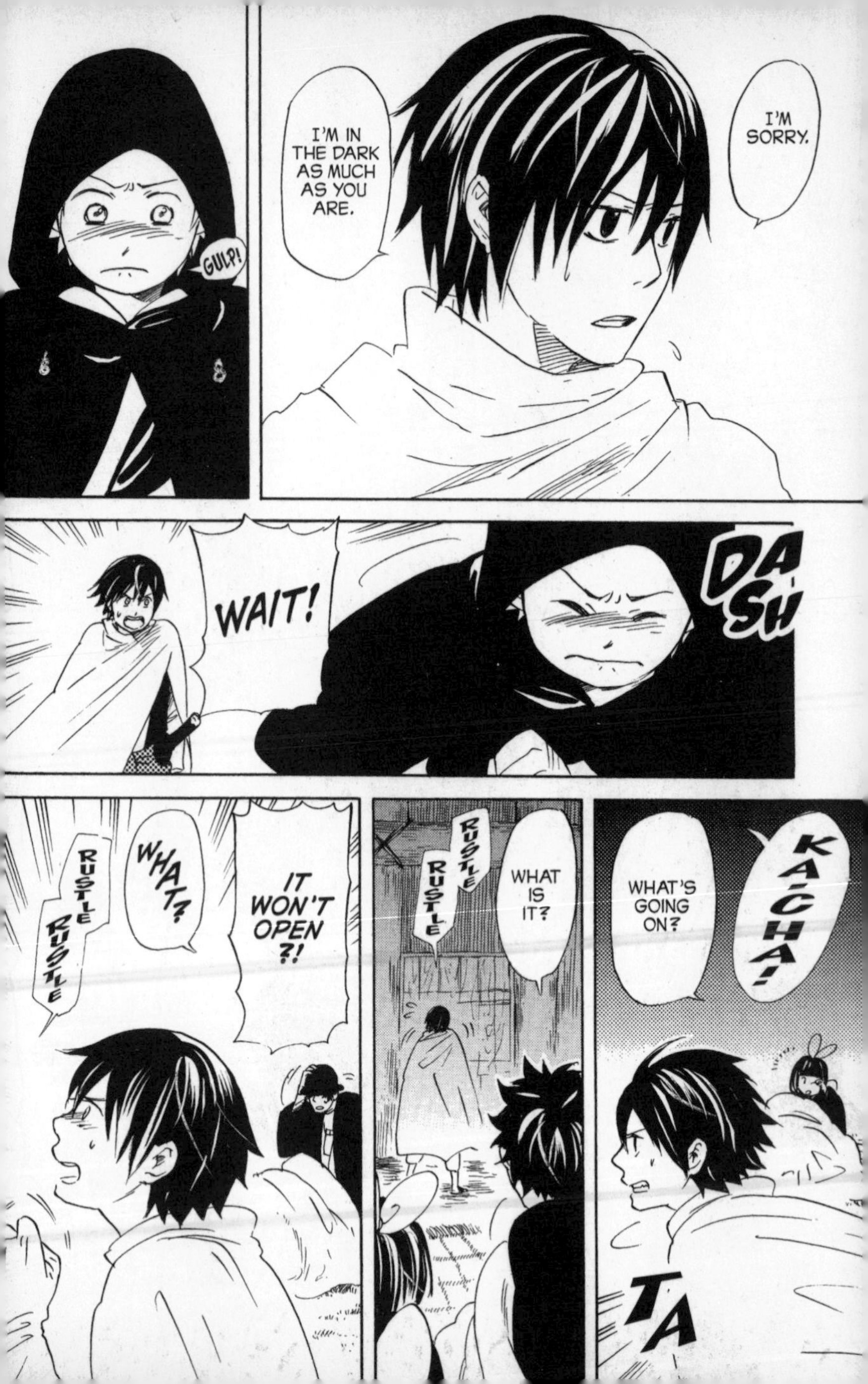
I'M SORRY.
I'M IN THE DARK AS MUCH AS YOU ARE.
GULP!
DASH
WAIT!
KA-CHA!
WHAT'S GOING ON?
TA
RUSTLE
RUSTLE
WHAT IS IT?
IT WON'T OPEN?!
WHAT?
RUSTLE
RUSTLE

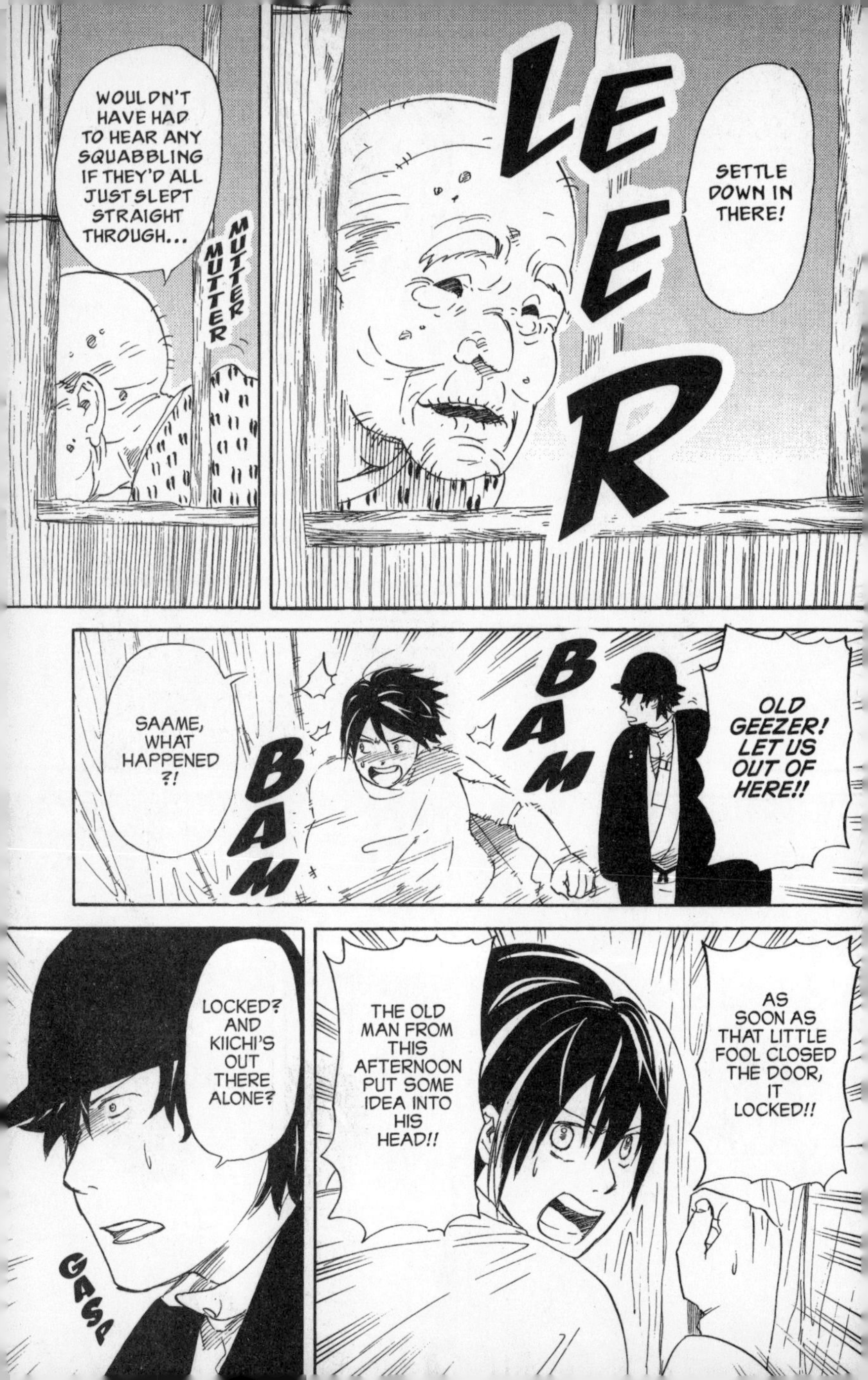
SETTLE DOWN IN THERE!
LEER
WOULDN'T HAVE HAD TO HEAR ANY SQUABBLING IF THEY'D ALL JUST SLEPT STRAIGHT THROUGH...
MUTTER MUTTER
OLD GEEZER! LET US OUT OF HERE!!
BAM BAM
SAAME, WHAT HAPPENED ?!
AS SOON AS THAT LITTLE FOOL CLOSED THE DOOR, IT LOCKED!!
THE OLD MAN FROM THIS AFTERNOON PUT SOME IDEA INTO HIS HEAD!!
LOCKED? AND KIICHI'S OUT THERE ALONE?
GASA

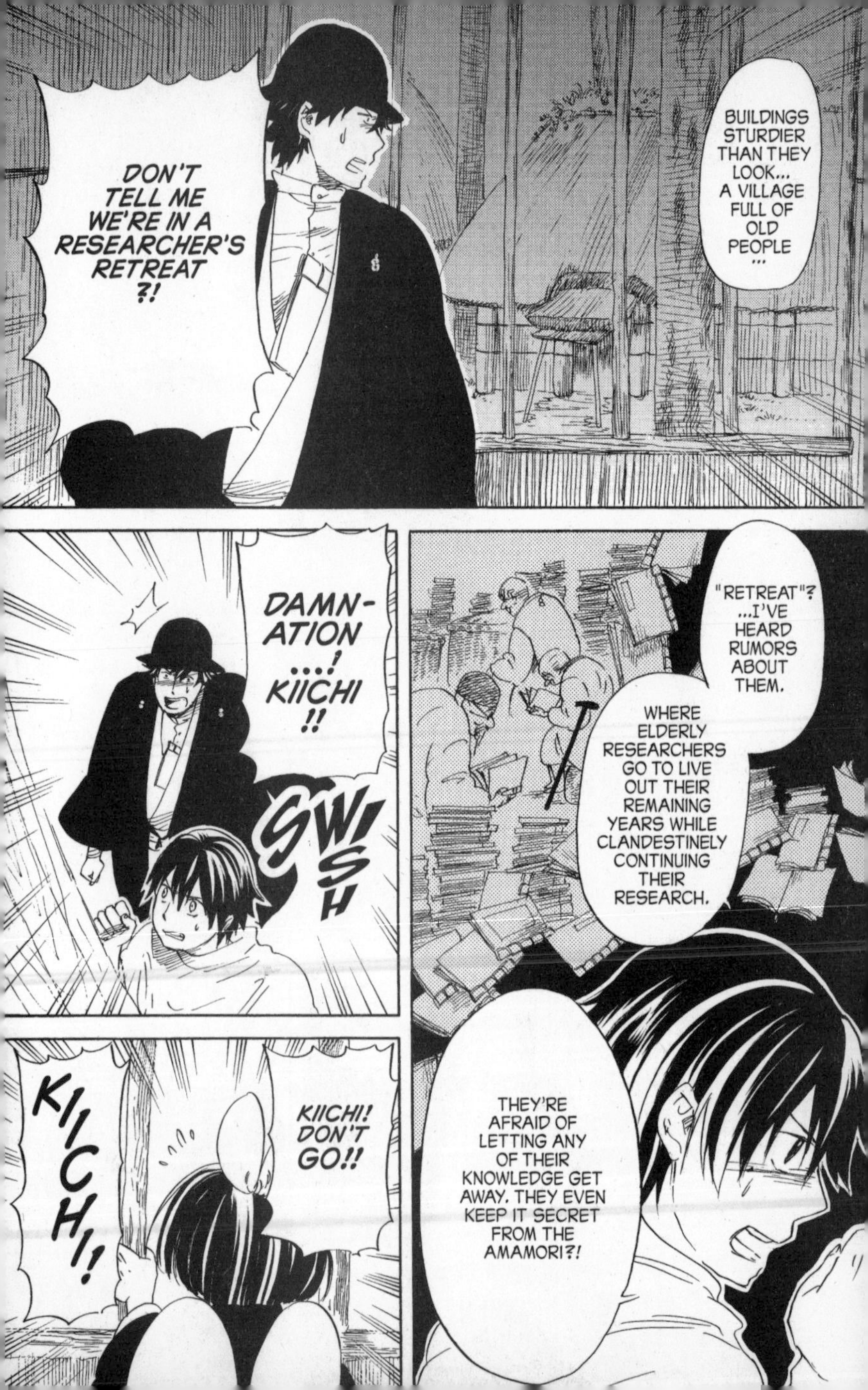
BUILDINGS STURDIER THAN THEY LOOK... A VILLAGE FULL OF OLD PEOPLE ...
DON'T TELL ME WE'RE IN A RESEARCHER'S RETREAT ?!
"RETREAT"? ...I'VE HEARD RUMORS ABOUT THEM.
WHERE ELDERLY RESEARCHERS GO TO LIVE OUT THEIR REMAINING YEARS WHILE CLANDESTINELY CONTINUING THEIR RESEARCH.
THEY'RE AFRAID OF LETTING ANY OF THEIR KNOWLEDGE GET AWAY. THEY EVEN KEEP IT SECRET FROM THE AMAMORI?!
DAMN-ATION ....! KIICHI !!
SWISH
KIICHI! DON'T GO!!
KIICHI!

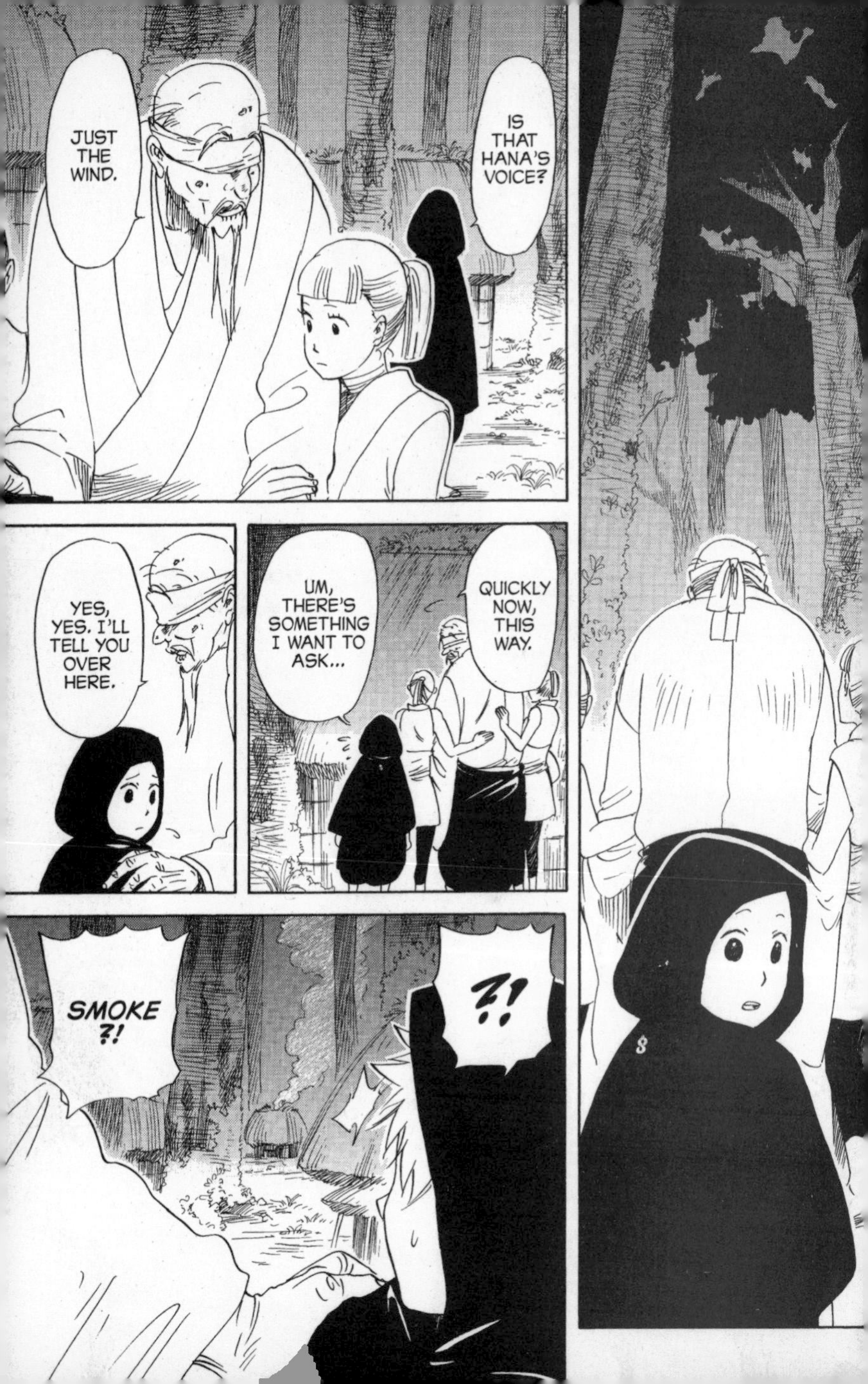
IS THAT HANA'S VOICE?
JUST THE WIND.
QUICKLY NOW, THIS WAY.
UM, THERE'S SOMETHING I WANT TO ASK...
YES, YES. I'LL TELL YOU OVER HERE.
?!
SMOKE ?!

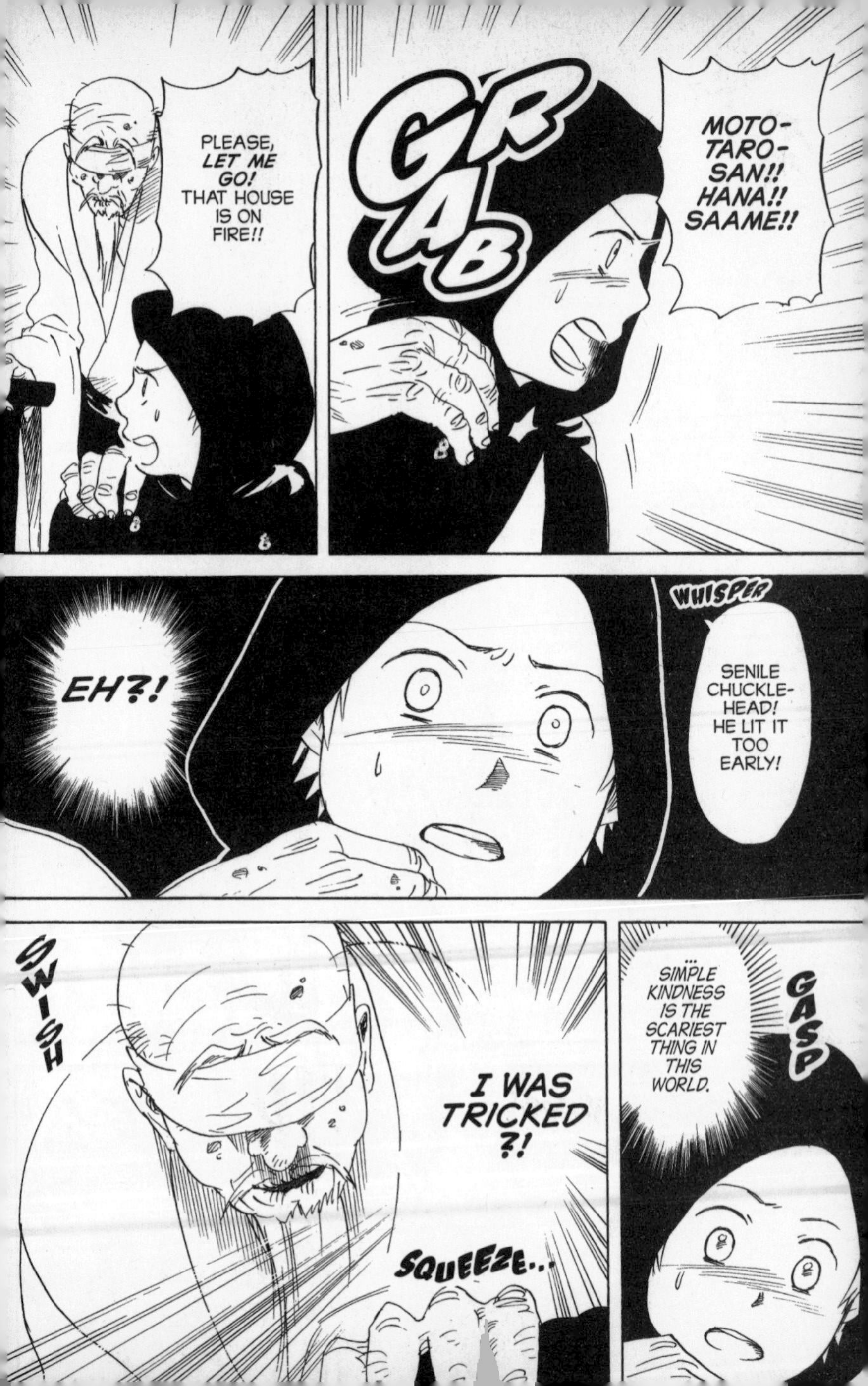
MOTO-TARO-SAN!! HANA!! SAAME!!
GRAB
PLEASE, LET ME GO! THAT HOUSE IS ON FIRE!!
WHISPER
SENILE CHUCKLE-HEAD! HE LIT IT TOO EARLY!
EH?!
GASP
...SIMPLE KINDNESS IS THE SCARIEST THING IN THIS WORLD.
I WAS TRICKED?!
SWISH
SQUEEZE...

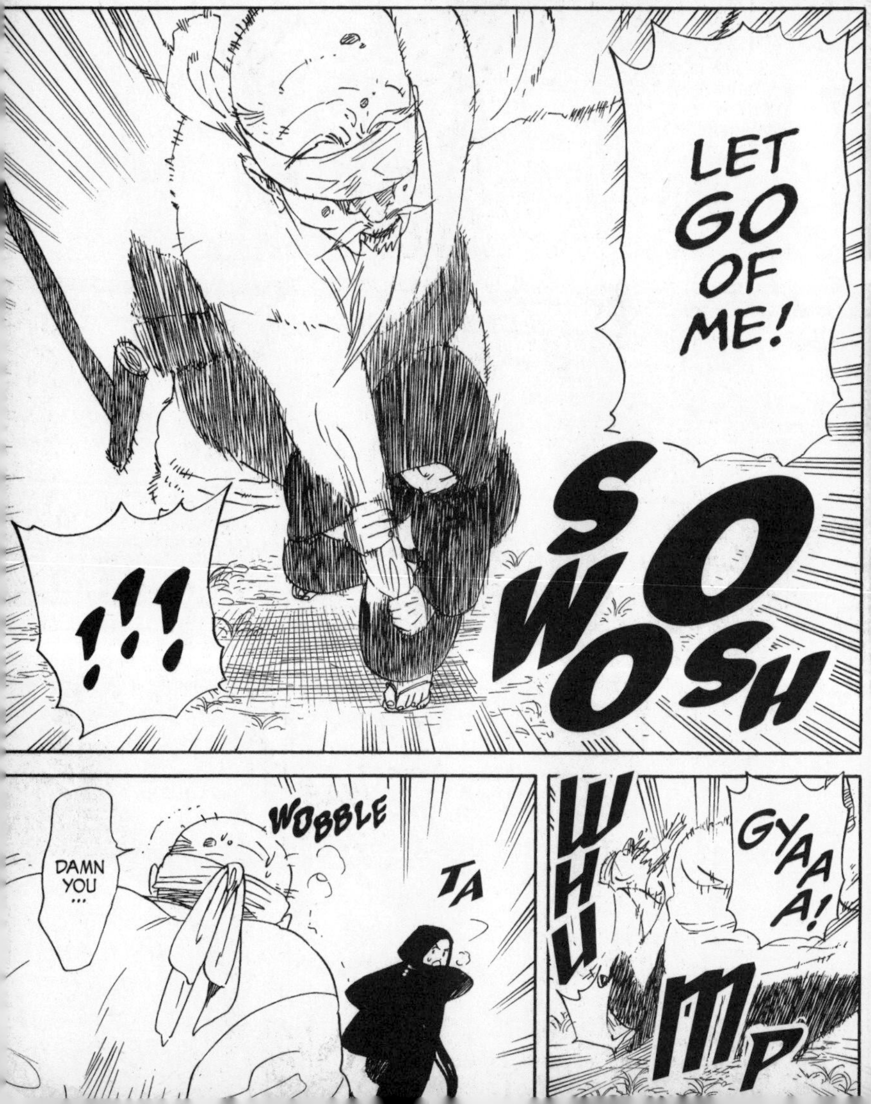
LET GO OF ME!
SWOOSH
!!!
GYAAA!
WHUMP
WOBBLE
TA
DAMN YOU ...

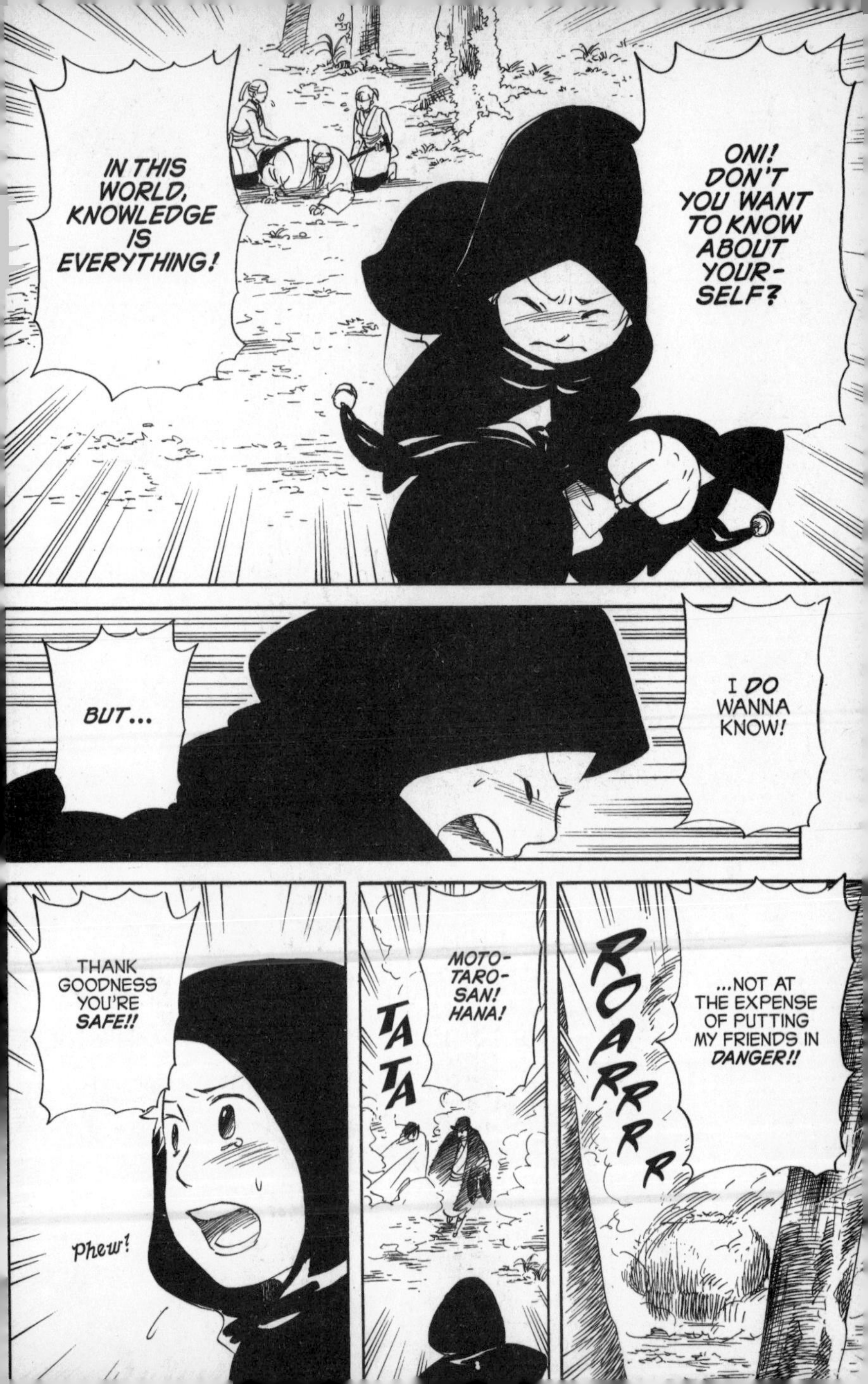
ONI! DON'T YOU WANT TO KNOW ABOUT YOURSELF?
IN THIS WORLD, KNOWLEDGE IS EVERYTHING!
I DO WANNA KNOW!
BUT...
...NOT AT THE EXPENSE OF PUTTING MY FRIENDS IN DANGER!!
ROARRRR
MOTO-TARO-SAN! HANA!
TATA
THANK GOODNESS YOU'RE SAFE!!
Phew!

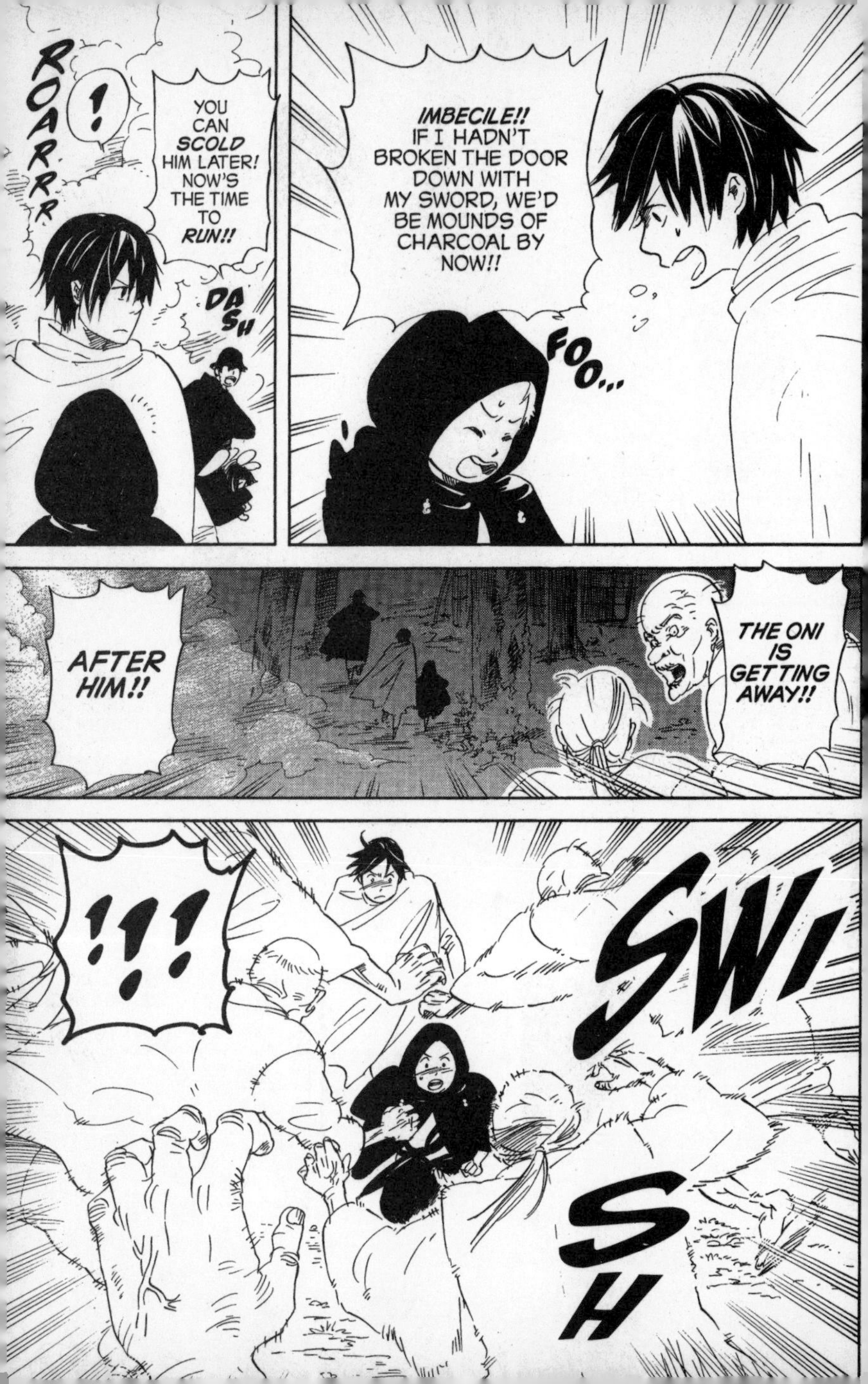
IMBECILE!! IF I HADN'T BROKEN THE DOOR DOWN WITH MY SWORD, WE'D BE MOUNDS OF CHARCOAL BY NOW!!
FOO...
ROARRR
!
YOU CAN SCOLD HIM LATER! NOW'S THE TIME TO RUN!!
DASH
THE ONI IS GETTING AWAY!!
AFTER HIM!!
SWISH
!!!

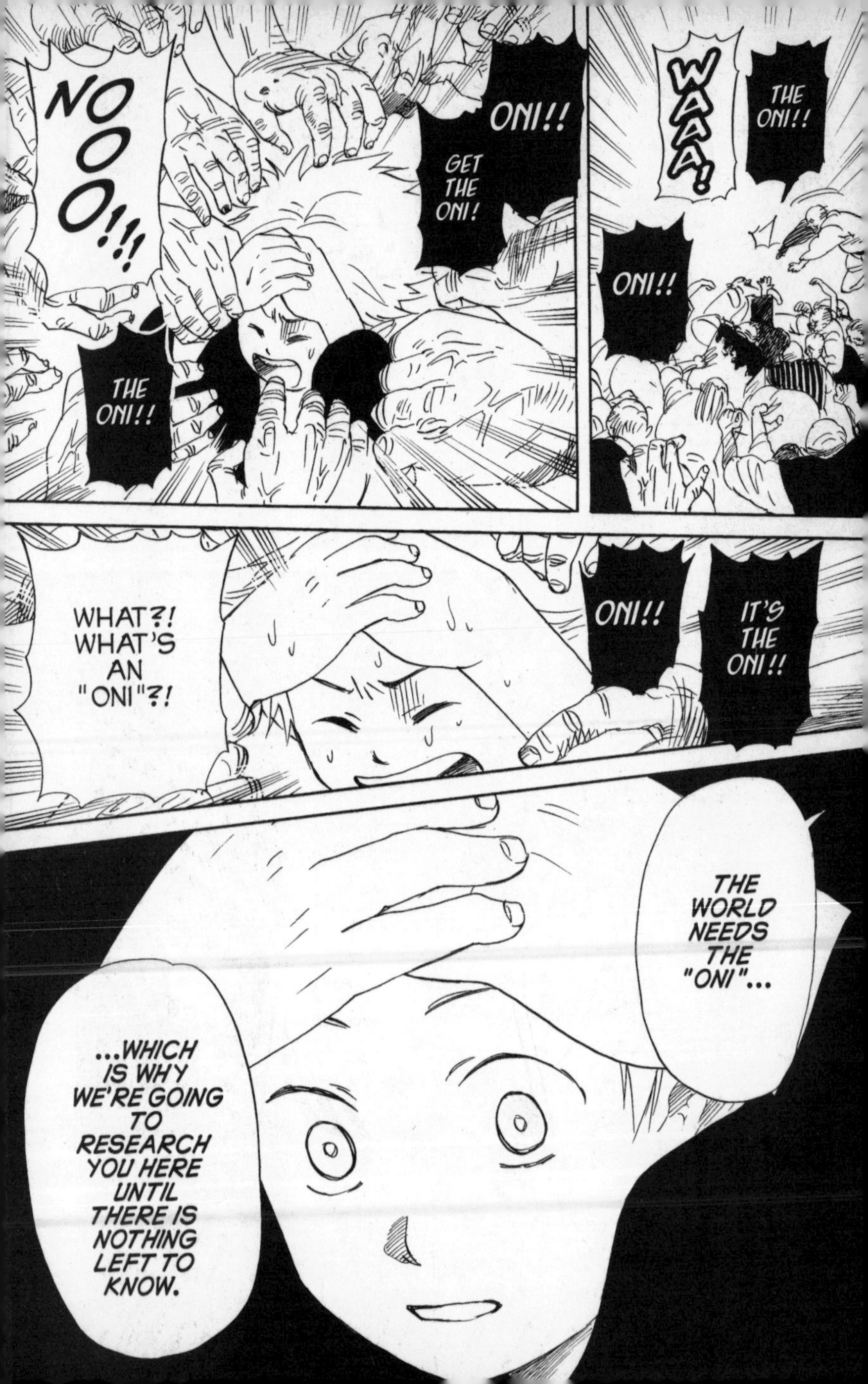
THE ONI!!
WAAA!
ONI!!
ONI!!
GET THE ONI!
NOOO!!!
THE ONI!!
IT'S THE ONI!!
ONI!!
WHAT?! WHAT'S AN "ONI"?!
THE WORLD NEEDS THE "ONI"...
...WHICH IS WHY WE'RE GOING TO RESEARCH YOU HERE UNTIL THERE IS NOTHING LEFT TO KNOW.

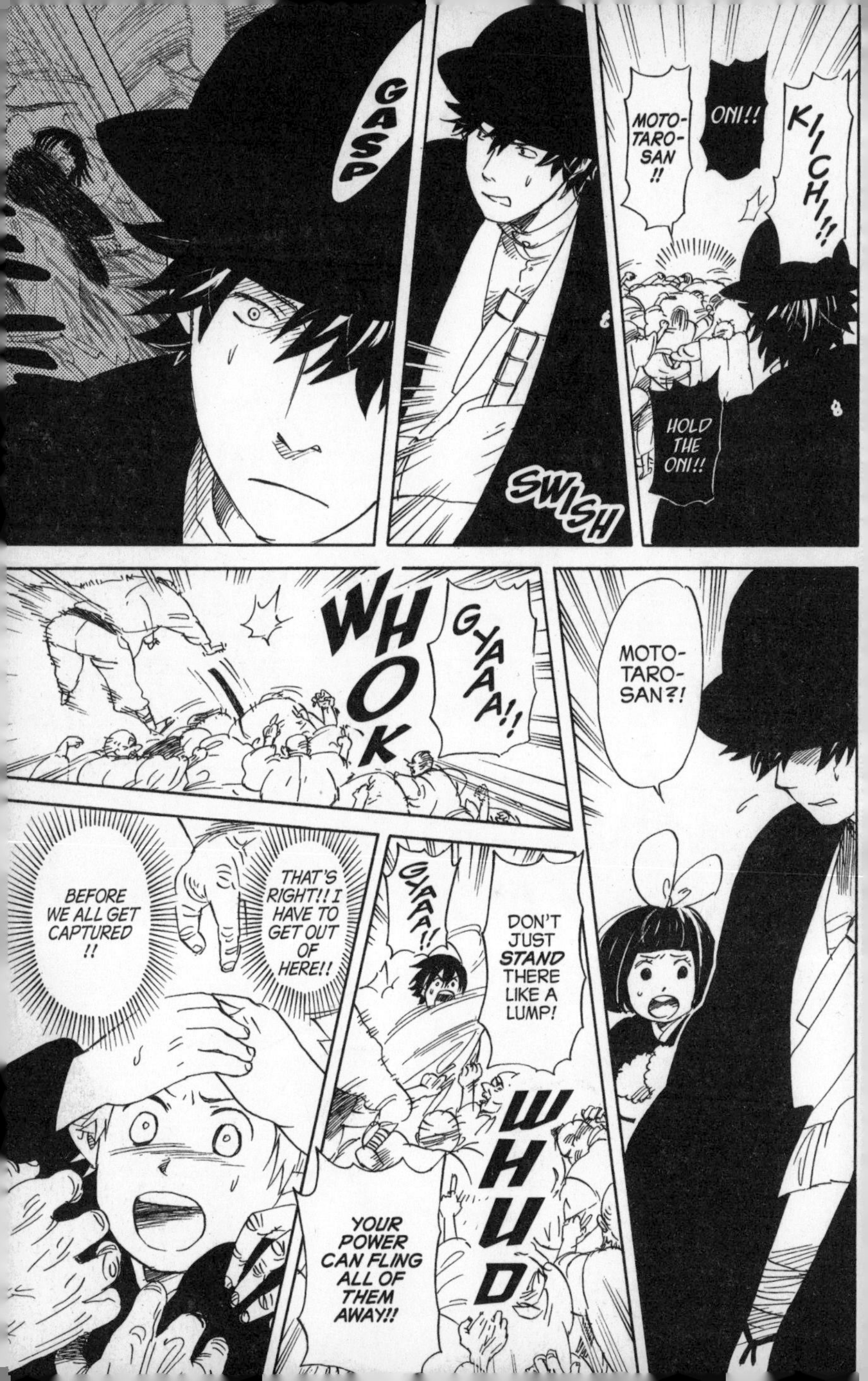

KIICHI!!
ONI!!
MOTO-TARO-SAN!!
HOLD THE ONI!!
GASP
SWISH
MOTO-TARO-SAN?!
GYAAA!!
WHOK
GYAAA!!
DON'T JUST **STAND** THERE LIKE A LUMP!
WHUD
YOUR POWER CAN FLING ALL OF THEM AWAY!!
THAT'S RIGHT!! I HAVE TO GET OUT OF HERE!!
BEFORE WE ALL GET CAPTURED!!

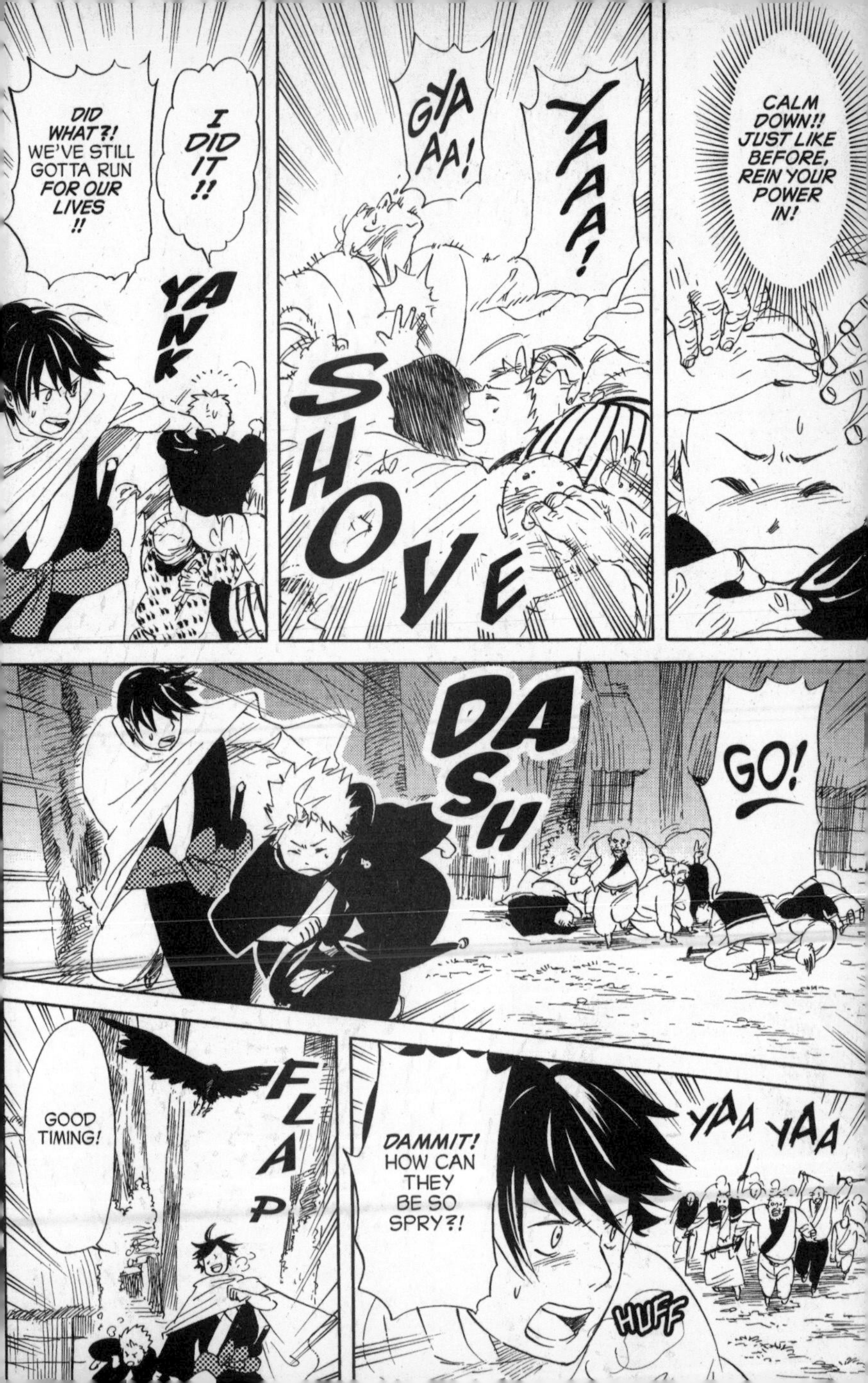
CALM DOWN!! JUST LIKE BEFORE, REIN YOUR POWER IN!
YAAAA!
GYAAA!
SHOVE
I DID IT!!
DID WHAT?! WE'VE STILL GOTTA RUN FOR OUR LIVES!!
YANK
GO!
DASH
YAA YAA
DAMMIT! HOW CAN THEY BE SO SPRY?!
HUFF
FLAP
GOOD TIMING!

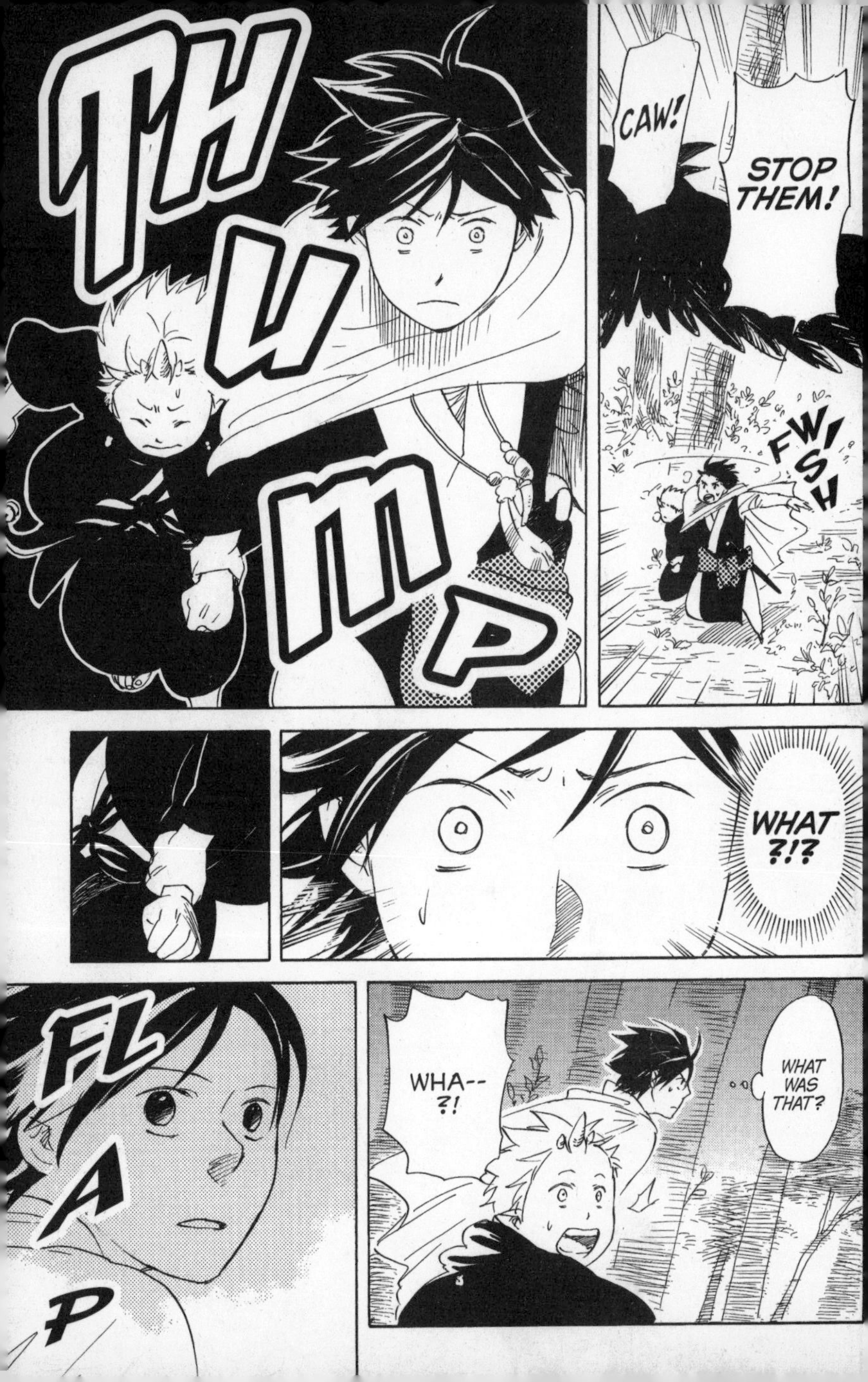
CAW!
STOP THEM!
FWISH
THUMP
WHAT ?!?
WHAT WAS THAT?
WHA-- ?!
FLAP

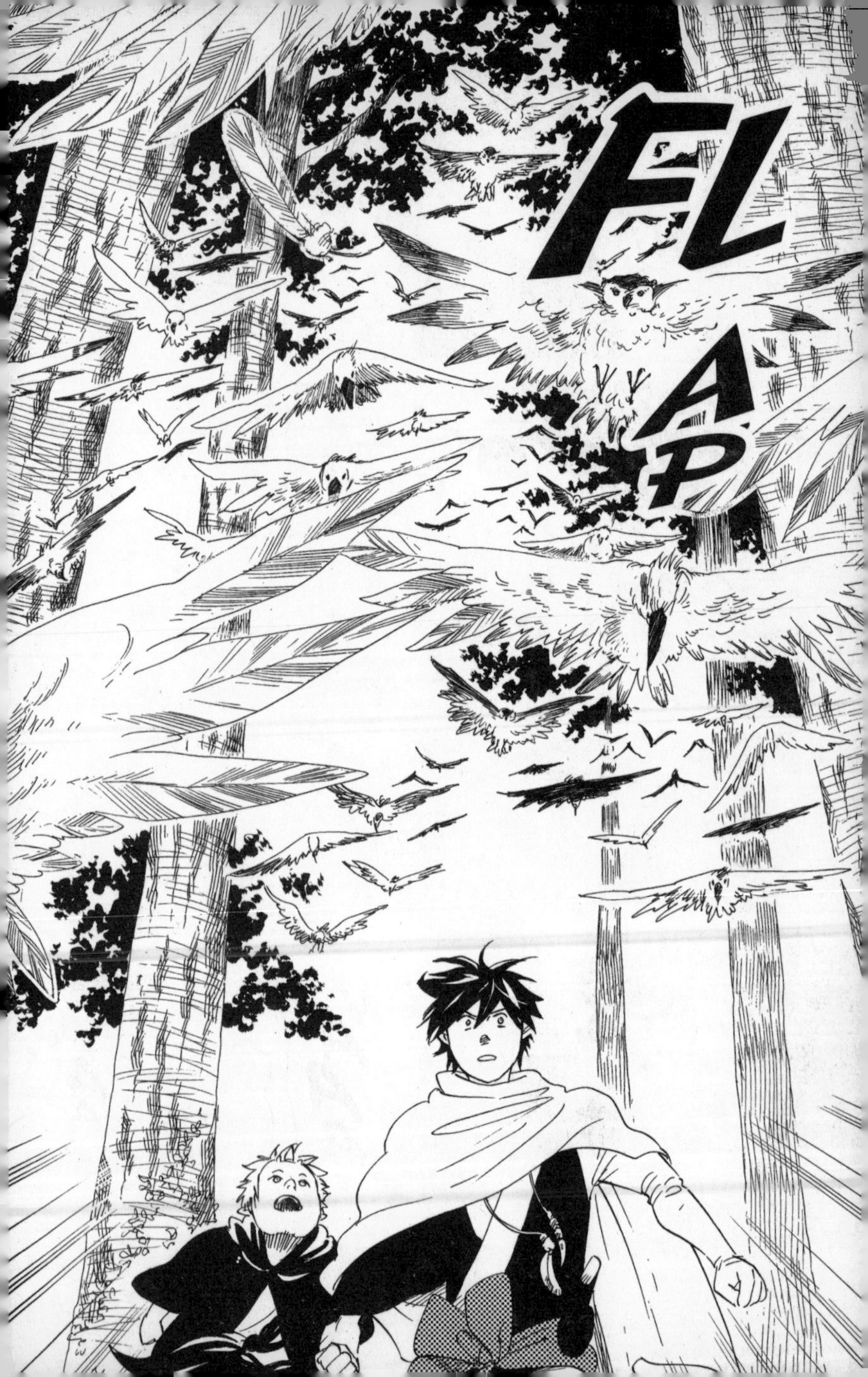
FLAP

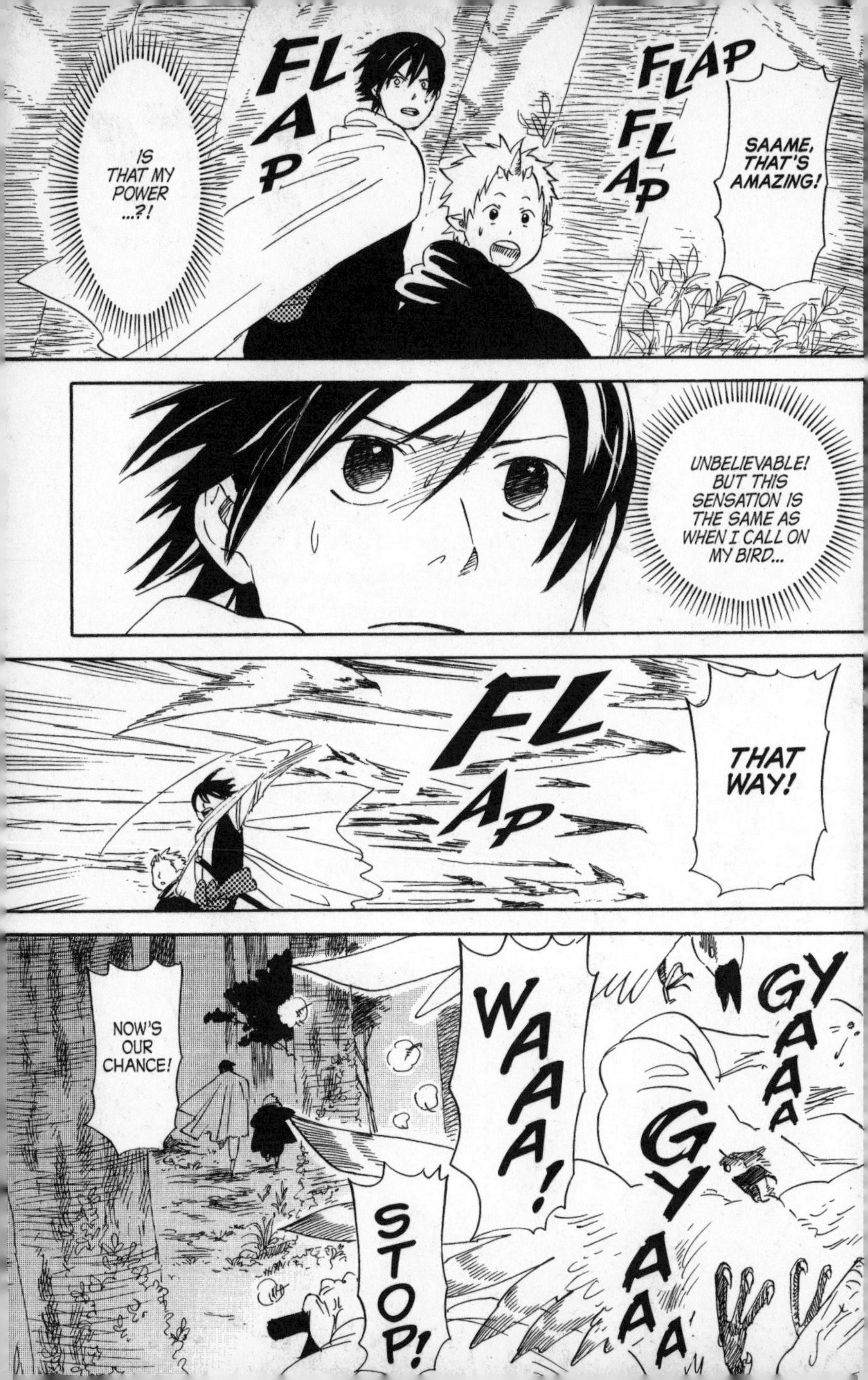
SAAME, THAT'S AMAZING!
FLAP
FLAP
FLAP
IS THAT MY POWER ...?!
UNBELIEVABLE! BUT THIS SENSATION IS THE SAME AS WHEN I CALL ON MY BIRD...
THAT WAY!
FLAP
GYAAA
GYAAA
WAAA!
STOP!
NOW'S OUR CHANCE!

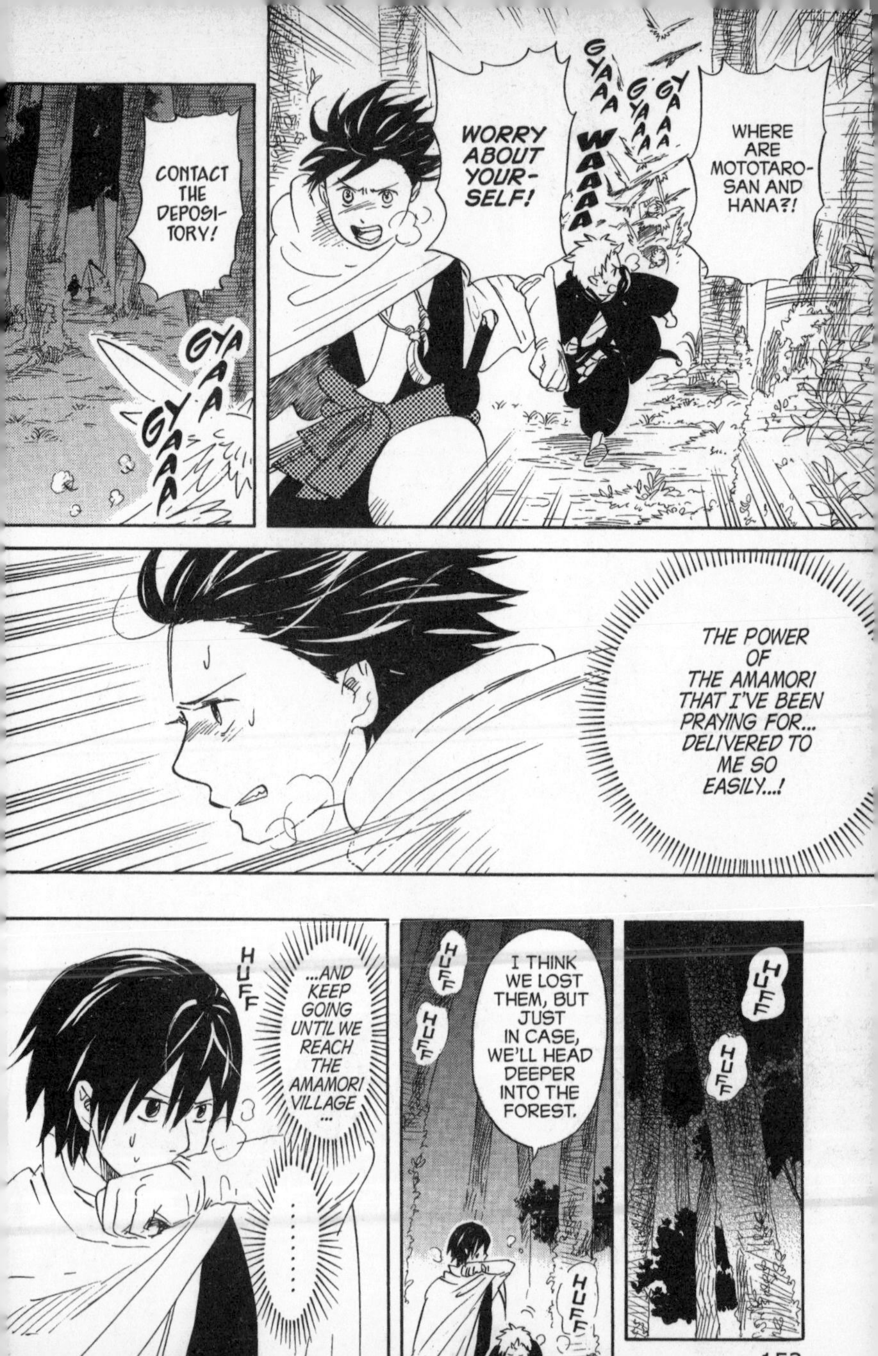
WHERE ARE MOTOTARO-SAN AND HANA?!
GYAAA
GYAAAA
GYAAAA
WAAAAA
WORRY ABOUT YOURSELF!
CONTACT THE DEPOSITORY!
GYAAA
GYAAA
THE POWER OF THE AMAMORI THAT I'VE BEEN PRAYING FOR... DELIVERED TO ME SO EASILY...!
HUFF
HUFF
HUFF
HUFF
I THINK WE LOST THEM, BUT JUST IN CASE, WE'LL HEAD DEEPER INTO THE FOREST.
HUFF
HUFF
...AND KEEP GOING UNTIL WE REACH THE AMAMORI VILLAGE ...
......

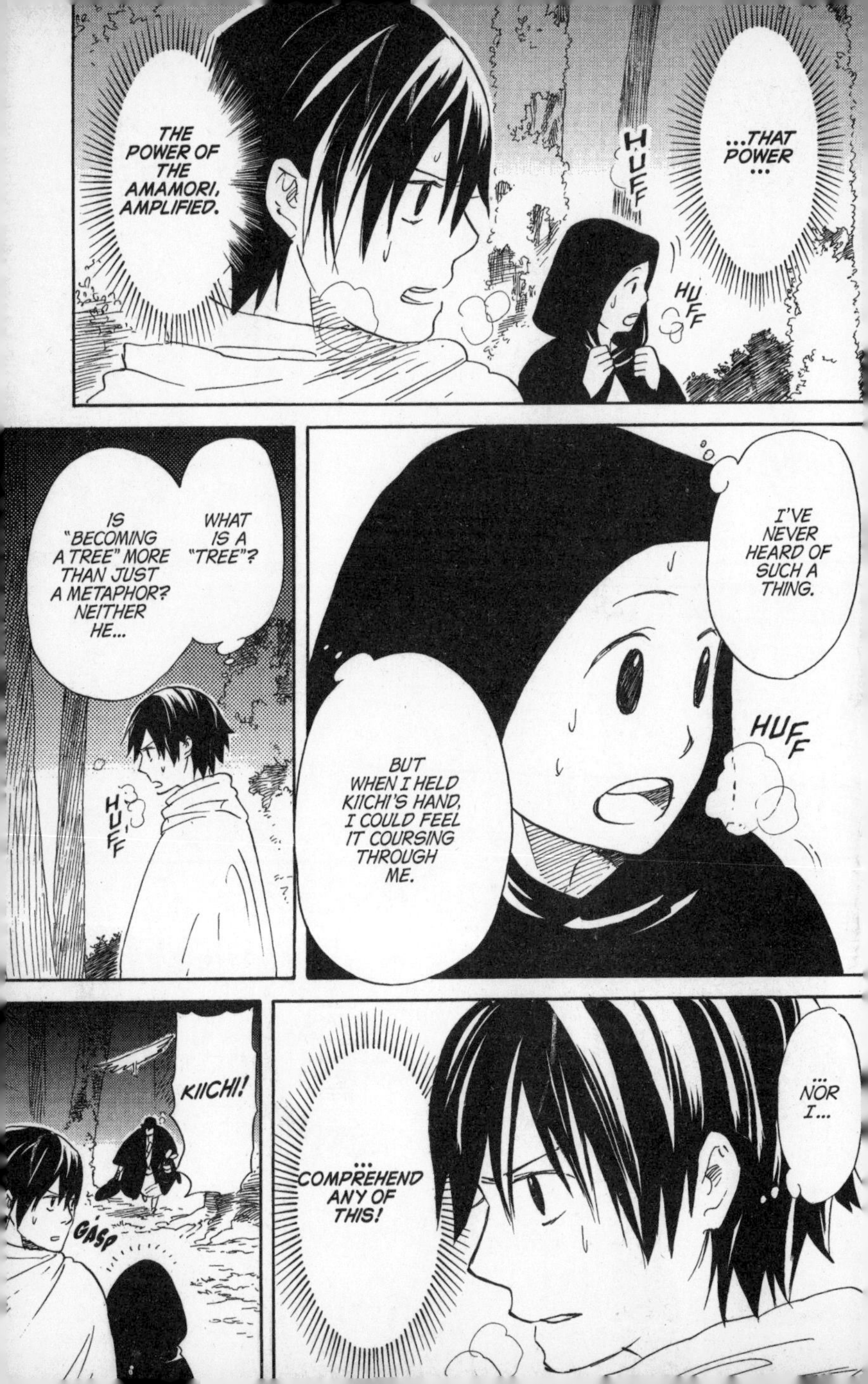
...THAT POWER...
HUFF
THE POWER OF THE AMAMORI, AMPLIFIED.
HUFF
I'VE NEVER HEARD OF SUCH A THING.
HUFF
BUT WHEN I HELD KIICHI'S HAND, I COULD FEEL IT COURSING THROUGH ME.
WHAT IS A "TREE"?
IS "BECOMING A TREE" MORE THAN JUST A METAPHOR? NEITHER HE...
HUFF
...NOR I...
...COMPREHEND ANY OF THIS!
KIICHI!
GASP

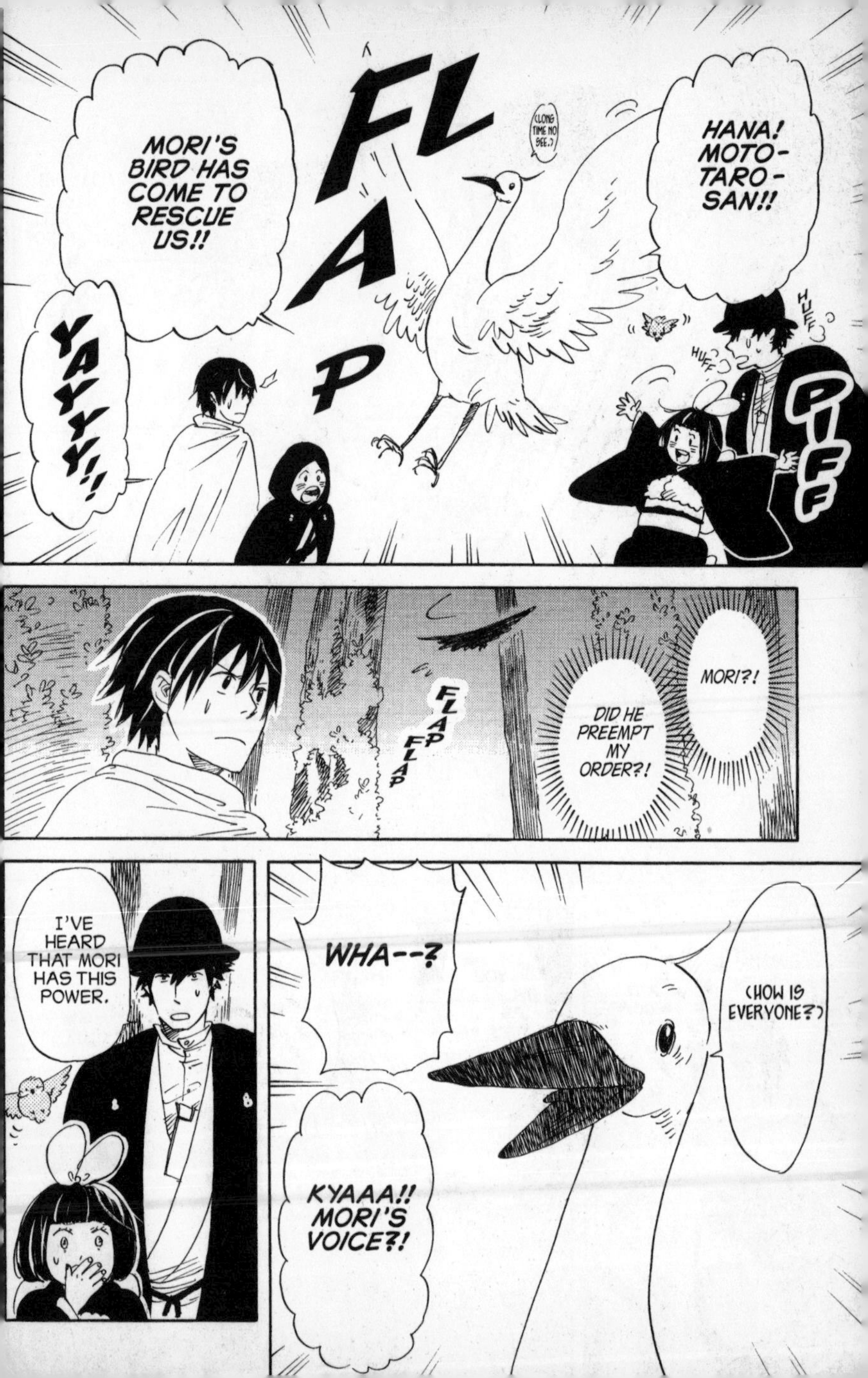
HANA! MOTO-TARO-SAN!!
PIFF
HUFF
HUFF
(LONG TIME NO SEE.)
FLAP
MORI'S BIRD HAS COME TO RESCUE US!!
YAYYYY!!
MORI?!
DID HE PREEMPT MY ORDER?!
FLAP
FLAP
(HOW IS EVERYONE?)
WHA--?
KYAAA!! MORI'S VOICE?!
I'VE HEARD THAT MORI HAS THIS POWER.

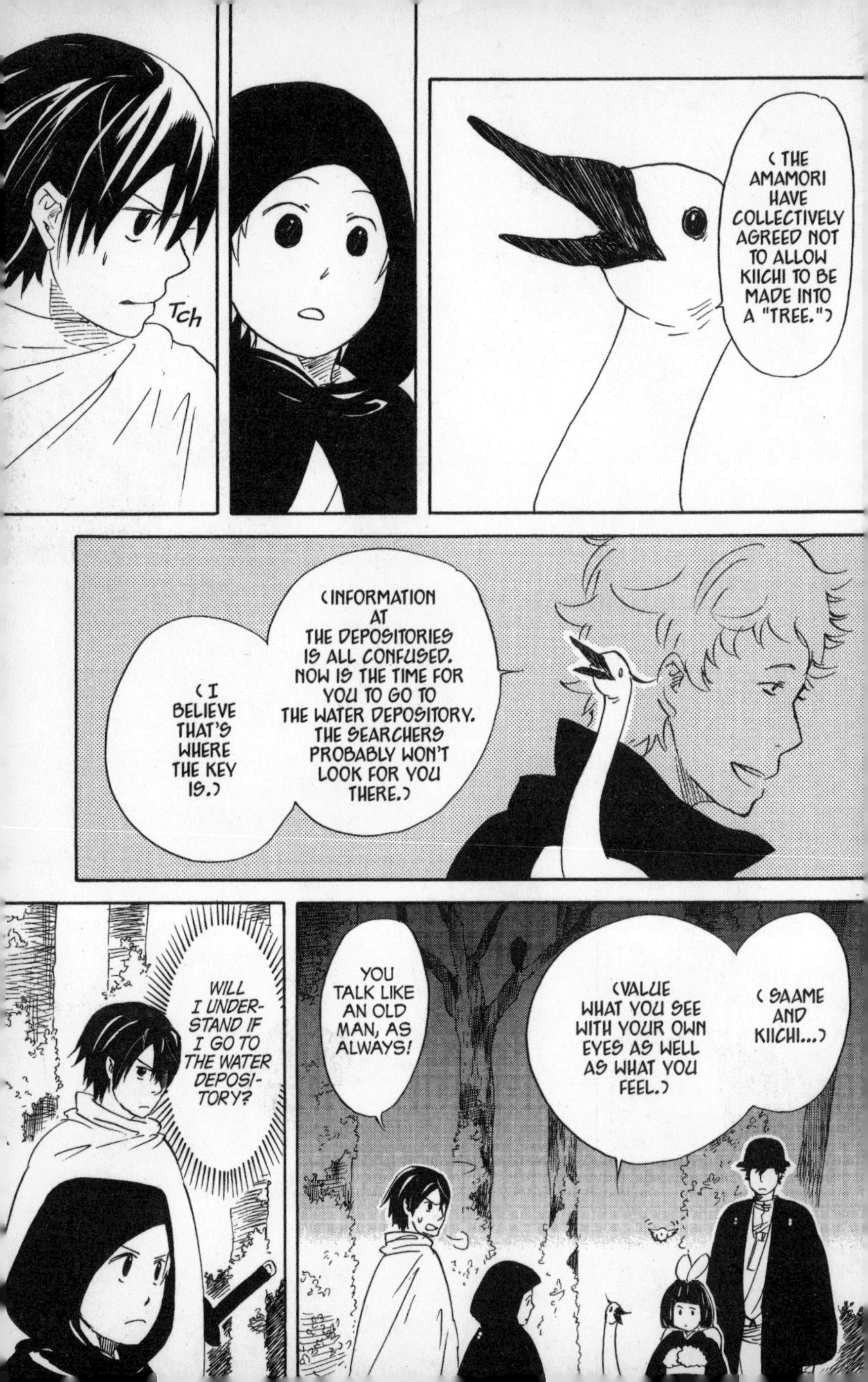
(THE AMAMORI HAVE COLLECTIVELY AGREED NOT TO ALLOW KIICHI TO BE MADE INTO A "TREE.")
TCH
(INFORMATION AT THE DEPOSITORIES IS ALL CONFUSED. NOW IS THE TIME FOR YOU TO GO TO THE WATER DEPOSITORY. THE SEARCHERS PROBABLY WON'T LOOK FOR YOU THERE.)
(I BELIEVE THAT'S WHERE THE KEY IS.)
(SAAME AND KIICHI...)
(VALUE WHAT YOU SEE WITH YOUR OWN EYES AS WELL AS WHAT YOU FEEL.)
YOU TALK LIKE AN OLD MAN, AS ALWAYS!
WILL I UNDERSTAND IF I GO TO THE WATER DEPOSITORY?

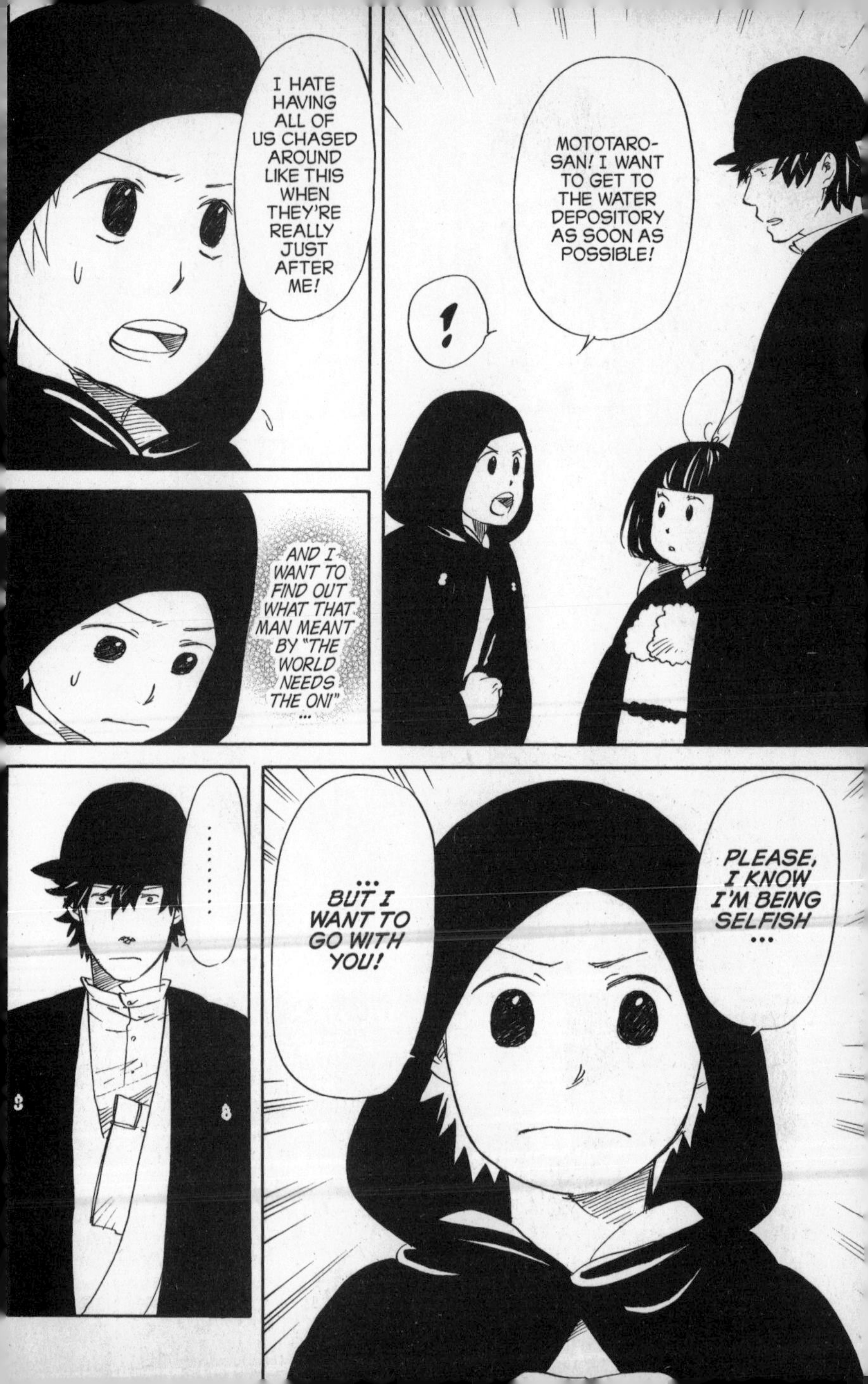
MOTOTARO-SAN! I WANT TO GET TO THE WATER DEPOSITORY AS SOON AS POSSIBLE!
!
I HATE HAVING ALL OF US CHASED AROUND LIKE THIS WHEN THEY'RE REALLY JUST AFTER ME!
AND I WANT TO FIND OUT WHAT THAT MAN MEANT BY "THE WORLD NEEDS THE ONI!"...
PLEASE, I KNOW I'M BEING SELFISH...
...BUT I WANT TO GO WITH YOU!
....

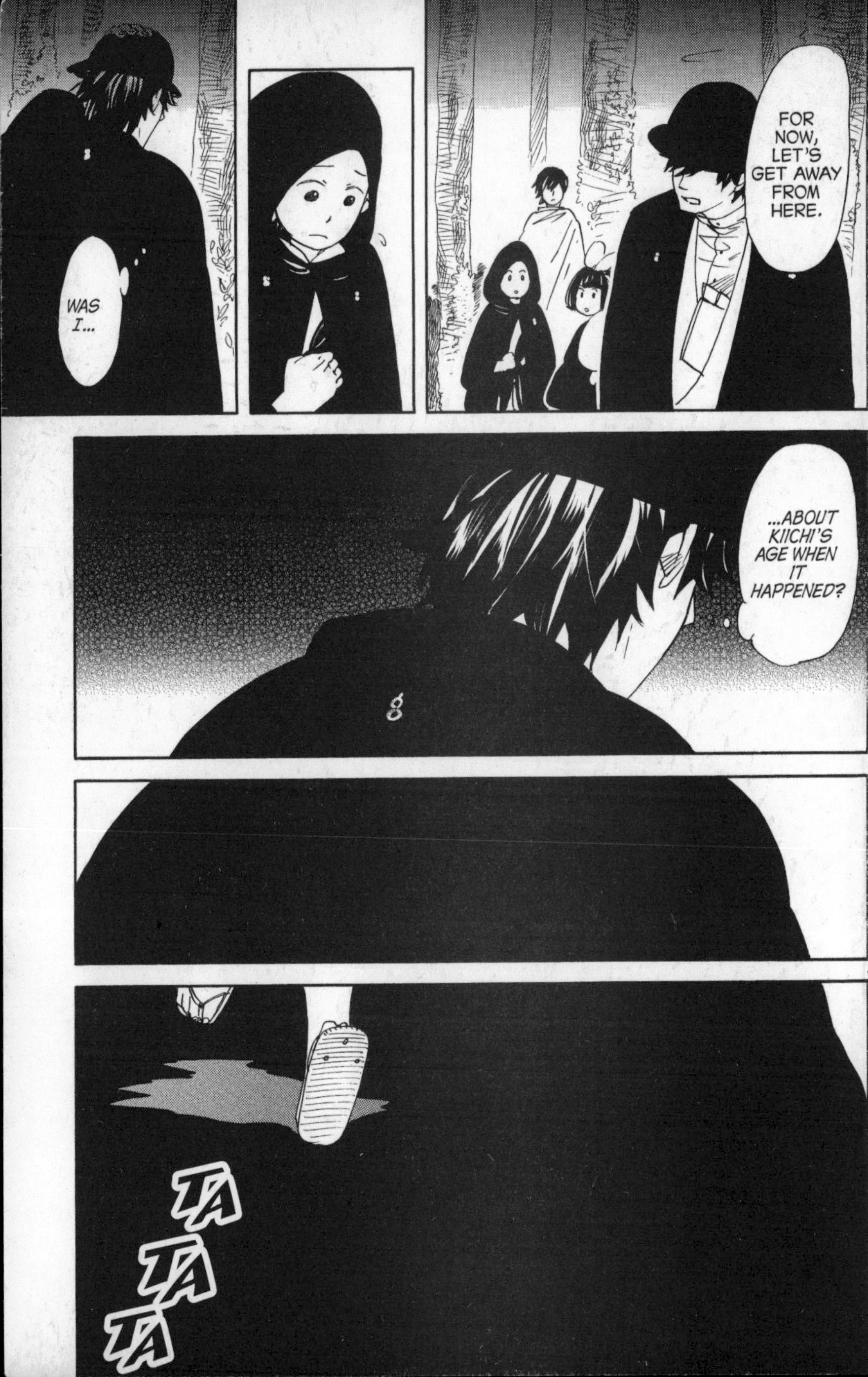
FOR NOW, LET'S GET AWAY FROM HERE.
WAS I...
...ABOUT KIICHI'S AGE WHEN IT HAPPENED?
TA TA TA

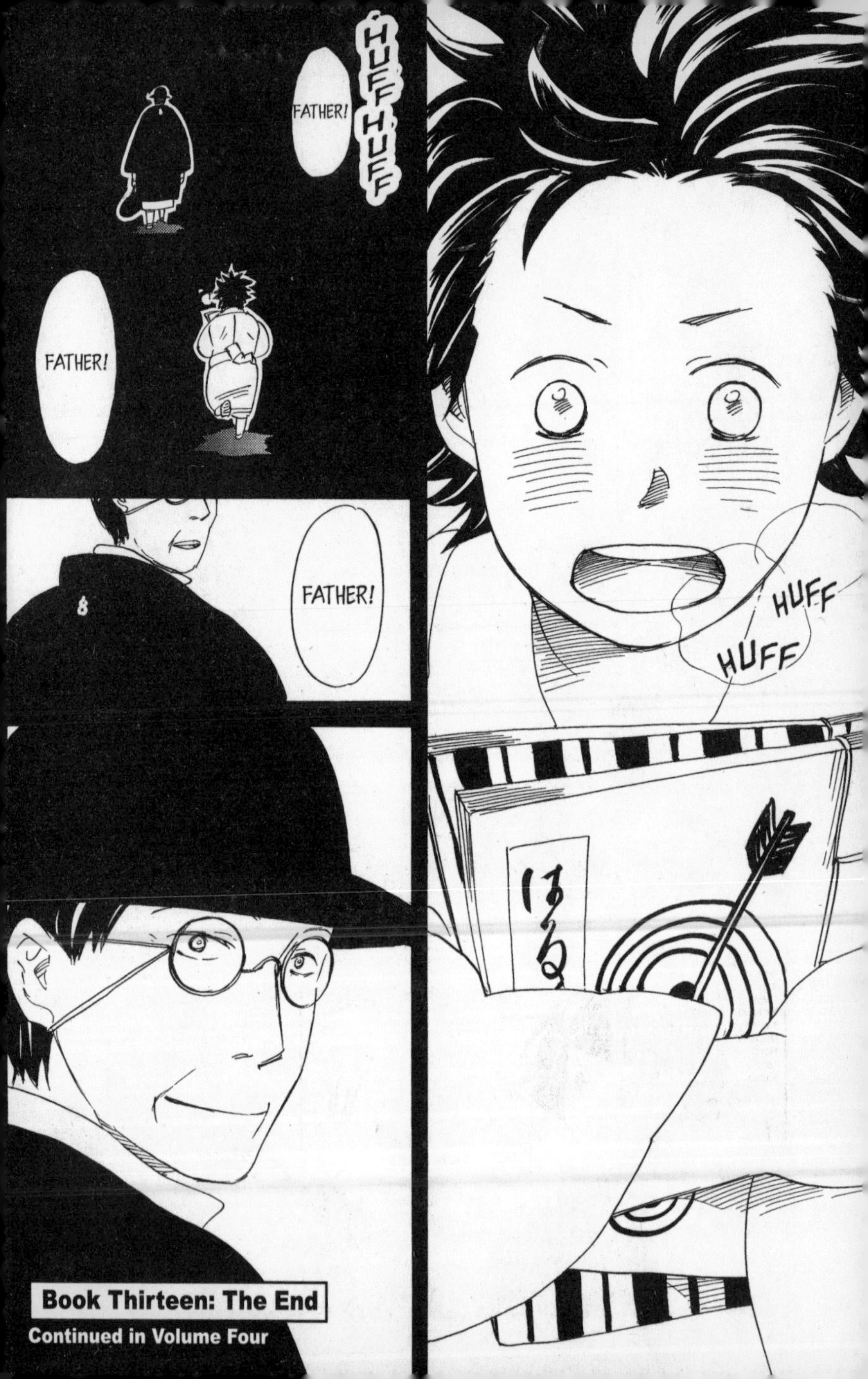
HUFF
HUFF
HUFF HUFF
FATHER!
FATHER!
FATHER!
Book Thirteen: The End
Continued in Volume Four